# Approaches to Teaching
# the *Song of Roland*

# Approaches to Teaching
# World Literature

*Joseph Gibaldi*, series editor

For a complete listing of titles,
see the last pages of this book.

*To Charles, fellow spirit, Leslie*

# Approaches to Teaching the *Song of Roland*

Edited by

## William W. Kibler

and

## Leslie Zarker Morgan

*With warmest feelings...*

*Best regards, Heinemann*

The Modern Language Association of America
New York    2006

For information about obtaining permission to reprint material from MLA book
publications, send your request by mail (see address below), e-mail
(permissions@mla.org), or fax (646-458-0030).

Library of Congress Cataloging-in-Publication Data

Approaches to teaching The song of Roland / edited by William W. Kibler and
Leslie Zarker Morgan.
p. cm. (Approaches to teaching world literature)
Includes bibliographical references and index.
ISBN-13: 978-0-87352-998-3 (hardcover : alk. paper)
ISBN-10: 0-87352-998-7
ISBN-13: 978-0-87352-999-0 (pbk. : alk. paper)
ISBN-10: 0-87352-999-5
1. Chanson de Roland.   2. Epic poetry, French—Study and teaching.   I.
Kibler, William W., 1942–   II. Morgan, Leslie Zarker.
PQ1522.A67 2006
841'.1—dc22        2006021701
ISSN 1059-1133

Cover illustration for the paperback edition:
Mort de Roland, Les anges emportent sonâme au ciel.
*Grandes Chroniques de France*. Bibliothèque Nationale
de France, fonds français 2813 (14th c.), folio 122v.

Published by The Modern Language Association of America
26 Broadway, New York, New York 10004-1789
www.mla.org

# CONTENTS

# PREFACE TO THE SERIES

In *The Art of Teaching* Gilbert Highet wrote, "Bad teaching wastes a great deal of effort, and spoils many lives which might have been full of energy and happiness." All too many teachers have failed in their work, Highet argued, simply "because they have not thought about it." We hope that the Approaches to Teaching World Literature series, sponsored by the Modern Language Association's Publications Committee, will not only improve the craft—as well as the art—of teaching but also encourage serious and continuing discussion of the aims and methods of teaching literature.

The principal objective of the series is to collect within each volume different points of view on teaching a specific literary work, a literary tradition, or a writer widely taught at the undergraduate level. The preparation of each volume begins with a wide-ranging survey of instructors, thus enabling us to include in the volume the philosophies and approaches, thoughts and methods of scores of experienced teachers. The result is a sourcebook of material, information, and ideas on teaching the subject of the volume to undergraduates.

The series is intended to serve nonspecialists as well as specialists, inexperienced as well as experienced teachers, graduate students who wish to learn effective ways of teaching as well as senior professors who wish to compare their own approaches with the approaches of colleagues in other schools. Of course, no volume in the series can ever substitute for erudition, intelligence, creativity, and sensitivity in teaching. We hope merely that each book will point readers in useful directions; at most each will offer only a first step in the long journey to successful teaching.

Joseph Gibaldi
Series Editor

# PREFACE TO THE VOLUME

The *Song of Roland* is one of the best-known medieval French literary texts. However, it is better known in excerpts and generalities than in its entirety. It poses difficulties to a modern college or university class because of its age, form, language, and subject—all characteristics that are related to scholarly issues surrounding the text.

Because of its importance to literary history, the *Song of Roland* is frequently taught in survey courses in both English and French by nonspecialists who may themselves have only encountered the text briefly. Scholarship about the *Roland* is extensive; like many canonical texts, the bibliography of secondary works is extensive, and translations and editions appear in many languages. It is difficult even for experts to keep up with the latest studies published throughout the globe. Where to begin, then, when preparing to teach it, whether for the first time or after many repetitions? This volume aims to help resolve an instructor's quandary.

To explore current practices in teaching the *Song of Roland*, the MLA distributed a questionnaire prepared by the volume's editors to all members of the Division of Medieval French Language and Literature as well as to a random selection of other MLA members. The editors also solicited responses from a few instructors outside the language and literature profession, as recommended by readers of early drafts of this volume. The thirty-two responses to the questionnaire came from college and university instructors at all levels; from all regions of the United States; in the case of one, from Canada; from those presenting the poem in English to freshmen; from those teaching it in Old French to graduate students; from those in language and literature; and from those in history. They represent, we believe, a fairly accurate cross section of methodologies and approaches. Many of the essays in the volume were first proposed by the respondents, but others were commissioned by the editors to address fully questions and concerns raised by respondents themselves. Not all approaches will appeal to every user of the volume, and some will be more helpful on one pedagogical level than another. Some approaches are straightforward and factual, whereas others are more speculative and potentially controversial. Each, we believe, can offer something of value to the teacher and student of the *Song of Roland*.

Contributors are primarily North American, as is the system to which the essays respond. Their essays treat specialized courses in which the poem is taught in the original Old French, in Modern French, in English translation, as well as survey courses in English or Modern French. However, since Britain shares the language of much of the United States and Canada, if not necessarily the educational system or literary approaches, three British scholars— all experts in their field—have graciously contributed to our volume. Continental critics are cited and will no doubt be the next step for those who continue in their studies of the chanson de geste and its progeny in the languages in which they were originally written.

The volume is organized into two parts and includes an audio CD. Part 1, "Materials," provides a descriptive analysis of materials available for teaching the poem, from editions through secondary and electronic items. The works listed derive both from suggestions submitted in the initial survey and from personal reflection and research by the editors. Readers should find particularly interesting the commentary on new editions of the *Chanson de Roland* derived from the online search for in-print French books. This allows instructors to depart from familiar but out-of-print editions for newer, cheaper, and available editions.

Online has become an important world, part 1 seeks to provide reliable information on Web sites. Additionally, multimedia materials that portray the importance of the *Roland* to Western Europe through art and music are reviewed. The accompanying audio CD provides readings in Old French according to three possible manners of presentation (since we do not know for sure how the poem was performed). Transcriptions of the texts presented and CD notes are included at the end of this section. Various forms of media, old and new, from comic books to computer games, are discussed in Leslie Zarker Morgan's "Audiovisual and Electronic Resources" to allow as wide a choice as possible in teaching materials, in methodologies, and in levels of instruction. In the world of self-guided instruction that the Internet makes available, we hope that this approach will introduce the joys of the *Song of Roland* to new audiences.

Part 2 of the volume, "Approaches," is subdivided into six sections: "Historical, Intellectual, and Literary Contexts"; "Avatars of the *Song of Roland*"; "Text, Language, and Poetic Techniques"; "The *Song of Roland* in the Classroom"; "Major Characters and Episodes"; and "Critical Approaches." With the exception of the last of these, the sections are intended primarily to give the instructor the necessary tools and background needed to present the text honestly and in context and to provide basic orientation for answering the questions most frequently asked of and about the poem. The final section offers a sampling of specific critical approaches to the *Song of Roland* from experienced teachers of the text at several levels and of different backgrounds. Readers might consult any of the sections separately, according to their current needs, and return at other times for inspiration in other courses or other semesters.

"Historical, Intellectual, and Literary Contexts" addresses the background of the *Song of Roland*. That background is historical both at the specific and general level. Thus it goes from, what really happened? when? how do we know? to the new historical contextual interests: what was the structure of the society that would cause people to be represented as acting in the way they do in this text? The question involves social structures from the concept of feudalism to the creation of oral and written versions of the *Roland* on the Continent and elsewhere. It also pertains to the more recent concern of social inclusion: the cultural context of western Europe at the time of the poem, surrounded and threatened by non-Christian Arabic groups. The epics of these groups are likewise colored by the times and can be examined in parallel with the epics of Christian Europe and, in particular, with those of the Carolingian empire.

"Avatars of the *Song of Roland*" addresses those who would continue their studies beyond the French tradition or who wish to link the *Roland* with its later developments. The essays in this section place the *Roland* in relation to literary works in Italy and Spain from the Middle Ages and Renaissance. But this section does not stop with medieval and Renaissance reception history; it continues to the rediscovery of the text and explores how France and Spain, in a time of nationalism and growth in the nineteenth century, greeted the rediscovery of the *Song of Roland*.

For those particularly interested in linguistic issues, the section "Text, Language, and Poetic Techniques" might be a first stop. It discusses both Anglo-Norman connections (the most famous version of the *Roland* is in Oxford, England) and issues of transmission. It also looks at the difficulty of translation into English and compares translated passages from different translators (this section expands the list of available translations in the "Materials" section for those concerned with teaching in translation). It is also a must-read for those wishing to review the oral versus written (in other words, traditional versus individualist) theories of composition, about which much ink was spilled during the twentieth century.

The section "The *Song of Roland* in the Classroom," is typical of the "Approaches" series and offers specific examples and discussion of results at different levels of instruction, from survey courses to upper-level French courses to history courses. These compare the *Roland* with other texts with which it is frequently read (*Beowulf, Hamlet*) and with elements of popular culture (*Lord of the Rings*). Certain essays include both discussion questions that the authors themselves use and reactions of students in their classes that might help readers prepare for the responses of their own students.

The essays in "Major Characters and Episodes" were primarily written as a result of questionnaire respondents' requests. Each essay summarizes a major issue either in literary or textual interpretation. We recommend these essays in particular because they treat not only many of the most disputed issues of the *Roland* in the past but also one rapidly developing area of research. Throughout the volume, whether one reads the entire book or dips into sections, one will notice returning themes that may be specifically addressed or just referred to in passing; many of these themes are discussed in this volume. Thus, Roland's *démesure*, taken for granted by some contributors (Everson, Black) and vigorously denied by others (Cook) is part of the received knowledge about the *Song of Roland* and is a concept frequently addressed in survey courses (see Warren; Engar, in this volume). But this is not a clear concept in the original text, as Catherine M. Jones emphasizes in her essay in this volume. She outlines step by step her class preparation, which aims to shock her students into considering Roland's actions differently. The Baligant episode has long been controversial, and scholars of different persuasions have tried to decide whether or not it is part of the "original" poem. Mary Jane Schenck carefully leads us through the critical history and then presents exercises to use with students in considering the episode's place in the poem's structure. Finally, Lynn Ramey's concluding essay in the section exemplifies how feminist criticism approaches medieval and Renaissance texts through historical and cultural methods.

The last section, "Critical Approaches," addresses both where *Roland* criticism comes from and where it may go. Two critics well known for their interpretations in volumes frequently cited in the surveys and critical literature on the *Roland* offer us shorter versions of their current insights on the poem, and three newer critics conclude with approaches relevant to current critical thought and methodologies. These are in part responses to questionnaires. Both Robert Francis Cook's and Eugene Vance's readings of the *Roland* were frequently cited as seminal to teachers' formation. Many respondents spoke of their concern with the violence that dominates the text. Others sought approaches that are beyond the textual and historical and that are more closely related to current literary critical concerns. We should note that the first proposal for this volume was delayed in submission by the 9/11 attack on New York City; therefore, many of the concerns and discussions in this collection reflect that event. Though we have tried to avoid too easily dated material, we feel that it is a sign of the viability of a text to be able to evoke passion in readers a thousand years later. Therefore, readers will find references to such current events in certain of these essays. The volume concludes with notes on the contributors, a list of the survey participants, and all works cited by the individual contributors.

In this volume, all citations of the original are from Ian Short's *La chanson de Roland* (1990), since it is the one most frequently cited by our respondents (for more information, see the first part of the "Materials" section, "Editions and Translations"). All translations are from Glyn S. Burgess's *The Song of Roland*, which is accurate, inexpensive, and readily available. Usually citations are by line numbers, and thus the words *line* or *lines* are not written. However, as is traditional when citing larger segments of the text, some citations may be by laisse, the strophic form of the chanson de geste (see Colby-Hall for more information), in which case "laisse" will be specified.

Several of the essays were first presented at the New College Conference on Medieval and Renaissance Studies in April 2004, in a session devoted to the volume; others were read at the annual meeting of the Medieval Institute at Kalamazoo in May 2001, in a session organized by the American Canadian branch of the Société Rencesvals, Teaching the *Song of Roland*. The enthusiastic response and overflowing audience there helped convince us of the need for this volume. Another paper was given at the annual meeting of the Medieval Institute in May 2004, again under the aegis of the Société Rencesvals.

In preparing this volume, we have received help from many sources. We thank most especially our colleagues who have collaborated in producing this volume, both those who took the time to painstakingly fill out the lengthy questionnaire as well as those who wrote, and rewrote, essays for the volume, patiently responding to our queries. We also wish to thank William Cowdery (Cornell University) for preparing a computerized copy of the melody by Alice M. Colby-Hall; Robert Eisenstein, director of the Five College Early Music Progam and founding member of the Folger Consort, for his technical expertise in assembling the final version of the CD and making other computerized copies of melodies performed; The Folger Shakespeare Library, Washington, DC, for providing a recording venue; and Mount Holyoke College for financial support. For assistance in preparing final copy, we are grateful to those colleagues who read and commented on sections, including Sophie Marnette, who, in reading an early version, made helpful suggestions. In addition, we express appreciation to the contributors, who, on occasion, generously allowed reorganization of their essays, even occasionally moving pieces of their writing to other sections of the book. We owe a special debt of gratitude to Joseph Gibaldi, director of Book Acquisitions and Development at the MLA and general editor of the series, for his helpful guidance through every step of preparing this volume. His interest even extended to attending the special session at the New College Conference on Medieval and Renaissance Studies devoted to the *Song of Roland* and to his teaching the text for the first time in many years. We thank also the anonymous readers of both the proposal and the completed essays for their many helpful criticisms, as well as the members of the MLA's Publications Committee for their careful consideration of our manuscript. And a volume on "approaches to teaching" cannot omit the most important of all, our students, who, in their responses and reactions, inspire us to continue seeking new information and appropriate ways of presenting the text with which we are so engaged in order to draw them in as well. We thank these listeners, contributors, readers, the MLA, and our respective institutions for enabling us to work on the volume. And we do so on behalf of future readers, because we know that the questions and thoughts reflected here are what render a literary classic such as the *Song of Roland* valuable through the centuries. Indeed, the poem lends itself to reexamining old questions with each generation and addressing contemporary concerns through the classic text.

WWK and LZM

# Part One

# MATERIALS

# Editions and Translations

### William W. Kibler

The *Song of Roland* is taught in college and university courses in the United States and Canada, in several departments and at different levels. For example, it can be used for lower-division students in a general survey of literature or as part of a freshman-level honors seminar on the epic, for upper-division students in French literature, or for graduate students in an introductory course or seminar in medieval literature or language. The choice of text will depend on the level at which it is taught, the language of instruction, and the purpose for which it was selected (that is, as a literary, linguistic, or historical document).

## French Editions and Translations

The *Song of Roland* found in the Oxford University, Bodleian Library Digby 23 manuscript is the most frequently edited text in Old French. The *editio princeps* was produced by Francisque Michel in 1837, whereas the first critical text was that by Léon Gautier in 1872. The first modern edition, accompanied by what is still recognized as the most elegant French translation, and which trumped all other editions and translations for many decades, was Joseph Bédier's La chanson de Roland, *publiée d'après le manuscrit d'Oxford et traduite par J. Bédier* (1921). Other widely respected and frequently cited editions are those by T. Atkinson Jenkins (1924; rev. 1929), Frederick Whitehead (1946), and Gérard Moignet (1969). In 1971, Cesare Segre produced the most thorough critical edition to date, the first to really consider seriously medieval French manuscripts other than Oxford as well as medieval translations. In what Segre calls a "synoptic" version, one can for the first time compare the Oxford text with the readings of all other medieval witnesses. This edition, originally published in Italian, was translated into French in 1989. A reprint of this edition, without the complete critical apparatus, was prepared for the French university exams of 2004 and 2005. It contains the Oxford text, Segre's original introduction and index of proper names, and a glossary by Bernard Guidot (Segre [2003]).

The other standard editions listed in the preceding paragraph are no longer in print, so teachers who wish to teach the *Roland* in French must rely on more modern editions. Currently available are three inexpensive translations into Modern French, with the Old French on facing pages. The earliest is the prose translation by Pierre Jonin, for the Folio Classique collection in 1979. Its introductory material and notes are the least useful of the three. Ian Short's edition with facing line-by-line translation was published in the Lettres gothiques collection by Livre de Poche in 1990. (In 1997 Livre de Poche published the translation alone in its Classiques médiévaux series.) The third edition and translation, by Jean Dufournet for Garnier-Flammarion (1993), is likewise line by line. This edition has the most detailed and useful introduction and notes of the three and also provides important historical background, including six appendixes that translate and analyze early chronicle passages relating to what actually happened in the Pyrenees. An abridged version of the translation alone has just appeared in a text aimed for French middle- to high-school-level students (presented by Patrice Kleff for GF Flammarion's "Étonnants Classiques"; see Dufournet [2003]).

Fully half the respondents who teach the *Song of Roland* in French, whether in Old French or in modern translation, use Short's edition and translation. It is appreciated for its availability, its reasonable cost for students, and its notes. Five respondents preferred the Moignet edition and translation for its more detailed notes but regretted that it is out of print. Most used Moignet's complete text ("texte original et traduction"), but one also used the extracts. The modern French extracts in Robert J. Berg and Fabrice Leroy, *Littérature française, textes et contextes*, were criticized by one respondent for giving "a somewhat skewed vision of the poem (e.g., near complete excision of Bramimonde and of Ganelon's trial)." Four respondents, who teach the poem in Old French in graduate-level courses, mentioned the 1924 Jenkins edition, which presents the text in standardized spelling and with an extensive, analytical glossary helpful to students new to Old French. This edition, however, has also been out of print for a long time. Gerard J. Brault's and Bédier's two editions and translations were each mentioned by a single respondent, as was Guillaume Picot's translation. Surprisingly, no one mentioned the Jonin or Dufournet editions and translations.

From our survey, it appears that Short's edition and translation has a virtual monopoly in the field. It is a very good choice, but teachers should be aware that it is an "interventionist" edition that has editorial changes intended to reflect more accurately the poet's original intentions, instead of simply reproducing the rather imperfect copy left to us in the Oxford manuscript. Editing any medieval text requires certain interpretative choices to be made by the modern editor, but this is greatly complicated in the case of the *Roland*, which exists in a number of distinctly different versions in Old French. One respondent noted: "To be honest, it is only in carrying out [recent] research that I have become aware of the true complexity of the editorial decisions involved in producing a *Roland* text. Because of this heightened sensitivity to the battles that have been waged over both general principles and specific lines, I will probably soon become more demanding of the edition I use."

Nonetheless, through all the battles, everyone acknowledges the superiority of the version found in the Oxford Digby 23 manuscript, which was discovered in England in 1835 by Michel, and, with only a handful of exceptions, all editions (and therefore all translations) are based on this copy. Although many early editors, notably Bédier (1921) and Moignet (1969), defended the Oxford text with all its difficulties, most modern editors admit that there are failings on the part of the scribe and seek to remedy these, usually with reference to the only other assonanced version of the poem, the Venice 4 (V4) manuscript. Even the most conservative editions count four or five lines from the V4 manuscript in the total line count of 4,002; these are lines 1389, 1615, 3146, 3390, and 3494 (this last line is counted but not printed by Bédier and Moignet!). Short adds these lines and alters the order of lines 1381–87 (in laisse 108), and displaces Bédier's and Moignet's laisses 113–14 to follow laisse 124. He likewise regularizes certain faulty lines and assonances. These changes are scrupulously indicated in the notes, so that the original order of lines in the manuscript can be easily reestablished, if one so desires.

Short's introduction, although succinct, is reliable. Short provides a line-by-line Modern French translation opposite the Old French verse original, in which he seeks to reproduce the rhythms and repetitions of the Old French. In this he largely succeeds. One respondent writes, "the translation is excellent," whereas another praises its "readability." In sum, readers of both the Old French and Modern French versions of the poem are well served by the Lettres gothiques text. Teachers looking for an option would do well, however, to consider Dufournet's edition and translation, which has particularly good complementary materials (introduction, notes, and appendixes).

The near-unanimous preference for the version of the *Song of Roland* in the Oxford Digby 23 manuscript has somewhat obscured the fact that the poem also exists in six other full-length manuscripts and three important fragments. They are

> Venice 4 (Biblioteca Nazionale Marciana, Fr. Z.4 [=225][1]), 6,011 assonanced lines (often referred to simply as V4)
> Venice 7 (Biblioteca Nazionale Marciana, Fr. Z.7 [=251]), 8,397 rhymed lines as edited (often V7)
> Châteauroux (Bibliothèque municipale MS 1), 8,201 rhymed lines
> Paris (Bibliothèque Nationale de France, fonds français 860), 6,828 rhymed lines
> Cambridge (Trinity College, R. 3.32), 5,695 rhymed lines
> Lyon (Bibliothèque municipale 743), 2,932 rhymed lines
> Lavergne fragment (Paris, Bibliothèque Nationale de France, nouv. aq. fr. 14658), 108 rhymed lines
> Bogdanow fragment (London, British Library, Additional 41295), 160 rhymed lines
> Michelant fragment (Paris, Bibliothèque Nationale de France, nouv. aq. fr. 5237), 352 rhymed lines

Other than Oxford, until recently only the assonanced Venice 4 manuscript had been satisfactorily edited according to modern standards. All seven French manuscripts were edited or photographically reproduced by Raoul Mortier; this edition, produced under difficult conditions during World War II, is very unsatisfactory and has recently been replaced by a new synoptic edition of all the manuscripts and fragments by a team of American and British scholars under the direction of Joseph J. Duggan (see Duggan et al.).

## English Translations

There was less unanimity on the choice of an English translation of the *Song of Roland*, although practical considerations again played a significant role. Respondents were about evenly divided in preferring either the new Penguin Classics translation by Glyn S. Burgess (based on the Whitehead edition) or the Frederick Goldin translation (based on Segre's 1971 edition), which is available in the stand-alone edition of the complete poem (1978) or extracted in the *Norton Anthology of World Masterpieces*. The earlier Dorothy Sayers translation, the W. S. Merwin translation, and the Robert Harrison translation were each mentioned by a single respondent. All these translations, as well as a newer translation by Patricia Terry, were listed as available for immediate shipment by popular book suppliers on the Web in June 2006. Goldin is more expensive than the competition but has an especially good introduction and notes; although his translation is still listed on *Amazon.com*, several respondents lamented that it is out of print. The popular Burgess translation is reasonable in cost, accuracy, and readability. The introduction and notes are less satisfactory overall than those by Goldin, but Burgess does reproduce in an appendix significant portions of the Old French text ("The Betrayal" [1–825], "Oliver v. Roland" [994–1109], "The Battle" [1188–1268], "Roland's Lament" [1851–85], "The Death of Roland" [2259–96], and "The Trial of Ganelon" [3750–4002]). The Brault student edition—a paperbound version of volume 2 of his analytic edition—is the only English translation to have the Old French text on facing pages. Two translations in the public domain and widely available on the World Wide Web, that in rhyming verse by John O'Hagan and that in assonance by Charles K. Scott-Moncrieff, are to be avoided.

Teachers and students using both Short's Old French or Modern French texts and Burgess's English translation will not fail to note that, although the line numbers mostly correspond, the laisse numbers are not always identical. This is another instance of the difficulties in editing the *Roland* alluded to above in the section on French editions and translations. Laisse beginnings usually involve a change of assonance, and this is generally marked as well by two-line red initials in the manuscript. The ends of many laisses in the *Roland* have the mysterious notation "AOI," which no one has ever explained satisfactorily. This notation occasionally occurs internally as well, and in those cases Burgess creates new laisses, whereas Short does not. Table 1 will help clarify the differences.

**Table 1**

| Verse | Mark | Laisse in Short | Laisses in Burgess |
|-------|------|-----------------|---------------------|
| 1403 | AOI | 109 | 109–10° |
| 2839 | AOI | 202 | 203–04 |
| 2981 | AOI | 214 | 215–16 |
| 3110 | colored initial | 226 | 228–29 |
| 3190 | colored initial | 230 | 233–34 |
| 3223 | AOI | 232 | 236–37 |
| 3231 | AOI | 232 | 237–38 |
| 3785 | AOI | 274 | 280–81 |

°Laisses 125a and 126 in Burgess correspond to 124 and 123 in Short.

## The Manuscript

The Digby 23 manuscript of the *Song of Roland* was written in England by an Anglo-Norman scribe, probably between 1125 and 1170. It is a simple, unimpressive manuscript with deletions, tears, stains, holes, and sewn repairs clearly visible. The text is written in a single column in ink that has faded to brown, with red two-line initials to mark the beginnings of most laisses. There are no miniatures or decorated initials, and the *Roland* is bound together with Calcidius's Latin translation of Plato's *Timaeus*, a manuscript of clearly different origin.

There are two facsimile editions of the manuscript, one in book format and in black and white (Samaran [1932]) and the other online and in color (*Bodleian*), which Leslie Zarker Morgan discusses below in "Audiovisual and Electronic Resources."

NOTE

¹This number designates the physical shelf collocation and is not the complete shelf mark or call number by itself. Fr. is an abbreviation for Francese.

# Readings for Students and Instructors
### William W. Kibler

## Background Studies

The alterity or otherness of the Middle Ages and of medieval mentality is frequently seen as a hurdle to approaching and understanding the *Song of Roland*. The basics of Western civilization are rarely taught these days, and, even in our modern environment of East-West confrontation, knowledge of the Arabic world and its culture is minimal at best. Many of the instructors who responded attempt to supply essential background through class lectures rather than assigned readings, especially on the undergraduate level. One instructor comments, for instance, "Frankly, I assign no background works because I realize that students here do not do additional reading." Typical of this group is Jeannette Beer's approach: "An introductory class explains literary and historical aspects that would otherwise be unfamiliar to modern students (assonance, epic formulae, feudal hierarchies, Crusading)." Nonetheless, when pushed, most instructors came up with fairly lengthy and often complementary lists of background and essential readings.

For instructors who prefer working from primary texts, two works basic to medieval thought are the New Testament and the Koran. To understand the philosophical and theological underpinnings of the Middle Ages, Boethius's *Consolation of Philosophy*, Augustine's *On Christian Doctrine* and *Confessions*, and Prudentius's *Psychomachia* are essential. More specific to the *Song of Roland* are Einhard's *Life of Charlemagne*, with its fascinating biographical details on the emperor and its brief and enigmatic mention of the Spanish campaign; Foulcher of Chartres's speech at the Council of Clermont, which launched the First Crusade; as well as Pope Urban's speech on the same occasion. These can be most conveniently found at the *Internet Medieval Sourcebook* (www.fordham.edu/halsall/sbook.html). Other epics sometimes taught in conjunction with the *Song of Roland* are Vergil's *Aeneid* and the Old English *Beowulf*. For other French epics that might profitably be studied alongside the *Song of Roland*, see Philip E. Bennett's essay, "Origins of the French Epic: The *Song of Roland* and Other French Epics," in this volume; for the Italian epic tradition and *Roland*, consult Jane E. Everson's contribution to this volume; for the Spanish tradition, see Matthew Bailey's essay; for other languages, see Joseph J. Duggan's essay, in this volume.

In addition to such primary sources, a number of secondary sources that provide basic intellectual and cultural background were cited. Specific areas in which background studies can be useful to both student and instructor in relation to the *Roland* are medieval history and culture, feudalism and chivalry, the Crusades and the Saracens.

Two medieval historians, Georges Duby and Jacques Le Goff, were named more than any others; both provide essential cultural context as well as hard historical facts. A number of books by Duby and Le Goff were cited, and all the key ones by both authors are available in English translation. Most often noted was Duby's *The Three Orders: Feudal Society Imagined*. Respondents also recommended Duby's *The Knight, The Lady, and the Priest: The Making of Modern Marriage in Medieval France; Love and Marriage in the Middle Ages; The Age of the Cathedrals: Art and Society, 980–1420;* and *The Chivalrous Society*. Works by Le Goff referred to were *Un autre moyen âge; Medieval Civilization, 400–1500;* and *The Medieval Imagination*. A more recent study by an American historian that has garnered interest is Constance Brittain Bouchard's *"Strong of Body, Brave and Noble": Chivalry and Society in Medieval France*.

The category of feudalism and chivalry overlaps with that of history and culture, so many of the works just cited are pertinent here as well. In addition, the class could be directed to Marc Bloch's classic study *Feudal Society*; Duby's *William Marshal: The Flower of Chivalry*; or Maurice Keen's *Chivalry*.

In the undergraduate classroom, Bloch is heavy going, and much of the exposition of feudalism continues to be presented through such shorter and less complex volumes as Carl Stephenson's *Mediaeval Feudalism* or, at a more advanced level, François Louis Ganshof's *Feudalism*.

On the Crusades, the classic works are Kenneth M. Setton, *A History of the Crusades*; Steven Runciman, *A History of the Crusades*; and Carl Erdmann, *The Origin of the Idea of Crusade*. On relations between Europe and Islam, consult Franco Cardini, *Europe and Islam*. On Saracens in the *Roland*, two articles are particularly illuminating: Sharon Kinoshita, " 'Pagans Are Wrong and Christians Are Right': Alterity, Gender, and Nation in the *Chanson de Roland*," and Deborah Streifford Reisinger, "The Other and the Same: The Ambiguous Role of the Saracen in *La Chanson de Roland*." Other works on Saracens in the epic that are worth consulting are Norman Daniel, *Heroes and Saracens: An Interpretation of the Chansons de Geste*, and Jacqueline De Weever, *Sheba's Daughters: Whitening and Demonizing the Saracen Woman in Medieval French Epic*.

## Basic Sources for Students

On the most basic level, entries in *Dictionary of the Middle Ages* (Strayer) or *Medieval France: An Encyclopedia* (Kibler and Zinn), such as Charlemagne, Feudalism, Song of Roland, chanson de geste, provide the bare essentials. Also accessible are the pertinent chapters in Urban T. Holmes, Jr., *A History of Old French Literature* (though now rather dated); in Simon Gaunt's *Retelling the Tale: An Introduction to Medieval French Literature* (ch. 1); and in Michel Zink, *Medieval French Literature: An Introduction*, translated by

Jeff Rider. Available only in French are the chapters on the *Roland* in Zink, *Littérature française du moyen âge* and in Emmanuèle Baumgartner, *Moyen âge: 1050–1486*. Along this same line, introductions to the student edition by Gerard J. Brault and to Frederick Goldin's translation were recommended by multiple respondents. Also named, but more difficult to find, are the introduction and notes to T. Atkinson Jenkins's and Gérard Moignet's editions. Finally, Duggan's chapter entitled "The Epic," in *New History of French Literature*, is a contextualized introduction.

Duggan has also compiled a useful annotated bibliography in English through 1976, *Guide to Studies on the* chanson de Roland. Although dated, it is organized to provide, as the respondent Michelle R. Warren noted, "a sense of the most debated episodes and issues." A more up-to-date annotated bibliography can be found in the *Bulletin bibliographique de la Société Rencesvals*, which has been published annually since 1958. The best source for a current online bibliography is the MLA Bibliography, available by subscription at most institutional libraries.

The reading that is by far the most frequently assigned to students is the chapter "Roland Against Ganelon" in Erich Auerbach's *Mimesis*. As Judith Haas pointed out, it is "useful to provide ways of talking about the strangeness of the language and the form." One book, available in English translation, stands out as being especially helpful for getting students engaged with the text and with the problems it poses: Pierre Le Gentil's *La chanson de Roland* (1955). It covers, in a series of well-organized chapters, all the main questions generally associated with the poem: the Oxford text, the historical event, authorship and date of the poem, the prehistory of the poem and its origins, the meaning and unity of the work, character depiction, and the artistry of the Oxford poem. Three other volumes, all by American scholars, were mentioned by multiple respondents: Eugene Vance, *Reading the* Song of Roland; Robert F. Cook, *The Sense of the* Song of Roland; and Peter Haidu, *The Subject of Violence: The* Song of Roland *and the Birth of the State*. The most enthusiastic comments were for Cook, who, according to Catherine Jones, offers "a close textual reading and reviews/refutes past interpretations." Paul Rockwell expands on this observation, noting, telegraphically, that Cook's "line-by-line analysis [provides a] good review of previous work. [His] common sensical approach [is] good for undergrad's understanding [and] helps [the] instructor organize citations for clarity of presentation." Three respondents mentioned George Fenwick Jones, *The Ethos of the* Song of Roland, whereas two preferred Karl D. Uitti's chapter on the *Roland* in *Story, Myth, and Celebration in Old French Narrative Poetry, 1050–1200*. A recent and accessible monograph in English by Wolfgang G. van Emden, entitled simply *La chanson de Roland*, is available in the Critical Guides to French Texts series, written originally for British undergraduates.

## Readings for Teachers

In addition to the readings listed above for students, with which an instructor should obviously be familiar, a number of other studies can be helpful for anyone teaching the *Song of Roland*. Two general works about the French chanson de geste cited by respondents are François Suard's concise *La chanson de geste*, in the popular Que sais-je? series, and Dominique Boutet's more discursive *La chanson de geste: Forme et signification d'une écriture épique du moyen âge*.

Among the most important studies of the *Roland* are Joseph Bédier's four-volume *Les légendes épiques*, in which he set forth his famous theory that the poems we have today were composed by individual poets in the late eleventh and twelfth centuries along the pilgrimage routes to Compostela. Prior to Bédier, "traditionalist" scholars of the nineteenth century had concluded that extant epics such as the *Roland* stood in a long line of narrative poems, often referred to as cantilenas, that were born on early fields of battle, or shortly thereafter, and then handed down orally over the centuries. But Bédier's clarity of style and persuasiveness led most critics to accept his "individualist" theories fully, at least until Jean Rychner and Ramón Menéndez-Pidal published their important studies in the 1950s. Rychner's *La chanson de geste: Essai sur l'art épique des jongleurs* (1955) draws on the oral theories of Albert Lord and others, which contend that the medieval world into which the chansons de geste were born created and consumed literature orally. Not only did audiences listen to the poems being recited, but their "authors" (the jongleurs) actually created them as they sang by drawing on traditional themes, motifs, and formulaic lines. Four years later, Menéndez-Pidal's La chanson de Roland *y el neotradicionalismo (origines de la epica romanica)* appeared and neotraditionalism began to carry the day, especially following the French translation of his opus, retitled La chanson de Roland *et la tradition épique des Francs*, the following year. After decades of study of traditional Spanish epic, during which he demonstrated that Spain cultivated short, totally oral poems, Menéndez-Pidal was inspired by Rychner's work to postulate that French epic must have undergone a similar oral stage. His ideas were refined and popularized by Le Gentil in what remains the key introduction to the poem (*La chanson de Roland*). This research revived the debate between traditionalists and individualists, adding an essential new element, orality. On the differences between oral and written cultures, a key concept in understanding the origins and composition of the epic, two works are useful: Walter Ong, *Orality and Literacy* and Brian Stock, *The Implications of Literacy*. Opposing arguments in the orality and literacy debate are well articulated by Duggan, who advocates a traditionalist or oralist approach, and William Calin, who sets forth an individualist approach, in a series of four articles published in 1981 in *Olifant* (see Duggan, "Mode" and "Théorie"; Calin, "Épopée" and "Littérature"). This debate is important, for how we view the very nature of the *Roland* depends on the side we take: are we dealing with literature at all (in the sense of works composed of letters) or with an ever-changing tradition of sung epic that has no definitive form but exists in a multiplicity of performances, one of which was accidentally preserved in each of the extant manuscripts? Given the six quite distinct versions of the *Roland* preserved in French (see Duggan's essay in this volume), this debate can lead to quite passionate and active class discussion. For the past half century, with some refinements from the oralists here and there, neotraditionalism has been the most widely accepted theory of the origins of the French epic.

Corollary to the quarrel between the individualists and traditionalists about the origins of the epic is the question of oral composition, which considers whether traditional poets composed their works orally using stock themes, motifs, and formulaic lines. Anyone reading the *Roland*, even in English translation, is struck by the repetition of stock phrases and the manner in which certain scenes are consistently organized. The most accessible and oft-cited study of this material is Duggan's The Song of Roland: *Formulaic Style and Poetic Craft*. A more specialized work is Edward A. Heinemann's *L'art métrique de la chanson de geste: Essai sur la musicalité du récit*, which is not focused solely on the *Roland*. Also useful for studying formulas, as well as individual lines and words, is Duggan's *A Concordance of the* Chanson de Roland.

A good way to engage students in the debate between oralists and traditionalists is to have them analyze in detail one or several of the groups of *laisses similaires* that occur in the Oxford poem. Such a study necessarily begins with Rychner, cited above, but two more recent discussions that offer opposing points of view are those by Gaunt in his *Retelling the Tale* (ch. 1) and by Suzanne Fleischman in "A Linguistic Perspective on the *laisses similaires*: Orality and the Pragmatics of Narrative Discourse." On the one hand, Gaunt argues that the Oxford *Roland* is a literate work by a cultured poet that was written down from its inception. Although it presents some of the external characteristics of oral style (formulas, invocations, *laisses similaires*, etc.), the Oxford version is a bookish production. Fleischman, on the other hand, proposes a linguistic rather than a literary analysis. She accepts that the *Roland* is a product of oral performance, if not necessarily of oral composition, and argues that the repetitive pattern of the *laisses similaires* (which she terms "overlay") is a device common in popular (i.e., oral) as opposed to learned (i.e., written) discourse. There are a number of other studies devoted to the *laisses similaires*, but Gaunt's and Fleischman's should serve well to begin the discussion.

Several books offer close readings of the *Roland*, laisse by laisse and sometimes line by line. By far the most frequently cited by respondents was Cook's *The Sense of the* Song of Roland. Also useful for close readings, for both instructors and students, is Brault's commentary volume that accompanies his

1978 edition; van Emden's monograph, *La chanson de Roland*; and Jean Dufournet's *Cours sur la* Chanson de Roland.

Recent years have seen a bumper crop of publications about the *Song of Roland* in France. *Roland*'s presence on the *agrégation* (a national exam that, if passed, allows one to teach at the high school level or at some universities in France) of both 2004 and 2005 certainly added to the number of volumes. Among the more useful are Jean-Pierre Martin and Marielle Lignereux's *La chanson de Roland*, which consists of a literary analysis by Martin and a linguistic study by Lignereux, each organized as a course, and Bernard Gicquel's *Généalogie de la* Chanson de Roland *suivi des sources et modèles*, which is devoted principally to sources that the *Roland* poet might have exploited.

Other studies, not specific to the *Roland*, were listed by several respondents as providing helpful background materials for teachers: Martín de Riquer, *Les chansons de geste françaises*; R. Howard Bloch, *Etymologies and Genealogies: A Literary Anthropology of the French Middle Ages*; R. Howard Bloch and Stephen G. Nichols, *Medievalism and the Modernist Temper*; Sarah Kay, *The Chanson de Geste in the Age of Romance; Plaisir de l'épopée* (ed. Mathieu-Castellani), which includes chapters on humor in epic and later uses of epic material; and Suard, *Chanson de geste et tradition épique en France au moyen âge*.

# Audiovisual and Electronic Resources

*Leslie Zarker Morgan*

Audiovisual aids can help make the *Song of Roland* more familiar by presenting the poem's cultural context and the sound of the text. The audiovisual aids recommended by respondents to our questionnaire can be divided into two categories: textual resources, which address either the written form of the poem or an oral rendition of it, and cultural resources, which discuss the art, architecture, geography, and texts that influenced the creation and reception of the *Roland*. I treat both categories below, listing multiple formats (e.g., CD, video) together in each category.

## The Physical Text: Manuscript and Facsimiles

To introduce the text to students, several respondents mentioned using a facsimile of the manuscript but did not specify which facsimile they use. Available facsimiles include the photographic reproduction produced by the Société des Anciens Textes Français in 1933 by Charles Samaran (originally produced in a limited edition in 1932 for the Roxburghe Club). More readily accessible is the complete reproduction of the Oxford manuscript online (see *Bodleian*). Unlike Samaran's published facsimile, it is in color (although this manuscript has no illuminations or historiated initials to admire) and easily navigable, which gives the user a sense of the original text. The online text is not the same as holding a manuscript in one's hands, but, since there are other manuscripts available for viewing at this site, one can get an idea of the quality of the Oxford *Roland*. When viewing the manuscript, one can click on "View All" to navigate the manuscript by folio. The initial thumbnail images (about a quarter of the actual size) can be selected to view images that are approximately five times larger than an individual folio.

Respondents noted that they use facsimiles of other versions of the *Song of Roland* or of the Charlemagne cycle to illustrate the literary tradition of that cycle. Salvatore Calomino, a professor of German, shows students a facsimile of the *Rolandslied* with illuminations (reproductions of the illustrations from the *Rolandslied* [Heidelberg, MS. P, Codex Palatinus Germanicus 112], in reduced-format facsimile prints [Werner]) to illustrate the text. Also available to illustrate literary tradition is a facsimile of a fourteenth-century Franco-Italian manuscript, the *Entrée d'Espagne*, which recounts the adventures of Charlemagne in Spain before the defeat at Rencesvals (*Entrada*).[1] The *Entrée* manuscript is interesting both for the variety of miniature styles within a single long text and for demonstrating later developments of the *Roland* tradition (see also in this volume Everson's "Roland in the Italian Tradition"). This facsimile, since it is made with heavy paper and careful binding in an attempt to reproduce the original, can help demonstrate the feel of a manuscript.

## Audio Resources

Other respondents reported using sound, either readings or sung versions of the text. Joseph J. Duggan's Web site originally included his singing part of the text, but it no longer does (for more about oral presentation of the *Song of Roland*, see Switten's "Teaching the *Song of Roland* in Upper-Level Courses," in this volume). A reading of laisses 1 and 66 of the *Roland* is available online (*Chanson* [2003]). The Internet connections are problematic; it took over an hour to download the software required, and then the files could not be read without a plug-in.

There is a recording on a two-LP set (*Chanson* [1961]). Practically no one uses LPs today, so these are of limited value. For those who can still use LPs, the two-record set is recorded by The Proscenium Studio of Montreal, under the direction of Lucie de Vienne, and is read in Old French. It includes a pamphlet, "Program notes and text," with an introduction that explains the impetus for producing the recording: a visit to a ruined chapel in the "Pass of Roncesvals." There is also a brief note on the French language, in sections titled "Rhythm," "French 'R'," "Psychological Aspects of Language," "AOI," and "Music." The edition read from and printed in the accompanying booklet is Joseph Bédier's. There is also a Modern French translation included, produced by the Proscenium Studio, as well as Dorothy Sayers's English translation. According to the notes and the jacket, this is a complete rendering, with laisses 1–47 on A1, 48–92 on A2, 93–160 on B1, and 161–291 on B2. However, the disc labels indicate that the first ten laisses are absent. Furthermore, the text and translations show that various laisses are skipped throughout the rendering. The background music—trumpet voluntaries at the start, for example—can be a bit distracting, but the idea of using different voices for the narrator and for the various roles certainly increases the drama. (For a discussion of how to use this sort of resource in class and possible student reaction, see Switten, "Teaching," in this volume).

An audiobook version of the *Song of Roland* was produced in 1998 by Kathleen Kent Watson (*Song*). It is narrated by Terry Burnsed and read by a full cast on two one-and-a-half-hour cassettes. It begins with a very brief introduction, then the first six lines in Old French are sung by Duggan. The rest is read dramatically in English and is based on the English translation by D. D. R. Owen, with minor cuts: most of the pagan boasts in laisses 70–78, the defeat of the pagan peers in laisses 96–105 and of many of the Christian peers in laisses 114–20, the enumeration of Charlemagne's troops in laisses 216–25 and of the pagan divisions in laisses 232–35, as well as parts of the battle in laisses 237–45. As with the two-LP recording, the use of background noises—frequent trumpet blasts, the deep roar of the olifant, horses whinnying, blows supposedly being struck in battle, wild animal noises to accompany Charlemagne's dreams, Gregorian chants when mass is mentioned, and the like—can be distracting. Nonetheless, overall this is a successful production that enables the modern audience to experience the poem orally, as it was originally intended.

Three other audio excerpts are available. *Roncevaux: "Echos d'une bataille"* combines narration in modern French with music of later periods (the "echo") to present the *Song of Roland* to a general public. *Medieval Romance Poetry: A Survey of Medieval Romance Literature* presents poems read in the original languages and in English verse translations. One side and the beginning of the second LP are devoted to a discussion and reading of the *Song of Roland*. *Bele Buche et Bele Parleure: A Guide to the Pronunciation of Medieval and Renaissance French for Singers and Others*, by Jeannine Alton and Brian Jeffery, includes a booklet with the text and basic information about the *Song of Roland*, as well as a cassette that contains a reading of the opening lines, the death of Roland, and parts of Charlemagne's lament on the death of Roland.

The recording of a radio program by Wolfgang van Emden, originally produced for the BBC, *Was Roland?*, includes a short reading from the first laisse plus the sound of an olifant and a selection from an oral presentation of Yugoslav poetry (van Emden). While no one today is absolutely sure how the *Roland* actually sounded, that it was read or sung aloud we do know, because various historians mention that a singer named Taillefer sang a "song of Roland" ("cantilena Rollandi") on the battlefield of Hastings in 1066 to encourage Norman soldiers (see, for example, the list of similar examples in Moignet, *Chanson* 16 [1969], who mentions William of Malmesbury and Wace; for more on the significance of this contention, see also Short, "The *Song of Roland* and England," in this volume). Van Emden's recording is also interesting since it includes an impassioned defense of the individualist side of the debate about *Song of Roland* origins but does not denigrate the traditionalist point of view.

Because accurate recordings are difficult to find, and because they go out of circulation quickly, we include with this volume a CD that features several performances of part of the *Song of Roland*. These are explained and discussed in Margaret Switten's essay "Teaching the *Song of Roland* in Upper-Level Courses" and in the section "Resources for Reading and Singing," at the end of the "Materials" section.

## Visual Aids

Separating the *Roland* from the culture that formed it, as for any work of literature, is difficult. Visual resources aimed at teaching students about the civilization that produced the *Song of Roland* can explain references in the text and help make the poem more comprehensible to modern readers.

## Maps and Illustrations

Respondents to the survey frequently mentioned maps as a useful teaching tool, though which maps instructors used were not specified; one respondent noted the lack of a high-contrast, reproducible map that could be used to illustrate the geography of the *Roland* (see the maps at the end of this section). Many respondents also indicated that they use slides to illustrate general medieval topics, from architecture to cultural artifacts, and that they introduce slides and postcards of Rencesvals (Roncevaux in Modern French, Roncesvalles in Spanish) and its region, Aachen (in Modern French, Aix-la-Chapelle), the Chartres Cathedral window, and the Bayeux Tapestry.

## The Bayeux Tapestry

The Bayeux Tapestry, whether shown in the form of foldout or slides, is a major artistic aid to the study of the *Roland*. Since it was produced shortly after 1066 and since the Oxford version of the *Song of Roland* is generally dated to about 1100, the warrior dress and actions shown in the tapestry provide a good idea of what the poet may have envisaged as he composed (see also DeVries's "Military History and Technology in the *Song of Roland*," in this volume). In addition, in it there is a small character labeled "Turold," who seems to be dressed as an entertainer. While not many scholars think this has anything to do with the Turoldus of the poem, it is nonetheless an interesting coincidence. There is a wonderful foldout version available at the Centre Guillaume le Conquérant in Bayeux (where the Tapestry is displayed), complete with labels of all scenes in French, English, and German (*Tapisserie*; for more complete information, see the section "Resources for the Bayeux Tapestry" in Switten's essay "Teaching," in this volume). In that foldout version, the Turoldus figure appears in the scene labeled number 10. Also available is a CD-ROM that contains a complete reproduction of the entire tapestry, together with the text woven into the tapestry, maps of the military campaign, and notes (Foys). A beautiful coffee-table book with the Bayeux Tapestry in color, including descriptions and commentary, is also available (Wilson).

## The Chartres Window

A stained-glass window devoted to the legend of Roland that is found in the cathedral of Notre Dame of Chartres is frequently used by instructors to demonstrate the popularity of the Roland story. This window (dated from the end of the twelfth through the first quarter of the thirteenth century) appears in the northeastern radial chapel and recounts the Roland legend. However, the window is not based on the Oxford *Roland*, and it therefore contains scenes not in the poem. It has also been questioned whether or not the twenty-two panels originally were mounted in a different order (Maines). For black-and-white schematic representations of the window panels, as well as comments on the order and history of the window, see Clark Maines, who also offers a bibliography of earlier studies of the window. In addition to postcards from Chartres, respondents indicated that Rita Lejeune and Jacques Stiennon's *La légende de Roland dans l'art du moyen âge*, as well as the translation (*Legend*), is invaluable for its photographs and artistic information (volume 1 is composed of text and color plates; volume 2 consists of black-and-white photographs and indexes). The translation's page numbers and illustrations correspond exactly to the original. For reproductions of numerous artistic works related to the *Roland*, Lejeune and Stiennon's work is unparalleled.

Several details of the Chartres window appear in Lejeune and Stiennon's volume 1 (my descriptions quote the English translation of Lejeune and Stiennon, though not always in its entirety): "Charlemagne, Roland and Archbishop Turpin leaving for Spain," plate 7; "Charlemagne praying for the fall of Pamplona," plate 8; "Roland taking the heathen city of Noble," plate 9; "Roland and the miracle of the flowering lances," plate 10; "Roland killing a heathen king in the fight following the miracle of the flowering lances," plate 11; "Roland and the giant Ferragut fighting on horseback," plate 12; "Roland killing the heathen champion Ferragut, achieving sanctity as shown by a halo," plate 13; "End of the battle of Rencesvals. Roland, mortally wounded, trying to break his sword Durandal, and blowing his horn to warn Charlemagne," plate 14. Lejeune and Stiennon's chapter 1, "The [L]esson of Chartres," which appears in the "Gothic Period" section, discusses the organization and meaning of the Chartres window, arguing that the Chartres stained-glass window is not based on the Pseudo-Turpin version (192–98).[2] They also discuss and compare the Chartres window in other articles (e.g., "Héros Roland"). Lejeune and Stiennon's conclusions both about the Chartres window and other artistic works related to the Charlemagne cycle have been criticized; the bibliography in the relevant chapter notes to the *Légende/Legend* will allow readers to pursue the points raised if they so desire (Lejeune and Stiennon, *Légende* 206; *Legend* 206). For an example and further bibliography of criticism about Lejeune and Stiennon's conclusions regarding the Chartres window, see V. Labande-Mailfert's review. The Chartres window's details are available on the Web; however, the sites change as course offerings in different universities change, so they are not listed here, though students and instructors can perform a search to find a current posting.

## Cultural Background

### Manuscripts and Paleography

Respondents also indicated that the manner of producing a manuscript, the transmission of text, and aspects of paleography in general are essential topics for teaching the *Roland*. Although the Oxford manuscript is a key document of French literary tradition, it is located in the Bodleian Library of Oxford University. Thus, the reasons for its survival and for its less-than-optimal manuscript state need to be explained to students familiar with books that are omnipresent in multiple editions and preserved in libraries. Learning about manuscript culture, from the production of writing materials to the script used, can add to students' appreciation of the "differentness" of the text. *The Medieval Book* (Shailor) and *The Making of a Manuscript* (Rigg), a video, allow students to follow the process of manuscript production and to understand the fragility of the medium and the expense required for its production. Both works show actual folios, codices, and writing implements. There are various videos available that discuss the history of manuscript and book production (e.g., Smeyers et al.), and another inexpensive and useful volume on manuscript production is *Scribes and Illuminators* (De Hamel).

### Artifacts

Other artistic aides that can be used in the classroom include images relating to the Roland legend, such as illustrations of artifacts from the thirteenth through fifteenth centuries. Illuminations from manuscripts of various texts (not necessarily the *Song of Roland*) are reproduced in editions of the *Roland*, in anthologies (e.g., Berthelot and Cornilliat 80–81), and in pedagogical editions of the *Roland*, such as the Nouveaux classiques Larousse series (Picot). Horns of the type used by Roland (e.g., the so-called Charlemagne's Olifant, which dates to the ninth century [Berthelot and Cornilliat 71]) and sword handles that might contain relics, as Charlemagne's and Roland's did, can also provide background information. A museum guide, such as the *Metropolitan Museum of Art Guide* (Howard) can provide numerous examples of artifacts contemporary to the writing of the Oxford version of the *Song of Roland*.

## Film and Television

There are several movies related to the *Song of Roland*. The film *La chanson de Roland* is cited on various film databases (Cassenti) and in *The Reel Middle Ages: American, Western and Eastern European, Middle Eastern, and Asian Films about Medieval Europe* (Harty 49, number 83). It has just been reissued on DVD and is available from bookstores and record stores. The film is difficult to follow without previous preparation, since it is a "story within a story"; it is not a straightforward recounting of the *Roland*, but rather the story is presented by a group of medieval pilgrims on the way to Santiago. The scenery is appropriately depressing—mountain passes in winter—and the characters a bit rough. Cassenti's *Roland* will need to be previewed carefully to determine whether it is appropriate for the intended audience, because of the representation of violence and scenes of other sorts, such as childbirth.

Teachers have attempted to produce their own videos, though these seem not to be generally available. For example, Alan Hindley and B. J. Levy document producing a *Chanson de Roland* for the Hull French Tapes (Hindley and Levy), but I have been unable to track this down.

Kevin Harty lists a number of other films related to the Roland tradition, many of which are from Italy. However, since those are more likely to follow Matteo Maria Boiardo's fifteenth-century *Orlando innamorato* ("Roland in Love") than the Oxford *Song of Roland*, they are not included here. A five-film series about the life of Charlemagne, *Charlemagne*, which includes the battle of Rencesvals in the fourth video, is no longer available but might be found in local libraries. The five films, in a popular format, draw from both historical and fictional sources (e.g., the *Song of Roland* and *Chanson des Saisnes* ["Song of the Saxons"]) and mix history and fiction indistinguishably. The result is a great story. The film includes some incidents not often mentioned in literature courses (e.g., Charlemagne's attempt to build a canal between the Rhine and the Danube, in order to link the North Sea and Black Sea), but it can muddy discussion for those unfamiliar with history.

Instructors can also use two films not directly related to the *Roland* that are effective teaching tools since they help in illustrating points about the tradition. William Paden teaches Oliver Stone's *Platoon* successfully as a modern contrast to medieval battle development and approach. I have used a *Star Trek* episode, "Darmok," in which the character Dathon, an alien-race (Tamarian) captain, communicates only in epic metaphor. Students were somewhat surprised but enjoyed a discussion of epic language as a result. Since the episode is 46 minutes long, it also fits well into class time (in my case 50 minutes), which is not true of feature films.

## Other Resources

Finally, comic books and computer games can help make the medieval world accessible to a modern, visually trained generation. Recently, an inspired undergraduate created a comic book in Japanese style (Amaya, Moon, and Ba) that illustrates Frederick Goldin's translation. There is also a computer game, *The Madness of Roland*, written originally as a separate CD for personal computers. The game is based on Boiardo's *Orlando innamorato* (for Boiardo, see Everson's "Roland in the Italian Tradition," in this volume); in it, a user takes the role of any of the main characters in the story and follows the plot from that character's perspective (Roach). I used the separate game as an outside activity for one course, Introduction to Medieval French Literature in English, asking students to comment on it both as a game and in relation to characteristics of epic and romance that we had studied. They enjoyed the assignment but found the game primitive, because they were not allowed to choose the character's actions at each decision point. Since the game is based on a literary work, the characters' choices are to a certain extent limited. Students did prefer the game to reading the text themselves, however. (Note that the version of the game we used was an early stand-alone version, on a Macintosh computer, which was in general unfamiliar to my students at Loyola College, who tend to use IBM computers. I have not had the opportunity to test newer versions; for information about the latest version, see www.hyperbole.com/full/serial/roland/roland.html.

There are many Web pages put up by school groups and individuals that provide translations of the *Roland* (now in the public domain) or general information about the poem and its context, sometimes of a questionable nature. Among the sites that are useful, there is a French Web site that gives information about various chansons de geste; in addition the site has a separate page about the *Chanson de Roland* (click on Toutes les chansons; La chanson de Roland). The ORB: *On-line Reference Book for Medieval Studies* contains a number of useful pages, among which are my own translations of a fourteenth-century Franco-Italian "Berta e Milon" ("Berta and Milone") and "Rolandin" ("Childhood of Roland" [see Morgan]). Also on the Web are useful links to historical sites like Einhard's *Life of Charlemagne* on Paul Halsall's *Medieval Source Book* site.

## Cultural Resources: Later Traditions Deriving from the Song of Roland

The later tradition of the *Roland* frequently derives from intermediary texts such as Ludovico Ariosto's *Orlando furioso*, rather than from the *Song of Roland* directly. Not only movies, as suggested above, but also George Frideric Handel's operas derive from Ariosto. Handel's last operas form a trio of Ariosto-based works: *Orlando* (1732), *Ariodante* (1734), and *Alcina* (1735). According to Iris Bass, more than one hundred operas owe their plots to the *Orlando furioso*. Compared with the *Roland*, Handel's *Orlando* has a greatly reduced number of characters, five: Orlando, Angelica, Medoro (her prince), Dorinda (a shepherdess), and Zoroastro (a magician). It is currently available in a two-CD version that includes an introduction, summaries of the scenes, and the arias, all translated into English, French, and German (see Handel [1996]). There is also a Oiseau-Lyre version on authentic instruments that I had to order from Canada, since it was not available in the United States; it took nearly a year to arrive (Handel [1991]).

Keeping up with useful audiovisual pedagogical materials is difficult. Audiovisual and technological resources are, unfortunately, more easily outdated than editions and textbooks. An introductory video about the *Song of Roland* has just been released as the manuscript for this volume is being typeset (www.filmsmediagroup.com/id/12572/The_Song_of_Roland.htm).    I would suggest therefore that the interested teacher might consult periodically *Studies in Medieval and Renaissance Teaching*, which, in the issue that arrived during this writing, contains an article entitled "Antar, an Islamic Counterpoint to Roland" (Stevenson). Similarly, the annual *Bulletin bibliographique de la Société Rencesvals* includes all articles on the romance epic, whether pedagogical in nature or purely research-oriented. The Web site of the Société Rencesvals provides links, including one to the archive of its journal *Olifant*, which can be used to investigate current hot topics or to follow historical discussions of all kinds. The current issues are available in many libraries through their online subscriptions. The Globe-Gate Project Web site, dedicated to French language, culture, and civilization, includes *Medieval French Heroic Literature*. It is maintained by Robert Peckham (aka "Tennessee Bob") and includes links to medieval French literature, language, and culture; it too can also provide updated references (see Peckham).

NOTES

[1]The reproduction is of Venice, Biblioteca Nazionale Marciana, Francese Z.21 (=257).

[2]For more about the Pseudo Turpin, see Bennett ("Origins") and Duggan ("Beyond"), in this volume.

# Resources for Reading and Singing

## *Musical Examples*

Ex. 1. *Laisse 1.* Music by Alice M. Colby-Hall, 2004 (CD Track 9)

Ex. 2. *Laisse 1.* Music adapted by Joseph J. Duggan (CD Track 10)

| Car - les li | reis, | nos tr'em-pe | - re - re | ma | - gnes, |
|---|---|---|---|---|---|
| Set anz tuz | pleins | ad es - tét | en Es | - pai | - gne: |
| Tres qu'en la | mer | cun-quist la | tere al | - tai | - gne, |
| N'i ad cas - | tel | ki de-vant | lui re | - mai | - gne; |
| Mur ne ci - | tét | n'i est re - | més a | frain | - dre |
| Fors Sar - ra - | gu - ce, | k'est en u | - ne mun | - tai | - gne. |
| Li reis Mar - | si - lie | la tient, ki | Deu nen | ai | - met; |
| Ma - hu - met | sert | e A - pol - | lin re | - clei | - met: |
| Ne s' poet guar - | der | que mals ne | l'i a | - tei | - gnet. |

Ex. 3. *Laisse 2.* Music adapted by Joseph J. Duggan (CD Track 11)

| Li reis Mar - | si - lie | es - teit en | Sar - ra | - gu | - ce: |
|---|---|---|---|---|---|
| A - lez en | est | en un ver - | ger suz | l'um | - bre; |
| Sur un per - | run | de mar - bre | bloi se | cul | - ched, |
| En - vi - run | lui | plus de vint | mi - lië | hu | - mes. |
| Il en a - | pe - let | e ses dux | e ses | cun | - tes: |
| "O - ĕz, sei - | gnurs, | quel pec - chét | nus en | - cum | - bret: |
| Li em - pe - | re - res | Car - les de | Fran - ce | dul | - ce |
| En cest pa - | ïs | nos est ve - | nuz cun | - fun | - dre. |
| Jo nen ai | ost | qui ba - tail - | le li | dun | - ne, |
| Nen ai tel | gent | ki la stü - | e de - | rum | - pet. |
| Cun - se -ilez | mei | cu - me mi | sai - vĕ | hu | - me, |
| Si m'gua - ri - | sez | e de mort | et de | hun | - te!" |
| N'i ad pai - | en | ki un sul | mot res | - pun | - det |
| Fors Blan - can - | drins | de Cast - tel | de Val | - fun | - de. |

Ex. 4. *Laisse 1.* Music adapted by Margaret Switten (CD Tracks 12 and 14)

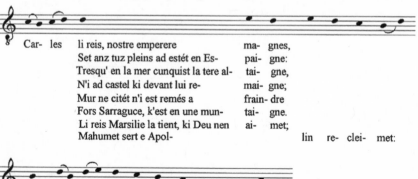

| Car- les | li reis, nostre emperere | ma- | gnes, |
|---|---|---|---|
| | Set anz tuz pleins ad estét en Es- | pai- | gne: |
| | Tresqu' en la mer cunquist la tere al- | tai- | gne, |
| | N'i ad castel ki devant lui re- | mai- | gne; |
| | Mur ne citét n'i est remés a | frain- | dre |
| | Fors Sarraguce, k'est en une mun- | tai- | gne. |
| | Li reis Marsilie la tient, ki Deu nen | ai- | met; |
| | Mahumet sert e Apol- | lin re- clei- met: |

Ne s' poet guar- der que mals ne l'i a- tei- gnet.

Ex. 5. *Laisse* 176. Music adapted by Margaret Switten (CD Track 13)

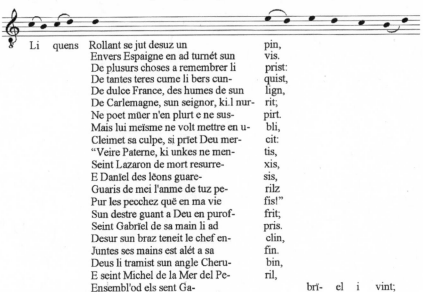

| Li | quens | Rollant se jut desuz un | pin, |
| | | Envers Espaigne en ad turnét sun | vis. |
| | | De plusurs choses a remembrer li | prist: |
| | | De tantes teres cume li bers cun- | quist, |
| | | De dulce France, des humes de sun | lign, |
| | | De Carlemagne, sun seignor, ki.l nur- | rit; |
| | | Ne poet müer n'en plurt e ne sus- | pirt. |
| | | Mais lui meïsme ne volt mettre en u- | bli, |
| | | Cleimet sa culpe, si prïet Deu mer- | cit: |
| | | "Veire Paterne, ki unkes ne men- | tis, |
| | | Seint Lazaron de mort resurre- | xis, |
| | | E Danïel des lëons guare- | sis, |
| | | Guaris de mei l'anme de tuz pe- | rilz |
| | | Pur les pecchez quë en ma vie | fis!" |
| | | Sun destre guant a Deu en purof- | frit; |
| | | Seint Gabrïel de sa main li ad | pris. |
| | | Desur sun braz teneit le chef en- | clin, |
| | | Juntes ses mains est alét a sa | fin. |
| | | Deus li tramist sun angle Cheru- | bin, |
| | | E seint Michel de la Mer del Pe- | ril, |
| | | Ensembl'od els sent Ga- | brï- el i vint; |

L'an- me del cun- te por- tent en par- re- ïs.

Translations

   LAISSE 1. Charles the king, our great emperor, / Has been in Spain for seven long years, / And conquered that proud land as far as the sea. / There is no castle which can resist him, / No wall or city left to be destroyed, / Except for Saragossa, which stands upon a mountain. / It is held by King Marsile, who does not love God; / He serves Muhammad and calls upon Apollo. / He cannot prevent disaster from overtaking him.

   LAISSE 2. King Marsile was in Saragossa; / He went into a garden, beneath the shade, / And reclines upon a slab of bluish marble / With more than twenty thousand men around him. / He summons both his dukes and his counts: / "Hear, lords, what misfortune weighs upon us; / The emperor Charles from the fair land of France / Has come to this country to destroy us. / I have no army to match his in battle, / Nor sufficient men to break his army down. / Give me counsel as my wise men, / And protect me from both death and shame." / There is no pagan who utters a single word in reply, / Except for Blancandrin from Castel de Valfunde.

   LAISSE 176. Count Roland lay down beneath a pine tree; / He has turned his face towards Spain. / Many things began to pass through his mind: / All the lands which he conquered as a warrior, / The fair land of France, the men of his lineage, / Charlemagne, his lord, who raised him. / He cannot help weeping and heaving great sighs; / But he does not wish to be unmindful of himself. / He confesses his sins and prays for the grace of God: / "True Father, who has never lied, / You who brought back Lazarus from the dead / And rescued Daniel from the lions, / Protect my soul from every peril / And from the sins which I have committed in my life." / He proffered his right glove to God; / Saint Gabriel took it from his hand. / Roland laid his head down over his arm; / With his hands joined he went to his end. / God sent down his angel Cherubin / And with him Saint Michael of the Peril. / With them both came Saint Gabriel. / They bear the count's soul to paradise.

Ex. 6. *Beatus vir* (CD Track 15)
*Liber usualis,* Psalmus 111, Tonus 7

| Intonation | Reciting pitch | Inflection (for long lines) | Reciting pitch | Mid-verse cadence | Reciting pitch | End cadence |
|---|---|---|---|---|---|---|
| 1. Be- a- | tus vir qui | | | ti- met Do- mi- num | in mandatis ejus | vo- let ni- mis. |
| 2. | Potens in terra erit | | | se- men e- jus: | generatio rectorum be- | ne- di- ce- tur. |
| 3. | Gloria et divitiae in | | | do- mo e- jus: | et justicia ejus manet in sae- | cu- lum sae- cu- li. |
| 4. | Exortum est in tenebris | | | lu- men re- ctis: | misericors et misera- | tor, et ju- stus. |
| 5. | Jucundus homo qui | | | | | |
| 5.. | miseretur et | com- mo- dat, | disponet ser- / mones suos | in ju- di- ci- o: | quia in aeternum non | com- mo- ve- bi- tur. |
| 6. | In memoria aeterna | | | e- rit ju- stus: | ab auditione mala | non ti- me- bit. |
| 7. | Paratum cor ejus | | | est cor e- jus: | non commovebitur donec / despiciat ini- | mi- cos su- os. |
| 8. | sperare in / Dispersit, dedit pau- | Do- mi- no, / pe- ri- bus | confirmatum / justicia ejus / manet in | sae- cu- lum sae- cu- li | cornu ejus exaltabi- | tur in glo- ri- a. |
| 9. | Peccator videbit et ira- sce- | tur, | dentibus suis fremet | et ta- be- scet: | desiderium peccato- | rum per- i- bit. |
| 10. Gloria | | | | Pa- tri, et Fi- li- o, | et Spiri- | tu- i San- cto. |
| 11. | Sicut erat in principio, et | | | nunc, et sem- per, | et in saecula saecu- | lo- rum A- men. |

**Translation**

Blessed is the man that feareth the Lord: he delights greatly in his commandments. / His seed shall be mighty upon earth: the generation of the righteous shall be blessed./ Glory and wealth are in his house: and his justice remaineth for ever and ever./ To the righteous a light is risen up in darkness: he is merciful, and compassionate and just./ Acceptable is the man that showeth mercy and lendeth: he shall order his words with judgment: because he shall never be moved./ The just shall be in everlasting remembrance: he shall not be afraid of evil tidings./ His heart is ready to hope in the Lord: his heart is strengthened, he shall not be moved until he look over his enemies./ He hath dispersed, he hath given to the poor: his justice endureth for ever and ever: his horn shall be exalted in glory./ The wicked shall see, and shall be angry, he shall gnash with his teeth and pine away: the desire of the wicked shall perish./ Glory be to the Father, and to the Son, and to the Holy Ghost. / As it was in the beginning, is now, and forever shall be: world without end. Amen.

Ex. 7. *Commemoratio brevis,* Seventh mode end cadence

Gloria... se- cu- lo- rum a- men

**Ex. 8.** *Aucassin et Nicolette,* section 1 (CD Track 16)
BnF fr 2168, fol 70

**Ex. 9.** *Aucassin et Nicolette,* section 33 (CD Track 17)
BnF fr 2168, fol 79

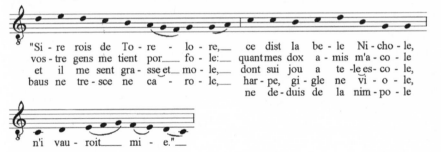

**Ex. 10.** *Le Jeu de Robin et de Marion,* line 729 (CD Track 18)
BnF fr 25566

Translations

*Aucassin et Nicolette*

SECTION 1. Whoever would hear good verse / Composed joyously by "Vielantif" / About two fair children, / Nicolete and Aucassin, / About the great sorrows he suffered, / And the valiant deeds he accomplished / For his belovèd with the fair countenance. / Sweet is the song, beautiful the tale, /And courteous and well composed. / No one is so depressed, / So doleful nor undone, / So gravely ill, / That, if he hears it, he will not be healed / And restored to joy / So sweet it is.

SECTION 33. "King of Torelore, my lord!" / So spoke fair Nicolette / "Your people think I am crazy: / When my sweet friend embraces me / And he finds me plump and soft, / I am in such a state / That neither dance, carole nor round, / Music of the harp, the gigue (stringed instrument) or the vielle, / Nor game of chess / Means anything to me.

*Le Jeu de Robin et de Marion*

"Audigier," said Raimberge, "I say shit to you."

Ex. 11. *Tu autem* (CD Track 19)
BnF lat 1139, fol 44

Translation

Our story/explanation must henceforth end; / I am tired, for the sound was too high. / Two priests rise to say the response; / Thou also God who art the glorious Father, / We pray Thee to remember us, / When Thou wilt separate the bad from the good.

Acknowledgments

The music computer files were prepared by William Cowdery for Ex. 1 and by Robert Eisenstein for Ex. 2-11.

Sources

The music for examples 8-11 is transcribed from the manuscripts indicated by the abbreviations above each transcription. The music for examples 8 and 9 comes from Paris, Bibliothèque nationale de France, fonds français 2168. The music for example 10 comes from Paris, Bibliothèque nationale de France, fonds français 25566. The music for example 11 comes from Paris, Bibliothèque nationale de France, fonds latin 1139. The texts and translations are taken from the following sources, which cross-reference entries in the works-cited list at the end of this volume. The text of the *Song of Roland*, laisses 1, 2, and 176, is from Short (*La chanson* [1990] 28, 30, 178, 180). The translation is from Burgess (*Song* 29, 104-05). The text and music of *Beatus vir* are taken from the *Liber usualis* (151-52); the translation is adapted from Palisca (26-27). Example 7 from the *Commemoratio brevis* is from T. Bailey (95). For *Aucassin et Nicolette*, sections 1 and 33, the text is from Walter (32, 138); the translations are by Switten. The text of the *Jeu de Robin et de Marion* is from Dufournet (124); the translation is by Switten. The text and translation of *Tu autem* are taken from *The Medieval Lyric* (anthology 1, p. 20.)

## *Track Listing for the Accompanying Compact Disc*

| Reading of the *Song of Roland* by Alice M. Colby-Hall | Time |
|---|---|
| 1. Introduction (lines 1–9) | 00:46 |
| 2. Army's Return to Gascony (lines 814–25) | 00:58 |
| 3. Roland's Refusal to Blow His Horn (lines 994–1092) | 07:20 |
| 4. Roland's Change of Mind and Blowing of the Horn (lines 1702–95) | 06:48 |
| 5. Roland's Death (lines 2297–396) | 07:10 |
| 6. Charlemagne's Lament for Roland (lines 2855–944) | 06:20 |
| 7. Aude's Death (lines 3705–33) | 02:12 |
| 8. Punishment of Ganelon and Closing Lines (lines 3960–4002) | 03:02 |

| Singing the *Song of Roland* | |
|---|---|
| 9. Laisse 1 (lines 1–9), melody by Alice M. Colby-Hall | 01:04 |
| 10. Laisse 1 (lines 1–9), music adapted by Joseph J. Duggan | 01:04 |
| 11. Laisse 2 (lines 10–23), music adapted by Joseph J. Duggan | 01:36 |
| 12. Laisse 1 (lines 1–9), music adapted by Margaret Switten | 00:56 |
| 13. Laisse 176 (lines 2375–96), music adapted by Margaret Switten | 02:32 |
| 14. Laisse 1 (lines 1–9), music as for track 12, with a vielle | 01:12 |

| Musical Models | |
|---|---|
| 15. *Beatus vir*, Psalm 111 | 02:40 |
| 16. *Aucassin et Nicolette*, section 1 | 01:06 |
| 17. *Aucassin et Nicolette*, section 33 | 00:46 |
| 18. *Le Jeu de Robin et de Marion*, line 729 | 00:08 |
| 19. *Tu autem* | 00:54 |

| Total Time | 49:08 |
|---|---|

Tracks 1–8: Alice M. Colby-Hall, recorded at Cornell University, Language Resource Center, Andrew Page, engineer. Tracks 9, 12–17: William H. Sharp, baritone, voice faculty, Peabody Conservatory, Baltimore, and for Track 14 Robert Eisenstein, vielle; recorded at the Folger Shakespeare Library, Washington, DC, by Robert Eisenstein, director of the Five-College Early Music Program and founding member of the Folger Consort, Washington, DC. Tracks 10–11, 18: Andrew Pidkameny, baritone, Hampshire College; recorded at Mount Holyoke College by Robert Eisenstein. Track 19: Paul Hillier, baritone, from *The Medieval Lyric, a Project Supported by the National Endowment for the Humanities and Mount Holyoke College*. Tracks 9–19 used with permission of Mount Holyoke College. Consultant for Old French, Alice M. Colby-Hall; consultant for Old Picard, Samuel N. Rosenberg, Indiana

University. CD coordinator, Margaret Switten; CD compilation and production, Robert Eisenstein. © 2006 The Modern Language Association of America.

## Notes to the Compact Disc

### Margaret Switten

The accompanying compact disc proposes ways of teaching the *Song of Roland* as oral poetry and sung language. It invites students to think of the "text" as carrying its message through sound rather than sight, through listening rather than reading. Since no *Roland* manuscript has musical notation, knowledge of language rests on surer ground than knowledge of music, but neither is perfect. The intention here is therefore not to demonstrate what the *Song of Roland* was "really like"; rather, we offer sonorous models that can help students appreciate the rich quality of the old language and listen to the efforts to recuperate the lost music proposed by the musical examples.

Tracks 1–8 are discussed in the essay by Alice M. Colby-Hall in this volume. These readings enable students to get a sense of the language and of the pulse and movement of the poetry.

Tracks 9–14 record the various approaches to reconstructing sung performance offered by musical examples 1–5. These are educated guesses. We have not attempted to perform the letters *AOI* that follow some laisses because there is a total lack of consensus on their function. Many aspects of medieval musical performance are lost to us. If music for the *Roland* had been notated, the notation of that period, and of a secular repertory, would have informed us about pitches (highness and lowness of notes), but not about other parameters such as rhythm or tempo. Voice quality is another variable. Texts speak of different types of voices, some full and rich, others not so full—as, indeed, we encounter natural voices today—but the kind of training that produces the modern singer was unknown in the Middle Ages. Our performances inevitably reflect modern performance strategies; through them, however, we hope to stimulate an awareness of sound for this work that we call a song.

Track 9 is a recording of a melody composed by Colby-Hall, performed by William H. Sharp. The melody, as she points out in her essay, is chantlike, recalling the essential musical environment of the period of the *Song of Roland*. The melody focuses on the note a, which by force of repetition almost takes on the function of a reciting tone, and closes on the final D. The melodic structure built on three units, two repeated throughout the laisse while the third serves as a concluding formula, resembles, though it does not exactly reproduce, the structure of the melody for the sung laisses in *Aucassin et Nicolette*.

Tracks 10 and 11 offer another type of reconstruction. The music for these performances is based on the single melodic line preserved in the play by Adam de la Halle, *Le jeu de Robin et de Marion*. Joseph J. Duggan has adapted this line to the metric system of the *Song of Roland* by reversing the two segments of the melody. This approach to singing the *Song of Roland* is akin to the view of the early-fourteenth-century Parisian theorist Johannes de Grocheo, who states that for the chanson de geste (*cantus gestualis* in his terminology), "the same melody ought to be repeated in all the versicles [verses]" (Grocheo 17). These tracks are sung by Andrew Pidkameny.

Tracks 12 and 13 turn to the chant, specifically to liturgical recitative and psalmody, for a way of performing the *Roland*. Liturgical recitative is flexible, yet it is structured by opening, mediant, and closing formulas and can be extended or contracted as needed. Psalmody, if strictly followed, however, would not serve for the chanson de geste, whose purpose and poetic structure are not like those of the psalms. Taking Psalm 111, *Beatus vir* (see description below), we have adapted it to performance of the *Roland*, attempting to maintain the flavor of psalmody without exact imitation. Because the *Roland* lines are short and regular, only the first portion of the melody is used: the opening gesture (intonation); the reciting tone; and the mid-verse cadence, slightly modified, except for the next-to-last-line of the laisse, which moves to the end cadence. Since psalms do not normally close anything but are usually followed by something else, their end cadences tend to be cursive rather than conclusive. A concluding line has therefore been devised for the adaptation, based on a seventh-mode cadence descending from e to G, to bring the reconstruction to a close on the final G. Musical example 7 shows such a cadence. (Compare transcriptions of the *Roland*, laisses 1 and 176, musical examples 4 and 5, with *Beatus vir* and the cadence from the *Commemoratio brevis*, musical examples 6 and 7. (For definitions and terminology used here, see Crocker 30, 54.) The adaptation also shows how slight shifts in the music can accommodate feminine (laisse 1) and masculine (laisse 176) line endings typical of vernacular verse and how performance strategies might differentiate between declarative and meditative laisse types. Although it is impossible to portray visual gestures through sound recording, we have tried to convey through vocal performance the animation that might have informed some performances. At the end of laisse 176, one might think of the stage directions for the twelfth century *Jeu d'Adam*: "whoever names Paradise should look at it and point to it with one hand" (qtd. in Schmitt 275; see also Brault, Song 1: 111–15). These adaptations were originally created by Margaret Switten, Project Director, with the staff members and participants during two NEH Institutes, each one entitled The Teaching of Medieval Civilization, held at Mount Holyoke College in the summers of 1981 and 1983. The singer is William H. Sharp.

Track 14 illustrates one possible way of using an instrument. That instruments were used at least in some cases seems likely (although early manuscripts have no written record of their usage). It seems likely also that the vielle would have been an instrument of choice (Page, *Voices* and *Owl*; Huot). Therefore, we have performed the version of laisse 1 on track 12 with vielle accompaniment. The vielle used in this performance was set in an open tuning, with the finalis of the mode doubled as the two lowest strings, the reciting tone as the next highest, and an octave above the finalis as the highest string. (For a different vielle tuning that could be used for the line from *Le jeu de Robin et de Marion*, see Page, *Voices* 129). William H. Sharp sings; Robert Eisenstein plays the vielle.

Tracks 15–19 illustrate some melodies that can serve and that we have used as musical models for singing the *Song of Roland*. They enable students to hear musical examples 6 and 8–11. Tracks 15–17 are performed by William H. Sharp, 18 by Andrew Pidkameny, 19 by Paul Hillier.

Track 15 is a performance of Psalm 111, *Beatus vir*, seventh-mode psalm tone with end cadence on d. The seventh-mode final would be G, but psalms did not always end on the final. In the context of psalmody, a mode may be defined both as a scale type and as a method of classifying chants by final pitch and range. Four notes were used as finals: D, E, F, and G. For each final there were two modes, one with a high ambitus (range), and the other with a low ambitus, thus creating eight modes. The seventh mode has a final on G (it is a scale starting on G and using—in modern terms—only the "white notes" on the piano) with a high ambitus, that is, it employs mainly the notes above the final. A psalm tone is essentially a recitation formula consisting of repetitions of a single pitch (the choice of which depends on the mode—for mode seven the reciting tone is d) preceded by an intonation and followed by a cadence, as described above for *Beatus vir*. Thus a seventh-mode psalm tone is a melodic formula constructed from and limited to the pitches of the seventh mode. *Beatus vir* was a focus of study at the NEH Institutes, hence its choice as a basis for singing the *Song of Roland*.

Tracks 16 and 17 contain a performance of two sung portions from *Aucassin and Nicolette*. This well-known thirteenth-century *chantefable* consists of sung parts and parts that are spoken, clearly indicated by the rubrics "or se cante" and "or dient et content et fablent." The sung portions have the same kind of laisse structure as a chanson de geste; the spoken portions are in prose. In the manuscript, indicated above the transcription, musical examples 8 and 9, the music is written out at the beginning and end of each section to be sung. It is generally considered that *Aucassin* is a parody; because it features two encounters with shepherds, *Aucassin* has been compared both with the *Jeu de Robin et de Marion* and with the lyric genre of the pastourelle (Butterfield 196–99). Certain melodic elements seem to support such interpretations: the short lines, which could lend themselves to a dancelike performance, contrast with the notion of epic, and the pitch of the last short line seems almost intentionally humorous. The *Aucassin and Nicolette* manuscript has preserved the music in nonmensural notation (without indication of rhythm), and we have so transcribed it. One may find transcriptions into modern rhythmic notation in editions by Mario Roques and Philippe Walter, as well as on the Umilta Web site (www.umilta.net/aucassin.html), which shows the complete work, original and translation, with manuscript images. It is clear from the musical notation that masculine and feminine line endings were respected, but there is no indication of what to do for laisses with an unequal number of lines, not counting the last short line. We have selected one section (number 1) with masculine line endings and an even number of lines (not counting the last) and one section (number 33) with feminine line endings and an uneven number of lines (not counting the last) to illustrate these different possibilities. The musical-repetition pattern for track 16 is an educated guess. (Other solutions in Stevens, *Words* 226; Chailley 27).

Track 18 illustrates the single line, 729, from Adam de la Halle's *Jeu de Robin et de Marion*, a play with lyric insertions. The music is in the manuscript cited above the transcription, musical example 10. (See Chailley 29 for a facsimile of the manuscript.) The work to which the line refers has been identified as a rather vulgar parody of an epic poem about Audigier (Dufournet, *Jeu* 151). It is sung in the *Jeu* by a peasant named Gautier who wants to show off his talent as a singer of chansons de geste. Thus Gautier identifies the line as coming from epic. He is immediately interrupted by Robin, who doesn't want to hear such garbage. Since we are dealing with parody, the status of the music is not clear. But most scholars consider this single line a useful model for performing chansons de geste. The notation in the manuscript cited, though it is not without ambiguity, could be interpreted rhythmically, and our transcription has so interpreted it.

Track 19, a recording of musical example 11, provides a model that was not directly used in the reconstructions on this compact disc. However, Jacques Chailley has argued that *Tu autem*, likely a versicle sung after the lesson of matins, could demonstrate links between liturgical chant and narrative poems, saints' lives especially, and also between chant and chansons de geste (see also Stevens, *Words* 247–48). The piece comes from a manuscript, formerly in the library of the Abbey of Saint Martial of Limoges, Bibliothèque nationale de France, fonds latin 1139, dating from around 1100. Persuasive reasons for attaching this piece to narrative romance genres are the use of decasyllabic verse and the language: Old Occitan. Repetitive patterns are not regular but show similarity to *Aucassin*. Chailley usefully compares its structure both with the melody from *Aucassin and Nicolette* and with the pronouncements about repetition made by Grocheo (Chailley 26–28).

# The Major Pilgrimage Routes to Santiago de Compostela

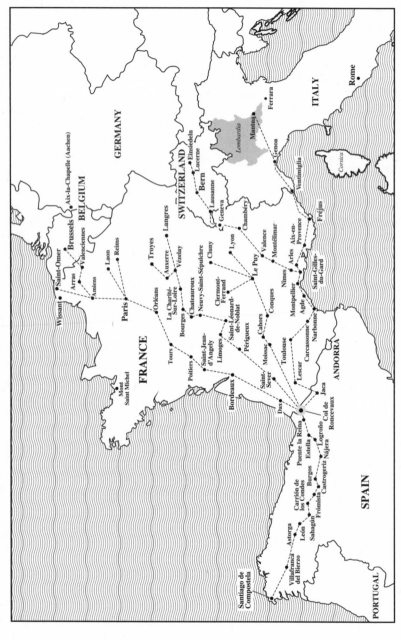

# The Rencesvals (Modern French Roncevaux, Spanish Roncesvalles) Area

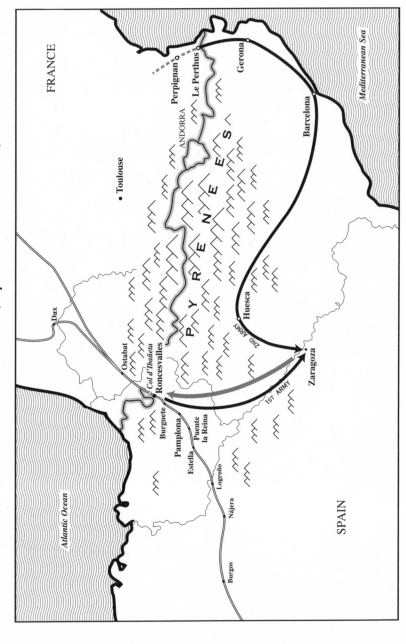

*Part Two*

# APPROACHES

# Introduction

*Leslie Zarker Morgan*

The responses to the MLA survey included college and university instructors who teach the *Song of Roland* to undergraduate, graduate, and mixed-level courses. The college and university instructors teach the text in English, French, and Old French, in excerpts and in its entirety. The courses in which they teach the poem vary from survey courses of French literature and culture to Western civilization, medieval history, and special-topics courses, including Literacy (Kinoshita), Law and Literature (Enders), Trial, Ordeal, and Desire (Warren), and Medieval Movies (Paden). Clearly the approaches to teaching these courses differ widely,,since the needs and interests of the institutions and instructors vary.

*Approaches to Teaching the* Song of Roland is divided into six sections: the first, "Historical, Intellectual, and Literary Contexts," includes essays that provide the factual underpinnings a nonexpert may find helpful: historical details, literary context (for example, other epics to demonstrate the *Roland*'s difference; other versions of the text; and analogues to the *Roland*, such as Arabic epic). Additionally, the two maps at the end of the "Materials" section were especially commissioned for this volume and can be photocopied and used in class to portray the sites mentioned in the *Song of Roland*.

The second section, "Avatars of the *Song of Roland*," both follows reception history of the text in other countries and examines the meaning of that reception. Charlemagne's activities ranged over much of what is now Western Europe, including the areas that now make up the countries Italy and Spain, and therefore those geographic areas possess a tradition of Roland and Charlemagne of their own. The presence of the character Roland or of figures and models of behavior based on the *Roland* form a core of literary activity that is still appreciated (and in some cases, still in active creation and presentation) today. An important part of reception is also the reaction to the rediscovery of the *Song of Roland* in France and its political and social significance in the modern sphere of nation states. Similarly, in Spain, Frankish actions and their meaning were interpreted through lenses appropriate to local pride. These approaches offer considerable scope for instructors to help their students think of political spin and its effect on literary instruction.

The third section, "Text, Language and Poetic Techniques," responds to the many requests of instructors answering our survey for information about the original language and how it sounded, as well as how the original sound and meaning are rendered into modern English. It should be noted that readings on the audio CD accompany this third section and exemplify Alice M. Colby-Hall's explanation of Old French oral technique.

The fourth, fifth, and sixth sections, "The *Song of Roland* in the Classroom,"

"Major Characters and Episodes," and "Critical Approaches," are practical sets of guidelines for how the *Roland* may be included in a syllabus. The "classroom" section places the *Roland* in contexts with other literary and historical works. "Major Characters and Episodes" responds to active student interest in people (heroes, antiheroes, and marginal characters or sidekicks) as well as to the emotional impact that the death of a close relative can create. These concerns are specifically integrated in the *Roland* text to emphasize the continuity and complexity of plot. The final section, "Critical Approaches," offers the instructor personal readings of the poem by teachers of advanced courses who implement critical approaches into their classes. These include readings by well-known and much-published critics as well as by younger practitioners who use recent methodologies to provide a new look at this classic text.

A number of essays or sections include questions and exercises that the authors have used in class and are generously sharing with us (see the essays in this volume by Burde; Schenck; Kinoshita; Switten). These in-class activities are tailored to different levels of instruction with varying purposes; some essays also include step-by-step suggestions for class discussion (Jones).

Instructors will consult different portions of the volume depending on their own familiarity with the text and on the nature of their class, and will not necessarily read the volume from cover to cover. In different years and for different levels of students, instructors who consult this volume may find some chapters more useful than others. It is frequently difficult to engage students in older literature. By appealing to personal emotional interest or to more recent historical epochs, by engaging in comparative approaches to literature from other geographic areas and eras, and by providing cultural background, the teacher of the *Song of Roland* can open a new world. We encourage all instructors to dip into various chapters, even though the subject may not seem initially related to a planned course, for the scholars who contributed these essays have all generously offered their expertise and materials to assist the ongoing discussion of the medieval *Song of Roland* and to inspire future students to think about the text, as well as about literature and its place in society.

# HISTORICAL, INTELLECTUAL, AND LITERARY CONTEXTS

# Will the Real Charlemagne Please Stand Up?

## Joel T. Rosenthal

Charlemagne stands as the dominant figure of what we might call the end of the early Middle Ages, and his long, successful, and immensely influential reign can be considered the bridge between the days of the Germanic (or "barbarian") tribal invasions and kingdoms and those of the feudal monarchies that resulted from the ninth- and tenth-century breakup of the Carolingian Empire. Charlemagne's accomplishments can be divided into several main areas: political and military expansion, legal and administrative consolidation, and—perhaps as the spiritual counterpart to these accomplishments—what we generally refer to as the Carolingian Renaissance. In addition, being crowned by the pope in 801 as "[t]he great and peaceful emperor of the Romans" (Scholz 81) gave Charlemagne a contemporary prestige, as well as a historical legacy, that was not to be matched by any other secular figure of the Christian West throughout the medieval centuries.

Charlemagne was very much the heir to the powerful state building of his grandfather (Charles Martel, de facto ruler of the Franks from 719 to 741) and his father (Pepin, who was ruler from 741 and who ruled as crowned king from 751 until his death in 768). At Pepin's death, in keeping with Germanic custom, the realm was divided between the surviving legitimate sons, Charles and Carloman. Fortunately for Charles, his brother died after three years of abrasive joint, or divided, kingship, and for over forty years Charlemagne was able to focus and direct the resources of his realm in order to achieve an amazing level of success in most of his enterprises.

The expansion of the Carolingian realm is perhaps the most striking, or at least the most obvious, aspect of Charlemagne's success. Charlemagne was at war in virtually every year of his reign, and, though occasionally he was called on to suppress an internal uprising or a separatist movement, the main thrust of his empire was conquest and expansion. Some of the wars brought territory directly and fully into the Carolingian realm, whereas others—farther from such favorite home bases as Aachen—established satellite and buffer states that turned potential threats and rivals into compliant if not amiable allies and helped guard the realm's outer borders. In the course of his many wars, Charlemagne added territory in virtually every direction, about doubling the substantial kingdom he and his brother had inherited. The course of conquest was uneven. While the Lombards pretty much fell before him in one great military swoop, and the Bavarians recognized his sovereign authority without a pitched battle, the great conquest of Saxony continued sporadically from 777 until 804, as Carolingian harshness—marked by deportations, mass executions, and the breakup of families and villages—plus forced conversion to Christianity fueled and refueled the fires of Saxon independence (or of perfidy, as the Franks told the story). When on his death Charlemagne left his kingdom to his only surviving legitimate son, Louis the Pious, he was turning over a stretch of territory that now included not just France but the northern stretch of Spain; western and central Germany; Italy down to the south of Rome; Austria; the Low Countries; the western Balkans; and Bavaria, along with the imperial title.

His Spanish ambitions show both his zeal to push forward and the limitations that distant enterprises placed on even Carolingian aspiration. Charles first went to Spain, at the behest of restive Muslim nobles and local princes, for the ill-fated expedition of 778. After his vast army took Pamplona, he turned his enmity on the Christian state of Asturias and on the Christian Basques, although promises that his presence would spark a widespread Muslim revolt against the caliph of Córdoba proved illusionary. But despite the defeat at Rencesvals and the death of Roland, there were further expeditions that eventually solidified a Spanish march beyond the Pyrenees and that provided the bedrock of a Christian Barcelona and the kingdom of Aragon. Though fierce Arab counterattacks in 793 might range as far north as Narbonne and Carcasonne in France, by Charlemagne's death his supremacy—usually represented on the ground by his son Louis, named as king of Aquitania and Septimania while still a child—was recognized as far south as Pamplona and Navarre as well as in the Balearic Islands.

Charlemagne's amazing record of military success rested to a considerable extent on his exceptional ability: tireless, at least in his younger days; doubtlessly charismatic and effective as a leader of men on the march and in battle; relentless and harsh in pursuit of such goals as the Saxon conquest; and knowledgable about how to utilize the well-organized system already in place. These traits can also be seen in his less dramatic but equally impressive efforts to impose a high level of administrative unity on his vast realm and its many peoples, languages, and local cultures. The numerous capitularies that have come down tell of Charlemagne's concern for organizing his armies (as DeVries spells out in this volume), for determining the economic potential and return of crown lands and those of other great landholders, for making nobles and powerful landholders accountable to traveling lieutenants who were directly responsible to him, and for supervising the uniformity and equity of local courts and justice, among other goals and projects. There were few areas of public life into which he did not inquire and impose himself, at least in intention. Between a peripatetic court, envoys entrusted with the power to convene local juries and to hold inquisitions into numerous issues as they made their rounds (the *missi dominici*), and an annual general assembly of both lay and ecclesiastical magnates, his long reach touched many corners of western Europe.

*Carolingian Renaissance* is a convenient summary term for the burst of intellectual, religious, and artistic life that flourished during this period, much of it directly encouraged by the court and directed by the eminent collection of intellectuals whom Charlemagne gathered as a brain trust or kitchen cabinet. While Alcuin of York is the most famous, and perhaps the most influential, of the circle of learned clerics who also turned their thoughts to affairs of state, men of ideas and letters were drawn from all over western Europe: Theodulf, bishop of Orleans; Paul the Deacon, from Lombardy; Einhard, from eastern Francia; among many others. We now see the revival of intellectual activity under Charlemagne not so much as a new movement, but rather as a focus on standardization and dissemination that was lavishly supported from the top down, and that reached in all directions. The text of the Bible, the basic scribal hand, the court style of manuscript illumination (coming to full flower in the reign of Charles's grandson Charles the Bald), political philosophy, theological discourse and definition, and poetry were all lines of endeavor that drew the attention of leading figures as they sought to blend late classical and patristic achievements into a new high culture. As Einhard tells us, Charles even had the legends of the Franks collected and set to writing, though these seem to have been destroyed by Louis the Pious, supposedly aghast at their pagan content.

Several aspects of Charlemagne's reign, and of the great ruler, merit additional comment. One concerns what we might think of as the cooperation or even the symbiosis between the church and the secular court or "the state." When Charles devoted much of his vast resources to the three decades of warfare needed to conquer and convert the Saxons, he was making a bold and innovative (if unlovely) statement regarding the militant expansion of Christianity. However, he was also heir to a dynastic tradition of close Frankish-papal relations; his two immediate predecessors had worked hand in glove with the papacy in support of Saint Boniface's missionary enterprises across

the Rhine and into the Low Countries. When Charles annexed the Lombard
kingdom, he was once again combining political self-interest with his role as
a supporter of the faith. His newly proclaimed kingship over the Lombards
made him a major player in much of Italy and gave him access to the Medi-
terranean and to the many Byzantine holdings that still dotted its shores.
Meanwhile, as a good Catholic he was relieving the papacy of the looming
and hostile presence of a Lombard regime that was still sympathetic to the
Arian heresy, with its long-proscribed view of the nature of Christ. When a
minor and disreputable pope, Leo III, placed the imperial crown on Charle-
magne's head during Christmas mass in Saint Peter's in 800, this bold step is
hard to read as anything other than a grand scheme devised by men like
Alcuin. They presumably saw how a temporary hiatus in the Byzantine line
of succession could be coupled with Charles's awesome record of martial and
domestic triumphs, his support of the Western Church, and his unparalleled
stature. It was an opportunity to stake a claim to political hegemony unheard
of in the West for four or five centuries. Charles, whether he sought to take
this step or whether in effect it was taken for him, did think so much of his
new title that older oaths of loyalty had to be resworn, or renewed, in order
to carry explicit recognition of his more exalted rank.

But against this narrative of success, occasionally interrupted but rarely re-
versed, we should pose some questions about the way we comprehend this
whole Carolingian world, before and after the papal-imperial coronation of
800. When we refer to the emperor as Charles or Charlemagne (Charles the
Great), we make him a Frenchman. If we look at the English scholarship
before World War I, we are more apt to encounter Karl (Karl der Grosse),
which makes Charlemagne a German—though this nomenclature turned out
to be too reminiscent of the kaiser, and it fell out of later usage. However, it
is important, in looking at Europe in the eighth century, to realize that Char-
lemagne was neither French nor German. He was a Frank, leader of the tribe
or people and king of what had become their territorial realm (and his title
was still as much personal or family property as an office in a modern sense).
Though his first language was a variant of a Germanic language, the continual
addition of territory made the realm more and more polyglot; the term *mul-
ticultural* may be anachronistic, but it can be used in this case if with caution.
While the widespread Carolingian world was united by one faith (though this
is easily overestimated), and by the clerical and administrative reliance on
Latin, it was mostly held together—for many years—by the overwhelming
presence of Charles himself. His achievements rested on the solid spadework
of his grandfather and father, but to a great extent they were personal tri-
umphs—triumphs of organization and good management, as well as of the
sword, but personal nonetheless. As a long-term entity the Carolingian Empire
was really beyond the resources of a ninth-century European state. It is easy
to blame Charles's son and grandsons for its dissolution. The marvel is that

he held it together as well, and for as long, as he did. More than ten modern nations lay within his boundaries.

Medieval historians are prone to lament the paucity of their sources, no matter what the topic. But when looking at Charlemagne, we have fairly rich ore—a testimonial to his administrative reforms and his towering stature: a life written by Einhard, who had known him; numerous well-informed (monastic) chronicles; a rich supply of administrative documents and edicts; along with the many literary and theological products of Carolingian cultural life. And beyond these traditional materials there is still the cathedral at Aachen, in which the Emperor lies, plus a wealth of numismatic and archaeological materials to flesh out various bits of the tale of material life. Not every question can be answered, of course, and we will always wonder how much whitewashing there is in what has been preserved—for example, the mystery about the disaster at Rencesvals. Nor do we have any serious "outsider" views of Charlemagne and his reign: the views of those who felt his wrath or who were crushed beneath the weight of his insatiable ambition. We can but speculate on Saxon, Avar, or Danish assessments of "the real Charlemagne." Nor, for all the edicts and capitularies, can we link those royal decrees about normative behavior and bureaucratic models with a good idea of what and how much actually got implemented. Frustration, failure, and never having enough time are always parts of the human condition, even when the view is from the palace.

A final tribute to Charlemagne's towering stature can be measured by looking at how quickly he became a figure of legend and at how widely this legendary swath cut across Europe. While any given tale, such as the *Song of Roland*, might ostensibly be about one of *his* men, Charles the Great was the figure who knit all such tales into a coherent whole. And unlike the long-ago Arthur of Britain, there were material remains, relics, and monuments from the historical Charlemagne to be found across much of Christendom, all lending credibility to his legendary persona. By the mid–ninth century, Notker, the Monk of Saint Gall, was depicting him as an omniscient and omnipotent military leader who could double up as a sort of citizen king, rubbing elbows with the downcast (see Thorpe). Whether we look at heroic German tales, or the *Karlamagnús Saga* (see Hieatt's edition) that made its way into the Icelandic literary corpus or the spin-off stories of his great vassals, Charlemagne assumed many guises, many roles. Tales were told of his journey to free Jerusalem, of his death as a martyr to the faith after he had reached some legendary peak of longevity, of wars in Africa, of tribute from afar, of his burial in an upright position on the imperial throne, and the like. The final accolade—revealing a good deal about wish fulfillment and the need to forge links between the secular and the spiritual and the heroic and the reachable—is perhaps his official canonization in 1165. And while Charlemagne is not much of a cult figure for hagiographic devotion these days, and while Vatican II was hard on these political and dynastic saints of the Middle Ages, we should keep in mind that the European Union gives a medal to the person judged to have done the most to promote a united continent: The Charlemagne Medal. The record, whether based on hard data from Carolingian Europe or on more malleable records and legends from a later day, still speaks for itself.

# Rencesvals: The Event

### William W. Kibler

Although the *Song of Roland* that we know today, almost exclusively through the Oxford University, Bodleian Library Digby 23 manuscript's version, is nearly entirely fictive, there is a grain of historical truth behind the poem that requires elucidation. In 711, less than a century after the death of the Prophet Mohammed in 632, Muslim armies under Tariq ibn Ziyad crossed the Pillars of Hercules, after which it was called Jebel al-Tariq (or Gibraltar), into then Visigothic Spain. After subjugating the Visigoths, they pushed as far north as Tours on the Loire in France but were defeated near Poitiers by Charlemagne's grandfather, Charles Martel, in 732 and driven back into Iberia. The rapid and widespread advances of the Muslim armies led to the establishment of essentially autonomous Islamic states in the conquered lands; the most powerful Spanish kingdom was governed from Córdoba in Andalusia. It brought with it civilization of the highest order, certainly much higher than that of the Carolingian kingdom to its immediate north. But all was not tranquil in the emirate of Córdoba, and in 777 the governor of Barcelona, Suleiman ibn al-Arabí, went to Charlemagne's court at Paderborn (Westphalia) and requested that the emperor come with an army into Spain to help in his rebellion against the first Umayyad emir of Córdoba, ʿAbd ar-Rahmān I (reigned 755–88). In exchange, he promised Charles the cities of Pamplona, Barcelona, Huesca, Girona, and Saragossa. Charlemagne accepted the offer and crossed the Pyrenees in April 778. He occupied Pamplona peacefully and received hostages from that town, as well as from Barcelona, Girona, and Huesca. Saragossa however refused, and Charles laid siege to the city. But after two unsuccessful months, learning of yet another Saxon uprising in the north, Charles set off back across the Pyrenees, taking hostage al-Arabí, whom he felt had betrayed the promises given at Paderborn. On the way back, Charlemagne destroyed Pamplona to keep its inhabitants from rebelling against him. This much is fairly clear, but what happened next varies with the source. It is certain that al-Arabí was freed in an ambush, perhaps led by his brothers and with the help of the Basques.

In the Royal Annals to 801, the "official" Carolingian history composed shortly after the events it recounts, we read that Charles came to Pamplona, received many hostages, destroyed Pamplona and subjugated the Basques and Navarese ("Hispani Wascones . . . et Nabarros" [Menéndez-Pidal, Chanson 526), then returned to France. This is official propaganda, with no hint of any difficulties in Spain. The Royal Annals to 829, composed about twenty-five years later, and not coincidentally after the death of Charlemagne (814), add some important details: at the summit of the Pyrenees, "the Basques ["Wascones"] were waiting in ambush; they attacked the rear-guard, causing great tumult and trouble in the whole army. Although the Franks were superior in arms and courage to the Basques, the difficult terrain and their lack of familiarity with mountain fighting, put them at a disadvantage. Most of the dignitaries of the royal court were slain and the supply wagons were looted." (Menéndez-Pidal, Chanson 526). No names are named, but the defeat is acknowledged.

In his *Life of Charlemagne*, composed in Latin in 830, Einhard provides a much more detailed account:

> [I]n recrossing the Pyrenees, Charles felt somewhat the perfidy of the Basques. The narrow route required his army to be stretched out in a long line. The Basques ["Wascones"] had set an ambush at the summit of the mountain: the spot, covered with thick woods, was ideal for the purpose. They swept down on the last supply wagons and the rear guard which was protecting the bulk of the army. They forced our men into a valley, attacked, and killed them to the last man. Then, having sacked the supplies, they dispersed rapidly in every direction under cover of nightfall. In their favor was the lightness of their armor and the nature of the terrain; the Franks, on the other hand, were slowed by their heavy armor and their position below the Basques. In this battle were killed the seneschal Eggihard, Anselm, a count of the Palace, [and Roland, duke of the March of Brittany,] along with many others.
>
> (qtd. in Bédier, *Légendes* 3: 193; my trans.)

I have placed the phrase concerning Roland in brackets, because it appears in the A family of Einhard manuscripts, but not in the B group. Some have argued that it was simply omitted in the B group, but Ramón Menéndez-Pidal makes a good case for its addition in the A family due to the increasing popularity of the epic hero (see Menéndez-Pidal, Chanson 287–91).

Various historical annals repeated or summarized this text over the next century, adding such details as Charles's seizing al-Arabí at Saragossa. One merits special mention: the Latin *Life of the Emperor Louis*, written in 840 by the Limoges Astronomer. After describing the battle, it concludes, "Those who were marching in the rear-guard were massacred in the mountains; since their names are well-known, I'll not repeat them here" (Menéndez-Pidal, Chanson 528–29).

It is clear that, shortly after the battle, stories began to be told. Official Frankish propaganda probably tried to suppress mention of the defeat, but it was too well known not to find its way into even the official record—after the death of Charlemagne. Since he was not an important official at court, Roland may not have figured in the earliest redaction of Einhard's official history, but his increasing popularity assured him a place in the second and subsequent editions.

The date of the battle is not given in any of the historical texts, but it can be deduced from the epitaph of Eggihard, one of the three victims of the battle mentioned by Einhard, found in a Latin manuscript at the Bibliothèque Nationale in Paris, fonds latin 4841. Here we learn that Eggihard died on 15 August and was buried in a church dedicated to Saint Vincent.

What precisely happened on 15 August 778? There are two types of sources: Latin and Arabic. We have seen that the Latin texts speak of an attack by Basques on Charles's rear guard but say nothing of the fate of the hostages. According to the Arabic sources, al-Arabí's sons, aided by Muslim forces, liberate their father. Ibn al-Athīr, in the thirteenth century, writes: "Charles became suspicious of Ibn al-Arabí and, seizing him, set off for his own lands. Once Charles had left Muslim lands and felt completely secure, Ibn al-Arabí's sons, Matruh and Ayshun, swept down on the Frankish king with their troops. They freed their father and returned with him to Saragossa" (Menéndez-Pidal, Chanson 520; my trans.)

The *Song of Roland* likewise reports an attack by Arabic forces on Christian troops. If this attack actually occurred, then the poem is in fact more accurate on this point than the Latin sources. What seems most likely, according to Menéndez-Pidal and most subsequent scholars, is that the attack was by both Basques and Muslims, that the supply wagons were pillaged, and that the hostages were freed. Far from being a simple raid on the supplies by a ragtag group of mountaineers, the 15 August 778 battle was a major defeat for Charlemagne's army by a coalition of Basque raiders and Muslim troops.[1]

The *Song of Roland* evokes poetically on several occasions the high peaks and deep valleys of the route across the Pyrenees that leads through Rencesvals. This terrain was favorable to quick skirmishes: small bands could ambush a larger army as it struggled up the narrow trail with its supply wagons and heavy weaponry. The Frankish army, which relied heavily on its swift cavalry was, in effect, paralyzed by the terrain. The strategies and tactics developed by Charlemagne's armies, especially the mounted shock combat that served him so well in other campaigns (and described in detail by DeVries, in this volume), were useless—or worse—in this setting. The ambushers allowed the main body of the army, with its heavy cavalry units, to pass unimpeded over the peaks and downwards toward France, and, when the attack came on the rear guard, there was no room or time for them to maneuver or return to help, because the route had undoubtedly been blocked. The Basques and Muslims probably rained down a torrent of javelins, arrows, and the like on the Franks, who found themselves teetering on the edges of deep gullies with nowhere to turn for protection. Their heavy armor, in the heat of an August day, was of little or no use; their horses had no room to charge; confusion, no doubt, reigned supreme. The rear guard was annihilated, their supply wagons were ravaged, and their prisoners liberated.

We have seen that certain Latin chronicles (but not the Royal Annals) mention the capture of al-Arabí, but none say what happened to him. There was probably an attempt early on to silence reports of this defeat, but it was so well known, so notorious, that the word of mouth eventually could no longer be denied. Legends and (who knows?) songs began to recall this event and to transform it, as the official chroniclers had been powerless to do, into a signal victory over the Arabs by Charlemagne and his armies.

NOTE

[1]The most detailed analysis of the events surrounding the battle of Rencesvals is that by Menéndez-Pidal (Chanson), who points out that it was both the Muslims and Basques who attacked the rear guard (205–09). See in particular chapter 6, "L'événement historique" (181–231). The Latin and Arabic texts are given in the "Appendice historiographique" (519–32). Another source where much of the historical discussion can be conveniently found is Le Gentil (Chanson [1955], esp. ch. 2).

# Origins of the French Epic:
# The *Song of Roland* and Other French Epics

## *Philip E. Bennett*

Although the *Song of Roland* is by far the most famous of Old French epics, and the most studied in courses across the world, it is far from being the only one. Nor is it, in the form in which it is usually studied, typical of the epic genre in French. Between 100 and 150 chansons de geste ("songs of deeds") survive from the Middle Ages in France, but most of them are so unlike the general conception of epic poetry that they do not figure in standard manuals on epic poetry produced for comparative literature studies. The stark monumentality of the *Song of Roland* (at least in the early, Oxford, version) may have its counterpart in the oldest parts of the *Song of William* and *Raoul de Cambrai*, but both of these poems were given continuations before the end of the twelfth century, comic and centered on the figure of the giant Reneward in *William*, romance-oriented in *Raoul*. Even *Roland* was reworked to late twelfth-century taste: the role of the tragic Aude was expanded, and Ganelon was given escape and pursuit sequences that followed the best traditions of popular adventure tales (see Duggan's "Beyond the Oxford Text: The Songs of Roland," in this volume). In the thirteenth century, magic and a mysterious view of the Orient became popular. These predilections are encapsulated in *Huon de Bordeaux*, whose hero is sent by a vindictive Charlemagne to Babylon, where he must kiss the emir's daughter and cut off the emir's moustache. Huon is helped in his quest by Auberon, King of Fairyland. This is only the most popular of the many chansons de geste, including all those contributing to the poetic biography of Charlemagne, that were modernized and rewritten as prose romances or chronicles in the fifteenth century, and then printed to provide the core of popular literature from the sixteenth to the eighteenth centuries. The story of Huon de Bordeaux and the figure of Oberon (as his name comes to be spelled) remained so popular at the time when the *Song of Roland* was forgotten (except by antiquarians) that they provided a central figure to Shakespeare's *A Midsummer Night's Dream* and the plot of Carl Maria von Weber's opera *Oberon*.

The origins of this prolific and diverse epic poetry are shrouded in a mystery that has kept controversy raging among specialists for over a century. It is known that in the early ninth century Charlemagne ordered the ancestral songs of the Franks to be collected and recorded (see also Rosenthal's "Will the Real Charlemagne Please Stand Up?," in this volume). If the project was ever undertaken is unknown; if it was, no trace of it has survived. In any case, such songs would not have been composed in the French Romance language but in the High German Frankish language, which continued to be spoken by the French aristocracy until about the year 900; we are reminded of this fact by the almost exclusively Germanic names of the heroes of chansons de geste. It is, however, this very Germanic aspect of the lost early poetry that has caused the controversy. Until the Franco-Prussian War of 1870, scholars took it for granted that French epic was simply a branch of Germanic epic. Gaston Paris accepted the views of German scholars that epics were the spontaneous productions of the people involved in the events recounted. He suggested that epics began as short ballad-like pieces (cantilenas) that were sung in celebration or lament immediately after the events; they were then transmitted orally from generation to generation, until they were finally copied as the poems we know into manuscripts in the twelfth to fourteenth centuries (*Histoire poétique* [1974]). Some Old French poems preserve in their fictions a character who sings such songs (*Raoul de Cambrai, Huon de Bordeaux*). In the *Song of William*, we learn that the hero, like a Celtic chieftain in more recent times, has a jongleur who accompanies him everywhere and who sings songs in praise of the hero's ancestors—ancestors who, it happens, are all heroes of surviving chansons de geste. The disaster of 1870 dramatically changed the attitudes of scholars in France, who immediately distanced themselves from the "barbaric" Germans and insisted that their epic poetry was purely home-grown on models drawn from classical Rome. It was Joseph Bédier who produced the most authoritative formulation of the idea that chansons de geste were written by individual poets collaborating with churchmen to provide poems celebrating French heroes of the struggle against the infidel to be sung to pilgrims on the main pilgrimage routes to Rome and Compostela (*Légendes*). Despite some controversies, Bédier's view remained the standard explanation of the origins of the Old French epic until the 1950s, when a number of scholars—Jean Rychner in Switzerland (*Chanson*), Ramón Menéndez-Pidal in Spain (Chanson), and Joseph J. Duggan in the United States (The Song of Roland: *Formulaic Style and Poetic Craft*)—revitalized the idea of the oral composition and dissemination of chansons de geste on the model of studies of Homeric and Serbo-Croatian epic by Milman Parry (*L'épithète traditionnelle dans Homère*; *Serbo-Croatian Heroic Songs*; *The Making of Homeric Verse: The Collected Papers of Milman Parry*) and Albert B. Lord. However, these scholars did not explicitly link Old French to early Germanic epic, being content to discuss the poems as traditional oral works in Romance culture. It was not until Joël H. Grisward published his study linking Old French epic to Indo-European mythology, invoking parallels in Celtic and Germanic epic, as well as in Greco-Roman and Sanskrit texts, that the old debates, and the old wounds, were reopened. There is still no consensus about the origins and development of chansons de geste, but scholars are now much more aware of the complex nature of these poems and of their relations to other European epic traditions.

Nor are the poems that have come down to us a unified corpus. Writing— and for once the verb is almost certainly correct—the prologue to his poem *Girart de Vienne* around 1180, Bertrand de Bar-sur-Aube lists three gests that, according to this account, compose the whole corpus of Old French epic. These gests, which we can interpret as "cycles," are referred to as the cycle of the king; of Doon de Mayence (who is the ancestor of all rebellious barons), also called the revolt cycle; and the cycle of Garin de Monglane (ancestor of the clan of faithful barons, whose most famous members are Aymeri de Narbonne and William of Orange), also called the William cycle. The cycle of the king contains the *Song of Roland*, but, like that of the rebellious barons, it is very hard to conceive of the loosely related songs that deal either with the early adventures of Roland and the prelude to Rencesvals (such as *Aspremont*, *Fierabras*, and Bertrand's *Girart de Vienne* itself) or with the difficulties Charlemagne faced following the death of his nephew as a cohesive cycle of the sort that the cycle of Garin de Monglane already was at the time Bertrand was writing.

Unlike the cycle of Garin de Monglane, which is conserved in two manuscripts that contain all twenty-four songs of the complete cycle, as well as in several others offering different but coherent selections of poems, only one manuscript survives that contains any number of poems from the cycle of the king. It is conserved in Paris, Bibliothèque Nationale de France, fonds français 860, and begins with a late redaction of *Roland*, followed by *Gaydon, Ami et Amile, Jourdain de Blaye*, and *Auberi le Bourguignon*. In *Gaydon*, Thierry d'Anjou, the vanquisher of Ganelon's champion, Pinabel, has to defend Charlemagne against further machinations of Ganelon's clan. *Ami et Amile* is an adaptation of the hagiographic theme of the mystical twins who by turns sacrifice themselves, like Castor and Pollux, for the other. *Jourdain de Blaye* is a sequel to the previous poem in the manuscript; it maintains the link to the royal cycle established by *Ami et Amile*, in which Amile is Charlemagne's son-in-law, since the hero, Jourdain, is the grandson of Ami, who substituted himself for Amile in a judicial duel against a member of Ganelon's clan. The core of the plot of *Jourdain de Blaye* deals with the unsuccessful attempt of a later generation of the family of the traitor from *Roland* to avenge what has become a series of judicial defeats for the clan. So far, the thematic link to *Roland* has oddly been Ganelon and his family's genetic predisposition to treachery, although only *Gaydon* actually picks up on narrative details from the earlier poem. The last song in the Paris manuscript, *Auberi*, breaks that link, telling instead of the circuitous way in which the nephew of Auberi, Gasselin, becomes duke of Bavaria and father of Naimes, Charlemagne's trusted counselor (for further discussion of these poems see Gaunt, *Gender*, ch. 1).

Bertrand's advertisement for his new poem, which is what his prologue amounts to, suggests a water-tight separation between cycles presenting the legendary deeds of various clans (the word *geste* has all these connotations in Bertrand's usage), but in historical terms this separation never existed—even the *Song of Roland* has among its characters Ogier de Danemark, Girart de Roussillon, and Richard le Vieux de Normandie. Ogier and Girart belong to what Bertrand calls the "Geste de Doon de Mayence" (van Emden, *Girart* lines 14–16), or revolt cycle, whereas Richard figures in many poems of both the cycle of the king and the cycle of Garin de Monglane. What is certain is that the twelfth-century audience members of *Roland* was expected to recognize these characters and recall their roles in other songs, so that the epic world of the song that it was hearing was extended by echoes of other songs to create the illusion of a broader autonomous universe. This epic universe is already fully formed, with a complete fusion of characters from each of Bertrand's cycles, in one of the earliest witnesses to the existence of French epic that we have.

In the mid 1950s, a note was discovered in a manuscript containing works by Saint Eucherius of Lyon; it had been added in a space left blank at the end of the copy (for a photograph, see Menéndez-Pidal, Chanson, plate 10). Since the manuscript was originally from the abbey of San Millán de la Cogolla in Castile, which is about twenty miles southwest of Nájera and is a main stopping place on the pilgrim road from Rencesvals to Santiago de Compostela, the note, which paleographers have dated to the early eleventh century, is now usually referred to as the *Nota Emilianense*. It gives a brief account of the events recorded in the *Song of Roland*, but from a very different perspective:

> In era .d.ccc.xvi. venit Carlus rex ad Cesaragusta. In his diebus habuit duodecim neptis; unusquisque habebat tria milia equitum cum loricis suis, nomina ex his *Rodlane, Bertlane, Oggero Spatacurta, Ghigelmo Alcorbitunas, Olibero* et episcopo domini *Torpini*. Et unusquisque singulos menses serbiebat ad regem cum scolicis suis. Contigit ut regem cum suis ostis pausabit in Cesaragusta. Post aliquantulum temporis, suis dederunt consilium ut munera acciperet multa, ne a ffamis periret exercitum, sed ad propriam rediret. Quod factum est. Deinde placuit ad regem, pro salutem hominum exercituum, ut Rodlane, belligerator fortis, cum suis posterum ueniret. At ubi exercitum portum de Sicera transiret, in Rozaballes a gentibus Sarrazenorum fuit Rodlane occiso.
>
> (Menéndez-Pidal, Chanson 390)

In the year 816 King Charles came to Saragossa.[1] In those days he had twelve nephews; each one had three thousand fully armored knights under his command. Among them were Rodlane [Roland], Bertlane [Bertrand], Oggero Spatacurta [Ogier Short Sword], Ghigelmo Alcorbitunas [William Hook Nose], Olibero [Oliver] and the lord Bishop Torpino [Turpin], and each one served the king in turn for one month with his war band. It happened that the king and his army lay siege to Saragossa ["Cesaragusta"]. After a while his men advised him to accept many gifts so that the army should not die of hunger but return home. This was done. Afterwards it pleased the king, for the protection of the

army, that Roland, a mighty warrior, should form the rear guard with
his contingent. But when the army was crossing the pass at Sicera, Ro-
land was killed by the Saracens in Rencesvals ["Rozaballes"].

(my trans.)

This note is an interesting mixture of material that will reappear in the
Oxford *Roland* and in the report of the event in Einhard's *Vita Karoli*. How-
ever, there is no role for Ganelon, no revenge for Roland's death, and no
Baligant episode; on the other hand, Charles does accept large gifts, presum-
ably from the Saracens, and it is Saracens, not Basques as in Einhard, who
attack the rear guard and cause Roland's death. Neither of the historical com-
manders of the rear guard in AD 778, Anselm and Eggihard, is mentioned at
all (Thorpe 64–65). It has been much debated whether this note and the forms
given to characters' names indicates the existence as early as c. 1000 of legends
(written or oral) or of a song (in French, Occitan, or Castilian) on the subject
of Rencesvals (Menéndez-Pidal, Chanson, 391–94).

The most significant aspect of the *Nota Emilianense* account of the Ren-
cesvals campaign is the transformation of the Twelve Peers into twelve neph-
ews whose rotating monthly service has clear calendrical connotations. More-
over, the selection of nephews named shows a mixing of cycles thoroughly at
odds with the doctrine of Bertrand de Bar-sur-Aube. Roland, Oliver, and Tur-
pin all belong, of course, to the *Roland* tradition, and Ogier too figures in the
Oxford version, although without a reference to his sword, Courtain—so called
because it was the first of three attempts by Wayland, the Germanic smith of
the gods, to forge the perfect weapon, and when he tested it, the point
snapped off so that the sword had to be reforged. The second of Wayland's
swords belonged to Raoul de Cambrai, and the final, perfect sword was Du-
rendal, Roland's sword. These details are available only in *La chevalerie Ogier
de Danemark*, a song usually associated, like *Raoul de Cambrai*, with the revolt
cycle. The last pair of heroes mentioned in the *Nota Emilianense*, William and
Bertrand, are uncle and nephew in the cycle that Bertrand de Bar-sur-Aube
names after Garin de Monglane. However, this cycle is just as often called by
modern critics the William cycle, because William is the most important hero
of a core group of seven poems in it, and he figures largely in most of the
other poems, which nominally deal with exploits of his various brothers and
nephews. William has many nicknames: Fierebrace (or Strong Arm, since he
dispatches some enemies with a blow from his mighty fist), Au Court Nez
(Short Nose in the poem *Le couronnement de Louis*, because the tip of his
nose is cut off in a fight with the Saracen Corsolt), and "of Orange" (which
associates him with the town that he captures along with the Saracen princess,
Orable, who becomes his wife under the baptismal name of Guibourc). In
only one poem is he called as here Au Courb Nez (Hook Nose). That song,
*La chanson de Guillaume*, survives in one manuscript from the first half of

the thirteenth century and recounts with variations the repeated battle of L'Archamp, in which Frankish forces commanded by William struggle with Saracens led by Desramé of Córdoba. Although elements of that song are known to be archaic, the form in which we have it cannot predate the mid–twelfth century. However, the presence of William, given the nickname Al-corbitunas in the *Nota Emilianense*, confirms that a version of his song was also being sung on the pilgrim road to Compostela in the early eleventh century.

The same promiscuous mixing of heroes from different cycles is found later in the twelfth century in *Le pèlerinage de Charlemagne*. The exact date of this poem is controversial, but the latest editors believe it to be no earlier than the 1150s (Burgess and Cobby 2), too late for the original audience of the Oxford *Roland*, but likely to have been familiar to audiences for the later rhymed versions. *Le pèlerinage* forms part of the prehistory of Rencesvals to the extent that at the end of the first part of the poem, detailing Charlemagne's purely fictitious visit to Jerusalem, where Charlemagne is given relics of the Passion by the Patriarch, he specifically receives the mission to wage ceaseless war on the Saracens. The poet specifies that Charlemagne fulfills this mission in the campaign in which Roland and the Twelve Peers died. The second part of the song sees Charlemagne just as fictitiously visiting Constantinople, where he enters into a burlesque competition with the emperor of Byzantium to determine which of them wears his crown more regally. This part of the poem also parodies the well-known epic motif of the heroic boast, in a scene in which the drunken Frankish heroes boast of bizarre ways they will humiliate their host (Bennett, *"Pèlerinage"*; Grigsby). Roland will blow his olifant so hard it will blow off the emperor's mustache; Oliver will make love to the emperor's daughter twenty times in a night; William "Fierebrace" will hurl a mighty stone ball and demolish the walls of Constantinople; Aïmer, one of William's brothers, has a cloak of invisibility like that of Siegfried in the *Nibelungenlied*, which he will use to steal the emperor's food literally from under his nose. Only Turpin is allowed a nonaggressive boast: this austere churchman dreams of being a jongleur, so he will ride standing up on three horses while juggling with a set of golden balls. This poem contains such a wealth of intertextual reference in both its parodic and its nonparodic parts that it gives us a clear idea of the epic culture of a late-twelfth-century audience: characters, story lines, themes, motifs all have to be recognized if the poem is to have its effect. So, indeed, must the controversy raised by the Church's condemnation of jongleurs have been a matter of popular knowledge and debate if the image of the archbishop of Rheims doing a circus turn was to have its full impact.

The major irony of Bertrand's prologue to *Girart de Vienne* is that the poem that follows intricately intertwines threads and characters from all three of the gests Bertrand has identified. Moreover, his poem is an adaptation of much older epic material, which very likely dates back to original historical events of the late ninth century. The effect is that the eponymous hero of his song is artificially incorporated into the William cycle, whereas the prototype for Girart, if he belonged to a cycle at all, would be associated with the revolt cycle. The legend of Girart probably finds its source in the struggles between Charles the Bald, king of the West Franks, and Girart, count of Vienne, who had previously been count of Paris and of Mâcon. Whatever the politics of the actual rivalry between Charles and Girart in the ninth century, that rivalry was soon transformed in epic legend into a prolongation of the struggle for independence by the Burgundians against the Franks, who had effectively colonized the kingdom of Burgundy in the sixth century. However, in Burgundy as in Visigothic Aquitaine, the sense of ethnic, regional separateness remained strong throughout the Middle Ages. Thus in the twelfth century the figure of a rebellious Girart emerges in three poems: in *Aspremont*, where he is known as Girart de Fraite (or d'Eufrate) and refuses at first to support Charlemagne's crusading campaign in southern Italy; in the Franco-Provençal *Girart de Roussillon*, where the eponymous hero is most closely associated with Burgundy and the question of allodial (free) and feudal (dependent) lands is most clearly debated in his constantly renewed war with Charles Martel; and in Bertrand's *Girart de Vienne*, where the emperor, once again Charlemagne, is shown to be aggressive and concupiscent. In Bertrand's poem, Girart's rebellion arises not from principles of landholding but from a personal insult: when, as part of the homage ceremony, Girart has to kiss the emperor's foot, the empress arranges that he kiss her foot instead.

The main purpose of the new version of Girart's legend is really to present the *enfances* (first deeds of arms) of Roland and to introduce Oliver and his sister, Aude, both of whom are in this poem assimilated to the family of William of Orange, since they are the children of Girart's brother, Renier de Genvres. Thus the climax of the poem is not the final capture of Charlemagne by Girart and his nephew, Aymeri de Narbonne, which leads to a resolution of the main plot. The climax is instead the duel between Roland and Oliver, which is intended to decide the legal positions of Girart and Charles, whose dispute is the result of an insult suffered by Girart and of Girart's subsequent renunciation of his oath of loyalty to the emperor. The duel, however, is interrupted by an angel instructing Roland and Oliver to become companions in the fight against the infidel.

To this extent *Girart de Vienne* belongs to the tradition of later twelfth-century poems offering a prelude to Rencesvals. *Aspremont* is effectively in the same tradition, since this song, which was certainly composed at the time of the Third Crusade (1189–92) and is inspired to some extent by Richard the Lion-Heart's intervention in Naples and Sicily, gives a prominent role to Roland, who has not yet been knighted. The young man not only saves his uncle Charlemagne's life, but in the course of the campaign captures from their original Saracen owner his sword, Durendal; his olifant; and his warhorse, Veillantif. *Fierabras*, another prelude to Rencesvals, is also classed with the

*Destruction de Rome* and *Le pèlerinage de Charlemagne* in the short cycle of the relics, so called because stories in this cycle deal in their own ways with the transfer of the relics of the Passion from the east to France, and particularly to the French royal abbey of Saint Denis. In *Fierabras*, which dates from between 1180 and 1200, we find a judicial duel between Oliver and Fierabras to settle the fate of Christendom reminiscent of that between Roland and Ferracutus in the Latin *Pseudo-Turpin Chronicle* of c. 1140 or the one between William of Orange and Corsolt in *Le couronnement de Louis* of about the same date. Fierabras is converted and joins the army of Charlemagne in destroying the kingdom of the emir Balan and in returning the relics captured in *Destruction de Rome* to Christian keeping. We find virtually all the Frankish personnel of the *Song of Roland* gathered in this poem, including Ganelon, who is not yet the traitor he will become. Additionally, the poem exploits a theme popular at the end of the twelfth century, since Aigremore, the capital of Balan, is taken as much because of the love of Balan's daughter Floripas for one of Charles's knights, Gui de Bourgogne, as it is by Charlemagne's military prowess.

Although one cannot say that two out of the three cycles identified by Bertrand really existed as fully integrated poetic projects in the Middle Ages, it is clear that poets thought in terms of relating poems thematically and by their characters. It is also clear that the legend of Rencesvals and the personality of Roland dominated epic composition in the later twelfth century almost as much as they dominate modern critical thought about the chansons de geste. Moreover, one can identify many more small groupings of poems than just the three mentioned by Bertrand. The Lorraine cycle details an endless feud between the Lorrainers from eastern France and the Bordelais from the southwest. The Nanteuil cycle, a heterogeneous group of poems related to the revolt cycle, brings the Nanteuil clan, over several generations, into contact with Girart de Roussillon, Ganelon, and other characters known from a variety of poems. The Crusade cycle begins, as many other epics seem to have done, in history, with a fairly faithful poetic rendering of the events of the first part of the First Crusade (1095–99) in *La chanson d'Antioche*, a version of which may have been composed by a participant in the Crusade, Richard le Pèlerin. The cycle then becomes increasingly fantastic in *Les chétifs*, *La chanson de Jérusalem*, and the series of poems portraying the family history of the first king of Jerusalem, Godefroi de Bouillon, who is portrayed as descending from the mythical *Chevalier au Cygne*, the swan-knight of Celto-Germanic mythology. It was perhaps this very mythologizing drive in epic that drove the evidently learned clerk Bertrand de Bar-sur-Aube to imagine the Old French epic organized into the numerologically perfect whole of three branches, of which, in trinitarian fashion, he made one poem.

The nature of the translations of Old French epics does not on the whole make it possible to study the poetic features of the texts, since in general, whether the translation is into verse or into prose, translators tend to suppress the repetitive formulaic aspects of the original compositions in the interests of readability for a modern public. However, general questions of thematics, traditional character presentation, narrative structuring, and how medieval culture and society relate to epic conceptions of the world can all be approached with the help of some good translations, most of which also have informative introductions. For those whose classes operate in French, the Lettres gothiques series published by Livre de Poche has some excellent bilingual editions, including a very useful compendium of the William cycle (Boutet, *Cycle*). In English, despite some of the limitations of the translation into verse, *Guillaume d'Orange: Four Twelfth-Century Epics* (Ferrante) offers a useful introduction to the cycle, as do the prose translations in *William, Count of Orange: Four Old French Epics* (Price). Individual poems from all three cycles have been translated by Michael Newth (*Aspremont*; *Heroes*), but these should be treated with care. An approach to epic on the borders of the cycle of the king; the revolt cycle; and mixing generic features of epic, romance, and hagiography can be made through *Ami and Amile* (Danon and Rosenberg; Weiss), and a similarly intergeneric text originally in Occitan can be found in *Daurel and Beton* (Shirley). An indication that the Middle Ages were prepared to find humor in even the most serious epic heroes and themes is found in the much translated *Pèlerinage de Charlemagne* (Picherit; Burgess and Cobby; Burgess, *Pèlerinage*).

NOTE

[1]The year referenced is in fact AD 778: the medieval Spanish "era" counted 38 BC, the year in which Julius Caesar assumed power in Rome, as year 1.

# Beyond the Oxford Text:
# The Songs of Roland

## Joseph J. Duggan

Students living in the age of copyright need to be taught about the medieval mentality that permitted, and in fact encouraged, poets, redactors, and scribes to adapt and revise freely the works that had been handed down to them. This creative license resulted in a variety of manifestations of what we often now consider an unalterable literary work, and these regenerations took on a spectrum of meanings. The critical tradition of the *Song of Roland* has focused obsessively on the Oxford version, of which two dozen editions have appeared since it was first published in 1837. This exclusiveness masks an extraordinary richness of the poem's medieval metamorphoses, which include six other substantial versions and three fragments in medieval French;[1] ten versions in other languages; and still other variations reflected in oral and written literary traditions, as well as in medieval art (Lejeune and Stiennon, *Legend*). Since none of these versions match one another, the assumption is that whatever others existed in the period also differed substantially. For medieval audiences, there was not one *Song of Roland* but a multitude of songs about the battle of Rencesvals, its antecedents, and its aftermaths.

## *Versions before Oxford*

That a literary legend of Roland and Oliver existed as early as the year 1000 is suggested by the practice of naming brothers, sometimes twins, Roland and Oliver (Aebischer, "Trois"). Furthermore, some three decades before the Oxford version of the end of the eleventh century, a Spanish version of the poem, known as the *Nota Emilianense*, was summarized in a manuscript copied around 1070, which contains essential elements of a literary legend of Roland that probably circulated in oral tradition (see Menéndez-Pidal, Chanson 390): the Twelve Peers, the traditional epithet of William of Orange (in its archaic form), the association of the sword Courtain with Ogier, Saragossa as a town resisting conquest, the name of the Pyrenean pass of Cize found in the Oxford text (lines 583, 719, 2929), and the first mention in any source of the place name Rencesvals (in the form Rozaballes). The forms of the proper names show that it is a summary of a Spanish text, and that it was a poem is indicated by the final nonetymological *e*'s on *Rodlane* and *Bertlane*, a feature only found in medieval Spanish epic and balladry. If a Spanish version of the *Song of Roland* circulated already in this early period (see below concerning a later version in Spanish, *Roncesvalles*), French versions were surely sung even earlier. (See Bennett, "Origins of the French Epic," in this volume, for the Latin text and translation of the note.)

## Versions in Medieval French

Six substantial manuscript versions in Old French, apart from the Oxford text, have survived in the modern period. These versions are parallel to the Oxford text up to the end of the battle of Rencesvals; however, they differ radically after that point. That three of them were copied in Italy in a mixed language known as Franco-Italian or Franco-Venetian, which was used only for literary works, indicates strong interest in the legend of Roland and Charlemagne among the Northern Italian public. This popularity is corroborated by a number of medieval accounts, the most striking of which is the report of an Italian jurist, Odofredo, that around the middle of the thirteenth century blind men were singing of Roland and Oliver in the public square of Bologna. Eventually, French singers, who must have been in some way disruptive, were forbidden from performing in Bologna in 1288 (Holtus, *Lexikalische* 52).

Of the non-Oxford versions, the most archaizing, even though it is not found in the oldest manuscript, is a fourteenth-century text in Franco-Italian, now in the Library of Saint Mark's in Venice, known as Venice 4. This 6,011-line version follows the textual tradition found in the assonanced Oxford text for its first 3,846 lines, which are also in assonance. After the episode of Baligant, Venice 4 deviates from the plot of Oxford with a 572-line rhymed narrative of how the young knight Aimeri is given the city of Narbonne in Languedoc, thus becoming Aimeri de Narbonne. This episode in Venice 4 was, confusingly, inspired by the mention of the town Nerbone in Gascony (see Oxford, line 3683),[2] which the French army passes on its way from Rencesvals to Aix-la-Chapelle (that is, present-day Aachen). Elsewhere in the chansons de geste, Aimeri and his wife give birth to seven sons, a lineage known as the Narbonnais, and their exploits are the subject of an entire cycle of epic songs, usually called the cycle of William of Orange after its most famous hero. (For more on cycles of chansons de geste, see Bennett, "Origins of the French Epic," in this volume.) After the taking of Narbonne, Venice 4 incorporates rhymed episodes that it shares with the five other substantial non-Oxford versions.

These texts are known after their current locations: Paris, Cambridge, and Lyon, which all lack the beginning of the text, and Venice 7 and Châteauroux, which are complete and descend from the same lost manuscript in a French that is heavily marked by Italian features. All five texts are in rhyme, although each also incorporates brief passages that descend from lost versions in assonance. The Lyon version lacks the episode of Baligant, which in the other versions occupies between 989 and 1,285 lines. The three rhymed fragments, ranging from 108 to 352 lines, are related respectively to Paris, Cambridge, and Lyon.

Venice 4 and the other five substantial non-Oxford texts contain a version
of the episode of Aude's death that is remarkably different from the brief
appearance of Aude in the Oxford text. In this more extensive episode, Char-
lemagne sends messengers to Vienne to summon Aude, who is Roland's be-
trothed and the sister of Oliver and who is living in the castle of her uncle
Girart in Vienne. Girart and Aude are to meet the army at Blaye. In the
meantime, Charlemagne leads his forces first to Saint-Jean-le-Vieux, where he
establishes a church in memory of Roland, then on to Sorde at the foot of
the Pyrenees. There Ganelon escapes, pursued by Oton, who recaptures the
traitor. The army then moves on to Blaye, from which Charlemagne sends a
delegation to Mâcon to fetch his sister Berte, Roland's mother (in the Paris
and Lyon versions her name is Gille). Messengers then arrive at Vienne and
inform Girart that he must accompany Aude to Blaye, where she will be
married. The party sets off from Vienne.

Aude has had a dream that she recounts to her uncle and to the cleric
Amaugin: a falcon carries her to a prominence, where she has a vision of
Roland and Oliver as they hunt. Roland cuts off the right foot of a lion. An
eagle then flies onto Aude's lap, making her feel as if she has fallen into an
abyss. The eagle carries off first her right breast, then her left. Charlemagne
arrives and takes her in his arms. A black cloud covers Spain, including the
French army at Rencesvals, as if the earth had opened up beneath their feet,
and the land itself burns. Aude sees Charlemagne's right arm and shoulder
torn away; she fears Ganelon's treachery.

Aude then tells about a second dream: she is left in a forest dressed only
in her shift. A bear attacks her, but a knight takes her onto his horse and
rescues her. She then sees Oliver and Roland hunting a stag and calls out to
them in vain. They tumble from their horses and the ground opens beneath
them. She sees Roland and Oliver lying side by side next to a pillar. A sparrow
hawk flies out of Aude's mouth and over Oliver's body, leaving her in a state
of anguish. After Aude's account, Amaugin consults a book of necromancy and
sees that the dreams reveal the deaths of Roland and Oliver, but to protect
Aude from this news the cleric tells her that the falcon represents Charle-
magne, the eagle a lady whom Roland will prefer to her, and the sparrow
hawk a child of Roland's to which she will one day give birth.

Meanwhile in Blaye, Charlemagne commands that the inhabitants conceal
their sorrow over the deaths of Roland and Oliver by dancing and singing so
as not to upset Aude. When she approaches the city, however, she is not taken
in by this subterfuge and demands to know what has happened. Charlemagne
offers to marry her to the duke of Normandy, but she refuses. He tells her
that Roland and Oliver have stayed in Spain among the Saracens and that
Oliver will marry Baligant's sister. In the meantime, Roland's mother has ar-
rived at Blaye, and Charlemagne tells her that the treachery of her ex-
husband, Ganelon, has caused Roland's death. Entering Blaye, Aude forces
the emperor to tell her the truth, and on hearing it she faints. When she

revives, she is led into a church to see the bodies; there, she lifts the shroud from Roland's corpse and faints again. She asks to remain alone with the bodies of Roland and her brother. When she addresses Oliver, God sends an angel down to tell her, in Oliver's voice, that she will join her brother in heaven. She leaves the church, confesses her sins, prays that she might die, and expires in Charlemagne's arms. Angels carry her soul to heaven. The body of this "only lady ever to die of love," in the words of the Châteauroux and Venice 7 versions, is laid out between the biers of Roland and Oliver (Duggan et al. 2: 775, line 7267; my trans.)[3]

The details of this expanded episode of Aude differ somewhat from version to version, occupying variously 776 lines in Venice 4, 995 lines in the composite text of Châteauroux and Venice 7 (available in Duggan et al., vol. 2), 894 lines in Paris, 916 in Cambridge, and 456 in Lyon. In contrast, the short episode of Aude in Oxford is only twenty-nine lines long (lines 3705–33). Students are interested to learn that Oxford is the only French version to restrict the role of Aude to the scene of her sudden death. The Oxford text, it turns out, is the sole French song of Roland that accords only a modicum of space to the roles of women.

Between the episode of Baligant and the extended episode of Aude, the texts in rhyme include two brief episodes, the miracles of the hawthorn bushes and the hazel trees. In the first of these, in answer to Charlemagne's prayer, God sends Saint Martin down to Rencesvals to turn the corpses of the Saracens into hawthorn bushes. When wood is lacking to make biers for the bodies of Roland and Oliver, a second prayer prompts God to make hazel trees grow expressly for this purpose. Those who make the pilgrimage to Santiago de Compostela, the texts assure us, can still see both of these arboreal manifestations of divine intervention. In teaching about the social function of the *Song of Roland*, one can stress the use of the poem as a marketing tool aimed at persuading pilgrims to visit the places associated with Charlemagne and Roland and to complete the pilgrimage to Santiago de Compostela in Galicia (an undertaking not mentioned in Oxford), one of the three most important destinations for medieval pilgrims.

In the rhymed texts, the French, having buried the three bodies, proceed on through Poitou and Touraine to Bonneval near Chartres, and then on to Laon, where Ganelon is tried—rather than at Aix-la-Chapelle as in the Oxford text. Ganelon denies the charge of treason, and Gondelboef the Frisian challenges him to a judicial combat. No sooner is Ganelon mounted for battle than he gallops off, attempting once more to escape. Gondelboef, however, captures him quickly, and the trial resumes. Ganelon admits to causing Roland's death but denies committing treason because he received no compensation in material wealth for his betrayal. Gondelboef then reveals that the French had captured a Persian from Marsile's army, who told them how Ganelon sold the rear guard to the Saracens. As in Oxford, Ganelon's kinsman Pinabel of Sorance arrives to defend Ganelon against the charge of treason in single combat against Roland's squire, Thierry. After the two champions swear on relics to the truth of their respective sides, Thierry kills Pinabel with a thrust of his sword, and the defeated champion's body is dragged to the top of a hill and hung. The next morning, after Ganelon confesses to the charge of treason, the barons discuss his punishment. Five proposals are made and rejected before Otoier of Boulogne suggests that Ganelon should be tied to horses and torn apart (as in Oxford), which is done. The ending lines of each version differ, but Oxford is the only text that mentions Vivien or Turoldus.

The differences among the various versions give the teacher the opportunity to illustrate the much discussed variability (*mouvance*) of literature in the Middle Ages, when poets, performers, and redactors composed variations on the substance of received works with no adverse literary or legal consequences. Oxford, which numbers Scotland, Ireland, and England among the conquests of Roland and Charlemagne (lines 372–73, 2331–32) but gives short shrift to Aude, is the most militant version, and its association with the Normans who had recently conquered England (Douglas) should not surprise. The common model of Châteauroux and Venice 7, fashioned in the late twelfth or early thirteenth century when courtliness was in full flower, gives the greatest attention to Aude (Duggan, "Épisode"), an aspect that was likely developed to appeal to a clientele of female listeners and—as literacy became more common among women—female readers. The least militant version is Lyon, which has the extended episode of Aude but lacks all trace of Baligant and his legions.

## Versions in Languages Other Than French

Variety also marks the transformations that took place in the extraordinary propagation of the literary legend of Roland in languages other than French. Among these are two Latin texts. The first purports to be an eyewitness account of the Battle of Rencesvals, the author claiming to be none other than Archbishop Turpin, who contends to have survived the fighting. This text composes chapters 21–29 of the mid–twelfth-century *Pseudo-Turpin Chronicle* (Smyser), which, in turn, is the fourth part of the "Book of Saint James," whose fifth part was a guide for travelers making the pilgrimage to Santiago de Compostela. Enormously popular and surviving in some two hundred manuscripts, the *Pseudo-Turpin Chronicle* appears to have been written by a French cleric working either in the monastery of Saint Denis or at Aix-la-Chapelle. Most medieval artistic representations of the Roland legend are based on this work (Lejeune and Stiennon, *Legend*).

The second Latin text, thought to have been composed in the early thirteenth century, perhaps in Germany, is a poem of 482 hexameters, the *Carmen de tradicione Guenonis* ("Song of Ganelon's Treason" [Paden and Stäblein]), which lacks the pursuit of the Saracens after Rencesvals; the episode of Baligant; and the trial, but not the punishment, of Ganelon.

A group of texts derives directly or eventually from lost Anglo-Norman versions. The earliest of these is the *Saga af Runzivals Bardaga* ("Saga of the Battle of Rencesvals"), the eighth branch of the *Karlamagnús Saga* (Hieatt), a compilation in Old Norse assembled for King Hákon Hákonarson of Norway (ruled 1217–1263). The first branch of this compilation, based on now lost French epic texts, is extremely useful for the teacher, since it recounts events from the death of Charlemagne's father, Pepin, to the eve of the battle of Rencesvals, including how Charlemagne engendered Roland in an act of incest with his sister, Gille, but omitted this sin when he confessed to his chaplain Saint Giles. This tale of incest, also told in the fourteenth-century *Tristan de Nanteuil* (Sinclair, lines 21705–10), is alluded to obliquely in the Oxford version's reference to Saint Giles (2095–98), where we are told that "he who does not know as much has not properly understood [the poem]" (Burgess, *Song* 2098). This legend makes it possible to interpret the poem as the story of how Charlemagne was punished for the sin of incest by the death of his firstborn son, Roland. The first branch of the *Karlamagnús Saga* also provides a motive for Ganelon's hatred of Roland, since it tells how the young knight was seduced by Ganelon's wife. The *Karlamagnús Saga* gave rise to similar compilations in Swedish, *Karl Magnus* (Kornhall), and Danish, *Karl Magnus' Krønike* (Hjort). Like Lyon, the Norse version lacks the episode of Baligant, but unlike Lyon it includes only the short episode of Aude's death.

The second text derived from a lost Anglo-Norman version is the Middle Welsh *Cân Rolant* (Rejhon), incorporated into the Welsh Charlemagne cycle, the *Ystorya de Carolo Magno*, composed in the thirteenth century. Its narration goes from the beginning of the French poem well into the battle of Rencesvals. However, since *Cân Rolant* replaces chapter 22 of the Welsh version of the *Pseudo-Turpin Chronicle*, it only extends as far as the first 126 laisses of the Oxford text.

The third text based on a lost Anglo-Norman version is the *Rolandslied* (Kartschoke; J. W. Thomas), a monument of German literature written around 1170 by a priest, Konrad, who claims to have translated the French into Latin before he rendered it into Middle High German. Konrad's work gives an ecclesiastical aura to the tale. From it derives the *Karl der Grosse* (Bartsch), written in rhyme by an author known only as "der Stricker." Additionally, a descendant of what must have been a rich Anglo-Norman tradition of *Roland* versions is the Middle English fragment of the *Song of Roland* (Herrtage).

*Ronsasvals* (Gouiran and Lafont), a song of Roland that differs greatly from the French versions and includes an admission by Charlemagne of his incestuous paternity, survives in the language of southern France, Old Occitan. Only a hundred-line fragment of the Spanish *Roncesvalles*, a text that was likely an avatar of the version summarized in the *Nota Emilianense*, is extant (Menéndez-Pidal, *Roncesvalles*; see also Bennett's "Origins of the French Epic," in this volume). A Middle Dutch version, *Het Roelantslied* (van Dijk), survives in fragments totaling 1,835 lines. The variants of *Roland* in medieval

Spain and in late medieval and Renaissance Italy are discussed by Matthew Bailey and Jane E. Everson in their contributions to this volume.

Teachers should stress the remarkable richness and cosmopolitan nature of the literary legend of Roland, the nephew—and, for some medieval transmitters, the son—of Charlemagne, one of the founding figures of the French nation. Most of the legend's medieval manifestations come from outside the boundaries of present-day France, including even several of the texts composed in medieval French, which were copied in Italy (Venice 4, Venice 7, Châteauroux) and in Anglo-Norman England (Oxford). As the poem was passed on by singers, redactors, translators, and scribes aiming to please widely divergent audiences, it was adapted in each period and according to the interests of each receiving culture to fit the mentalities and narrative needs of different times and places.

NOTES

[1]All the *Roland* texts in medieval French mentioned in this essay can be found in Duggan et al.

[2]Line numbers given for the Oxford version are consistent with Burgess's and Short's editions.

[3]"Ne fu mais dame qi morist por amor."

# Feudalism in the *Song of Roland*

## George T. Beech

A knowledge of feudal customs in eleventh-century France is important for understanding both the details in and narrative of the *Song of Roland*. The poem dates from a period when feudal institutions and attitudes had permeated French aristocratic society, and this is evident in many aspects of the story—not that the poet consciously describes them. On the contrary, he takes it for granted that, like himself, his auditors will be so fully acquainted with things feudal that no explanation is needed, which can sometimes leave the modern reader mystified. My purpose in this essay is to call attention to the basic elements of French feudalism reflected directly and indirectly in the poem.

The story of the *Song of Roland* concerns one small segment of French society, the nobility or aristocracy, to the exclusion of the majority of the population: peasants and townspeople, not to mention clergy (other than Archbishop Turpin) and members of the religious orders. The anonymous author occasionally identifies his characters as members of this class with terms such as noble, baron (*barun*), knight (*chevaler*), and lord (*seignor*), but often does not bother to do so, presumably because their social rank is, to him at least, self-evident. Equally self-evident to the author is that the noble members of Charlemagne's army are, in addition to being his subjects, linked by personal relationships to the king as his dependents or vassals. These personal relationships involved service to a lord in return for which a vassal received lands (fiefs) in compensation. In the poem the terms *seignor* and *vassal* (and their derivatives *vasselage* and *vasselement*) serve to identify the two principals in feudal relationships, as, for example, when Ganelon angrily retorts to Roland that, "You will not go in my place; You are not my vassal and I am not your lord" (295–96). More often the author wants to stress that Roland (and others as well) is a good (*bon*) noble, a valiant (*vaillant*) vassal. An equivalent term to vassal, but one used less often, is *hom* (*homme*, or *man*), which also means the dependent of a lord.

A derivative of the term *hom* is *homage*, or the oath of submission of a vassal to his lord, which was part of the ceremony by which a man entered formally into a dependent (feudal) relationship with a superior. The only explicit reference to this act in the story is Ganelon's prediction that King Marsile will become Charlemagne's vassal, "with his hands clasped in yours he will become your vassal [*hom*]" (223), a reference to the dependent placing his hands between those of his new lord as a sign of his submission. Traditionally the vassal then swore an oath of fidelity (fealty) to his lord.

Having received homage and fidelity, the lord then reciprocated by investing (act of investiture) his new vassal with the fief (also called an *honor*) agreed on in advance, usually land and sometimes also a castle or castles, depending on the lord's social rank. In the case of monarchs, part of an entire kingdom could be held as a fief. When negotiating with Marsile as Charlemagne's envoy, Ganelon promises that the French king would give Marsile half of Spain as a fief: "He wishes to give you half of Spain as a fief" (432). The other half would go to Roland (472). Fiefs were normally lifetime tenures and could be passed on to one's male heirs, who then became vassals of the same lord or his successors. When he is about to leave for Muslim Spain as Charlemagne's ambassador to Marsile, Ganelon, apprehensive he will be killed on this mission, designates his son Baudoin as his successor as vassal to the king and specifies: "To him I bequeath my honours and my lands" (315).

The reception of a fief imposed a number of obligations on the vassal vis-à-vis his lord, all of which can be grouped under the heading of service. No one puts it more succinctly than Ganelon, who, when on trial for his life, asserts to the judges: "For the love of God, listen to me, barons. / Lords, I was in the army with the emperor; / I served him *in faith and in love*" (3768–70; my emphasis). For Roland service means total dedication and self-sacrifice in his lord's interests: "For his lord a vassal must suffer hardships / And endure great heat and great cold; / And he must lose both hair and hide" (1010–12). To avoid conflict of interests when a man held fiefs from more than one lord, the custom of liege homage developed, where service was owed to the grantor of the most important holding: "They bewail their sons . . . and their liege lords" (2420–21).

The obligation to serve one's lord "in faith and in love," an obligation emphasized by the oath of fidelity sworn by the vassal, was a critical element in the relationship between the two men. Indeed, two differing interpretations of what that obligation meant and entailed causes the conflict leading to the disaster at Rencesvals, the central event of the poem. Charles's accusation at the opening of the trial—that Ganelon had betrayed Roland, Oliver, and the 20,000 French killed in that ambush—amounts to an accusation that Ganelon had broken his oath of fidelity to his lord, the king (3752–57). Vigorously denying this charge, Ganelon claims that he has served Charles with faith and love (3769–70). Ganelon does not deny having informed Marsile or having helped him plan and carry out the massacre of the French. Instead he argues that his was an act of revenge against his nephew Roland for having "conceived a hatred for me / And [having] nominated me for death and woe" (3771–72). Furthermore, he justifies his action by pointing out that he had defied Roland publicly and that Charles himself had witnessed this act of defiance:

> "Lord," said Ganelon, "this is all Roland's doing;
> As long as I live I shall have no love for him.
> Nor Oliver . . .
> Nor the twelve peers . . .
> I challenge them here, lord, in your presence." (322–26)

As strange as it may seem, Ganelon appears to be arguing that his right to vengeance for a wrong done to him privately takes precedence, if expressed publicly, to his commitment to loyalty to his lord and king, even at the cost of thousands of lives. Charles rejects this defense, but Ganelon's guilt is not formally decided until his champion loses in a duel (for more discussion of the meaning of Ganelon's trial, see Mickel, "The Implications of the Trial of Ganelon," in this volume).

In twelfth- and thirteenth-century France, service meant, above all, military assistance, and vassals were required to answer their lord's summons and to fight in his army, providing a certain number of armed knights (dependent on the size of their fiefs) for a certain number of days each year. The French nobles in Charles's army in Spain are carrying out their feudal obligation of military service to their lord, though the author is not explicit about this, nor does he speak of their owing a specific number of days annually. In addition to requiring military service, lords called on their vassals to consult with them—to advise and consent—regarding future policies and strategies. Thus, to decide how to respond to Marsile's envoys, who have come to Charles's royal court to present the Saragossan king's proposal that he leave Spain, Charles "summons his barons to conclude his council" (169).

Another aspect of feudal counsel was the vassal's duty to serve as a judge in his lord's court in the adjudication of disputes, of alleged crimes, and of general cases involving himself and his fellows in relation to their superior. The denouement of the *Song of Roland* presents a detailed example of feudal court service in the trial of Ganelon. After his victory in Saragossa, Charles returns to Aix-la-Chapelle and prepares to try Ganelon on the charge of having caused the defeat at Rencesvals. "Charles summons vassals from many lands" (3743), then, at the opening assembly, he charges them with their task: "Lord barons . . . / Give me a true judgement with regard to Ganelon" (3750–51). These men serve as the jury to which first Ganelon (3957–58), then his kinsman Pinabel (3780–92), address the defense. The author then describes the members of the council consulting among themselves (3793–806). They first recommend to the king that the charge against Ganelon be dropped (3808–13), but later they advise that he be torn to pieces and his kinsmen be hanged (3947–51).

In contrast to this unusually detailed depiction of court service, the poem offers nothing on the feudal aids, that is, the monetary obligation of a vassal to help pay for his lord's ransom in case of his captivity, for the knighting of his eldest son, and for the marriage of his eldest daughter. Nor does it emphasize the obligation of the lord to protect and look out for the interests of his vassals. The nearest it comes to mentioning this duty occurs in Naimes's exhortation to Charles to "[a]rm yourself and shout out your battle-cry / And ride to the aid of your noble household. / You can hear clearly the distress cry which Roland sends" (1793–95). This is his reminder that the king should now go and rescue his vassals.

A survey of the entire *Song of Roland* reveals that the author refers relatively rarely, and then unevenly, to practices, customs, and beliefs that modern specialists write about in their works on feudalism and feudal society. This is not, however, because of their insignificance in the literary world he creates but because they constituted a reality so basic that no explanation was needed.

# Military History and Technology
# in the *Song of Roland*

## Kelly DeVries

From *The Iliad* to *Cold Mountain* war stories have been popular. Undoubtedly this is because the heros whom war stories portray exhibit all the best human qualities in the midst of the worst human violence and depravity. There is also usually a distinct good (the hero or his heroic comrades) and a distinct evil (the enemy or traitor). The military struggle allows the good to face and defeat the evil, while providing a setting in which the hero can struggle against his own fears and weaknesses. Inevitably these struggles are as important to the hero and his role in the war as they are to his and his comrades' victory, although ultimately, and almost always, the hero must lose his own life, now that he is unencumbered with the frailty with which he was struggling, to ensure that victory. What technology he wore and wielded and what strategy and tactics he followed may be secondary to the hero's plight, but they are important aspects of the setting and thus allow us to understand the war story better.

The *Song of Roland* is one of the most popular medieval war stories. Well known is its influence in medieval French literature in general and on the legend of Charlemagne in particular. Less well known, but equally important, is its influence on the recruitment and maintaining of the Crusades. Yet few scholars have approached or taught the *Song* as a war story, although in my experience almost all students see it as such. This often leads to confusion about what is going on and whether it mirrors the reality of medieval military conflict, either that of the time of Charlemagne or later. The purpose of this essay is to discuss what can be taught about the military history and technology of the *Song of Roland*. It is divided into two parts: the military technology found in the *Song of Roland* and the military strategy and tactics demonstrated by the actions of the combatants.

## Military Technology

Most war stories not only do not present an accurate portrayal of the strategy and tactics of the conflicts of their times; they also frequently exaggerate the death and destruction of the engagements written about. Yet, for a reason I do not fully understand myself, and one that cries for more investigation, the authors of war stories almost always portray an accurate depiction of the military technology being used at the time of the story's composition, if not at the time of its setting. That the author of the *Song of Roland* knew the arms and armor of the soldiers of his time is reflected in the accuracy of his war story. However, his determination of military strategy and tactics and his depiction of the death and destruction on a battlefield does not differentiate between the arms and armor of the Christian and Muslim armies. This suggests that, although he was well versed in the military technology of his own side, he had not seen any foreign armaments—and might not have thought that any were being used.

It is also fortunate that medieval arms and armor had changed little from the time of Charlemagne to the period of the *Song of Roland*'s composition, making the dating of the work less important in this regard. Significant alterations in personal military technology—arms and armor—do not occur until the late thirteenth through fifteenth centuries. Well before his death, Charlemagne established the norms for arms and armor throughout his very large realm, and these would not be radically changed by the Viking invasions, Norman conquests of Sicily and England, or the launching of the early Crusades. Artistic and archaeological evidence suggests that, although styles and sizes might vary, the purpose, manufacture, and capabilities of the military technology, both offensive and defensive, did not change. In addition, Charlemagne tried to maintain dominance in the normalization of military technology throughout his realm by placing restrictions on the sale or exportation of Carolingian military technology outside of Francia, but eventually these norms would also be found in England, Scandinavia, and Spain. The Crusades, because of the diversity of the participants, would continue to normalize military technology; they would also ultimately provide a technological thrust toward new technology, although primarily in the area of fortification construction and artillery, technology not evidenced in the *Song of Roland*.

## Armor

Charlemagne recognized very early in his reign that the defensive requirements of his large realm and his desire to conquer lands beyond its borders required a highly regulated professional army. He thus needed a strict military organization and an army that was well armed, both offensively and defensively. The first extant law to state this as a policy was the *Capitulare missorum* of 792/93, which demanded that all benefice and office holders in the Carolingian realm possess full armor and shield as well as a horse and offensive weaponry. This was followed in 802/03 by a capitulary again charging these nobles to have their own helmets and body armor, known to the Carolingians and mentioned in the *Song of Roland* as *byrnies*. Finally, in 805, the law was made even more specific. In this capitulary, Charlemagne required any man in his empire who held twelve *mansi* of land to have his own armor and to serve as a horseman in Charlemagne's army; if any such man failed in his duty, both his land and his armor would be taken.[1] Infantry soldiers were not so well protected, although the Capitulary of Aachen, proclaimed in 802/03, did require them all to carry a shield.

The main defensive armament of the Carolingian army, although it is not suggested as such in the *Song of Roland*, was the shield. It was also the least expensive armor, and thus all soldiers, even horse archers, were required to carry it. A shield and lance together cost three times less than a helmet and six times less than a *byrnie*. Carolingian shields were round, concave, and made of wood, and at least some were covered, perhaps on both sides, by leather. They were rimmed with metal, and metal strips were sometimes added for extra strength. A dome-shaped metal boss was set in the middle of each shield with a grip running across the underside and attached both to the boss and to the wood; a strap was also connected to the grip, allowing the soldier to sling the shield across his back when transporting it. Carolingian shields were much larger than other early medieval shields, measuring between 52 and 80 centimeters (approximately 21 and 32 inches) in diameter; thus they protected more of the warrior's torso, with the largest shields able to cover the body from the neck to the thighs.

The second most prominent armor of a Carolingian soldier was a helmet. Carolingian helmets were made of metal, however generally not out of a single piece of metal, and were of varying designs. The most common of these, as portrayed in many artistic sources (no archaeological exemplar has yet been excavated), consisted of a cap encircled by a wide rim. The rim rose to a point at the forehead and tapered toward a pronounced neck guard at the rear of the helmet. A strengthening band descended from the top of the helmet and intersected the rim at a button or large rivet. This band also served as the helmet's crest, with some illustrations showing a feather attached to it. A less common design was the *spangenhelm*. More rounded than other Carolingian helmets, the *spangenhelm*, of which both artistic and archaeological examplars exist, consisted of a framework formed by a single headband on which were attached six or more metal bands, known as *spangen*. This framework was then filled with metal or horn plates.

A final defensive armament of the Carolingian army was the *byrnie*. To the Carolingian soldier, the *byrnie* was his most highly valued piece of armor, not only because of its cost but also because no enemy he met on the battlefield would have one. Indeed, as early as 779, Charlemagne had forbidden the sale of this armor outside the realm; in 803, he added a declaration that soldiers were forbidden even to give it to a merchant who might sell it to a potential enemy. It does appear, however, that *byrnies* eventually did make it into the armaments of some Avars, Muslims, Bretons, and Vikings. There is some dispute among historians as to what exactly constituted the Carolingian *byrnie*. Again, relying only on artistic and some literary sources because of the lack of an archaeological exemplar, some claim that it was a heavy leather jacket with metal scales sewn onto it and that it was long, reaching below the hips and covering most of the arms. This would not make the *byrnie* a unique garment, since scale armor, the *lorica squamata*, had been worn since the fall of the Roman Empire. Most other historians, myself included, believe instead that the Carolingian *byrnie* was a coat of mail, long enough to cover the thighs and upper arms. Warriors might also have been outfitted with a mail hood, or coif, over which their helmet would sit. Finally, the Carolingian *byrnie* might have had a mail ventail, or bib, hanging from the neck that, when raised and attached to the helmet, provided neck and lower face protection. The ventail is specifically mentioned twice in the *Song of Roland*, at lines 1293 and 3449, and is also what is meant when the helmets are described as being "laced up."

Leg guards and greaves appeared during the Carolingian period, worn by the most wealthy of Charlemagne's horsemen. Also emerging for the first time were arm guards and gauntlets, later to be common armor for all cavalry; Charlemagne also forbade the sale of these armaments to foreigners. All these body armaments are depicted in Carolingian illustrations and in the Bayeux Tapestry. They constitute the basic armor worn by Charlemagne, Roland, and their comrades and enemies in the *Song of Roland*, although the author frequently adorns the armor of the more wealthy and heroic horsemen with precious metals and gems; these would not have been present on any battlefield armor of the Middle Ages.

Carolingian military policies remained dominant throughout the ninth and tenth centuries. The army continued to be primarily a well-armed cavalry-based force, and each soldier was protected by a long *byrnie*, which by this time was definitely composed of mail; a segmented, wide-brimmed helmet; and a large round shield made of wood and leather. This mail *byrnie*, called by different names, remained the primary body armor into the late Middle Ages. The shield and helmet changed in style, but not in manufacture, sometime during the late tenth and early eleventh centuries, although there is no evidence available to explain these changes.

Since the shield was round, it did not protect the full body of the horseman, leaving almost his entire leg exposed to enemy attack. At the same time, its large size made it unwieldy for a cavalry soldier to maneuver easily during battle. These problems were solved by making the shield long, narrow, and kite-shaped, with a rounded top and pointed bottom, similar to those depicted in the Bayeux Tapestry. The Bayeux Tapestry also shows that these shields were gripped in a variety of ways by a series of leather straps (or *enarmes*), which are riveted onto the insides of the shields. The most frequent of these grips consists of a loose strap draped around the soldier's neck, with a shorter strap grasped by his hand. Horsemen carry their shields consistently on the left side and their lance on the right; infantrymen also carry their shields in the left hand. Finally, on the Bayeux Tapestry shields are frequently decorated, although there seems to be no consistency or heraldry in these decorations. Among the designs that appear are birds, dragons, wavy crosses, diagonal lines, and saltires; the boss and rivets were sometimes incorporated into the pattern. It may be that designs referred to in the *Song of Roland* were inspired by such artistic representations, rather than those found on Carolingian shields or depicted in heraldry. However, this is one military subject that necessitates a correct dating of the text, since heraldry began to develop in Europe in the twelfth and thirteenth centuries. Artistic sources demonstrate that the kite-shaped shield of the Bayeux Tapestry was the most prominent shield carried by troops, infantry, and cavalry until the beginning of the thirteenth century and was, therefore, the most likely shield carried by the soldiers of the *Song of Roland*.

It is less easy to speculate on the reasons for change in helmet design. Perhaps the wide helmet was too complex in its construction, or perhaps it was simply too difficult to avoid losing during the pressure of battle. At any rate, the segmented, wide-brimmed Carolingian helmet evolved into a more simply constructed and tightly worn conical helmet. The early Carolingian helmet and shield continued to be used, but only infrequently, until the twelfth century and are shown in artistic sources to have been worn by non-Western European armies, such as Romans and Muslims, or by that special iconographic figure of military evil, Goliath. The segmented conical helmet, sometimes with a nasal guard, is also seen in most of the exemplars that remain from the period, some of which also show signs of having once been attached to mail ventails. The segmented conical helmet would not be replaced until the thirteenth century by what became known as the "Great Helm" and is undoubtedly the type of helmet worn by soldiers on both sides in the *Song of Roland*. Again, however, the adornment of the helmets and shields of these soldiers' battlefield armors must be considered a nonhistorical literary invention.

## Arms

### Swords

The most celebrated weapon in the *Song of Roland*, although not on the historical battlefield, is the sword. Swords were valued throughout the Middle Ages, as evidenced not only in literary texts, like the *Roland*, but also in historical, artistic, and archaeological sources. Such sources report that swords were intricately made, expensive to own, and generally passed down from generation to generation. They were also frequently named, with Roland's Durendal equaling that of Arthur's Excalibur in fame. The sword was the weapon of leadership, an effective military tool as well as a ceremonial object. Often it would be given to a boy as a gift at birth or at his naming. The child would grow up playing with it and with other, lighter swords, until the gift sword became a weapon he could wield with strength and agility. At other times, the sword would not be presented to the boy until he had reached manhood. As such, it stood as a symbol of the end of childhood and the birth of the warrior. Such inherited swords were a family treasure that had been passed down from one warrior to the next, a token of past wars fought and past victories won. This need not have been a complete weapon but could also be the shattered fragments of an ancestor's sword. Once obtained, the sword became the warrior's constant companion. He carried it into the king's hall or at council, although it could never be drawn. He used it when swearing an oath, when fighting in a duel or, of course, when in battle. At night it hung above the warrior's bed, and, at his death, the sword would either be buried with him or passed on to his son or close relative. The honor of the sword and, consequently, of its bearer is unique in its medieval prominence and explains why Roland chided Oliver for continuing to fight with his lance after the initial charge had been levied; the lance simply did not hold the same honor as the sword for such noble warriors.

The medieval sword was a carefully and intricately made weapon and was so cherished by its maker that he often inscribed it with his name. Forged of pattern-welded steel of the finest ore, a sword's fabrication often took an extremely long time. First the smith, or an associated ironworker, produced a strong bar of steel, which was heated until red hot, then reduced in thickness by hammering. At the same time, the edges and as deep a groove down the center of the blade as possible, aimed at decreasing its weight but not its strength, were also shaped. The heating and hammering were repeated until the desired thickness was achieved. Once the fabrication was completed, the sword was ground, first by a rough grinding stone and then by finer stones and files, until a fine sharpness had been achieved. The cross-guard, grip, and handle were added, and the sword polished. Modern attempts at replicating medieval swords have shown that it is extremely difficult to reproduce the high quality of this early workmanship.

In Charlemagne's many capitularies that refer to weaponry, the sword is always prominent. When a man owned a warhorse, he also had to own a sword; in fact, in many sources the sword is reported to be the cavalry soldier's primary weapon. But while a new emphasis on ownership of the sword was present in Carolingian Europe, and the numbers of these weapons increased dramatically, the swords themselves had not changed much from earlier medieval examples. The only change that seems to have been made to Carolingian swords was in the shape of the long-sword blade. Earlier swords had edges that ran parallel for most of the length of the blade, converging only at the end to form a point. In the beginning of the ninth century, this construction was changed so that the blade's edges began to taper gradually from the hilt to the tip. This shifted the center of gravity closer to the sword grip and made the weapon more maneuverable and easier to handle in combat but at the same time did not lessen the strength of the blade itself. Carolingian swords were almost always inscribed with the name of the maker, and, sometimes for the most wealthy and noble owners such as Charlemagne and his champions, the hilt was decorated with gold; silver; gems; jewels; and, as with Charlemagne's and Roland's swords, religious relics. Scabbards were probably made of wood and leather and also decorated, although none have survived, and they were hung on a sword belt around the waist. The sword was primarily a cavalry weapon, to be used in close combat, although infantry soldiers also might carry one—if they could afford to—since it was the most expensive offensive armament.

## Spears, or Lances

Although not as renowned as the sword, the spear, also called a lance when carried on horseback, was the most commonly used weapon of the Middle Ages. Unlike all other weapons, the spear or lance could be used by both the infantry and cavalry as a hand-held thrusting weapon or, when thrown, as a missile. The spear's provenance is prehistoric and its use throughout premodern times is discussed by all contemporary authors and illustrators of war stories. Charlemagne's insistence on establishing a standardized weapons policy for his troops began with the spear/lance. As early as 792/93, the *Capitulare missorum* required the lance as a weapon for all horsemen. A similar command was echoed in capitularies decreed in 804 and 811. The infantry was to be outfitted likewise with a lance, as directed in the Capitulary of Aachen in the year 802/03. This is also evidenced in artistic sources, all of which show the spear as the predominant weapon carried by both the Carolingian cavalry and infantry. The Carolingian lance was not a missile weapon. Both artistic and literary sources confirm that it was only thrust at the enemy, whether its bearer was on foot or on horseback.

With the military changes instituted by Charlemagne, the spear took on a new importance in warfare. Yet using the lance only as a thrusting weapon when mounted made the warhorse merely a fighting platform and did not incorporate either its power or speed into the attack. This was accomplished only when the lance was held fixed under the horseman's arm in a couched position. Then, as the horse charged an opponent, the lance blow was delivered by a combination of the lance, the rider, and the horse, thus producing a far greater impact to the attack than a manual thrust ever could. This type of warfare has been called *mounted shock combat* by modern historians, a term that correctly recreates what must have been an extremely forceful and "shocking" attack. It clearly impressed medieval writers, many of whom recount this form of combat in graphic detail, as apparent in the *Song of Roland*, with its description of breaking shields, bursting hauberks, cut bones, and torn-away spines, leaving the victim soulless and hurled far from the point of contact (see, for example, lines 1198–205 or 1225–30). Although certainly exaggerating the effects of such a blow, the anonymous author of the *Roland* has quite clearly shown the impression that contemporaries had of mounted shock combat, an impression that caused many to flee the battlefield without a blow being made. There is some uncertainty about when mounted shock combat was first practiced. It might not have been used by the Carolingian cavalry, but it certainly and obviously was the chief form of cavalry warfare by the time of the *Song of Roland*.

To perform mounted shock combat effectively, significant technological changes were made to the lance. No longer was an infantry spear, with its light wood shaft and small iron head, sufficient to withstand the impact required of the couched lance. The typical cavalry lance was made of strong, hard wood, about four meters in length; its leaf-shaped metal head had two cutting edges and a sharp point. It was also generally outfitted with a wing attachment behind the lance head (a *pennon*). This limited the lance's penetration, preventing the thrust of the weapon from imbedding itself too deeply in an opponent's body or armor, so the lance could be easily extracted. A flared restraint was attached to the end of the lance to keep it from being driven backward beneath the wielder's arm. Finally, a handgrip was often added.

Stirrups were also required, as was a saddle with a high pommel and cantle. The stirrup was a simple device, created by the mere addition of a rigid wood, rope, or metal tread at the end of a strap descending from the saddle into which the horseman's feet would be placed. Yet its impact on cavalry warfare was far greater than its simple technology. The stirrup increased the cavalry soldier's stability and added new dimensions to his fighting tactics, especially to mounted shock combat. The European origin of stirrups is disputed, although stirrups were certainly being used by horsemen at the time of the composition of the *Song of Roland*. The saddle with high pommel and cantle appeared at the beginning of the twelfth century. Before this, the saddle had been made of rigid flat leather, which replaced the ancient horse blanket and riding cushions but provided little further lateral stability. It only prevented the rider from falling off his horse but did nothing to help him in combat. With the addition of a high wraparound cantle, which sat against the rider's back and prevented him from being thrown over the horse's rump, and of an equally high pommel, which not only protected the rider's genitals and lower stomach but also kept him from being thrown over his horse's head, the cavalry soldier was now able to use the full power of his horse to provide a mounted shock lance attack without being toppled from his steed.

**Bows**

The bow is not used in the military engagements of the *Song of Roland* but is mentioned as a tool for delivering an oath. It is thus difficult to know what type of bow would be used by the armies of *Roland*'s Charlemagne. Medieval archers fired several different types and sizes of bows. By the time Charlemagne's professional army was established, the bow was often used. Some suggest that this was a result of Charlemagne's wars against the Avars and Slavs, tribes that had used bows since ancient times; their proficiency with the weapon, although not decisive against Charlemagne's soldiers, may have inspired the Carolingians to adopt it. In the Capitulary of Aachen in 802/03, Charlemagne ordered that the bow become the army's chief infantry weapon, demanding that infantry soldiers carry it along with a spare string and twelve arrows (the contents of one quiver). He followed this in 806 with a decree that each horseman also be equipped with a bow as well as several quivers of arrows. Both decrees were reiterated in an 811 capitulary.

The Merovingian Franks had used D-shaped longbows that were perhaps as long as two meters. Charlemagne had his army also use shorter recurved bows. Thus both bows were probably common in the Carolingian army. Both types of bows continued in popularity through the twelfth century, when crossbows began to replace them in Europe, except in Spain and England. The variety of arrows in use is indicated by the discovery of both barbed and nonbarbed arrowheads in archaeological excavations. The quiver was probably made of wood and leather, and artistic sources portray it as covered with a domed lid to protect the arrowheads; a long strap allowed it to be slung across the archer's back.

That bows are not used by Charlemagne or his champions in the *Song of Roland*, as with other literary characters, most notably the knights of the Round Table, has often been explained as a noble prejudice. While this bias undoubtedly exists in the *Roland* and other literary works, it is far from factual: medieval kings and nobles employed numerous archers in their armies, and many members of the nobility surely were themselves trained to use bows.

## Warhorses

Although the medieval warhorse itself cannot be called a military technological device, many of the accoutrements used to breed and outfit the warhorse, without which the horse's importance might have been diminished, were indeed products of technology. The warhorse was perhaps the most important piece of military equipment owned by a medieval cavalry soldier. Not only was military status conferred by ownership of a horse but also a soldier's role in medieval society was established by the expense of owning and maintaining a horse. Heavily armored cavalry, like that depicted in the *Song of Roland*, began to influence the conduct of medieval warfare in the eighth and ninth centuries, when the early Carolingian rulers—Charles Martel, Pepin II, and Charlemagne—instituted laws establishing more and better cavalry units for incorporating into their forces. By the eleventh century, as represented by the conquests of southern Italy and England and by the Crusades, heavy cavalry had become the dominant arm of every medieval army.

As cavalry began to dominate the battlefield, modifications in breeding began to change the warhorse. In the early Middle Ages, there was no need for a specially bred horse. With changes in technology, as well as with the increasing weight of armor, a better bred, stronger, and heavier horse was required. Known by the twelfth century as a destrier, the horse also had to be capable of training for either the tournament or the battlefield, although rarely would a rider use the same horse for both duties. This meant the selective breeding of a warhorse from Bactrian or Arabian stock through an intricate process over a long period of time. Eventually this produced a horse 17 hands tall (approximately 173 centimeters [69.2 inches]), with strong bones and a sturdy, short back (medieval horses had conventionally measured 12–13 hands, or 122–32 centimeters [49.2 inches] in height), one capable of carrying a heavily armored soldier into a battle or a joust. These are the warhorses ridden by the cavalry soldiers on both sides in the *Song of Roland*.

## Strategy and Tactics

For many years it was thought that no medieval military leader could be compared with ancient, early modern, or modern generals. If this were true, then medieval strategy and tactics were nonexistent. However, recent studies have begun to restore the military reputations of such stellar medieval generals as Charlemagne, Robert Guiscard, William the Conqueror, Saladin, Richard the Lionheart, Edward III, Henry V, and Joan of Arc. Of these Charlemagne may be the greatest. He deserves this honor if for nothing else than because he "never lost a battle," although, as the *Song of Roland* points out, his armies suffered at least one battlefield defeat, so perhaps the correct assertion should be that Charlemagne "never lost a campaign." Of course, it is a historical fact that he did not conquer all of the lands with which later legends would credit him, in particular the Holy Land. However, he did attack and conquer the Bretons, Frisians, Avars, Saxons (several times), and Lombards. He also pushed the Danes behind their protective *Danewerk* and the Muslims out of southern France and behind the Pyrenees, leading to the capture of Barcelona and, in 778, the destruction of Pamplona. These conquests gained for Charlemagne an empire over which he would be accorded the title emperor by Pope Leo III on Christmas day, 800.

### Strategy

Strategy determines conduct on a military campaign, in contrast to tactics that direct an individual military action, most often a battlefield or siege. The Romans have always been considered supreme strategists against whom medieval military leaders paled in comparison. But Charlemagne certainly imitated the strategy of the Romans, which he learned through military manuals, such as that written by Vegetius, and historical examples, such as those written by classical chroniclers. In addition, the great leader of the Franks created his own original strategies, determined by the enemies he faced and the terrain over which he fought.

Charlemagne summoned his armies to fight in nearly every one of his forty-two years on the Frankish throne, and all of these campaigns were used to extend the borders of the Carolingian kingdom. These military feats were accomplished by Charlemagne as he realized the power of a diverse, professional force. Because such a force needed to be large, Charlemagne required all the property holders of the realm to participate in military service, either by serving themselves or by outfitting and paying for a suitable replacement. Even subject peoples were required to fill the ranks of Charlemagne's army. However, they were always commanded by Frankish nobles. The cavalry was supplied by members of the more wealthy noble class who could afford the expensive armaments and horses. They were required to muster for any long campaign and lost their lands and titles if they failed to come in support of Charlemagne. When not required to fight in a campaign, they were put in command of a garrison along the borders of Spain or Saxony.

All soldiers were required to take an oath of fealty to Charlemagne. This was the first time since the fall of Rome that such an oath had been required. In doing this, Charlemagne secured a viable, legal means by which military service could be obtained from men who were previously not required to serve him. He also guaranteed a loyalty that earlier leaders had not been able to realize.

Charlemagne used his large army to successfully invade the numerous surrounding peoples listed above. This meant knowing how his enemies recruited their soldiers, how well trained and well led they were, and whether they were cavalry or infantry-dominant forces. He knew these details because he employed a large number of well-paid spies. Without this information, his campaigns might have ended less successfully.

In invading neighboring lands, Charlemagne maneuvered his forces to take advantage of the weaknesses of his enemies' defenses. He preferred avoiding battles, choosing strategies that would bring submission without endangering his troops; these included a large amount of raiding, pillaging, and destruction. Especially targeted were non-Catholic structures, idols, relics, and artifacts, for Charlemagne always contended that his armies fought with God on their side and that it was his responsibility to bring Catholicism to the populations he defeated. As his armies always contended against non-Catholics, Charlemagne also always went into his campaigns with the pope's blessing, and he responded, largely through forced baptisms, with the largest numbers of new converts for Catholicism since the days of Constantine and Clovis.

Charlemagne also knew the value of a wise defense. He built several large fortifications along the borders of his kingdom, and he established a very good signaling system to call for reinforcements anywhere in the large empire. He also bribed certain enemy chieftains, most notably those of the Danes, to remain at peace with his empire. Most important, Charlemagne's army could and would respond to any upheaval in his realm and to any threat outside it.

While no military leader from the ninth century to the end of the Middle Ages could compare strategically with Charlemagne, several learned from and imitated his expertise to wage their own campaigns with what even modern historians describe as good strategic generalship. Even more significant for the teaching of the *Song of Roland* is the recognition that the author knew of Charlemagne's strategic skills and sought to emphasize them. The author does not hide that Roland lost the battle of Rencesvals and that he seems not to have known his enemy's movements before they attacked—a strategic faux pas. Roland's error, however, duplicates the historical event, which the author lays at the feet of the traitor, Ganelon, who is supposed to be scouting the opponents. Charlemagne's own strategy, shown later in the epic, is much better and, of course, leads him and his forces to victory.

## Tactics

Part of Charlemagne's strategic brilliance was that he fought few battles. When he did, however, his Carolingian army was almost invulnerable. His tactical system of advances used the heavy cavalry troops to the full extent of their capability, even against lighter, swifter armies. How these heavy cavalry soldiers actually operated on the battlefield is hard to determine from Carolingian sources. It is improbable that they used the couched-lance mounted shock combat discussed above; most historians believe that the earliest date it could have been used in battle is the middle of the eleventh century, if not a century later. After that time it quickly became a tactic universally employed throughout western Europe. This is clearly seen in the large number of artistic sources from the period that depict the cavalry lance held in a couched position. Contemporary chronicles also report that the lance was the principal offensive weapon of the Crusaders in the Holy Land, where the first attack was always a mounted shock combat charge. In England, the 1181 Assize of Arms decreed by Henry II specifies only the lance as a required weapon for horsemen in battle, whereas a similar requirement was ordered of all cavalry soldiers in Italy by the middle of the thirteenth century. Spain, Germany, and France also practiced the battlefield use of mounted shock combat. Of course, for this study it is important to note that it is the primary battlefield cavalry tactic portrayed by the author of the *Song of Roland*.

Despite its obvious simplicity, mounted shock combat was not an easy form of warfare to learn, and cavalry soldiers were compelled to train for many years before they could wield the lance with dexterity and skill. There was no better place to learn the art of the couched lance than at a tournament, and from the twelfth century on there were sufficient tournaments held for everyone to learn his craft well. In the twelfth and thirteenth centuries, jousters at these tournaments generally used the same lances as they would on the battlefield, with the sharp lance head removed and a blunt coronal replacing it if fighting in a tournament *à plaisance* ("for pleasure" or practice); in a tournament *à outrance* ("to the death"), which more explicitly imitated warfare, the sharp warhead remained. The coronal prevented the lance head from piercing an opponent's armor, although the impact was still usually forceful enough to knock him from his steed. Indeed, it might well be that the author of the *Song of Roland* gained his knowledge of mounted shock combat more from viewing tournaments than from witnessing any actual battlefield warfare.

Mounted shock combat would be delivered by lines of horsemen charging into the infantry or cavalry lines of their opponents. Such a charge relied primarily on delivering its shock, but if the charge could also be delivered in a tightly packed order, such a shock could be made all the more powerful. Only the hardiest opponent could avoid turning and fleeing from the battle-field, and many battles were decided when just such a rout occurred. Sometimes no blow needed to be delivered. And that, too, proved to be a very effective tactic.

That mounted shock combat eventually failed for Roland and his companions at Rencesvals should not be an indication of its failure as a real-life tactic. From the time of the introduction of the first heavy cavalry units until 1300, victory in nearly every military engagement was tied to heavy cavalry and its eventual tactical use of mounted shock combat. Even after the infantry victories of the early fourteenth century, the mounted warrior, known as a knight in most histories, remained the dominant part of every medieval army.

While the *Song of Roland* was written some time after the actual battle of Rencesvals and reflects the time of its composition, its depiction of armor, arms, strategy, and tactics is heavily informed by the changes in the art of war and military technology initiated by Charlemagne. These were made to emphasize the heavy cavalry unit as the main arm of the military. From his time until the late Middle Ages, heavy cavalry-dominant armies with their mounted shock tactics gained victory in nearly every battle. Even when this began to change during the later Middle Ages, the mounted warrior continued to represent the highest ideals of military society through their nobility and chivalry. Eventually, however, the reality of warfare caught up with these "knights," whose role in it began to change with the advent of new infantry tactics and weapons, including gunpowder artillery, and they too became legend, as Roland, Charlemagne, Ganelon, and others had earlier.

NOTE

[1]See Loyn and Percival for an English translation of the capitulary.

# The Postcolonial Classroom: Teaching the *Song of Roland* and "Saracen" Literature

## Barbara Stevenson

The search for diversity that has been a focal point for the academy in recent years has also become an important issue for teachers and scholars of the Middle Ages, as the publication of Jeffrey Jerome Cohen's *The Postcolonial Middle Ages* illustrates. To avoid silencing and orientalizing the other, Cohen argues that medieval studies must "[d]isplace the domination of Christianity" and "[d]ecenter Europe" (7). However, abandonment of the subject position rooted in the Christian West has proved difficult: as Cohen himself notes, the essays in his book are mostly about Britain; furthermore, the teaching of and scholarship on the *Song of Roland* has equally been Eurocentric, despite the central role that the Saracen (a medieval word that often implies Muslim) plays in the epic. The *Song of Roland* is either situated with other French texts or, in crosscultural anthologies and studies, paired with other Christian European epics, such as *Beowulf* or *El Cid*. Even postcolonial readings of the *Song of Roland* tend to be Eurocentric, as William Chester Jordan observed when responding in a special issue on racism for the *Journal of Medieval and Early Modern Studies*. As an English professor who teaches undergraduate-level world literature survey courses in translation, I try to rectify this imbalance by juxtaposing the *Song of Roland* with Arabic-Muslim literature. With such juxtapositions, both professor and student can begin the journey together to meet the other on neutral ground.

In introductory courses students' knowledge of medieval literature may be limited to King Arthur's pulling the sword from the stone. Thus the teacher must first provide historical context for the complex Christian-Muslim relations of the Middle Ages, through the reading of relevant chronicles and other primary documents. One crucial aspect of this contextualizing involves medieval religious practices and beliefs. Gospel accounts of the birth, death, and resurrection of Jesus, declared as the Son of God, contrast with the Koran's sura on Marium (chapter in the Koran about Mary, mother of Jesus), which describes the life of Jesus as a holy prophet of God whom Christians misconstrue as God's son and as a manifestation of God himself. Consequently, Islam questions whether Christians are true monotheists because of their doctrine of the Holy Trinity and whether their worship of Jesus (especially the image of the crucifix) and statues of saints constitutes idolatry. Just as medieval Muslims perceived Christian belief and practice as pagan idolatry, so medieval Christians felt about Islam. Nicetas in the ninth century compared Muslims who worshipped the Kaaba (the black stone shrine in Mecca visited by pilgrims) with pagans who worshipped stone images of Venus, an opinion shared by later Christians, which culminated in thirteenth-century canon law declaring Islam a later manifestation of Greek and Roman paganism (Camille 139–40). In describing the medieval Christian orientalizing of Islam, Edward Said states, "Islam becomes an image whose function was not to represent Islam itself but to represent it for the medieval Christian" (qtd. in Camille 135). However, this statement proves equally true for the medieval Muslim.

As both the *Song of Roland* and tales from *The Arabian Nights* demonstrate, medieval Christian and Muslim literatures mirror one another in their othering of the rival religion. Traditionally scholars have given the famous framed tale collection—whose various English titles include *The Arabian Nights*—scant attention because it consists of popular and vernacular oral tales, not serious written literature. Though manuscripts survive, they lack the elegance of formal, classical Arabic and may have served as notes for storytellers as opposed to finished literary products. However, *The Arabian Nights* caught the attention of such imperialists as Richard Francis Burton, who in 1885 published the only complete translation in English. Although superseded by Husain Haddawy's superior translation, Burton's remains the only complete translation and contains the most relevant tales depicting Muslim-Christian relations. Even if critics question the quality of Burton's translation, they have largely accepted his theory of the formation of the anonymous tale collection: the core of the tales, including its frame, is of Persian origin dating from pre-Islamic times; around the 800s an expansion of the core began in the area roughly corresponding to modern-day Iraq; additional tales were added up through the 1500s, particularly in Egypt (Irwin). Therefore, the tales embody the evolving attitudes of the Muslim world from the Middle Ages into the early modern era.

In class I have students discuss the ways *The Arabian Nights* and the *Song of Roland* both denounce the opposite religion. Sometimes I put students in small groups for discussion, whereas other times students individually bring to class a list of similarities as preparation for a general class discussion. Listed here are some examples of the Muslim other and Christian other found in the texts. The perversion of Islam as a medieval Greco-Roman paganism surfaces many times in the *Song of Roland*, from the opening laisse in which Marsile rejects God in favor of Muhammad and Apollo until the destruction of "statues" and "idols" in synagogues and mosques by Charlemagne's men (lines 3662–65). *The Arabian Nights* denigrates Christianity as a false religion of "Plurality" as opposed to Islam, seen as the true monotheism of "Unity." For instance, in the short tale of "The Prior Who Became a Moslem," a young Muslim falls in love with a Christian woman and refuses to leave her, even though he is beaten by locals. Impressed by his devotion she asks, " 'Wilt thou enter my faith that I may marry thee?' He cried, 'Allah forbid that I should put off the faith of Unity and enter that of Plurality!' " (Burton 1708). A true godly and earthly lover, he will abandon neither his faith nor his beloved. After he dies, she has a dream of Paradise, which she can enter to be with the young Muslim should she convert to Islam. She dies shortly thereafter, and a group of Muslims take her body after the townspeople are unable to lift her for Christian burial. Impressed by the miracles, a monk converts to Islam. The conversion to Islam through love resembles Charlemagne's insistence that the Saracen queen, Bramimonde, convert to Christianity as a result of favorable interactions with Christians, not of force. Subsequent Charlemagne romances, like the Middle English *The Sowdone of Babylon*, feature Saracen princesses who convert to Christianity because of their love for a knight. *The Arabian Nights* contains other tales of Christian damsels who convert, often because they wish to be with their Muslim lover. Conversion narratives include the long romances "King Omar bin al-Nu'uman and His Sons Sharrkan and Zau al-Makan" and "Ali Nur Al-Din and Miriam the Girdle Girl" and the short tales "The Moslem Champion and the Christian Damsel," "The Man of Upper Egypt and His Frankish Wife," and "The Christian King's Daughter and the Moslem."

The most extreme form of demonizing the other comes in battle scenes in which enemies are not just idolatrous pagans but grotesque creatures (often giants), a portrayal that dehumanizes the other and distances the audience so that they will not have sympathy for these warriors when they die. The sprawling romance of "King Omar bin al-Nu'uman and His Sons Sharrkhan and Zau al-Makan" offers comic battlefield scenes that contrast ironically to those in the *Song of Roland*. (At one point Sharrkhan is losing a battle to the Franks— and then he learns that all those skilled knights are in fact Christian damsels, one of whom he loves.) In one episode the Christian knights prepare themselves for battle against Sharrkhan by dousing themselves with holy water and ointment, which, in fact, are urine and excrement from the great patriarch of the church: "Now the incense . . . was the excrement of the Chief Patriarch, the denier, the defiler of the Truth" (Burton 688). Luka, the Christian champion, is monstrous: "he was foul of favour, for his face was as the face of an ass, his shape that of an ape and his look as the look of a malignant snake . . . and blacker than night was his blackness and . . . grimmer than the leopard was his ugliness, and he was branded with the mark of the Infidels [the cross] on [his] face" (Burton 689). Sharrkhan wins the battle when he kills Luka by spearing the sign of the Cross that is in the center of his forehead: "[Sharrkhan] sped at him a second throw-spear which smote him and the point fell on his forehead, in the very centre of the sign of the Cross, and Allah hurried his soul to the Fire and Dwelling-place dire" (Burton 691). The *Song of Roland* echoes *The Arabian Nights'* description of enemies as monstrous black giants and evil heathens, descriptions that align the enemies with Satan (and in some cases that mock racial difference): "Out in front rides a Saracen, Abisme; . . . / He does not believe in God, the son of the Virgin Mary; / And is as black as molten pitch. / He loves treachery and murder" (lines 1470–75). In short, both Christian and Muslim literatures resort to propaganda to legitimize their quest for hegemony, both in religion and in territory, during the time of the Reconquest and Crusades.

Despite their religious differences, pilgrimage was important for both medieval Christians and Muslims. Relevant pilgrimages for the literature under consideration are Christian visits to Roland's tomb on the way to the shrine of Saint James at Compostela and to the "hanged poem" of Antara (also known as Antar) on the walls of Kaaba in Mecca, which was ridiculed by medieval Christians as pagan idolatry. These two popular pilgrimage sites are important because they feature the heroes of the epics the class will read and demonstrate that these secular warriors had become associated with religion during the Middle Ages.

The best known story of Antar and the one most frequently translated into English stems from the historical ʿAntara, who was a poet. According to Peter Heath's book *The Thirsty Sword*, the poem *The Life of Antar* (*Sīrat ʿAntar*) "purports to recount the life story of the famous pre-Islamic poet and warrior ʿAntara ibn Shaddad [who lived during the late sixth century AD]. The historical ʿAntara was a half-caste slave [his father was Arabic and his mother an African slave] who won freedom and fame through his poetic and martial abilities and ended life as a respected member of the northern Arabian tribe of ʿAbs" (Heath xiv). The poet Antara becomes famous for his "hanged poem," so called because he had to fight his lover's rivals and enemies to hang this love poem on the walls of Kaaba in Mecca (Heath 142). So famous does the legendary figure of Antar become that Muhammad was reported to claim that Antar was the only Arab from the past he wished to meet (Heath 7).

In terms of composition, the *Song of Roland* and *Life of Antar* share striking similarities. From our perspective, both Roland and Antar are minor, shadowy historical figures who inexplicably become major epic heroes. However, they illustrate how literature typically formed in the Middle Ages from its origin in oral storytelling to its later development into a written tradition—a creative process largely alien to modern audiences. After discussing with students what is known about the actual Roland and Antar, I review common theories of oral composition that help account for the transformation of minor historical figures into major epic heroes. No doubt the presence of Roland's tomb and Antar's poem at popular pilgrimage sites helped fuel the early oral tradition. In his *Gesta Regum Anglorum* of 1126, William of Malmesbury claims that the *Song of Roland* was chanted at the Battle of Hastings so that the French forces would be inspired in their fight against the Anglo-Saxons (Le Gentil, *Chanson* [1969] 18). Although there is no way to verify this claim, the account shows that aside from becoming a written epic, the story of the battle at Rencesvals was also recited aloud. Similarly, poems and chronicles of the historical Antar of pre-Islamic Arabia form the basis of both a popular oral and literary tradition of epic fiction. One version of the Antar cycle consists of fifty-five volumes (Norris, *Adventures* 42), and present-day storyteller Abu Shadi of Damascus takes one year to recite the complete cycle of Antar. Not surprisingly, no complete English translation exists, so I use excerpts from H. T. Norris's *The Adventures of Antar*, which focuses on Antar's exploits in

Africa. (It is an expensive hardback, so professors may wish to place the book on reserve for students to consult or to arrange for copied selections for student purchase.)

Then as we read the epic literature, I encourage students to look for parallels. Norris has written about these parallels, and he believes that the present version of *Antar* was completed by 1350, possibly in Spain, which explains why *Antar* reflects the influence of medieval European heroic literature, although Norris and other scholars have been unable to uncover a direct link between the creators of the *Antar* and the *Song of Roland* (Norris, "Arabic Folk Epic"). Of the possible parallels that could be mentioned, I limit the discussion here to the ways these two imperialist texts portray characters as God's champions to justify invasion and conquest.

Both epics signal the beginning of a major episode through the use of prophetic dreams. These symbolic dreams foreshadow a significant plot development. Antar dreams that "a black whelp had come from my loins. . . . it rose up against me in the shape of an eagle, sharp in beak and claw. It flew skywards. . . . It fell upon me like a blow of fate. It dashed against me and buried its claws in my shoulders. It pulled me and threw me upon my back. I was at its mercy" (Norris, *Adventures* 97). Antar turns to a counselor to interpret the dream. The interpreter notes that the eagle symbolizes war, so the dream is a prophecy of war. Of course, this is true, but it is much more. The black whelp from his loins indicates that he will battle his own African brethren, who will first fight against him, but with whom he will eventually be reconciled. In the *Song of Roland* it is Charlemagne who has the prophetic dreams about a war, symbolically revealed through animal imagery. For instance, in one of his dreams, "In his right arm he is bitten by a vicious boar. / From the direction of the Ardennes he saw a leopard coming; / It attacks his body with great ferocity" (lines 727–29). Charlemagne's dream possesses elements similar to Antar's: a hound that indicates a relative (Roland) and beasts that symbolize war (the Saracen attack on Roland's rear guard). Aside from serving the literary purpose of foreshadowing, the prophetic dreams also suggest that the upcoming wars fulfill a divine plan.

The action in both epics is triggered by requests that the heroes feel they cannot refuse. Ghamra, a secondary wife to Antar, requests that he help her regain territory conquered by an enemy in the Sudan. Like Roland's chivalry, Antar's heroism is centered around service: helping women and the weak against aggressors, loyalty to family and to allies. In the *Song of Roland* when Charlemagne asks his barons to decide who will stay with the rear guard as the Franks return home from Spain, Ganelon volunteers his stepson Roland. Although Roland realizes that Ganelon is setting him up for defeat, he "spoke like a true knight: / 'Lord stepfather, it is my duty to love you. / You have appointed me to the rearguard' " (752–54). Thus, the heroic code of pre-Islamic bedouin Arabs shares some commonalities with the feudal chivalry of medieval France. Furthermore, Antar is obligated to take revenge on Ghamra's attackers, just as Charlemagne avenges the death of his nephew Roland by defeating the Saracens and putting Ganelon on trial for treason. The obligations imposed by relatives in the two epics lead to war. And, as typical of heroic feats, these battles involve journeys: Antar leaves the Arabian peninsula for northern Africa, and Roland and Charlemagne are in Spain fighting Saracens. The ensuing imperialist aggression appears to be an honorable act to fulfill obligations to family, clan, and nation.

Each epic has moments of divine intervention that reinforce the point that God, not the heroes, succeeds. In the *Song of Roland* the angel Gabriel descends to take Roland into heaven after the Saracen ambush. Next, Charlemagne's prayer of a miracle is granted so that the sun stands still to allow the Franks to avenge the ambush. Finally, Gabriel rouses Charlemagne to action when it appears that Baligant may be victorious: "When Charles heard the sacred voice of the angel, / He has no fear or dread of death; / Strength and awareness return to him. / He strikes the emir with his sword from France . . . / Slicing through his head and spilling out his brain" (lines 3612–17). With the defeat of Baligant, the Franks regain Spain for Christianity. In *Antar*, Antar cannot claim victory for avenging his wife until he defeats the supreme overlord of Africa, the Negus. But Antar does not have a "fight to the death" encounter with the Negus that Charlemagne does with Baligant; instead, Antar battles the Negus's right-hand man, Al-ʿAbd Zinjīr, who, in the same vein as the *Song of Roland* and *The Arabian Nights*, is depicted as a monstrous pagan giant: "From the army of the Negus there sallied forth a knight. . . . No eye had seen one mightier than his frame nor more terrifying. He was like a flattened date palm or the stump of a burnt palm tree. . . . His voice echoed in the mountains, 'If your vile knights have no stomach for this fight then summon your protector to fight me. I have sworn by mighty Saturn that I shall leave him as a carcass in the dust' " (182). The fight between Antar and Al-ʿAbd Zinjīr continues for seven days; just as the giant almost crushes Antar, Antar has a vision of the future Muhammad, which gives him the strength to kill the giant: "I was blessed by good fortune, by courage and with the aid of that Prophet about whom continuous tales are told and who will appear at the end of the age, Muhammad" (185). With that vision, Antar summons all his strength to chop off the head of his opponent. The heroes' ultimate triumph over the enemy, then, is a triumph of religion, of one god over another.

The connection established in *Antar* between the Negus of Africa and Muhammad, although fictive, evokes important historical moments for the audience, just as the battle of Rencesvals resonates with a medieval Christian audience aware of the Reconquest and Crusades. Negus is the title given to the Christian kings of Ethiopia; during Muhammad's lifetime the Negus agreed to take in Muslim refugees who were being persecuted for their religion. The narrator of the folk epic adds this commentary:

> Mankala [the Negus] believed in our lord Muhammad and sent gifts to him, among them the standard of the eagle. . . . It is the fashion of the kings of countries that the ruler of the land of Ethiopia is called the Negus. . . . We have only commented on this expression "the Negus" so that our hearer may know that "the Negus" was not only in Antar's days, but also in the days of the Prophet.                                    (177)

This commentary accomplishes two goals: it connects Muhammad with the epic hero, Antar, through the character of the Negus and it insinuates that the historical Negus, a Christian king, may actually have been a convert to Islam. The epic revises history so that the kings of Africa and their peoples willingly convert to Islam and invite the Arabs to serve as overlords.

Such an invitation is hinted at in the resolution of the conflict between Antar and the Negus. After Antar captures the Negus in battle and then holds the Negus captive, he learns that his own mother, an African who was kidnapped and enslaved by his father, is a paternal aunt of the Negus. The two are then reconciled, and Antar returns home victorious. Though a spectral presence only, Antar's African mother cements the peace between the Negus (the representation of Christianity and Africa) and Antar (the representation of Islam and Arabia), a sentimental rendering of the Islamic empire's colonization of Africa and enslavement of kidnapped women. Likewise, a peaceful, if sentimental, resolution occurs in the *Song of Roland* when Charlemagne decides to take the Saracen queen, Bramimonde, to France, where she converts to Christianity. Nevertheless, the two epics' presentations of this religious victory differ considerably. Antar's success in Africa anticipates the future victory of Islam in Africa; however, Roland's battle ends in his defeat and death because of the treachery of the Saracens and of Ganelon. The triumph comes when Charlemagne avenges the death of Roland, thereby destroying idolatry in Spain and converting many to Christianity. Roland's death is not in vain.

Many epic episodes make up the Antar cycle, but only a few have been translated into English. Unfortunately, the episodes that most closely mirror the *Song of Roland* in which Antar battles the Franks and other Crusaders have not yet been translated. However, as Arabic-Islamic scholars make more translations available, teachers and students will have more opportunities to examine representations of the other in medieval literature.

# Roland in the Italian Tradition

*Jane E. Everson*

Tracing the tradition of the *Song of Roland* in Italy involves surveying at least four centuries of Italian literature and making reference to a large number of texts, some well known but others much less so. There is also an extensive bibliography of secondary literature. Most undergraduates, and many graduate students, can be expected only to engage in some detail with the best-known texts, such as the *Orlando furioso* of Ludovico Ariosto, a work that they invariably find extremely enjoyable and stimulating once they have been inducted into it. However, if they are to understand properly the generic tradition to which the *Orlando furioso* belongs and the material it incorporates, Ariosto's aims, and how the work was received by its immediate audience, as well as its subsequent influence on English and European literatures, they must be given an overview of developments in the genre of poems about Roland, from the first arrival of these in Italy to their full flowering as an independent tradition in the later fifteenth and early sixteenth centuries. Inevitably this introduction will be nothing more than an overview—it is not realistic to expect students at this level to read several long poems or the related criticism. In this essay I present an approach that I have been using for many years and that successfully provides students with essential points to ensure their reading of Ariosto is firmly founded. My introduction to the study of the *Orlando furioso* usually covers both the tradition of poems about Roland and Charlemagne and the tradition of Arthurian romance, which fused together to produce the form known in Italian as romance epic. In keeping with the theme of this volume, however, I shall concentrate only on the tales of Roland and Charlemagne. A fuller discussion of the historical development of the whole genre can now be found in my monograph (see Everson, *The Italian Renaissance Epic*).

## Introduction into Italy

The *Song of Roland* arrived in Italy very soon after the date of the oldest French manuscripts. Sculptures in churches in Verona dating to the early twelfth century represent Roland and the paladins in battle against the Moors, evidence that artists had knowledge of the tradition and that they transmitted the story to Italian onlookers and then drew on their audience's familiarity with it. Such acquaintance with the story of the *Roland* would have reached an Italian public orally, through recitations and performances by traveling entertainers who often accompanied merchants and pilgrims along the major trading routes. The most famous evidence for knowledge and dissemination of the *Song of Roland* in Italy before the date of the earliest surviving Italian texts is provided by Dante in the *Divine Comedy*. Roland is first referred to in *Inferno* 31.16–18, where Dante draws on the account of Roland's death at Rencesvals and his sounding of his horn there to convey the terrible sound of Nimrod's horn, which Dante hears as he descends into the pit of hell. Shortly afterward, Dante, appropriately, refers to Ganelon among the traitors (*Inf.* 32.122). Ganelon (Gano in the Italian tradition) is already the archetypal traitor—to country, family, and religion—for Dante and for his public. Not only Roland but also Charlemagne, William of Orange, and Rainouart are found in the heaven of Mars (*Par.* 18.41–48) as examples of holy warriors martyred in defense of the Christian faith. Like all his contemporaries, Dante would undoubtedly have heard recitations of the chansons de geste in public places, but he was also familiar with written forms of these texts. As Antonio Viscardi writes: "an important part of Dante's literary culture is made up of the widespread literary diffusion of the chansons de geste; at least as far as the *Song of Roland* is concerned, Dante was a careful and sympathetic reader of this work" (811; my trans.).

## Forms of Language, Style, and Meter

The language in which the *Song of Roland* was recited in Italy in this early period was certainly hybrid, a mixture of French (or langue d'oïl) with Italian forms, reflecting both the linguistic origins of the genre and the needs of the audience. Nevertheless, though pronunciation and grammar might both show strong Italian influences, the oral texts presumably retained the original meter and laisses, which are also preserved in the first written forms produced in Italy.

The popularity of the whole tradition of French narratives concerning Roland, the paladins, and Charlemagne in Italy at the end of the thirteenth century is attested by a series of important manuscripts (now in the Marciana library in Venice) that were probably written for the Gonzaga family in Mantua and that were certainly kept in their library until the end of the Renaissance. These contain, among other narratives, two versions of the *Song of Roland* (Venice 4 and 7). These manuscripts are in French but have been copied in Italy by Italian scribes. The text thus shows, as did the oral recitations in Italy, levels of interference that vary depending on the scribe's knowledge of the original, the care in transcription, and the intended audience. As far as the content of the narrative is concerned, there are of course some differences between the Venice manuscripts and other versions of *Roland*, but broadly speaking the aim is still to transmit the original narrative of Roland's last battle in the pass of Rencesvals (see Duggan, "Beyond the Oxford Text," in this volume). Nevertheless, other texts contained in these Gonzaga manuscripts already reveal modifications and developments, in both the character of Roland and the narrative of the campaigns, which depart progressively from the French original to constitute a native Italian tradition.

## Roland Narratives in Italy

The reference to Dante brings us to the beginnings of a genuine, native, original Italian tradition of narratives based on the *Song of Roland*. These can be divided into two or three main groups, which for convenience can be described as the Spagna (literally, Spain) group, the Aspromonte group, and the genealogical group. All of these had their origins in France in the French tradition but were rewritten in Italy and over time underwent various modifications. I shall concentrate here on the Spagna group, since those most closely link thematically to the *Song of Roland*, although for a full understanding of themes and ideas in the poems of Matteo Maria Boiardo and Ariosto, reference should be made to the Aspromonte tradition too (for a brief survey of which see Everson 32–35).

## The Spagna Tradition

One of the most important foundation stones of the whole tradition in Italy is the early-fourteenth-century epic poem nowadays entitled the *Entrée d'Espagne*, dated somewhere between 1320 and 1340. This anonymous poem was written probably in the region of Padua-Verona, perhaps by a cleric, certainly by a well-educated individual. Though the author was an Italian and a younger contemporary of Dante and was writing for an Italian public, the *Entrée* is still composed in the hybrid linguistic form known as Franco-Venetian (or Franco-Italian) and in the traditional laisses. The *Entrée* is the first of an important series of narratives developed in Italy that are devoted to narrating the whole of Charlemagne's seven-year campaign in Spain before the battle at Rencesvals. The surviving poem can be divided into three sections. In the first part, the poet tells of the invasion of Spain and the first campaigns against Marsilio, the long and important duel of Roland against Ferrau, and the sieges of Nájera, Noble, and Pamplona. At the beginning of the second part, Roland is upbraided by Charlemagne for his rash campaigns, and in a spirit of pique and hurt pride goes off to the Middle East, where he serves as a mercenary captain for the sultan and is involved in a series of adventures between military campaigns and pilgrimage. In a section of the narrative that is now missing, Roland liberates Jerusalem and converts the sultan. The last section opens with Roland's pilgrimage to the Holy Places and the marriage of the sultan's daughter Dionés before Roland returns to Spain and is reconciled with Charlemagne. The poem ends here, with the campaigns still in progress, but with the death of Roland having been prophesied by a hermit.

The open-ended nature of the *Entrée d'Espagne*, a feature that was to be typical of the Italian Carolingian narratives, almost immediately invited a sequel or continuation that could carry the story forward to the death of Roland. This is the narrative normally referred to nowadays as the *Prise de Pamplune*, by Niccolò da Verona, which takes the story to the conclusion of the siege of Pamplona. Between the 1340s, when Niccolò da Verona was writing, and the 1420s, a whole series of Spagna narratives were composed, only some of which survive. These include a prose version, generally referred to as *Li fatti di Spagna*, dated to the late fourteenth century, and the *Rotta di Roncisvalle* (a retelling of the original Roland narrative). The tradition of these narratives culminates in the great poem titled *La Spagna in rima*; the oldest surviving manuscript of *La Spagna* is dated between 1420 and 1430, but it undoubtedly transmits elements of earlier versions from both prose and verse accounts.

This interaction of prose and verse accounts of the Spagna narrative is extremely complex (see Catalano; Everson 116–19), but it is important for revealing how the tradition of the *Song of Roland* was transmitted in Italy through the course of the fourteenth century, from the Franco-Italian laisses of the *Entrée* to the wholly Italian *cantare* of *La Spagna in rima*. In this poem much of the narrative of the *Entrée* from a hundred years before is retained, but there are also modifications and additions. *La Spagna in rima* is made up of four constituent sections: the entry, the narrative originally developed in the *Entrée d'Espagne* of the early campaigns in Spain up to the siege of Noble; Roland in the East and his adventures, campaigns, and pilgrimages there; the capture of Pamplona from the original *Prise* account; and the narrative of the battle of Rencesvals from the Italian versions such as the *Rotta di Roncisvalle*. The fourth section, however, has some curious additional material, involving the interaction of Roland and Charlemagne with spirits and demons. The continuing siege of Pamplona is eventually won using the Lombard siege engines after a Saracen plan to flood the Christian camp fails. It is at this point that *La Spagna in rima* proceeds to narrate the story of the *Song of Roland*, from the embassies sent to Marsilio through to the death of Roland and the Twelve Peers, the trial of Gano, and the death of Alda.

It is apparent even in summary that the character of Roland in these Italian fourteenth-century narratives undergoes significant changes: his name is modified, changing from Roland to Orlando; his behavior becomes, certainly on occasion, less noble and admirable—he is often rash, quick-tempered, impatient, given to dissimulation and disguise, and deceitful toward both Saracens and Charlemagne—yet at the same time he acquires characteristics typical of the chivalric romance, an equally popular genre in Italy in this period. He is given physical attributes that encourage mockery by other characters and that would have provoked laughter in the audience—for example, he is consistently described as squinting and physically unprepossessing. He is often cold and uninterested in women yet capable of passing infatuations with Saracen women. He emerges as an expert in theology and a gifted preacher and linguist, capable of preaching to the sultan more successfully than either Saint Francis or Saint Anthony, since his preaching, unlike theirs, results in wholesale conversion. Yet he also dabbles in magic and communes with spirits. His character is emphasized through the development of a number of foils: not only Oliver (Ulivieri) but also and increasingly in the fifteenth century Astolfo (the boastful English knight) and Terigi (the faithful squire).

## The New Meter: Ottava Rima

By the time of *La Spagna in rima*, narratives concerning Roland and Charlemagne were no longer being composed in Franco-Venetian, although there is plenty of evidence that such narratives were still being read in the original French, or in Franco-Venetian versions. French had been replaced by regional forms of Italian, and much more importantly, the old meter of assonanced laisses had been replaced by the new, native Italian *cantare* of eight-line rhyming stanzas: ottava rima. The invention of this form is often attributed to Giovanni Boccaccio, who employed it in his early vernacular verse narratives, *Il Filostrato* and *Il Teseida* in the late 1330s. Certainly the use of this form by Boccaccio and by his fellow contemporary Florentine Antonio Pucci, author of short romance poems in ottava rima, was decisive and influential. In the space of a generation, between the mid-1340s and the 1370s, narratives of both the Arthurian and Carolingian traditions were recast in this form. Ottava rima was crucial to the success of the epic of Charlemagne and Roland in Italy; a dynamic and flexible narrative unit, it was also well adapted to memorization and oral recitation.

## The Flowering of the Roland Tradition in Italy

The three great exponents of the Carolingian narrative tradition in verse, the story of Roland in Italy, are Luigi Pulci (1432–1484), Boiardo (1441–1494) and Ariosto (1474–1533), three writers whose approach to their material and handling of it reveal the creativity, inventiveness, and diversity of the genre at the height of the Renaissance and the revival of classical culture.

## Pulci and the *Morgante maggiore*

The *Morgante* (c. 1461–1481) is the first of the Renaissance narratives of Roland and is the one most closely linked, at least on the surface, to the tradition just outlined. There is a modern translation by Joseph Tusiani and good critical studies by Mark Davie and Constance Jordan. Pulci's stated aim is to rewrite the narrative of Charlemagne and Roland in a language and style worthy of his sophisticated Florentine audience; indeed he claims to be writing at the behest of the mother of Lorenzo de' Medici (*Morgante*, canto 1, stanza 4). In constructing his narrative, Pulci draws on the existing tradition of *cantari* about Charlemagne and Roland and in particular on a popular poem now known from the location of the manuscript as the *Orlando laurenziano*. For much of his poem Pulci follows the narrative of this *cantare* closely. The *Orlando laurenziano*, however, does not narrate the culmination of the story of Roland and the defeat at Rencesvals, and Pulci is thus diverted from his original stated purpose. The *Morgante*, like the *Orlando* on which it is based, is concerned with a series of adventures involving Roland, Oliver, and various other knights—some imported from other narrative strands, like that concerning Rinaldo (Reynaud). These adventures are mainly military campaigns in various parts of the eastern Mediterranean and oscillate between relatively serious pitched battles and sieges, on the one hand, and comic, ludicrous, erotic, and mock heroic exploits, on the other. Spice is added to the narrative by the character of Morgante, a giant and companion to Roland, whom he converts in the first canto. Morgante is an antihero, sympathetic yet idiosyncratic (he fights with a huge bell clapper for example and pays scant attention to the rules of chivalrous engagement in combat). Morgante is present in Pulci's source, but Pulci extends this antiheroic theme, inventing the character of the half-giant Margutte, who figures in a long episode with Morgante (cantos 18–19). This is a delightful tour de force of verbal wit, scurrilous jokes, and ingenious tricks that ends with the death of Margutte, who literally bursts from laughing too much (*Morgante*, canto 19, stanzas 148–50). Roland is now no more than one hero among many, and not always the most prominent or attractive. To give students some idea of this part of the *Morgante*, I encourage them to read the first canto and the Margutte episode.

This reworking of the *Orlando* constitutes the first, longer section of Pulci's poem (twenty-three cantos)—the original published version. But Pulci was aware that he had not fulfilled his original aim of narrating the battle of Rencesvals and the final victory of Charlemagne. After an interval of a few years, he continued his poem, adding five more cantos and thus making a bigger *Morgante*, hence the full title *Morgante maggiore*. Here in these last five cantos he draws on a version of the *Rotta di Roncisvalle* and on *La Spagna in rima*. Pulci does indeed narrate the ambush, battle, and death of Roland and his peers at Rencesvals (cantos 26–27; it is worth asking students to read these so that they can compare Pulci's account with previous ones). Yet even in this more serious section, Pulci's natural verve takes over. As if sensing that the straightforward account of Rencesvals is now rather stale, he invents the participation in these campaigns of Antea, queen of Babylon (an old flame of Rinaldo), and notably the flight of Rinaldo on the back of the devil Astarotte from Egypt to Spain, in the course of which the devil instructs Rinaldo in comparative religion and the correct understanding of the Christian faith (canto 25, stanzas 232–44).

Pulci's *Morgante* reflects both the interests and personality of its author and of the Florentine humanist milieu in which it was composed. Pulci often seems little interested in the content and structure of the narrative. His chief interest is in language, style, and expression. Verbal dexterity, puns, jokes, equivocal use of language, neologisms and the use of words and phrases out of context, proverbial sayings turned to new ends and skillful rhymes, rhetorical tropes, and the parody of popular cantari techniques are what Pulci delights in and are where the greatest merits of the *Morgante* lie. Pulci's unorthodox, even heretical stance with respect to the Christian religion, and the philosophical and metaphysical discussions of Lorenzo's Florence are apparent not only in the debate between Astarotte and Rinaldo but also in Margutte's scurrilous parody of the Credo (canto 18, stanzas 115–42), well analyzed by Davie. The expanding world, voyages of exploration, an interest in new inventions like printing, the material world, and the good life are also notably present in the narrative. Even in the last section, Roland is often absent from the narrative. However, the treachery of Gano and his hostility to Roland have now been expanded and multiplied many times over, providing the chief structural link across the twenty-eight cantos of the poem.

### Boiardo and the *Orlando innamorato*

Pulci's near contemporary, Boiardo, writing at the Este court in Ferrara, takes a very different, almost diametrically opposed approach to the material of Roland and Charlemagne. Orlando's name appears in the title of Boiardo's poem, but the traditional narrative of the *Song of Roland* has effectively completely disappeared. This is apparent even in the epithet Boiardo gives Orlando: *innamorato* (in love). Although Orlando had been portrayed as in love before in the Italian tradition (see for example *Il Morgante*), he had never before been characterized as consistently infatuated with one woman, Angelica, as Boiardo makes him.

The *Orlando innamorato* is a complex poem, but it is absolutely essential for an understanding of Ariosto's *Orlando furioso*. Boiardo left his poem unfinished and with many narrative threads in suspense on his death in 1494.

Ariosto (among several other writers) takes up this same unfinished narrative and aims to conclude all the various narrative elements. Ariosto thus expects his readers to remember the exploits of many characters in the *Innamorato*, and indeed the opening stanzas of *Orlando furioso* make clear that the reader is expected to know the story so far (see canto 1, stanzas 1–5). For the modern reader this is much more of a problem than it was for Ariosto's immediate audience, but in addition to the outline of the contents of the *Orlando innamorato* given here, the student and teacher can refer to a modern translation of the *Innamorato* (Ross) and to a synopsis with extracts produced for the Italian reader by Gianni Celati.

The *Orlando innamorato* was composed in two, possibly three, distinct phases that correspond to the three books into which it is divided and that, like the *Morgante*, were published in two different states. The first two books (sixty cantos) were written mainly in the 1470s and published in 1483; the story of Orlando's infatuation was not complete, and soon afterward Boiardo began a third book, but progressed much more slowly and had only completed eight and a half cantos when he died a decade later. The narrative is structured around three campaigns of war, plus the story of Orlando's love for Angelica, which also has a fourth military campaign attached to it. The first campaign of war (book 1) is that of of Gradasso, king of Sericana (Sri Lanka), who attacks Charlemagne with the aim of conquering more territory and especially of acquiring Orlando's sword and Rinaldo's horse, both potent talismans. The second war (book 2) is the invasion of France by Agramante, king in North Africa. This is designed to avenge previous defeats and the death of relatives in earlier campaigns such as that of Aspromonte. The third war (book 3) consists of the campaign of Mandricardo, Lord of Tartary, to avenge his father Agricane (killed by Orlando in book 1) and to acquire various mythical items of armor. The poem opens, however, with Angelica's appearance at the court of Charlemagne during a truce between Christians and Saracens. She appeals for help because her city, Albraca, in central Asia, is besieged by would-be suitors. All those present are at once infatuated with Angelica and offer their services, but Orlando is most seriously affected. The narrative of the first two books thus oscillates between widely dispersed locations: France, Africa, and central Asia. The siege of Albraca is eventually abandoned in the course of book 2, and Orlando returns with Angelica to France. Into this already complex narrative, Boiardo also introduces a dynastic theme centered on the character Ruggiero, ancestor of the house of Este, patrons of both Boiardo and Ariosto. Boiardo does not develop this theme very far, but it does allow him to introduce some important points taken up by Ariosto: the prophecy of Ruggiero's early death; the attempts by Ruggiero's guardian, the magician Atlante, to hide him away from the war and thus from his death (bk. 2, canto 16); and the meeting and mutual love of Ruggiero and Bradamante (bk. 3, canto 5). The *Innamorato* also introduces a large number of secondary stories and characters, many of which Ariosto continues and concludes. These include Origille, Norandino and Lucina, Brandimarte and Fiordiligi, and Alcina. The Moorish kings of Spain—Marsilio, Isolieri, Serpentino, and Grandonio, who constitute a central core of Saracen characters in all the stories of the Roland tradition in Italy including the *Morgante*—appear in Boiardo's first book, but then become progressively less important and scarcely figure at all thereafter. Only Ferrau, or Ferraguto, remains a prominent player through the *Innamorato* and into the *Furioso*.

The narratives of Charlemagne and Roland (as well as those of Arthur) were particularly popular at the court of Ferrara and much read and enjoyed there. Boiardo's main aims in composing the *Innamorato* are thus primarily to provide a new set of stories in this popular genre and to entertain and delight his fellow courtiers. Boiardo himself was interested in the processes and traditions of storytelling in various genres (he produced versions of Herodotus's *Histories* and Apuleius's *Golden Ass*). He also brings together in *Orlando innamorato* motifs and themes from many different types of literature, including both classical and romance. But the diverse material of his narrative themes and of his sources often seems to overwhelm both writer and reader. One very striking difference between Boiardo and his successor Ariosto, however, is in the relation of the poem to external, historical reality. Although the *Innamorato* is dedicated to Duke Ercole d'Este, Boiardo makes little reference to the contemporary members of the family; there is little comment on matters external to the poem. Above all, when real warfare intrudes on Boiardo, he interrupts his poem, most dramatically and finally in 1494, on the invasion by Charles VIII of France that initiated the Wars of Italy.

## Ariosto and *Orlando furioso*

With *Orlando furioso* the tradition of narratives about Charlemagne and Roland in Italy reaches its greatest flowering. *Orlando furioso* is a monument of European literature and has had an enduring influence on many different forms of culture: literature, painting, opera, and film.

Throughout his adult life Ariosto was a member of the court of Ferrara, and it was there that he composed the *Furioso*, between 1505 and 1515. His poem was first printed in 1516 and dedicated to Cardinal Ippolito d'Este, brother of the duke, Alfonso I. This first version numbered only forty cantos. Ariosto subsequently revised his poem, producing a second edition in 1521 and, more important, an expanded version, of forty-six cantos, in 1532. Unlike Pulci, however, the additional six cantos are not added en bloc at the end of the previous poem. Rather, Ariosto inserts the additional material at various points in the poem, weaving it together to form a seamless whole.

Ariosto starts from the unfinished poem of Boiardo and takes up both the main themes of that poem and many of the secondary stories. He simplifies and unifies the war themes, retaining the invasion by Agramante and making

Gradasso and Mandricardo subordinate players in it. Orlando's infatuation for Angelica continues to provide the principal theme of love, to which are linked many other stories of lovers, both successful and unsuccessful, happy and tragic. Ariosto elaborates considerably the story line about Ruggiero and Bradamante as ancestors of the Este family, giving these two characters a prominent place in the narrative and concluding his poem with the celebration of their wedding. He also uses this dynastic narrative to convey praise and flattery of the contemporary members of the family and especially his patron, inserting at regular intervals visions and prophecies concerning the future descendants of Ruggiero and Bradamante. Ariosto is a master of the narrative technique known as *entrelacement*, or interweaving; he succeeds in keeping control of all the various narrative threads, skillfully advancing them in tandem and convincing the reader that he, the poet, knows just where everything is going. As a result it is much easier to read the *Furioso* than the *Innamorato*: Ariosto does not let his reader get lost!

In addition to interweaving the three principal themes and ensuring that they progress evenly, Ariosto weaves into his poem a large number of secondary stories, some closely integrated with the main characters, others less so. Some of these stories allow Ariosto to conclude unfinished stories from the *Innamorato*: for example, the tale of Norandino and Lucina (*Furioso*, canto 17) and of Ricciardetto and Fiordespina (canto 25). Others, like the story of Alcina (canto 6–8), are carried forward from the *Innamorato* but developed very imaginatively, and very differently probably, from Boiardo's original intentions; whereas others, like the stories of Ginevra (cantos 4–6) and of Adonio (cantos 43), are new to the narrative. Ariosto links all these stories to one or more of the main narrative threads through motifs, emphases, and common themes, such as jealousy, deceit, illusion, and the deceptiveness of the senses. He also uses the stories to illustrate the behavior of principal characters. Thus Orlando, for example, deluded in his infatuation for Angelica, encounters examples of faithful, mutual love like that of Olimpia (cantos 9–10) and Isabella (cantos 12–24) but does not see the contrast between his infatuation and their love. In the very center of the poem, between cantos 23 and 24, the conflict of illusion and reality, self-deception and forced recognition of the truth, comes to a destructive climax when Orlando, confronted with the truth of Angelica's love for another man, goes completely mad.

*Orlando furioso* seems, in its narrative development, a long way from the *Song of Roland*. None of the military campaigns of Ariosto's poem take place in Spain, and the culminating combat takes place on the island of Lampedusa in the Mediterranean (*Furioso*, canto 41), not in the pass of Rencesvals. Charlemagne plays only a spasmodic role in the poem, and Gano is scarcely present at all. And yet in making Orlando mad, Ariosto is forging a direct link back to one of the original aspects of Roland's character: his *desmesure*, his refusal to listen to reason or appreciate and act on common sense. In the *Song of Roland* that irrationality is exemplified in the final battle. In the poems of the

Spagna tradition, it is present in Roland's hot-tempered intolerance and exaggerated responses; in the *Furioso* the lack of *mesure* or self-restraint in Orlando's infatuation for Angelica ends by depriving Orlando altogether of his reason, making him insane. As if to underline the link between Orlando's *furia* and his earlier *desmesure*, the only part of the poem set in Spain is a short episode during Orlando's wild wanderings as a berserk madman.

Ariosto absorbs and takes further the thematic developments of his two predecessors. The narrative episodes range across a vast terrain, but, unlike those of Pulci's *Morgante*, Ariosto's knights do not go adventuring in the Middle East as mercenaries of Saracen rulers, nor, as in Boiardo's poem, do they spend a considerable portion of their time in central Asia in similar roles. Ariosto thus turns away from a·staple of the tradition from the time of the *Entrée d'Espagne*, substituting instead a more Eurocentric or Mediterranean-based geography. Unlike the previous tradition, in which groups of knights were often linked in series of such adventures, Ariosto's principals tend to act alone. There is thus a clear division made between the serious business of the military campaigns involving whole armies and the individual adventures of the paladins, which range from comic to tragic.

In composing his poem Ariosto draws on a wide range of sources. Like Boiardo, he combines and further enhances the fusion of Carolingian and Arthurian narrative traditions and draws on traditions of classical literature and vernacular fiction. Ariosto carries this syncretic process even further, absorbing also contemporary issues—such as humanist debates and discoveries and the development of artillery (damned by Orlando, *Furioso*, canto 9, stanzas 88–91). If *Orlando furioso* is the culmination of the Italian tradition of tales of Roland, it also marks a watershed. Writing in the period of the Wars of Italy, in which the French were the invaders and enemy, Ariosto is obliged to face up to the conflict between reality and fiction that had defeated Boiardo and that his other predecessors by and large had never had to face. Ariosto does this in a number of ways: most importantly in his handling of the war narrative, but also in his constant association of fiction with contemporary reality and his awareness that warfare is not always glorious and heroic. The ways in which he manages this conflict are discussed by C. P. Brand in a monograph originally written for students as a guide to Ariosto and his work, which remains the most useful work I can recommend for approaches to teaching this author and his work.

## Ariosto and English Literature

*Orlando furioso* was an immediate success and rapidly became a best seller, first in Italy, and soon after in many other European countries. It has been translated into English many times; the history of translations into English is well summarized by Barbara Reynolds in her introduction to the Penguin translation of Ariosto's major work. All translators of *Orlando furioso* into English have to grapple with the difficulty of rendering ottava rima naturally and fluently in English. The most successful translation of the *Furioso* into English remains, even today, after five hundred years, the very first: that of John Harington, godson to Queen Elizabeth I. His translation was first published in 1591; it was reprinted several times in the twentieth century. Like many Elizabethan translators, Harington takes a creative approach to the task. His knowledge of Italian is excellent, but more than any other translator of Ariosto, he aims to render the flavor, spirit, and tone of the original as well as (and equal in importance to) the meaning of the words. He is also aware of the interests and needs of his own contemporary public in Elizabethan England. In fulfilling these aims as translator, he subtly abbreviates Ariosto's original, sometimes by cutting out whole stanzas (the Este family genealogy for example), but more often simply by condensing passages of narrative or description to give a more concise, more English and pragmatic feel to the work. He also subtly modifies points of content and style. Geographic references, for example, are changed to appeal to an English audience, and comments on the pope and Catholicism are rendered acceptable for the Protestant English milieu. Harington frequently alters the balance of dialogue and narrative in both directions, replacing direct speech in Ariosto's original with narrative description and vice versa. The result is a work that can be read very successfully on its own but that does not work well as a student crib, a need best fulfilled by the modern translations of either Reynolds or Guido Waldman. Nevertheless, it would be interesting to ask students who are reading the *Furioso* in the original to compare passages of the original with Harington; such an exercise is very revealing of Ariosto's style as well as of Harington's ideas about translation. Harington's version of the *Furioso* is contemporary with Spenser's *Faerie Queene*, and I would suggest that students who are studying Spenser as a major text should be urged to use Harington's translation. Doing so usefully highlights not only Spenser's debt to Ariosto and the Italian tradition but also the important differences, not least in the vexed question of allegory. For students interested in the links to modern Italian literature, Italo Calvino's digest of the poem is recommended.

# Roland in Spain

## Matthew Bailey

The thematic material related to French epic song is generally referred to in Spain as the *materia carolingia* (Carolingian themes), and it enjoys a rich history. Among the Carolingian themes, the most notable influence on Spanish epic narrative is the *Song of Roland*, and the study of its influence leads to interesting insights about the dissemination of epic narrative across cultures and the formulation of a national epic discourse.

The first written reference to the *Song of Roland* in Spain is found in a single folio of manuscript Emilianense 39, Real Academia de la Historia, Madrid (the text is available in Alonso 9; for the text and English translation, as well as a complimentary discussion, see also Bennett's "Origins of the French Epic: The *Song of Roland* and Other French Epics," in this volume). It is a brief passage that had gone unnoticed because the folio on which it is transcribed had become separated from the original manuscript. Dámaso Alonso, who discovered and introduced the text to scholars in 1954 as the *Nota Emilianense*, dates it to 1075, although all previous paleographers, including non-Spaniards, had dated the manuscript itself to 951 or earlier (Alonso 70–77). In any case, the manuscript and the *Nota* predate the oldest surviving manuscript of *Roland*.

The *Nota* is a brief summary of a unique version of the *Song of Roland*. It offers enough details to distinguish itself thematically and to suggest its assimilation and dissemination by Spanish bards. For instance, Roland has not yet reached the primacy of later versions of the tale. The affirmation that the king had twelve nephews ("habuit duodecim neptis" suggests a lesser role than the one reserved for Roland alone in the *Chanson*.[1] Each nephew had three thousand horsemen with loricas, or cuirasses ("tria milia equitum cum loricis suis"), making them equal. In the same regard, the grouping of Bertran, Ogier, William, and Archbishop Turpin with the renowned peers Roland and Oliver is unique, as is the reference to each one of them serving one month of the year in the king's bodyguard ("unusquisque singulos menses serbiebat ad regem scolicis suis"). Dissemination of the tale by Spanish bards is suggested by the Spanish-sounding names and epithets that Ogier and William have acquired ("Oggero spata curta, Ghigelmo alcorbitunas"), also a clear indication of their prominence.

And yet Roland's legendary status is affirmed as well. The *Nota* reports that it pleased the king, for the security of his entire army, to place Roland, his best warrior, in the rear guard of the army ("placuit ad regem pro salutem hominum exercituum, ut rodlane, belligerator fortis, cum suis posterum ueniret"). And as the army passes through Cisa ("portum de sicera transiret"), the *Nota* recalls only the death of Roland at the hands of the Saracens in Rencesvals ("Rozaballes"). The marked singularity of Roland's death and the details of place offered in the passage indicate that the annotator is framing an event of epic proportions. By way of contrast, the compilers of the Carolingian annals wrote history, and in the *Vita Karoli* they offer no specifics of place; the Basques carry out the destruction of the French rear guard, and Roland and two other notables are identified among the many who were killed, "Eggihardus regiae mensae praepositus, Anselmus comes palatii, et Hruodlandus Brittannici limitis praefectus, cum aliis conpluribus interficiuntur" (Roncaglia 229).

The *Nota Emilianense* is an excellent text for focusing the attention of students on the oral dissemination of medieval epic narrative. Its dating prior to the earliest manuscript copy of the *Song of Roland* indicates that it summarizes an oral source. Its preservation on parchment by a cleric associated with the scriptorium at the monastery of San Millán de la Cogolla is a testament to its popularity in the Spanish Rioja. The use of Spanish-sounding epithets indicates that the narrative experienced a life of its own in Spain and is not simply the transcription of the French tale into Latin. These factors point to an oral transmission of the tale of Roland, probably by way of the Camino de Santiago pilgrim route from France into Spain. Such an itinerary would explain the more precise geographic details of the *Nota* and the less hostile view of the Basques than in the Carolingian annals (for relevant map see Zamora Vicente 132; see also the map of major pilgrimage routes in this volume). The monastery of San Millán and its literary production have long been associated with the nearby pilgrim route, and it was no doubt a place where a heroic tale of French warriors fighting Muslim warriors would find favor among clerics and pilgrims alike (Dutton 12). The oral performance of such a tale would serve to entertain pilgrims and other paying lodgers at the monastery.

The *Roncesvalles* fragment represents another manifestation of Carolingian themes in Spain and may be more familiar to nonspecialists. It also provides an opportunity to examine issues related to the oral dissemination of epic narrative as well as to the refinement of a national epic discourse in Spain. The *Roncesvalles* fragment is composed of some one hundred verses (see Gómez Redondo). The first verses present Charles eulogizing the dead Bishop Turpín (lines 2–4), then demanding to know from the dead Oliveros where Roland lies (18–22), and finally directing his lamentation to Roldán. Another fourteen verses (83–96) relate the lament of Aimón on finding his son Rinalte lying dead on the battlefield. In the final four verses Aimón and Beart throw cold water on Charles to revive him from his swoon (97–100). The fragment was put to parchment at the end of the thirteenth century. The verses are preserved on two parchment folios that seem to have been sewn together, probably to make a handbag or folder (Gómez Redondo 139).

From this brief description it seems clear that the *Roncesvalles* fragment resembles the passage in the *Song of Roland* in which Charles laments the tragic death of Roland at Rencesvals (lines 2870–944). It should also be evident that the tale had an evolution of its own in Spain, as evidenced in a number of peculiarities in the Spanish fragment. Perhaps the most striking difference involves the references to the French heroes' heads, suggesting that they were severed from their bodies. The first example occurs in the conversation between the emperor and Bishop Turpín's head: "raçonó se con eylla como si fuese bivo" ("he spoke to it[2] as if he were alive";[3] line 1).[4] Similarly with Oliveros the poet writes: "El buen emperador mandó la cabeza alçare, / que l'alimpiasen la cara del polvo y de la sangre, / como si fuese bivo començólo a preguntare" ("The good emperor ordered his head picked up [or raised], / that they clean his face of the dust and the blood, / as if he were alive he began to ask him"; 15–17). And again in the case of Aimón as he prepares to speak to his fallen son Rinalte, we are told: "alçóli la cabeça, odredes lo que dirade" ("he raised [or picked up] his head, you will hear what he will say"; 87). Roldán was evidently spared the fate of his fellow warriors, as Charles makes clear when he refuses to accept his death: "Non vos veo colpe nin lançada por que oviésedes male; / por eiso non vos creo que muerto sodes, don Roldane" ("I see no wound from sword or lance that harmed you; / that's why I don't believe you that you are dead, don Roland"; 45–46).

Perhaps the best evidence that *Roncesvalles* is indeed describing severed heads can be found by examining another Spanish epic, the *Siete infantes de Lara*. This narrative develops to even better effect the gruesome motif of severed heads in connection with seven young nobles, all brothers (Alvar). In this tale the father, Gonzalo Gustioz, is asked by his Muslim captor Almanzor to identify eight heads of Castilian nobles killed in combat. While cleaning them of blood, don Gonzalo suddenly recognizes them as the heads of his seven sons and their tutor. He lines them up in the order of their birth and proceeds to pick up their heads one by one, starting with the oldest and ending with the youngest. He cleans their faces of dust and blood and speaks lovingly of the character and unique attributes of each one. The phrasing is similar to the *Roncesvalles* fragment: "alimpiólas muy bien del polvo e de la sangre") ("He cleaned them very well of the dust and the blood"; Alvar 57); "razonóse con ella como si fuese bivo" ("he spoke to it[5] as if he were alive"; Alvar 61). As don Gonzalo finishes his spoken epitaph of each son, he kisses the son's head and sets it down with the others.

Charles, called "Carlos el emperante" in *Roncesvalles* (line 7), also speaks in a memorializing fashion about Bishop Turpín: "Bueno pora las armas, mejor pora ante Jhesu Christo, / consejador de pecadores" ("Good at arms, better at praying to Jesus Christ, / counselor to sinners"; 2–3). For Oliveros Charles employs a simple epithet, "caballero naturale" ("natural knight"; 18), and then for Roldán offers more detail: "Tanto bueno amigo vós me solíades ganare" ("so many good vassals you gained for me"; 37). Also Aimón briefly reminisces about his son's physical strength: "¡Qué cuerpo tan caboso! Omen non vio otro tale" ("What an excellent body! Man has not seen another like it"; 88). The similarities between the circumstances and the expression of the laments suggest a common narrative thread running through the *Roncesvalles* and the

most emotional narrative of Castilian epic, the *Siete infantes*. The greater
detail and the steadier focus of *Siete infantes* may indicate that the motif of
the severed heads originated with that narrative and only later was incorpo-
rated into the *Roncesvalles* fragment or that it was simply a better fit for that
story than for the tale of Roland.

Also unique to the *Roncesvalles* fragment is the reference to Aimón la-
menting the death of his son Rinalte, neither of whom participate in the battle
in the *Song of Roland*, and the details of Carlos's lament for Roldán, in which
he recounts his own youthful adventures and then Roldán's upbringing, first
victories and the wounding of Carlos at Zaragoza (Gómez Redondo, lines 54–
76). Together these details point to a hybrid narrative that reflects a variety
of sources brought together over a period of time in which the narrative was
modified to remain popular and influential.

For a reader accustomed to the heroic narratives of medieval Castile, the
long lament of Charles in the *Song of Roland* seems decidedly unheroic. The
Cid sheds a few silent tears but never cries out or faints. Lament is the subject
of the entire *Roncesvalles* fragment, which makes it seem an aspect of French
epic that Spanish audiences appreciated but ultimately rejected for their own
national heroes. The glaring exception to this perception is Gonzalo of *Siete
infantes*, who is captive in Córdoba and therefore unable to exact the revenge
that would restore his honor. A comparison of these sentiments is helpful in
reaffirming the connection between *Roncesvalles* and *Siete infantes*.

At the beginning of *Roncesvalles* the death of Bishop Turpín leads Carlos
to lament his own fate: "quién aconseyerá este viejo mesquino / que finca en
grant cuita" ("who will help this miserable old man / who is left in great dis-
tress"; lines 5–6; similarly 42, 53). This altered state also manifests itself in
the king's reaction on seeing Roldán: "El rey cuando lo vido, oít lo que faze: /
ariba alçó las manos por las barbas tirare; por las barbas floridas bermeja sayllîa
la sangre" ("The king when he saw him, hear what he does: / he raised his
hands to pull on his beard; / from his flowing beard the blood ran red"; 30–
32). Carlos also makes several references to wanting to be dead in place of
Roldán or to join Roldán in death; for example: "yo era pora morir e vós pora
escapare" ("I was meant to die and you to escape"; 36); "Con tal duelo estó,
sobrino, agora non fues' bivo" ("I am in such pain, nephew, if only I weren't
alive"; 77); "Agora ploguiés al Criador, a mi Senyor Jhesucristo, / que finase
en este logar, que me levase contigo!" ("Now it please the Creator, my Lord
Jesus Christ / that I die in this place, that he take me with you!"; 78–79).

Once again, in *Siete infantes* we find a clear connection to *Roncesvalles*,
this time in the sentiments expressed by the bereaved father Gonzalo: he pulls
out his hair ("mesando sus cabellos e las barbas de su faz" ["He pulls out his
hair and the beard on his face"; 76]), he laments his old age and his fate
("Viejo so mesquino para estas bodas bofardare" ["I am too old and miserable
to celebrate this wedding"; 77]), and he faints away after his lament ("en esto

comediendo, amortescido se ha" ["Reflecting on this, he fainted"; 165]).[6] Otherwise in the Spanish epic, the vanquished enemies of the Castilians are the only ones who behave this way. In the learned epic *Poema de Fernán González*, the Muslim general Almanzor expresses a death wish after the devastation of his army: "el mj grran poder es muerto e catyvo / pues ellos muertos son, para qué fynco yo vjuo" ("my great army is dead and captive / since they are dead, why do I remain alive?"; López Guil, lines 266c–d]). Fernán González also uses the sentiment rhetorically to strike fear in his men as he rallies them to battle, "Es desamparado de todo byen el cavtyvo, / mas dize muchas veces que non querrya ser nasçido" ("The captive is bereft of any good, / and says many times that he wishes he were not born"; [433a–b]). This last statement brings to mind the captive Gonzalo and sheds some additional light on how his lament might have been conceived by a Castilian audience of the time.

Another indication of the long-standing popularity of the *Song of Roland* and its related themes in Spain is found in two legendary figures, Bernardo del Carpio and young Rodrigo Díaz (not yet known as el Cid). Their response to the Carolingian incursion against the Muslim reflects the emergence of something akin to national pride on the part of the Leonese (Bernardo) and the Castilians (Rodrigo). The Bernardo del Carpio narrative is found in a number of thirteenth-century Latin and vernacular chronicles, although later vernacular chroniclers indicate that they take some of their material from contemporary oral narratives, "Et algunos dizen en sus cantares et en sus fablas que fue este Bernaldo" ("And some say in their songs and their stories that it was this Bernaldo"; Menéndez-Pidal, *Estoria* 2: 351, column a, lines, 21–22). In brief, Bernaldo is adopted as an infant by his maternal uncle king Alfonso II, the Chaste (reigned 791–842), who then imprisons his father and sends his mother to a monastery. Alfonso becomes vassal to the emperor Charles in exchange for his assistance in fighting the Muslim, and Bernaldo, infuriated, marches to Zaragoza to defend the city and King Marsile against the French invaders. In the battle of Rencesvals that ensues, death befalls Roland, Count Anselm, Guirald, "he of the emperor's table," and many other men of the high nobility of France, "don Roldán, et el conde Anselmo, et Guiralte el de la mesa del emperador, et otros muchos omes de los altos omes de Françia" (Menéndez-Pidal, *Estoria* 2; 353, column b, lines 44–47). In a later version, Bernardo is sent to France and is received in the court of Charles II, the Bald, because he is the son of Charlemagne's sister, Timbor.

The Castilian response to the Carolingian epic is manifested in the deeds of the young Rodrigo Díaz as celebrated in the *Mocedades de Rodrigo*, a late-twelfth-century epic narrative (for the text see M. Bailey 189–216). Rodrigo's fifth and final deed in his quest for manhood before marriage is the invasion of France. Rodrigo alone is compelled to action after King Fernando I receives a letter signed by the king of France, the patriarch, the pope, and the German emperor demanding that Spain pay them tribute as a vassal state. Rodrigo rallies Spain to invade France and eventually defeats and captures the count of Savoy, who offers Rodrigo his daughter and only heir as ransom for his freedom. Rodrigo then hands her over to King Fernando, demanding that he "embarraganad a França" ("make France your mistress"; M. Bailey, line 988). Rodrigo then marches all the way to Paris and demands to fight the Twelve Peers. In the end the French did not expect to fight a warrior as great as Rodrigo and exact a truce from the Spanish by unexpectedly baptizing the love child of Fernando and the Savoyard.

No doubt a version of the *Song of Roland* entered Spain with pilgrims en route to the shrine of Saint James the apostle in Santiago de Compostela, along the Camino de Santiago, also known as the Camino Francés. This was manifested in writing as early as 1075. Most likely, as the tale evolved orally in France it also evolved into Spain. French pilgrims continued to introduce new versions of the narrative into Spain and to take back with them details from the Spanish tale. The important motifs and heroic sentiments of the story of Roland not readily found in the autochthonous narrative tradition insinuated themselves into the Spanish epic. Also, a growing pride in Spain's own warrior culture led to the formulation of nationalistic sentiments that produced novel responses to the legend of Roland and the Twelve Peers.


NOTES

[1] All quotations from the *Nota* are from Alonso 9.
[2] This is feminine, as in *cabeça*.
[3] The word *bivo* is masculine.
[4] Quotations from *Roncesvalles* are from Gomez Redondo; translations are mine.
[5] Feminine.
[6] Quotations from *Siete infantes* are from Alvar.

# A Competitive Edge:
# Franco-Hispanic Rivalry and
# the Origins of the *Song of Roland*
### Kimberlee Campbell

## Reception History as Pedagogy

When I teach the literature of the Middle Ages, and in particular a literary
monument such as the *Song of Roland*, I devote a session or two to the
question of reception history. Such a history can be traced through literary
texts—the Spanish *romanceros* and Ludovico Ariosto come to mind—as well
as through historical and critical commentary. A brief presentation of this kind
will help the students conceptualize the *Roland* as something other than a
museum piece famous for its symmetry. The reception history completes stu-
dents' understanding of the text by allowing them to see how the words,
structures, and story can have a political and social impact, often in ways never
imagined by the original artist.

The students who take the survey course in which I most often teach the
*Song of Roland* consider themselves modernists, with little interest, at least
initially, in things medieval. For them, the *Roland* models a world at an im-
possible remove from their own. I introduce the concept of reception history
in reverse chronological order, starting with a warm-up exercise during which
students talk about their own knowledge or experience of medieval stories,
customs, or artifacts. The co-constructed corpus of knowledge can then be
mined for the values and purposes of the stories. From there, it is an easy
step to a formalized critical appraisal of important readings of the *Song of
Roland*. This work can be done as a series of short case studies, since it is
more important for students to grasp the multiplicity of uses for narrative than
it is for them to retain a coherent chronology of reception. I generally devote
one lecture to the detailed analysis of an interesting set of readings. For a
subsequent class, or in the form of a short paper, students are asked to re-
search and present their own case studies.

## Background to a Case Study

For my lecture, I most often select authors from one of the most interesting
moments in the long history of the reception of the *Song of Roland*: the
nineteenth century, when literary scholarship succeeded in imposing itself as
a discipline largely by association with history and politics, in an era of bur-
geoning nationalism in Europe. Literary scholars on that continent were in a
position to contribute substantially to the nationalizing rhetoric. In France,

for example, Louis-Napoléon's minister of education, Hippolyte Fortoul, was quick to create a chair for the study of language and literature at the Collège de France, commenting that he wanted to "encourage research that, in looking back to the ancient and glorious traditions of the country, would inspire national sentiment" (Dakyns 34). A heroic past lent weight and legitimacy to a nineteenth-century present in search of itself. Spatial constructs of national identity were reinforced by this temporal model of the collective self as a community expressed through shared history. As no less an authority than Gaston Paris himself put it: "Literature is the expression of national life; without national literature, that life is incomplete" (Poésie 99).[1]

In terms of a study of the reception history of the *Roland*, this era is rich in interpretations that edge the narrative toward propaganda. Nineteenth-century medieval scholars framed the quest for a legitimizing past in competitive terms, defining the collective "self" in opposition to an "other" whose physical and historical proximity permitted no quarter. The Franco-Germanic conversation, recounted in part in *Medievalism and the Modernist Temper*, is perhaps the most well-documented example of such a politico-literary rivalry (Bloch and Nichols). Less well known, but even more interesting for students given the vehemence of the rhetoric on both sides, is the dialogue between French and Spanish scholars. I need only recall Théodore de Puymaigre's devastating assessment of Spanish literary history—"The study of old Castilian literature is in some measure an appendix to work on our own [French] literary history" (1: 2)—to make the political agenda clear to my students.[2] This was a dialogue in which national and even racial superiority became a game of superlatives in time, in which *earliest* and *best* were synonymous. The lacunae and ambiguity of medieval records permitted a great deal of latitude with respect to critical interpretations; archival opportunities of this kind were not lacking on either side. In the context of this generalized rivalry, the emblematic importance of the *Song of Roland* stands out. Researchers focused on finding and laying claim to the original version that would legitimize collective identity. The stage was set for a Franco-Hispanic debate that cut to the core identity of both nations.

## The Case through French Eyes

I might begin my lecture with texts selected from the French side of the debate: Gaston Paris's reasoning is clear and consistent throughout his career, from his doctoral thesis, the *Histoire poétique de Charlemagne*, published in 1865, to his Collège de France discourse on the *Song of Roland* and French nationalism ("*Chanson*"), an obvious topic in 1870, to editions of *La littérature française au moyen âge*. For Paris, "France had, with respect to neighboring nations, an accepted role of intellectual, literary and social initiation and leadership" (*Littérature française* 32).[3] The genesis of most European national literature, according to Paris, was heavily influenced by the French chanson de geste and, more specifically, by the *Song of Roland*. In the best tradition of *translatio imperii*, then, France assumed the mantle of classical civilization, which it then transmitted to other European cultures. This sequence reflected the French ethnic predisposition to epic composition—a predisposition not granted to all nations: "On the contrary, [epic] is found only amongst a small number of Aryan peoples.... It is incorrect to speak of Egyptian, Jewish, Arab, Finnish or American epics; this name does not fit the monuments to which it has been applied" (Paris, *Histoire* 2–3).[4] Even those peoples who are "Aryan," a term that would appear to be synonymous with "European" for Paris, may lack an indigenous epic narrative, for want of favorable historical and social circumstances. This is the case for the Iberian peninsula. Paris notes that "Spain had no epic" (*Histoire* 203),[5] underlining the unequivocal nature of this assessment by refusing even to discuss it: "Skilled critics have demonstrated this fact ... ; we do not need to go back over this material here" (*Histoire* 203).[6] By framing his refusal to admit the possibility of a Spanish epic as a critical commonplace, Paris rhetorically bars discussion. The impersonal formulation underscores the universally known nature of his commentary. The *Cid* might have constituted an obvious stumbling block with respect to this line of reasoning, but Paris makes quick work of it in his introduction, relegating its mention to a parenthetical comment in which he sets it aside (*Histoire* 9). In *La poésie du moyen âge*, Paris makes it clear that he considers the *Cid* a work derived through imitation of French sources (54). Having stripped Spain of any vestige of an indigenous epic, Paris is then free to expound on his primary subject, the history of the Roland material in Europe, in its peninsular dimensions.

That the Roland material was present on the Iberian peninsula was never at issue, given the quantity of archives referencing the narrative available to researchers in the nineteenth century. The essential question, then, was how this material might reflect a consciousness of national or ethnic unity and, inevitably, of the relative worth of nations as measured against their counterparts. For Paris, the evidence of French leadership, if not superiority, was clear, if, as he contended, Spanish bards generally contented themselves with the simple repetition of French epic material: "Most of the time, they simply repeated ... the songs of the French jongleurs" (*Histoire* 205).[7] Spain would be by inference derivative, or secondary, a clearly pejorative characterization. There is however substantial development of the Roland material on the Iberian peninsula, if narratives featuring Bernardo del Carpio, Roland's Spanish counterpart and sometime foe, are taken into account (see also Bailey's "Roland in Spain," in this volume). Paris does address this material, integrating it into his argument by reading it not only in terms of the earliest-best paradigm, which gave the French a competitive edge in the race to an authorizing antiquity, but also as evidence of a collectivized character flaw. The Spanish are guilty of vanity, letting their pride take precedence over the truth, at least of the narrative, if not of history: "Gradually, they had Spaniards take part in the action, then they gave them the better role, and ended by making Bernardo del Carpio the enemy and conqueror of Roland, sacrificing the unifying, religious idea of the poem to their patriotism" (*Histoire* 28).[8] Paris maintains an air of patient but condescending tolerance toward the Spanish foibles, understanding, although not necessarily condoning, the apparent Spanish rejection of narratives that "all the same did not flatter Castilian pride" (*Histoire* 206).[9] In the last analysis, then, the Spanish are both unoriginal and vain, whereas the French, in a comparison no less powerful for being implicit, occupy the moral and aesthetic high ground, thus reinforcing, with respect to a specific other—the Spaniard—the position of eminence claimed for the French "self" in Paris's introduction.

Like his countryman Gaston Paris, Léon Gautier, that other great nineteenth-century French scholar of the Middle Ages, saw in the Old French chanson de geste a source of collective identity and heroic unity. The subtitle of Gautier's *Les épopées françaises*: *Étude sur les origines et l'histoire de la littérature nationale*, underscores the link between nationalism and the epic. Gautier certainly conceives of his professional mission in these terms, as he notes in the introduction to his second edition, in 1892. He says that if he could

> revive in some measure love for the cherished French nation . . . if the name of Roland . . . has served to rally souls smitten with true patriotism . . . then it is not without some consolation that I will put down my pen.
> (1: viii)[10]

Gautier's comment recalls Fortoul's call, made some forty years earlier, for literary scholarship that would contribute to the contemporaneous discourse of nationalism. Indeed, the sense of the profound importance of this literature to the collective consciousness of self persists long after the Romanticism out of which the idea was born has faded away.

With respect to the Roland material in Spain, Gautier's assessment is essentially identical to Paris's. While Gautier refrains from Paris's absolutes, he nonetheless avoids the question of the *Cid* and proceeds down the same analytic path as his colleague, from repetition to imitation to rejection and to the invention of the spurious (from the French point of view) character of Bernardo del Carpio. Gautier's less formal presentation of the genesis of the Bernardo material inclines to the supercilious at times in its attempt to dramatize literary history:

> In the end, they revolted against the celebration of the glory of only the great French emperor. . . . All French, not one Spaniard. It was scan-

dalous. . . . And Roland, that eternal Roland? After all, wasn't he beaten
at Roncevaux, and by Spaniards maybe?                    (2: 330–31)[11]

The Spanish are described as being jealous of the French; they become bitter.
This pejorative lexicon combined with the theatrical tone of Gautier's history
effectively removes the Bernardo legend from the realms of noble patriotism
to relocate it in the far less lofty sphere of petty envy; the Spanish people,
unable to accept the legend in all its aesthetic and emotional, albeit foreign,
beauty, are so crass as to substitute their own clearly inferior narrative to satisfy
the demands of pedestrian competitiveness. Despite his deprecation of the
Bernardo material, Gautier admits to an admiration for Spanish culture, yet
what he would seem to admire most are those Spaniards who have the good
taste to appreciate the French! He endorses his Spanish counterpart's book,
Manuel Milá y Fontanals's *De la poesía heróico-popular castellana*, because
that author had the intelligence, as Gautier puts it, to "repair all of the literary
outrages that Spain had unknowingly inflicted on the [French] national epic"
(2: 343–44).[12] For Gautier, then, intelligence is tantamount to recognizing
French superiority by acknowledging the authority of French epic.

## The Spanish Point of View

Moving to the other side of the Pyrenees, it is clear that Spain is at something
of a disadvantage, for although there is archival evidence supporting the ex-
istence of French chansons de geste in Spain, the converse is difficult to argue.
The game must be played entirely on the Spanish side of the court, so to
speak. For this reason, rhetorical strategies are not simply mirror images of
those already examined; rather, the tactics adopted by Spanish scholars must
take into account the sometimes vexatious geographic and literary reality of
the Spanish Middle Ages. That said, the larger goals of establishing a collective
sense of national identity and validating that identity in the international arena
remain the same. Consequently, much of the language extolling the medieval
epic hero as an iconic archetype of self is similar, although on the Spanish
side of the Pyrenees the name evoked is most often that of the Cid: "the
Spanish people look at this hero from their tradition and their history, illu-
minating the past, infusing new life into the present and enriching the future
with the marvelous seed of his exploits" (Amador de los Ríos 3: 52).[13] Waxing
lyrical in his enthusiasm, José Amador de los Ríos, the author of the multi-
volume *Historia crítica de la literatura española*, is not the only Spanish in-
tellectual to recognize the potential political importance of epic heroes in the
context of contemporaneous nationalism. His countryman and colleague Pas-
cual de Gayangos, in his *Libros de caballerías* remarks on "the patriotic sen-
timents of the Spanish people who find solace and delight in the incredible

deeds of Bernardo del Carpio, and the glorious acts of the Cid and of other national heroes" (vi).[14] In Gayangos's formulation, Bernardo del Carpio takes his place at the side of the Cid, as a Spanish hero, rather than as the evidence of Spanish inferiority, as he was for French scholars.

The trans-Pyreneen ambiguity of Bernardo del Carpio is in fact at the heart of the Franco-Hispanic rivalry. The Bernardo material is at issue precisely because of its connection with the *Song of Roland*; for, if the epic is ennobling, empowering, and authorizing for the French, the same effect does not necessarily obtain in different geographic or social situations. Borrowing, imitation, or reaction to the original is read as evidence either of aesthetic ineptitude or of an inglorious local history. French intellectuals saw it as evidence of both, and thus were unable to resist the temptation of adopting a mocking tone toward Bernardo. Spanish scholars, on the other hand, had the delicate task of interpreting their literary history in a way that validated Spanish national pride. In this regard, they were faced with the relative paucity of extant epic texts in Spain as well as a significant corpus of references to a legend that was clearly linked to the totemic, but foreign, *Song of Roland*. Reactions and strategies were multiple. The most obvious approach, perhaps, was to minimize the importance of the Bernardo material in Spanish literary history while accentuating that of the *Cid* and related works. This Amador de los Ríos did in his literary history: although the legend of the Cid is in some sense on display in the *Historia* because it is the topic of not one, but several chapters, and because it figures in the chapter headings and subheadings, the Bernardo material appears only in the body of the study, invisible to the casual reader.

The Bernardo material could be made less obvious; it could also be made more "Spanish." Given the uncertainty of dates and references in the field of European epic, this is not an unreasonable gambit, Amador de los Ríos characterizes Bernardo as the bastard son of a princess of Asturias and a count of Saldaña, that is to say, an entirely Spanish hero. According to Amador de los Ríos, it is not until later that Bernardo's genealogy is revised to link him to the house of Charlemagne. Bernardo's Frenchness would therefore represent a corruption of the earlier, truer, more Spanish version of Bernardo's lineage.

In the case of the Bernardo materials, Spanish intellectuals often made a virtue of necessity: rather than try to minimize the legend, scholars at times simply seized the proverbial bull by the horns, emphasizing the Spanish pride evidenced not only in the narrative itself but also on the part of those bards who used their skills to answer their French counterparts. Bernardo was therefore read as a natural and eminently noble response to invaders of all stripes and, in fact, as a force for the unification of Spain. For example, Marcelino Menéndez y Pelayo speaks of the impulses of wounded Spanish pride, which protested "not only through the voices of the monk of Silos and the Archbishop Rodrigo but also through the national epic . . . Hispanizing it in such a way that rather than an imitation or continuation, it was a living protest against all foreign invaders" (1: 206–07).[15] His analysis of the genesis of the

Bernardo legend is just the opposite of Paris's and Gautier's: far from being a petty, unimaginative reaction to the authoritative French version of the narrative, the Bernardo material represents, on the contrary, an empowering demonstration of the strength and resolve of the Spanish people, thus contributing to a positive Spanish model of self.

Beyond the often eloquent arguments justifying the Bernardo legend in the context of Spanish nationalism, which, despite their effectiveness, must still be recognized as a form of defense, Spanish scholars also went on the offensive. If collective identity was validated by the originality and antiquity of the so-called national literature, then each cohort was vulnerable with respect to the age and inspiration of that literature, a point of logic that did not escape Spanish critics. And indeed, few of them missed the opportunity to recall the Germanic ancestry of the heroic ethos exemplified in the chanson de geste. Gayangos, reviewing the history of chivalric novels of Carolingian inspiration, noted, "chivalry, as an institution, was without doubt Germanic in origin" (iv).[16] Milá y Fontanals, commended by Gautier for his reequilibration of medieval literary history, nonetheless commented, "the spirit of the French epic was that of the classes of Germanic origin, who remained Germanic with respect to their ideas and their customs, even when they had adopted the language of the vanquished" (455).[17] Finally, Menéndez y Pelayo concluded, "this poetry, while French by language, was at times German and at others Celtic in origin" (201).[18] For these authors, the *Song of Roland*, far from being the sterling original compared to which the reactive Bernardo must be found wanting, was itself a narrative to be understood in terms of history—a history that did not support the mythologizing *translatio imperii* by virtue of which the French nation would be vested with the leadership of a new European civilization, as Paris had suggested.

## Research Projects and Presentations

By bracketing reception history and politicized ethnicities, the foregoing case study gives students a concrete example of narrative coopted by ideology to use as a guide for their own analyses. Before assigning individual projects, however, I find it useful to distribute selected portions of the critical texts comprising the sample case study, so that students, working together, may construct a typology of discourse strategies. When suggesting projects, in addition to nineteenth-century historians and critics, I also suggest appropriate literary texts, from the *Karlamagnús Saga* (translated into English by Hieatt or into French by Togeby and Halleux) to Victor Hugo. And of course, this unit would not be complete without some mention of the *Song of Roland* itself as an interpretive reading of the events at Rencesvals. Bringing the critical focus full circle, a reception history that reads *Roland* through Einhard or Urban II encourages the unpacking of the political and social agenda inscribed in the aesthetics of *Roland*, thereby enhancing my students' understanding of the text in its social and historical context.


## NOTES

[1]"[L]a littérature est l'expression de la vie nationale: là où il n'y a pas de littérature nationale, il n'y a qu'une vie nationale imparfaite." All translations in this essay are the author's.

[2]"[Q]u'une étude sur l'ancienne littérature castillane est en quelque sorte un appendice aux travaux dont notre propre histoire littéraire a fourni les éléments."

[3]"La France eut à l'égard des nations avoisinantes un rôle partout accepté d'initiation et de direction intellectuelle, littéraire et sociale."

[4]"On n'en trouve au contraire que chez un petit nombre de peuples âryens. . . . C'est à tort qu'on a parlé d'épopées égyptiennes, juives, arabes, finoises, américaines; ce nom ne convient pas aux monuments qu'on a ainsi désignés."

[5]"L'Espagne n'a pas eu d'épopée."

[6]"D'habiles critiques ont démontré ce fait . . . ; nous n'avons pas à y revenir ici."

[7]"La plupart du temps ils ont simplement répété . . . ce que chantaient les jongleurs de France."

[8]"Insensiblement ils firent intervenir dans l'action des Espagnols; puis ils leur donnèrent le plus beau rôle, et finirent, sacrifiant à leur patriotisme l'idée religieuse et unitaire de ces poëmes, par faire de Bernard de Carpio l'ennemi et le vainqueur de Roland."

[9]"ne flattaient pas de même l'orgueil castillan"

[10]"raviver un peu l'amour pour la chère patrie française . . . si le nom de Roland . . . a pu servir de ralliement aux âmes éprises d'un véritable patriotisme . . . ce n'est pas sans quelque consolation que je déposerai ma plume"

[11]"On se révolta à la fin de n'entendre célébrer . . . que la gloire du grand empereur de France. . . . Tous Français; pas un Espagnol. C'était scandaleux. . . . Et ce Roland, cet éternel Roland? Est-ce qu'en somme, il n'avait pas été battu à Roncevaux, et par des Espagnols peut-être?"

[12]"réparer un jour tous les outrages littéraires que l'Espagne avait inconsciemment fait subir à notre épopée nationale"

[13]"[m]ira el pueblo español á este héroe en los confines de la tradicion y de la historia, iluminando lo pasado, infundiendo nueva vida á lo presente y fecundando lo porvenir con los maravillosos gérmenes de sus proezas"

[14]"los patrióticos sentimientos del pueblo español hallasen solaz y deleite en las increibles hazañas de Bernardo del Carpio, en los gloriosos hechos del Cid y otros héroes nacionales"

[15]"por boca del monje de Silos y del Arzobispo don Rodrigo, sino que, invadiendo los campos de la épica nacional . . . españolizó la leyenda en términos tales, que más que imitación o continuación fue protesta viva contra todo invasor extraño."

[16]"[L]a caballería, considerada como institucion, es á no dudarlo, de orígen germánico."

[17]"[E]l espíritu de la epopeya francesa era el de las clases de orígen germánico y que

estas se mantuvieron germánicas en gran parte de sus ideas y de sus costumbres aún cuando hubieron adoptado el habla de los vencidos."

[18]"[E]sta poesía, aunque francesa por la lengua . . . era germánica unas veces y otras céltica por sus orígenes."

# The *Song of Roland* in Nineteenth-Century France

## Mark Burde

Over the past twenty years an understanding of the reception of the *Song of Roland* in nineteenth-century France has rightfully come to be seen as integral to a full appreciation of the work's richness and power. Familiarity with the social and cultural appeal that the *Roland* held for the citizens—especially the learned ones—of one of the world's paradigmatic nation-states can encourage students to reflect on issues as broad as the social function of national artistic monuments and the mutually convenient alliances struck between literature and ideology or as focused as the process by which seemingly arcane questions of textual editing could become freighted with considerable cultural importance. As in the study of language change, the history of the *Song of Roland*'s reception can be divided into its internal and external components. External history here will encompass the ways in which the *Roland* spoke to a French collective imaginary and stoked an often-urgent nationalism; internal history addressed at the end of this essay will by contrast pertain to the more technical philological negotiations by which a more or less standard text was produced from a clutch of imperfect manuscripts. In both cases the physical and philological prowess of a single competitor nation—Germany—was an ever-present consideration driving the thoughts and writings of French philologists and literary critics: internally, a scientific philology pioneered by German scholars would influence the editing of the *Roland*, whereas externally, such milestones as the integration of the work into the French school curriculum can be attributed in large measure to the traumatic defeat France suffered at the hands of the Prussians in 1870.

However central "the German question" to nineteenth-century *Roland* reception, though, it is crucial that students be made aware of the full range of issues and concerns for which this work became a nodal point. At stake was not only French (in)security in the face of modern-day German might but also the very roots of French identity in a complex ancient soil of Latin, Celtic, and Germanic makeup. With its repeated recourse to the terms *France*, *Francs*, and *Français*, the *Roland* seemed to promise insights into vexing sociopolitical questions of national origins and early national consciousness. More broadly, the *Roland* also established France's relation to wider European cultural traditions, for as a national epic comparable in function and even quality to the works of Homer and Vergil, the *Roland* stood France favorably in relation to Greco-Roman heritage. The numerous medieval translations and adaptations of the *Roland* into other European languages, moreover, suggested a French cultural preeminence coterminous with the history of French culture itself. Politically, observers as diverse as Romantic poets, staunch republicans, and traditionalist Catholics were beguiled by the prospect of gaining access to an ancient popular voice preserved, fossil-like, in the *Roland*, all to radically different—sometimes opposing—political ends. Finally, it is important to note the rarely acknowledged (at the time) but ever-present colonialist context for reception of the *Roland* in this period: if Roland's defeat became a consoling analogue to the cataclysmic events of the Franco-Prussian War of 1870, Charlemagne's ultimate victory over the armies of the non-Christian world seemed to portend and legitimate such French expansionism as the invasion and eventual annexation of Algeria, beginning in 1830.

This partial list of components to the external history of the *Roland* suggests a useful generalization, namely that nineteenth-century readers gravitated toward two forms of use value they found in the work: first, a testimonial, documentary, and sociological value indissociable from the assumed conditions of the poem's production and based on the presumption of a certain degree of evidentiary reliability and second, a moral, exemplary, and hortatory value, rooted in plot and characters and endowed, especially, with obvious pedagogical applications. Students may be surprised to learn that the category of purely aesthetic and artistic value accorded the work—the *Roland* as epic masterpiece—was of lesser concern for much of this period, but many commentators before Joseph Bédier were in fact only too happy to applaud the text as the kind of unadorned, virile, and innocently raucous work that their theories led them to associate with the genesis of national poetic production.

What, then, were the specific forms that this reception took, and how did they evolve over time? How did the *Song of Roland* come to be called a national epic, and what exactly did this term mean? Nineteenth-century reception of *Roland* can be considered to occupy the 130 or so years separating the Revolution from World War I and is divisible into four stages: Revolution to 1837, 1837 to 1850, 1850 to 1870, and 1870 to World War I. In the first of these periods, the phrase *Song of Roland* meant nothing more than a tantalizingly enigmatic literary reference made by a number of medieval historians. According to these chroniclers, the conquering Normans at Hastings in 1066 had either sung or heard performed such a song (vaguely designated as a "cantilena Rollandi" in the Latin works) to buoy their spirits for battle. When Francisque Michel published the first complete edition of the now-famous Oxford *Roland* manuscript in 1837, he devoted part of the introduction to a defense of what he acknowledged was an idiosyncratic choice of title on the grounds that he had possibly unearthed the mysterious work referred to in the chroniclers' accounts of Hastings. However indulgent the smile that current-day scholars might reserve for such fervent literalism, it is worth noting that if today we speak of "the Song of Roland" rather than "the poem of the Battle of Rencesvals" or any of a half-dozen other plausible designations for this untitled and anonymous work, it is because Michel chose to link the work to an originary (if probably apocryphal) act of commemoration. That is to say, well before the French state brandished the *Song of Roland* in its cultural war with Germany, the work's first editor assumed that the work had been performing martial service ever since its supposed participation in the epic downfall of the Anglo-Saxon dynasty, when a group of French-speaking warriors chose to invoke Roland's legendary heroism.

To many of Michel's readers, however, the term *song* had a resonance that far exceeded the bounds of any given time and place. For them the term conjured up the misty origins of national voice in a long-lost popular and bardic tradition. This Romantic interpretation defined the second period of *Roland* reception, which stretched from the publication of Michel's 1837 edition to the appearance of the second major edition produced by François Génin in 1850. This period is characterized by a largely enthusiastic embrace of the *Roland* in private circles by poets, scholars, and critics who, under clear influence of German Romantic poetics, did not hesitate to go a step further than Michel and, with unabashed patriotic fervor, to brand the *Roland* a national treasure. Although none of the reviews devoted to the Michel edition names Friedrich Wolf, Johann Herder, or the brothers Grimm, the influence of their ideas is evident in the recourse to descriptive phrases such as "untamed ruggedness" ("une sorte de rudesse sauvage"), "noble, Homeric simplicity" ("une noble simplicité homérique"), and "this precious national relic" ("cette précieuse relique nationale"), all found in an 1837 review article published by the *Journal de Paris* (Amiel 1; my trans.).

If the second phase of *Roland* enthusiasm was characterized by the initiative of enlightened individuals motivated by Romantic poetic nationalism, the third phase (1850–70) saw the French state suddenly warm to the work, with a concomitant precision and refinement from 1850 onward, in what might be called the nationalistic use value made of the poem. Fifteen years earlier the Ministry of Public Education had been under the direction of the eminent historian François Guizot, a man sensitive to the need, in the wake of decades of political turmoil and antagonism, to create a historical narrative that celebrated a shared French national heritage. Guizot's idea of a national epic resembled not the *Song of Roland*, with its flights of poetic fancy, but a thirteenth-century Latin verse work on the life of King Philip Augustus (1165–1223) entitled *La Philippide* and depicting, among other things, the French victory over German and Flemish foes at Bouvines in 1214. (Instructors teaching in French have the possibility of comparing the *Roland* with short passages of *La Philippide*, which Guizot published in the 1820s in a prose translation for a general readership.) Thus for Génin, a successor official of the same ministry, to publish a "critical text" of the Oxford *Roland* manuscript accompanied by a lengthy introduction and to distribute copies of it, at governmental expense, to hundreds of journalists and other arbiters of taste was an event of no small importance.

Génin's edition proved to be a turning point for the sharpening and focusing of the nationalistic interpretation of the work. The subject of the *Roland*, he declared in his prologue, "is national for the French as much as the events of the Trojan War were for the Greeks" (v).[1] Whereas only one of Michel's reviewers had made mention of the poem's repeatedly invoked epithet of "douce France" ("fair land of France"), it now became commonplace for commentators to call attention to the work's apparent equivalence of patriotism with love of land. The conservative critic and future Académie Française inductee Ludovic Vitet, for example, devoted a lengthy article to asserting in part that the incantatory return of "douce France" distinguished this work from all other French medieval epics. Although cool toward Génin's effusive comparison of the *Roland* with the Greco-Roman epic tradition (Old French being for him a language barely out of its swaddling clothes), Vitet advanced *Roland* reception significantly by ascribing singularity in the broadest possible terms: just as the *Roland* stood out among all other French epics for its unique manifestation of nationalistic devotion, its very fact of creation distinguished France from all other European peoples of the time, none of which, Vitet opined, had been capable of such a feat. This paradigm of French cultural precociousness and exceptionalism would become a crucial intellectual building block underlying discussion of the biggest single issue to preoccupy *Roland* scholars of the latter half of the century—the question of poetic creation and transmission (assumed to be oral) in an environment of uncomfortably similar northern European Germanic peoples. If the medievalists Léon Gautier and Gaston Paris could later unabashedly trace creation of the *Roland*—the French national epic—to the spontaneous lyricism of *Germanic* warriors, it was under the reassuring caveat that Christianization and the passage of the Rhine had imparted no small degree of civilization to these proto-Frenchmen.

The fourth and final phase of nineteenth-century *Roland* reception was inaugurated by two highly influential essays composed by Gautier and Paris as they endured the Prussian Siege of Paris in the winter of late 1870. With the streets having grown unsafe for stray dogs and speculation about the edibility of exotic zoo animals rising day by day, these two leading medievalists turned themselves toward a sober assessment of the *Song of Roland*'s significance to the history of the French homeland. Paris's thoughts, entitled "The *Song of Roland* and French Nationality," were first delivered orally from his post at the Collège de France in December of 1870; Gautier's much longer, 200-page "History of a National Poem"—coincidentally dated the same day as Paris's lecture—would constitute the introduction to his hugely successful 1872 deluxe edition of the poem. Despite this disproportionality in length, Paris's political and social reflections constitute the less polemical of the two treatments.

After opening with a plea for dispassionate scientific inquiry, Paris presents the central thread of his thoughts, namely a distinction drawn between empire and nation, the first (Rome's, Napoleon's) being a coldly artificial political construct held together by force and prone to sudden disintegration, the second (the Celts, the Germans, the Poles, the French, and so on) being a warmly organic entity traversed by strongly affective bonds. The *Song of Roland*, asserts Paris, was composed at a self-reflexive moment when the French nation, newly formed from a fusion of Frankish and Gallo-Roman subgroups, paused to take stock of itself. As such the poem lends itself to a political analysis that can offer a ray of compensatory hope against the darkness of the moment. The universal sine qua non of nationhood being for Paris the love of homeland, he finds a profound sentiment of national unity to be everywhere evident in the *Roland* and encapsulated in particular in the "divine expression" that is "douce France." This term, he maintains, is envied by the Germans, who are incapable of locating anything similar in their own national poetry (*"Chanson"* 108).

Declaring literature to be the most durable repository of national identity, Paris concludes that French readers returning to the *Roland* can find much in their beloved epic to inspire them with pride and hope. For one thing, the poem illustrates France's age-old dual strengths of unshakable unity and messianic cultural preeminence (early conversion to Christianity and early embrace of the Charlemagne legend, to name two manifestations). To those who lend an ear, however, it also whispers an almost oracular formula for robust national identity: pride in land, sense of national honor, and love of national institutions. Only on this last score does the France of 1870 fall short, Paris declares, hinting at the recent collapse of the Second Empire, but through a conscientious return to full appreciation of its medieval heritage the country can repair the damage and ensure that Frenchmen make themselves known as "the sons of those who died at Rencesvals and of those who avenged them" (*"Chanson"* 118).[2]

If Paris emphasized pride, Gautier gravitated toward prejudice. Although aimed in part at specialist readers, attested by the ample footnotes, his lengthy introduction often lapses into an almost conversational style and contains numerous populist asides. At one point Gautier even harangues any Germans he imagines to be in earshot with a startling apostrophe conforming to the "we were civilized when you were still forest savages" topos. Naturally, the *Roland* is offered as the primary evidence of the legitimacy of the assertion. The by-now commonplace synechdoche whereby hero embodies homeland ("Roland is France personified") is, moreover, put to propagandistic ends in a remarkable paragraph where Gautier unfavorably compares soulless German militarism to the bellicose ideals vaunted by the *Roland*. Turning the ghastly machinery of modern belligerence against itself, Gautier imagines a macabre and ludicrous juxtaposition between the purest exemplar of human courage and the reality of a nineteenth-century industrial warfare initiated by Germany. Roland, he writes,

> would today have no chance of prevailing, nor even of dying heroically. Courage has been abolished and replaced with science: war is waged chemically. . . . Roland, before our huge canons, would die basely, exactly like a coward. Take me back to the eleventh century, take me back to my French epic of yore.          (*Chanson* [1872] lxxvii–lxxviii)[3]

This passage is striking not merely because it adds the *Roland* to the ample list of works in which moderns have long sought chivalric escapism or because it celebrates what one critic has called the "expression of the French genius for doomed gallantry" (Taylor, "Was There" 35) but also because it makes the *Roland* ethos speak to specific concerns of a particular time and place in ways that suggest that the ultimate affront to a Roland-France adept at lyrically beautiful heroism in the face of overwhelming odds is to be ignominiously gunned down by a mortally prosaic Prussian killing machine.

Gautier's faith in the *Roland*'s exemplary and moral value ("it inspires love of France," he wrote)[4] made him into the preeminent lobbyist for inclusion of the work in school curricula, and it was in no small measure thanks to his efforts that the work began to appear on secondary school reading lists in 1880 (it had been added to the program of the state *agrégation* exam for teachers in 1877). Since the late 1830s school manuals had made brief mention of Roland's death as recounted by the historical chronicles, but instruction in the history of France was not obligatory at the primary level until 1867 (Amalvi 92). It was really only after Gautier's 1872 edition and translation that the preeminent literary account of the battle was readily available. Suddenly, in the wake of a spectacular defeat that saw the capture of the head of government, Napoléon III, and the traitorous surrender of a key defender of the country—François Bazaine—the *Roland* promised a wealth of salutary lessons for the young people, who, as one pedagogue put it, "today represent the hope of the fatherland and who, tomorrow, will constitute its force" (Bouchor 3).[5] These lessons encouraged students to love their country the way Roland's valiant and loyal comrades in arms did, not to be discouraged by the treacheries of the Ganelons of the world, and to plot and exact their revenge. These last two lessons were, to be sure, rarely stated explicitly, but the conclusion was doubtless hard to escape in the decades of a generalized thirst for vengeance following the defeat of 1870.

It would be an oversimplification, however, to characterize the *Roland* as having served only to foment jingoism over Alsace-Lorraine and to fuel interminable Franco-German squabbles. Some educators, in fact, used the pedagogical problems presented by the work's harshness as a springboard for introspective social commentary. In the introduction to his 1899 verse translation of the work, destined for use mainly in secondary schools, Maurice Bouchor frankly admitted the dubious edificatory value of such plot elements as judicially administered torture and forced religious conversions. Rather than doctor the text's depiction of the fate of Ganelon or, as a Protestant editor had previously done, censor the violent conversion of the Saracens, Bouchor, a popular poet, chose to indict his own day as hardly less prone to intolerance and barbarity. Evoking the recent flare-ups of anti-Semitism in the ongoing Dreyfus Affair, he wrote:

In the year of grace 1898 shouts of "Death to Jews!" were heard in the streets of Paris as well as Algiers, and scenes of savagery were witnessed. Whatever the causes of these aberrations, they revealed a fanaticism every bit as despicable as that of the barbarous ages.

(Bouchor 13n3)

Not just in religious but also in racial terms, Bouchor's colonialist contemporaries were equally unjustified in claiming to judge the convictions—"naive" yet "sincere," Bouchor wrote—of the their medieval ancestors:

We no longer force pagans to choose between baptism and death; in fact, we hardly speak of pagans at all anymore. But we believe in "inferior races" and we do not hesitate to impose our domination on them as often as we can. By what right? Daring not to speak of the right conveyed by might, we invoke the right of the more civilized.

(Bouchor 13–14)[7]

Nonetheless, as France drew near another epic clash with Germany in 1914, it was none of these lofty sentiments that prevailed. Rather, the pedagogical establishment valued the *Roland* for its depiction of a tightly knit Germanic *comitatus*, a social model deemed useful and applicable to a modern nation-state. It has even been suggested that so successful was this inculcation of Rolandian virtues in the latter-day chivalric warrior class that a fight-to-the-death mentality was nearly disastrous for France in World War I battles in which a more level-headed concern for logistics and even retreat, if necessary, would have been preferable (Benton 245).

As for the internal history of *Roland* reception I evoked above, the heart of the issue resides in a *Roland* peculiarity: unlike England's *Beowulf* or Spain's *El Cid*, the French national epic survives in multiple manuscript redactions that admit of comparative and even reconstructive editing techniques. Although overt nationalism rarely surfaced in *Roland* editorial work, it is undeniable that it was German innovations—and a specifically German scientific idealism in particular—that drove progress in the field for fifty years, beginning in the 1860s. Systematic recourse to non-Oxford manuscripts, for example, was pioneered by Theodor Müller in his 1863 edition, and nine years later Édouard Boehmer would be the first editor to recast the Oxford manuscript's Anglo-Norman forms and grammatical idiosyncrasies into an idealized and "pure" Continental French. Both Gaston Paris's popular volume of grammatically regularized *Roland* extracts, first published in 1887, and T. Atkinson Jenkins's full-length 1924 edition, reprinted in 1977, would follow Boehmer's editorial lead.

Common to these approaches was a model of manuscript classification that privileged the Oxford *Roland* version over its half-dozen competitors on aesthetic and formal grounds, making relatively limited and localized modifications to it. Beginning in the 1870s, however, a considerably more controversial form of textual intervention was adopted by German philologists, who, in the name of scientific objectivity and editorial empiricism, attempted to reconstruct the putative source text of the admittedly flawed Oxford *Roland* manuscript. In so doing, they set numerous later redactions on equal footing with the earliest one. Making humanistic concerns for literary value subservient to linguistic laws and to anachronistic notions of grammatical regularity, Edmund Stengel published a *Roland* text in 1900 that, to the horror of literary critics, "improved" on the Oxford manuscript not just by rearranging verses and laisses but also by weighing down its spare verbal frame with five thousand extraneous words gleaned from the more prolix later Continental redactions. Such exercises in philological restoration would meet sustained rebuttal by critics such as Frederick Bliss Luquiens and especially Joseph Bédier, who devoted the final work of his career ("Édition") to defending an extremely Oxfordcentric model of *Roland* editing.

This reception narrative, substantial portions of which have been recounted in detail by Christian Amalvi, R. Howard Bloch ("First Document"), and Joseph J. Duggan ("Franco-German Conflict"), among others, is likely to appeal to students' natural curiosity for historical contextualization, whether modern or medieval. Happily, the specifically Franco-German tensions that serve as leitmotif here have become quaintly outmoded, but the more fundamental question of the power and appeal of a work that speaks to a nation's sense of self is of timeless relevance. On this score, the *Roland* can serve as springboard to many more broadly ranging discussions about mythologizing and national identity.

NOTES

[1]"[i]l est national pour les Français autant que l'étaient pour les Grecs les événements de la guerre de Troie." All translations are mine unless otherwise noted.

[2]"les fils de ceux qui sont morts à Roncevaux et de ceux qui les out vengés"

[3]"Roland, d'ailleurs, n'aurait aucune chance aujourd'hui de vaincre, ni même de mourir héroïquement. On a supprimé le courage, qu'on a remplacé par la science: la guerre se fait chimiquement. . . . Roland, devant nos gros canons, mourrait vulgairement et tout comme un lâche. Ramenez-moi au XI$^e$ siècle, ramenez-moi à ma vieille Épopée française."

[4]"[e]lle fait aimer la France" (vi [1887])

[5]"qui sont aujourd'hui l'espérance de la patrie et qui, demain, seront sa force"

[6]"En l'an de grâce 1898, on a entendu crier *Mort au Juifs!* dans les rues de Paris aussi bien que dans les rues d'Alger. Des scènes de sauvagerie ont eu lieu. Quelles que fussent les causes de cet égarement, il révélait un fanatisme aussi odieux que celui des âges barbares,"

[7]"Nous ne contraignons plus les païens à choisir entre le baptême et la mort; même, nous ne parlons plus guère de païens; mais il y a, pour nous, des 'races inférieures,' et nous n'hésitons pas à leur imposer notre domination, toutes les fois que cela nous est possible. De quel droit? Nous n'oserions pas invoquer le droit du plus fort; nous alléguons le droit du plus civilisé." Also quoted in Amalvi 104.

## APPENDIX
### Study and Discussion Questions for the Tradition
### of the Song of Roland in Nineteenth-Century France

1. Does the national mythology of your native country include a bellicose hero seen to embody the nation or national character? If so, in what social context did this person first become widely known? How has appreciation of this character been influenced by periods of crisis or rapid social change?
2. Make a list of battles that mark important moments in the history of a given nation (such as Hastings, Agincourt, Gettysburg, Little Big Horn, Kosovo, or Thermopylae). How many narrative accounts of these events are you aware of? How do victors represent events in ways different from those of the losing side? (On these issues see Rosenberg.)
3. Do figures doomed to catastrophic failure or certain death (such as John Brown, General Custer, Nathan Hale, D-Day soldiers) claim a specific category of meaning in the American national consciousness?
4. It is sometimes said that the Song of Roland is to the French national mythmaking what the Western film genre is to American self-understanding. How might this be true?
5. Research the history of the composition of the painting depicting George Washington crossing the Delaware River (see, for example, Groseclose). To what ideological use did the painter intend to put the work, and how has its subsequent meaning evolved over time? What parallels or divergences do you see with the history of French appreciation of the Song of Roland?

# The *Song of Roland* and England

## *Ian Short*

Given the age-old and perennial animosity between France and its neighbor across the Channel (the French and the English have always been "the best of enemies"), it is ironic that the French national epic should have come to be known, at least among scholars, as the Oxford *Song of Roland*. This geographic reference is, in the first place, to the British university city whose venerable library, the Bodleian, currently houses its sole surviving text. It serves also to remind us, in the second place, that Britain was actually the cradle of this particular version of the epic, since the poem owes its very survival to an Insular (Anglo-Norman) scribe who copied it into a modest, not to say downright shabby, manuscript there. This he did sometime in the course of the twelfth century, some think toward 1130, others toward 1170. The manuscript has almost certainly remained in Britain ever since. While the likelihood is that the poem itself originates from the Continent, no other copy of this particular version has come down to us, thus giving the Oxford text the status of a truly unique literary artifact.

The Oxford *Roland* manuscript, Oxford, Bodleian Library MS Digby 23, is today bound with what seems an incongruous bedfellow, a twelfth-century Latin translation of Plato's cosmological treatise *Timæus*. Attached to *Timæus* is the name of its thirteenth-century owner, one Master Henri de Langley, a canon who between 1246 and 1268 held land from the king in Oxfordshire and Shropshire and who bequeathed his book to the Augustinian abbey of Oseney in Oxford. It is extremely doubtful whether at this stage the *Roland* manuscript already formed part of the same book as *Timæus*. By 1622, however, the two texts were already one book and belonged to the library of

Thomas Allen (died 1632), who passed it on to Kenelm Digby, who in his turn presented it to the Bodleian Library in 1634. The Oxford *Roland* next surfaces in 1775 when the Anglo-Saxon scholar Thomas Tyrwhitt saw and identified it, and then again in 1817 when the British Chaucerian John Conybeare announced a study of it that was never to appear. An immigrant refugee from the French Revolution, Gervais de la Rue, studied it in more detail in his *Essais historiques* of 1834, but it had to wait another three years before reaching a wider public and finally being published. Francisque Michel, a young cultural envoy from the French Ministry of Education, came to Oxford in 1835 for this purpose, and the first ever edition of the Oxford *Song of Roland* appeared under his name two years later in Paris.

Michel had been sent to reclaim an important and emblematic part of his country's cultural heritage. He had come, as a latter-day Continental scribe, to make a copy of a poem of truly outstanding literary quality that, seven hundred years earlier, had crossed the Channel in the same direction and been saved for posterity by the intervention of a not very skillful Anglo-Norman copyist. In so doing, Michel contributed, along with the Abbé de la Rue, to inaugurating Anglo-Norman studies and a scholarly tradition of Anglo-French cooperation and shared endeavor that continues in amity and mutual respect to this day.

Unique it may be as a literary object, but the Oxford *Roland* manuscript is not unparalleled, since there are other medieval French epics that owe their existence today to Insular rather than Continental copyists. Such a state of affairs is not altogether surprising to anyone familiar with the corpus of manuscripts written in the French vernacular during the twelfth century, since, for reasons that remain to be elucidated, an unusually large percentage of these are of Insular, rather than of Continental, origin. Nor is the fact that French was being used at this time in England particularly unexpected for anyone who knows that, in the wake of the conquest of England by William, duke of Normandy, in 1066, the Anglo-Norman dialect of medieval French had become both the vernacular and the written language (together with Latin) of the country's ruling baronial elite. English, of course, remained the majority mother tongue of the common people, but their lack of access to literacy and a dearth of English-speaking literary patrons meant that, in terms of written survival, their language suffered a temporary eclipse.

Little or nothing is known of the early development of Insular French (Anglo-Norman), and we are forced to fall back on conjecture and hypothesis in an attempt to fill the gaps in our knowledge. Although the invasion of England in 1066 is commonly referred to as the Norman Conquest, the colonizers did not in fact form a particularly homogeneous social group. The Norman army actually comprised significant contingents of Bretons as well as of Flemings, but since Anglo-Norman is not in any sense a hybrid dialect, it is to be assumed that its sociolinguistic core, as it were, resided within the immediate environment of the ducal court. William's principal residence in the 1060s, and the effective seat of an essentially itinerant government, had been Caen. Lower Normandy was also where the estates of the principal ducal vassals were situated, and after the conquest the fifteen or so most powerful magnates recorded in the Domesday survey as immediate tenants of the king in England were, with two exceptions, all Normans whose Continental lands lay within this same geographic area. There seems, moreover, to be significant correlation between the present-day dialects of the Lower Normandy region and Anglo-Norman.

Although it leaves its first written traces in some of the spellings of the Domesday Book in 1086, Anglo-Norman becomes a tangible reality only in the first third of the twelfth century at the hands of the earliest Insular French poets Benedeit, Philippe de Thaon, and Geffrei Gaimar. From their texts it is clear that Insular French, at least in its literary mode, already possessed a number of dialectal characteristics that contributed to differentiating it from its Continental (Norman) counterpart. Distinctive among such features was the tendency to interchange the sounds /y/ and /u/ (*fut* and *fout*, to take one notorious example), to allow rhymes such as that between *enseigner* and *peiner*, and the sporadic assimilation of lexical items from English.

When dialectal features appear in a particular poet's rhyme words, philologists feel justified in assuming that they belong to the deeper linguistic level of the author's phonetic bedrock. They draw a distinction between this and the more superficial layer of a text's orthography (spelling system) that they see as being attributable to the latest in a long line of different scribes through whose hands the work has passed. The theory is that, although a scribe copying someone else's poem might well, in some semiautomatic way, rewrite it in his own regional spelling system, he is unlikely to extend this intervention to adapting into his own dialect forms originally selected by the poet to rhyme in a different dialect. It is the absence from the Oxford *Roland* of any of the specifically Insular rhymes found in (admittedly later) Anglo-Norman literature that invites the conclusion that, though it has clearly been copied according to Anglo-Norman scribal conventions, the poem was not originally composed in that dialect.

If, however, the Oxford *Roland*'s composition falls within the eleventh century and predates the dialectal separation of Continental and Insular Norman, it could just as well have originated from either country. Dating it, however, is no easy task. It seems more than likely that the Oxford *Roland* in its present form was composed after 1066, since it is not difficult to read William the Conqueror between its lines. Charlemagne, we are told (lines 372–73), crossed the sea and conquered England, holding it by personal tenure and establishing there the so-called Peter's Pence payment to Rome, while Roland boasts (2331–32) of having added Scotland and Ireland also to the emperor's English territory. That an earlier, pre-Conquest version of the *Roland* existed, however, is suggested by William of Malmesbury, Henry of Huntingdon, Gaimar, Wace, and Benoît de Sainte-Maure, all of whom talk about the Norman troops advancing at Hastings singing a song about Roland (see W. Sayers). The most persuasive internal evidence for dating the present Oxford version is what appears to be an allusion, in line 2503, to the finding of the Holy Lance at Antioch in 1098, but this can, of course, be interpreted in a variety of ways.

The relation between language and identity is a complex one, but the status of Anglo-Norman as the idiolect of a politically powerful minority in the multilingual Britain of the twelfth century means that it must have served first and foremost as a means of expressing a sense of belonging to an elite stratum of society (less than one percent of the total population, it is estimated) and of indicating separate ethnicity and group identity. This is one of the reasons, incidentally, for the dialect's remarkable longevity and the fact that it far outlived its natural lifespan by being artificially preserved through to the fifteenth century and even beyond. In the 1140s, however, the incomers' descendants were already referring to themselves as English, and by the same date—at the very latest—most would have been bilingual. In the twelfth century, their imported French was used not only as a vernacular but also as the vehicle for a diverse, flourishing, and, above all, innovative literature. However one might explain the four decades of literary silence between the Conquest and the accession of Henry I in 1100, Anglo-Norman literature, when it does get under way, immediately lays claim to an impressive series of precocious developments vis-à-vis the Continent: the earliest appearance in French literature of the rhymed chronicle (Gaimar), of eyewitness historiography (Jordan Fantosme), of the Celtic-inspired narrative (Benedeit), of scientific (Philippe de Thaon) and scholastic (Sanson de Nantuil) texts, of biblical and administrative prose, of monastic rules, the earliest named patrons of literature, and the first women writers. While romance as a literary genre is well represented (*Horn, Haveloc*, Thomas's *Tristan*, Thomas of Kent's *Alexander*, and *Ipomedon* and *Protheselaus*, by Hue de Rotelande), epic literature constitutes a special and somewhat anomalous category.

That French language chansons de geste were known and appreciated in Insular circles is made clear not so much by their production by Anglo-Norman poets as by their textual transmission by Anglo-Norman scribes. In addition to the copying of the Oxford *Song of Roland*, the sole surviving texts of the *Pèlerinage* (or *Voyage*) *de Charlemagne*, of the *Chanson de Guillaume*, and of *Gormont et Isembart* are the handiwork of Insular scribes, whose isolated copies of them prove to have saved these twelfth-century epic poems from oblivion. But there is no evidence that any of these texts were actually composed in Britain. Even if it were true, as has been argued, that an Anglo-Norman redactor was responsible for part of the *Chanson de Guillaume*, neither the extent of the supposed intervention nor the evidence adduced to substantiate it is sufficient to warrant calling the text an Anglo-Norman epic. The first, indeed the only, Anglo-Norman epic belongs to the middle of the thirteenth century at the earliest and consists of no more than a continuation of the Continental *Destruction de Rome*, which was conceived as an introduction to the *Chanson de Fierabras*.

Among the explanations that have been advanced to explain the curious phenomenon of Anglo-Norman manuscript preservation, the hypothesis of Insular literary conservatism has enjoyed a particularly long critical life. According to this much-repeated and questionable theory, the peripheral geographic position of Britain (peripheral, one supposes, in relation to Paris, though Paris had little or no literary importance before the closing years of the twelfth century) resulted in archaic taste in Insular circles and the preservation there of old-fashioned and out-of-date versions of Continental texts. To explain the preservation of medieval France's oldest chanson de geste in England, it is not, however, necessary to resurrect the peripheral conservatism hypothesis. The well-documented precocity and inventiveness of twelfth-century Anglo-Norman literature would argue, if anything, in the opposite direction. That other early chansons de geste, *Gormont et Isembart*, the *Pèlerinage de Charlemagne* and the *Chanson de Guillaume*, also happen to survive in isolated Insular copies might just as well indicate that twelfth-century Britain was a particularly safe haven of conservation for highly valued epic as well as other manuscripts, and not some archaic backwater out of the mainstream of Continental literary production and a depository for outdated texts.

This does not, however, explain why the epic is so exceptionally underrepresented in Anglo-Norman literary production. Answers to this are likely to be found either at the level of transmission and preservation or at the initial level of composition. It is entirely possible, in other words, that the vagaries of manuscript survival or accidental manuscript loss mean that this particular genre simply failed to survive in anything like the numbers that would have been expected. More popular in its appeal, and more integrated into the oral tradition, than the exclusively written romance, the epic might well also have circulated in less durable forms and in more vulnerable copies. However, the relatively large number of epic texts recorded as having found refuge in English monastic libraries does not particularly argue in favor of such an explanation.

When the problem is reformulated and shifted onto the production level, and if we make the initial assumption that few or no French epics were ever composed in Insular circles, the issues at once become more complex. Why were the social and literary considerations governing epic production in medieval France not applicable to Anglo-Norman Britain? Of the hundred or so extant chansons de geste, almost all are thematically associated, in one way or another, with what today we would call French national politics, more specifically with feudal and dynastic questions involving France's monarchy or its Carolingian past. In other words, as popular historiography the epic poetry of France had a more or less exclusive Continental focus, and this would not, without radical modification, necessarily appeal to and hold the interest of an

Insular public. Although French epics were, of course, sometimes copied for Insular consumption, and though the narratives of Thomas of Kent, for example, or Jordan Fantosme or the *Horn* poet show their authors' familiarity with and mastery of French epic discourse, Anglo-Norman literature seemed to be able to do without an epic of its own. This naturally does not mean that Insular poets had no interest in or avoided such themes as heroism and honor, baronial aspiration, genealogical legitimation, or dynastic disputes, but when it came to treating such subjects, they had no need or motivation to copy Continental models. Instead they were able to turn to their own romance, which, unlike its Continental counterpart, was a broad and flexible enough category to embrace a wide variety of literary as well as political subject matter. The *Romance of Horn*, for example, manages to accommodate, within its adventure-quest structure, not only heroism, exile and return, genealogy, folklore, territorial conquest, and warfare but the obligatory love interest as well. Anglo-Norman literature did not, in other words, have an epic genre for the simple reason that it did not need one: its Insular romance functioned also as an epic.

Anglo-Norman literature does, however, boast—to summarize—the oldest copy not only of the *Song of Roland* but also of other chansons de geste belonging to the first age of French epic production. All are Insular copies in that they share a number of spelling conventions, such as *tut* for what in Continental French would be *tot*, *flur* for *fleur*, *cevaler* for *chevalier*, *camp* for *champ*, *unkes* for *onques*, and so forth, but none can be shown actually to be Insular compositions—which is not, of course, to say that the *Roland* survived in Britain only in a single copy. There can be no doubt that a (rather than the) *Song of Roland* was widely known in twelfth-century Britain. The Welsh *Cân Rolant* looks as if it goes back to an Anglo-Norman copy, while Pfaffe Konrad's Middle High German *Ruolandes Liet* may well have owed its existence ultimately to Henry II's eldest daughter Matilda. In Insular literature, contemporary writers repeatedly use similes involving Rencesvals, Roland, and Oliver, and in secular society parents can be found giving the baptismal names Roland and Oliver to their sons. The English monarchy, however, was never to set its seal of approval on the name of Roland in the same way as Henry II's son Geoffrey, and Henry VIII did by choosing Arthur as a fitting baptismal name for their sons and heirs. A glorious hero of medieval France he might have been, but for the British Roland was never anything more than a distinguished visitor to their shores.

# Translating the *Song of Roland* into English

## Patricia Terry

As their work progresses, translators become increasingly aware of how much a literary text is attached to its own language. There is pleasure in this, but also deep frustration. We would like to think that students could be invited to read our work as if it were the original, but translators know better than anyone else how far this is from the truth. So instructors cannot simply rely on a translation but must try to bridge the gap between it and the original. The purpose of this chapter is to offer some suggestions for doing so in teaching an English version of the *Song of Roland*. I will be giving examples of the work of four translators, including myself, to show a variety of legitimate, and sometimes idiosyncratic, approaches.[1]

The English-speaking translator of this poem starts with one encouraging advantage: in sound and accentuation Old French is closer to English than it is to modern French, with its smoother rhythm and gentler tonalities. But if students are given an opportunity to listen to a reading of the *Song of Roland* in the original, they will inevitably be struck by a dramatic quality that even the most emphatic English cannot provide (the CD accompanying this volume can be used, for example). The strong consonants of Old French make the individual words stand out, and every line functions as an isolated element. Each stanza, called a laisse, forms a discrete dramatic unit, set apart by its content and also by assonance. Working against these staccato elements is a hypnotic, drumlike rhythm. While the paratactic lines, and the laisses, segment the drama, bringing into focus one aspect at a time, the ground bass of the rhythm never stops its forward march.

It might seem that the ten-syllable lines of the *Song of Roland* could readily be reproduced in English, but that ease is deceptive. For readers accustomed to poetry in English, decasyllabic lines might look like iambic pentameter. This latter meter is capable of an immense variety of effects, but something stiffer and more primitive is required to reproduce the Old French epic meter, which is characterized by a marked caesura after the fourth, occasionally the sixth, syllable and a stress on the tenth. In addition to these two fixed accents, there will usually be two, variably placed, secondary ones.

> Ne plácet *Deu* ne ses séinz ne ses *angles*
> Que já pur *mei* pérdet sa valúr *France*!
> Mélz voeill murir qu'a húntage remaigne.
> Pur bén ferir l'emperére nos *aimet*.   (Segre [1989] 1089–92)

In contrast, iambic pentameter will have five variously accented syllables and no fixed caesura. Without a particular stress on the last syllable, the lines will tend to flow into each other. A short passage from *Henry the Fifth* will illustrate the English ten-syllable line:

> If we are mark'd to die, we are enow
> To do our country loss, and if to live,
> The fewer men, the greater share of honor.
> God's will! I pray thee wish not one man more.    (4.3.20–23)

A translator, seeking an equivalent for the Old French epic meter, will want to make sure that the fourth or sixth syllable of each line is stressed. However, unless that syllable can be followed by a comma, the emphasis may not be noticed by the reader. In an attempt to make the stress more apparent, I introduced an actual space:

> Tell me the way    Count Roland can be killed.    (581)

This is a very typical example. Although the sense of the line suggests emphasis on "way," if it were printed without a space:

> Tell me the way Count Roland can be killed,

the word "way" is unlikely to receive a primary accent, and the line would tend to have five beats rather than four as in Old French.

The translator must also find an equivalent for the laisses, each one unified by assonance, that is, each line ending in the same vowel sound. Most modern translators have decided that to reproduce the assonance in English requires too much distortion of the syntax. But abandoning assonance weakens the sense of drama, since each laisse is isolated from the next not only by its particular line endings but also by a resounding conclusion. Sometimes the mysterious letters *AOI*, which fortunately need no translation, add further emphasis. To approximate these effects, I tried to end each line with an accented syllable. I also set a rhymed couplet at the end of each laisse, again, like the interpolated space, a solution that substitutes an English device for the actual practice of the French poet.

The translator may attempt to reproduce something of the poetic quality of the text or aspire, as does Glyn S. Burgess, simply to be both accurate and readable (*Song* 27). In either case, the instructor will need to convey what is inevitably missing: the excitement that is inseparable from the actual Old French words, the accumulating momentum of the poem.

The *Song of Roland* is concerned primarily with events. Its syntax is unadorned, so that the slightest departures from plain English word order seem inappropriate. The vocabulary of the poem is also resolutely simple, urging the translator to avoid overly sophisticated words. For example, in his address to the French just before the battle begins, Roland is said to look at the

Saracens *fierement*, ("fiercely"; 1162), and then his gaze at his own men is described as *humeles* (1163). I agree with Gerard J. Brault that humility cannot be the stance of a war leader; *humeles* indicates rather Roland's appreciative connection to his men (Song 1: 186). However, under the circumstances, Brault's "amicably" seems rather understated. After much consideration, I translated *humeles* as "respectfully." I think that the meaning is accurate, but now the word strikes me as somehow too modern, perhaps a bit overdone. A work of literature can be finished, a translation never!

Instructors should remember that phrases that seem very expressive to an experienced reader may seem dull to someone encountering them for the first time. The celebrated description of the pass at Rencesvals simply says that the mountains were high and the valleys dark. The only color mentioned is a grey-brown:

> Halt sunt li pui e li val tenebrus,
> Les roches bises, les destreiz merveillus.   (814–15)

Variants of these lines recur later in the poem: when Charles is returning to Rencesvals, when Roland is close to death. The words, plain as they are, have a symbolic resonance. The idea of high places to be conquered occurs in the very first laisse, Saragossa on its mountain. *Tenebrus* evokes not simply darkness, but dangers concealed in the shadows. (Other than in a repetition of the line quoted, *tenebrus* occurs only once more in the poem: Roland's eyes, when Charles finds his body, are *tenebrus* [2896].) The consonants in *roches bises* are harsh, the color dull and unwelcoming. *Destreiz* are not simply narrow places; the word also means "hardship," "stress," "pressure." *Merveillus* means wondrous, awesome, and also terrible. The translator, trying to choose words from which these implications can emanate, constantly risks being either too prosaic or making too overt an appeal to the reader's emotions. Students may like to compare the following examples:

> High are the hills and the valleys dark,
> The rocks dull-hued, the defiles filled with horror.   (Burgess)

> The mountains are high and the valleys are shadowy,
> The rocks dark, the defiles frightening.   (Brault)

> High are the hills, the valleys tenebrous,
> the cliffs are dark, the defiles mysterious.   (Goldin)

> High are the hills,   the valleys shadowy,
> The cliffs rise grey,   the narrow ways hold fear.   (Terry)

Sometimes the coincidence of intensity and simplicity is caused by the way the significant words fall so perfectly in the line. After Charles, with the help of a miracle, has pursued the victorious pagans to their destruction, he finds himself "en Rencesvals, la o fut la bataille" (2854).

The balance of that line cannot be reproduced in English, if only because "battle" ends in an unaccented syllable. (The mute *e* of *bataille* is not counted and simply prolongs the diphthong.) The words *la* ("there") and *o* ("where") have the same meaning as their English equivalents, but the shorter words do not detract from the strength of the two nouns. *Was* is weaker then *fut*; the French verb pinpoints an event in past time, which *was* does not. *Fut* is thus more emphatic in meaning as well as sound. The following examples will show a variety of attempts to deal with these considerations:

> "At Rencesvals, where the battle took place." (Burgess)
>
> "at Rencesvals, where the great battle was." (Goldin)
>
> "There where the battle    was fought at Roncevaux." (Terry)

Although these translations differ from one another, the sense of line 2854 is the same in all versions. In another example of a perfectly balanced line, the famous "Rollant est proz e Oliver est sage" (1093), the word *proz* has a wide range of meaning, including, in some contexts, *wise*. *Proz* can also refer to valor or simply to worthiness. Translators will inevitably be influenced by whether they think that wisdom, religious fervor, an extreme sense of feudal obligation, or personal pride motivates Roland's decision not to ask for Charles's help in fighting the multitude of Saracens. Although *proz* and *sage* seem to offer a contrast between Roland and Oliver, the next line unites them as examples of surpassing courage. Brault translates *proz* as "worthy"; Goldin uses "good," which suggests that Roland's most fundamental characteristic is his virtue; Burgess writes "brave," which is appropriate but is also characteristic of Oliver, and indeed of all the Franks. To make a more emphatic statement of the difference between Roland's *proz-dom* and Oliver's wisdom, I refer to him as a hero. All these translations suggest a point of view. Goldin's is made explicit in his introduction: "An epic necessity . . . bestows dignity on men and events, for it removes them from the vanity of a personal will, and identifies them with a divine intention" (17).

It could be argued that *proz* should be translated the same way in every case, although I have seen no English translation that does so. The circumstances in which the word appears suggest various nuances of worthiness, but the meaning of the poem, however one understands it, would not be changed if they were all subsumed under "worthy" or "brave."

No single translation will accurately render the omnipresent word *pur*, although most of the time its meaning is simply "for," as in *pur son seigneur.* But T. Atkinson Jenkins, in his glossary, lists nine meanings that "for" can express, the most important of which is "because of," occurring in fifteen lines (356). Line 1090 offers a very clear example of this meaning: *Que ja pur mei perdet sa valur France!* ("That France should ever lose its fame because of me"; Burgess) Here there is no possibility that *pur* could mean either "for me" or "for my sake."

In laisse 140, Roland weeps for the Franks who have died and praises them. He recognizes that he cannot protect the few left alive and feels that he has failed their trust. However, if *pur mei vos vei morir* (1863) is translated "for me" or "for my sake," it suggests that the Franks are dying for a cause that is merely personal. In my reading of the poem, this would be either presumptuous or incorrect. "Because of me" admits that Roland is responsible but leaves room for the interpretation that he could not have done otherwise than he did.

*Pur* is also used in elliptical phrases often difficult to translate with similar brevity. *Ja pur murir ne vus en faldrat uns* (1048) means "Not one of us will fail you for fear of death" (Burgess). *Pur vasselage suleie estre tun drut* (2049) means "You used to love me, because you knew me brave" (Terry).

A number of Old French monosyllabic words are like exclamation points. *Ja* has several meanings, all less emphatic in English: "just now," "at once," "behold," "indeed" (as in *ja pur murir*). *Ainz* means "rather," "in contrast," but the Old French word is much more energetic than these. *Mar(e)*, which may come from *mala hora,* concisely expresses the idea that something that seemed to be fortunate ultimately was not:

> Li empereres tant mare vos nurrit!   (1860)
>
> The emperor raised you for this terrible hour!   (Goldin)
>
> The king's own household,   alas! brings him to woe.   (Terry)

"Si mare fumes nez," say the pagans: "we were born for such misfortune!" (Brault). When Roland sees Oliver dying, he, for the first time, loses a sense of what to do ("or ne sai jo que face"). And he adds, "Sire cumpainz, mar fut vostre barnage!" ("Was such great valor destined to be cut down!"; 1983; my trans.). Oliver's equal, he says, will never be seen on earth; Oliver's last words before he dies bless his companion, Roland. So, beyond right and wrong, their love for each other prevails.

In the rather laconic language of the poet, occasional adjectives of description acquire a rare intensity; the recurrent *cler* stands out against much darkness. Although it always refers to an aspect of light, *cler* has many different meanings and overtones. It occurs first in line 59 in reference to the Saracen's homeland: *clere Espaigne la bele*; in Brault's translation, "fair Spain, the beautiful." It evokes what the pagans most fear to lose. The parallel expression, *douce France*, "the fair land of France" (Burgess) is somewhat less poignant. Turoldus sometimes portrays the Saracens as more eloquent than the Franks, and always more powerful in numbers. The ultimate victory of the Franks must depend entirely on the rightness of their faith.

One of the most frequent occurrences of *cler* describes blood and is usually translated "bright." Helmets are *cler* ("shiny"). Often the day is *cler*, or the night. The sound of trumpets is *cler*, and the sound of the olifant. A verbal form indicates the horn's effect on the French: *esclairet* ("it sets their hearts on fire"; Goldin). This verb is used similarly in a passage describing the Saracen Margariz of Seville whom ladies loved for his beauty: "Not one of them sees him without becoming all aglow" (Brault). Turoldus must have loved this pagan himself, since Margariz is the only one who does not die on the battlefield. When Charles watches the single combat that will decide the fate of Ganelon, he cries, *E! Deus, . . . le dreit en esclargiez!* (3891). Goldin translates this as "make the right between them clear!" and Brault as "let justice blaze forth!"

The translation of *cler* becomes more subjective when it refers to a face. An emir's face is *fier e cler*: "fierce and open" (Brault), "fierce and fair" (Burgess), "lit up with pride" (Golden), "serene and bold" (Terry). The emir Baligant's face is *mult cler*—"very fair" (Burgess), "very clear" (Brault), "full of light" (Golden), "a brightness in his face" (Terry). Roland's face is *cler*, "radiant," and so is Charles's.

Another reference to light, unique in the poem, is used in praise of Charles and spoken, interestingly, by Ganelon:

> De tel barnage l'ad Deu enluminét,
> Meilz voelt murir que guerpir sun barnét.   (535–36)

> God put the light in him of such lordliness.
> he would choose death before he failed his barons.   (Goldin)

> God has made so much valour shine forth from him,
> That he would rather die than forsake his men.   (Burgess)

> By God's grace, honor   illuminates my lord:
> He'd rather die   than break faith with his court.   (Terry)

The poem is indeed ablaze with light, gleaming on armor, on Charles' sword, Joyeuse, which is brighter than the sun; the clear light of day; the light on the sea as Baligant's ships travel through the night; the radiant faces of warriors. English cannot offer one word for *cler*, which, in the Old French, makes connections between all these occasions. It may, however, suggest the triumph over shadows that is the central theme of the poem.

The *Song of Roland* offers translators an enigma in its last line: *Ci falt la geste que Turoldus declinet*. The poem that Turoldus recites, that he relates, comes to an end—or it comes to an end because Turoldus has no more to tell or because Turoldus has fallen ill. I tried to imitate the frustrating vagueness: "Here ends the poem   for Turoldus declines." Goldin lists many of the possible meanings, ending with: "Here ends the source that Turold turns into poetry." But only in the mind of a translator is "declinet" vague or ambiguous. The final word of the poem, a statement Turoldus is making about himself, must have been carefully chosen. It would surely have had a clear and precise meaning, obvious to him, but, alas, out of our reach.

NOTE

[1]Unless otherwise indicated, quotations from the *Song of Roland* are taken from the translations by Gerard J. Brault, Glyn S. Burgess, Frederick Goldin, and Patricia Terry.

# Orality and Textuality:
# Reading and/or Hearing the *Song of Roland*

## Philip E. Bennett

In the debate that has set individualists and (neo) traditionalists against each other for nearly a century now, both sides have been able to cite abundant evidence from the *Song of Roland* in support of their case. On the one side is the question of the "building blocks" of which the poem is composed: formulas, verses divided into semiautonomous hemistichs, motifs, and themes (Rychner, *Chanson*; Duggan, Song [1973]). On the other are a wealth of allusions and compositional devices that betray a "bookish" education on the part of the *Roland* poet (Chiri; Auerbach; Siciliano). Approaches to analyzing the *Roland* based on presuppositions about the literacy of the poet and his audience have implications for studying and teaching the poem. Before considering those implications, however, we must look closely at the concepts of literacy and illiteracy and their applicability to the society that produced the *Roland* and similar works. It will also be necessary to consider the relation, if any, between a particular mode of composition—oral or written—and the presence in the text of stereotyped units of composition.

The first real problem a modern reader has in approaching the question of literacy in medieval European society is that, with the advent of universal elementary education in the nineteenth century and the assumption that all who had gone successfully through this process of education could read and write, a definition of literacy based on those twin abilities became the norm (Stock, *Listening*). The minimum test in contemporary European society for writing is usually the ability to write and sign one's name, whereas reading has become defined in terms of a "reading age." Those who fail to pass the hurdles set by society are then classed as "backward" (although the judgment is usually dressed up in euphemistic administrative jargon). The consequence of this for studying cultures remote in time or space is that cultures that do not practice literacy in the current Western European manner are considered "primitive," with all the ambivalence that the word contains (Stock, *Listening* 10, 141–44). This was certainly the view of the Romantic traditionalists of the late nineteenth and early twentieth centuries, for whom Old French epic poetry, as the product of an unlettered Germanic or Germano-Celtic folk, was marked by a virile purity untainted by the decadence implicit in the imitation of alien, classical models (Ker). Such views have led to anachronistic accusations of racism, latent or explicit, against Paul Meyer, Gaston Paris, Max Müller, and other scholars of their generation (Ridoux). Another frequent accusation against traditionalists is that formulated by Michel Zink of using the words *people* and *popular* indiscriminately to mean both a national and a social group, so that they are both, either simultaneously or alternately, racist and propounding a class prejudice (*moyen âge*). The natural conclusion for Zink is that there is no such thing as popular literature in the French Middle Ages. Joseph Bédier's reclassification of Old French epic as the product of literate authors, or of nonliterate authors aided by literate clerics (*Légendes*), was partly motivated by a desire to recuperate these poems for a cultural canon defined in terms of high literacy by the classics-based curriculum of late-nineteenth-century universities. The "primitivist" view of epic survived Bédier's attack to reemerge in its purely sociological guise in standard twentieth-century literary histories, in which the chansons de geste were relegated to the status of old-fashioned, nonaristocratic literature once the literate romance had established itself as the fashionable literature of the cultured aristocracy in the last quarter of the twelfth century (Southern, ch. 5). This view of the evolutionary relation between epic and romance has been challenged by Sarah Kay (*Chanson*), whereas the oral nature of twelfth-century romance, including the works of Chrétien de Troyes, has been posited by Evelyn Birg Vitz.

Although it cannot be demonstrated to be part of Bédier's intention in writing *Les légendes épiques*, his notion of a collaboration between jongleurs and clerics does immediately reveal a fundamental flaw in this model of twelfth-century literacy. Until at least the end of the thirteenth century, to be literate meant strictly to have a clerical, Latin education and was divorced from any sense of being able to read or write in the vernacular. This was especially true in communities like France whose mother tongue was a Romance language: communities that spoke a language more remote from Latin (Anglo-Saxon England, the Germanic communities east of the Rhine) had developed a culture of the vernacular book from as early as the ninth century. This certainly had an impact on Anglo-Norman England and may account for why many of the earliest works of French literature—the *Life of Saint Alexis*, Geffrei Gaimar's *History of the English*, the *Song of Roland* itself—were either composed in England or first copied into manuscripts there (for more on French tradition in Britain, see Short, "The *Song of Roland* and England," in this volume). Moreover, those who produced epics, like the audiences for them, lived with an awareness of the importance of the Latin book as a repository of classical, ecclesiastical, and biblical texts.

This awareness of the written word and its high cultural status in the twelfth century is amply demonstrated in the text of the *Roland* itself. Although Ganelon is sent with an oral message to Marsile and given a staff and a glove as tangible symbols of his role as representative of Charlemagne's authority, he is also given a letter bearing the emperor's seal. This may function symbolically like the staff and the glove, and it is unclear from the poem whether anyone reads it (Bennett, "Ganelon's"), but its role in stressing the authoritative nature of the transmitted word is undeniable (Clanchy 245, 307–17; Stock, *Listening* 144–48). The numbers of pagans killed by Roland, Oliver, and Turpin are certified by reference to "charters," "records," and the Frankish Annals in a pair of overmarked lines (1684–85). The Old French word *geste* (translated as "history" or "annals") appears several times in the poem, often spoken by a character to guarantee a reputation or an event; three times it is given a capital letter by editors (lines 1443, 2095, 3262).[1] In the first and last of these lines the word is accompanied by the learned form *Francor* (from Latin *Francorum*), so that the whole formula *Geste Francor* seems to invoke quite unequivocally the official Latin history of the empire. Line 2095 is particularly interesting from the point of view of the interrelation of textuality and literacy in the *Song of Roland*, since the written authority of the annals is supported by the testimony of an eyewitness: "So say the annals and the man who was on the field." Line 2096 reveals that this "man" was actually Saint Giles (died 710 AD), whose words are themselves preserved in a charter—a fully worked-up document—in Laon. Thus is the oral witness also given divine sanction while being retranslated into authoritative text. The most celebrated use of *geste* in the poem occurs of course in line 4002. The interpretation of *geste* here is highly controversial, but the person responsible for the text in the Oxford manuscript seems to want to give the version of Turold the authority of written history. The reverence for the written word, possibly intensified by the fact that to be literate meant having a Latin education, did not mean that most people in the twelfth century owned or read books. Methods of producing books, which were written longhand in a stylized script with many words either abbreviated or represented by the kinds of conventional symbols later associated with shorthand and with the text presented in continuous unpunctuated blocks meant that reading was even more of a specialist skill than it is today. Writing was also not an accomplishment that most aristocrats or wealthy bourgeois would aspire to themselves: it was a menial task imposed on monks as a discipline from the early days of monasticism (Stiennon 87–88, 159–69). Indeed, until the end of the twelfth century almost all books produced in France or in Anglo-Norman England were copied in monasteries, even if by that date the work was done by itinerant laymen working as scribes (Watson), which explains why so few works of vernacular, secular literature survive in manuscripts from that period.

This is, of course, not to say that members of the upper classes could not or did not read or write either in Latin or in the vernacular, although evidence is scanty and indirect. We may, for instance, deduce that the copy of the Saint Albans Psalter prepared for the private devotions of the English noblewoman and anchoress Christina of Markyate in the mid-twelfth century, which contains the *Life of Saint Alexis* in Anglo-Norman French, was written for her personal use and implies her ability to read at least the French text (Pächt, Dodwell, and Wormald). In literature, the scene in *Yvain* by Chrétien de Troyes in which a young woman reads a romance to her family is well known (Kibler, *Arthurian Romances* 362), as is the exchange of letters between Tristan and King Mark in Beroul's *Tristran*, in which Tristan has his letter written by a hermit, and Mark has it read to him by a chaplain at his court (Gregory, lines 2357–620). In a scene that is probably willfully archaizing in the late-thirteenth-century *Roman de silence*, the king of France passes a letter he has received to his chancellor to read, but the letter, a counterfeit substituted for the original by the queen of England, was written by the queen herself, who had good reason not to dictate it to a third party (Roche-Mahdi, lines 4315–416). Returning to the twelfth century and to history, one can also be reasonably confident that the letters of Heloise to Abelard, if they are genuine, with their references to her regretting that Abelard would not let her live with him as his whore, would have been written by her own hand, not dictated to a nun of the Paraclete, of which Heloise was by then abbess. There is certainly no doubt that Heloise could write and also read in several languages (Radice; Pernoud).

Although, as the example from Chrétien shows, most people received literature aurally, it is clear that twelfth-century society was not an illiterate society; indeed no such society had existed in western Europe since before the establishment of the Roman Empire. It was a paraliterate society, one that used books and in which professionals who specialized in reading communicated culture orally to a wider public. The nearest twentieth-century parallel may be the way in which the classics of English literature are conveyed to the widest audience through television series like Masterpiece Theatre or Classics Illustrated comics.

It is this paraliterate cultural situation that probably leads to the rhetorical use by several Old French epic poets of the topos of the found manuscript, which remained a staple of literature well into the nineteenth century as a device for certifying both the authenticity and the autonomy of the story being told. And yet, precisely because of the cultural position of twelfth-century society, we cannot dismiss as purely rhetorical allusions to manuscripts from Saint Denis (e.g., Bateson, lines 11–13; Jacques Thomas, lines 1–10; Le Person, lines 5–6) or, as in the *Roland*, to the Frankish Annals as sources for poems or for episodes within poems, even if we would not give such allusions the weight Bédier wanted to give them for polemical purposes (*Légendes*). By the same token the Old French epic belongs to a culture that in both its Latin and vernacular forms remains fundamentally oral. Not only was literature of all sorts passed on by reading and reciting aloud or, as is regularly indicated in the epic, by singing, but teaching in church and school and knowledge of the law were also essentially oral.

It is therefore not surprising that the *Song of Roland* bears the signs of what has been taken to be orality (Stock, *Listening* 142). It is important to emphasize "what has been taken for orality," because our only knowledge of the poem comes from written sources, most particularly from the manuscripts that have transmitted to us the different versions of the poem. For those who consider the *Song of Roland* to be essentially the product of oral transmission—effectively of oral composition, since the songs will have been re-created from a bare outline of a story at every singing—these manuscripts have been presented as merely accidental transcriptions of individual performances (Rychner, *Chanson* 19–22, 26–36; Calin, "Épopée"; Duggan, "Théorie"; Stock, *Listening* 8, 35). The key to identifying such oral composition in the epic is not just the presence of formulas in the works but a particularly high density of formulas compared with works known—one should really say "assumed"—to have been composed in writing from the beginning (Duggan, *Song* [1973]). This high density of formulas in the text is coupled with a text that varies much more from manuscript to manuscript than is found in courtly romance, for example, so that, although *variance* or *mouvance* have been posited as the essence of medieval literature (Zumthor 18–36; Cerquiglini, *Éloge*), the extremely volatile nature of the epic text has been held as another proof of the recreation of the song by different singers. Now both of these aspects of epic composition have proved controversial. The question of variation has been tackled by Wolfgang van Emden (" 'Bataille' "; *Chanson* 10–13), who has shown that the variants revealed by the manuscripts of Old French epic are qualitatively different from those recorded from singings of Serbo-Croatian epics by Milman Parry, whereas they are only quantitatively different from those of the manuscripts of Chrétien de Troyes. It is, as can be seen from any number of critical editions of Old French epics, just as possible to establish a *stemma codicon* of the *Song of Roland*, *The Coronation of Louis*, or of *Aye d'Avignon* as it is of *The Knight with the Lion* or *The Romance of the Rose*.

That epic poems were sung in the twelfth century is not a matter of doubt, unless we wish to disregard every reference, both internal and external to the poems themselves, to such performances. What must remain a matter of doubt about that period is whether the existence of high densities of formulas, however defined within a chanson de geste, can indicate oral composition. Jean Rychner (*Chanson* 150–53) indicates that the *Song of Roland* in the Oxford version should not be taken as a model of oral composition, because of the sophistication of its compositional structures. One might also point out that the *Roland* is notable for not including those appeals to the audience ("my lords") and the deictic formulas ("see," "hear," etc.) that are so typical of later epics. Since the poem with the highest formula count in Duggan's survey (*Song* [1973]) is the *Prise d'Orange*, which, in the only form in which we can read it, is undoubtedly a written product dating from 1190 at the earliest (Régnier 90), one has to ask if these formulas, like the other motifs investigated by Jean-Pierre Martin (*Motifs*), are not simply marks of epic rhetoric. As Martín de Riquer suggested, the Old French epic seems to have led a double life, both oral and textual, in the later twelfth century, and the example of the Oxford manuscript of the *Song of Roland* leads us to believe that this was true much earlier than that ("Épopée"). Brian Stock's illuminating observation that by the twelfth century "an invisible scripture seemed to lurk behind everything one said" (*Listening* 20) encapsulates very well the dual nature, oral and textual, of the *Roland*.

The very opening line of the poem in the original Old French: "Carles li reis, nostre emperere magnes" ("Charles the king, our emperor, the great"; my trans.) by its use of a tmesis—placing the first part of Charlemagne's name at the start of the line and the last part at the end of it, framing his titles of king and emperor—announces in a way no clerically educated person in his audience could fail to notice the claims of the poet to belong to a tradition of Latin rhetorical composition. The last line of the poem offers a similar co-nundrum, if we make the usual assumptions of those who equate oral com-position and transmission with illiteracy. In the original the line reads, "Ci falt la geste que Turoldus declinet," which Glyn S. Burgess translates as, "Here ends the story which Turoldus relates" (*Song*). Gerard J. Brault offers, "Here ends the story which Turoldus tells" (Song). We have already considered the probable learned connotations of *geste*, and the last word of the line raises similar questions of cultural suppositions. If we ignore the almost jocular interpretation of the line, "the legend runs out here because Turold is sick" (but why should we, since it gives *declinet* its literal meaning?), the most obvious meaning for the word, taken straight from the Latin schoolroom, is the one borrowed from the study of grammar: "recite the parts of a substan-tival paradigm" (Lewis and Short 521; Godefroy 9: 283). The definition "tell a story," given in dictionaries (Tobler and Lommatzsch 2: col. 1257; Godefroy 2: 446), depends entirely on the word's appearance in line 4002 of *Roland*. Given that we can have no idea of the exact relation of "Turoldus" to the poem we have just read, all we can do is note that a good Norse name, Thorhold, has been given a Norman or Anglo-Norman form and tricked out with a Latin ending. The effect of this bounding of the song by complex Latin references and allusions is to invite the reader or listener to treat what has just been presented as text, whatever features from oral traditions of com-position have been deployed.

Taken at face value as part of the traditional technique of oral composition and transmission, the various building blocks of which the poem is constructed may speak to an audience in a variety of ways. Formulas, as well as providing a possible aid to improvised composition, signal to the audience that the poem belongs to a certain genre and mark the poem with a particular singer's "fin-gerprints": because traditional singers as well as authors have their own "style" (Finnegan 6), analysis of formulas always needs to take into account those formulas that are peculiar to the individual song and those that belong to the corpus of poems. Most important, formulas provide a stylized depiction of action and of character, which works by making reference to iconic models instead of by generating realistically individualized people and events (Kay, "Character"). Finally, formulaic composition, combined with paratactic sen-tence structure, contributes to the way in which the audience identifies with the poem's message by generating a hieratic, hymnlike incantation. The motifs, constructed of sequences of laisses, particularly those involving the incremen-tal repetitions of similar and parallel laisses, add to this incantatory effect while providing a pause in which the hearer catches his or her mental breath before the story moves on. Examples include sequences presenting the two scenes in which Roland and Oliver argue about blowing the horn to summon aid or in which the dying Roland tries to break his sword while recalling his exploits. The placing in parallel of council scenes, first in the Saracen camp, then in the Frankish one, like the regular insertion of such set pieces as laments for fallen warriors, with their stylized gestures of stroking or pulling the beard, the literal repetition of messages two or three times, or weeping and fainting by one or more characters provide a ritualized narrative that combines with the smaller units of stereotyped compositions to involve the audience in the celebration of the song's narrative (Uitti 115–27).

Much of this, of course, applies even if we consider the song as text, whether we envisage a poet composing orally or with wax tablet and parchment. This is inevitable, since virtually the whole audience for a song will receive it aurally however it was composed. What may change from our point of view is that we can see the formula as a structuring device. So the regular recurrence of the invocation of the seven years spent by Charles's army in Spain and returning phrases such as "high are the hills" and "what does it matter?" act as refrains characterizing different phases of the song's unfolding. Repetitions involving groups of between three laisses (Blancandrin's conversation with Ganelon about Charles, for example, in laisses 28–30) and ten laisses (the sequence where the Twelve Peers kill their Saracen counterparts: laisses 94–103), like explicit references to seven years spent in Spain, to the Twelve Peers, or to the thirty hostages for Ganelon, take on numerological significance, whether or not we identify them with Christian and Trinitarian interpretations of the text (MacQueen; Uitti, ch. 2). There are also more complex patterns of similar and parallel laisses at the poem's most crucial moments (the "first horn scene" at laisses 82–86; Roland's death scene, laisses 170–75), which may carry particular symbolic weight. Such sequences provide a monumental moment of lyric stasis, in which narration gives way to evocation, rather like a slow-motion sequence in an action film. They also allow reflection on the complexities of a situation and may be taken as a form of narrator's commentary, even though the narrator's voice does not intrude, since the audience is inevitably removed from the forward thrust of the narrative to concentrate on what the poet regards as significant.

There is one final level of which we must always be aware when interpreting an Old French epic such as the *Roland*, whether for ourselves or for our students. We inevitably come to the poem as text, and as a text fixed in its form by print and therefore capable of indefinite reproduction without variation and of being known in that form to different audiences in widely separated areas and times. This was not the experience of medieval audiences, for each of whom there was a different *Song of Roland*, whether we think of it as a literary product known through the manuscript that happened to be available to the audience or as an oral product known through the version of a particular singer. Only in one way does our experience of the *Roland* as text replicate that of the medieval audience, since the view we have of the poem depends in large measure on the edition or translation through which we approach it: reading the poem in the edition by Bédier, T. Atkinson Jenkins, Ian Short, or Cesare Segre will give very different views of the poem, as will approaching it through the translations of Dorothy L. Sayers, Brault, or Burgess, for, as Segre has pointed out, such editions and translations represent only a "working hypothesis" enabling us to get just a little closer to the medieval artifact (Segre, "Corrections" 277).

NOTE

[1]*Geste* is capitalized at line 1443 by Bédier (1921) and Short (1990), and at lines 2095 and 3262 by Bédier (1921), Short (1990), Gautier (1887), and Moignet (1969), although because *geste* is the first word of line 3262, the capital may have a simple typographic explanation.

# Teaching the *Song of Roland* as Oral Poetry: Phonetics and Metrics

*Alice M. Colby-Hall*

I first read the *Song of Roland* many years ago with the help of a facing-page translation in Modern French and was rather disappointed in the text as poetry because it lacked the forcefulness and grandeur I had expected. Later, however, after I had studied the historical phonetics of French and could use the publications of Édouard Bourciez and Jean Bourciez, Pierre Fouché, and Mildred K. Pope to reconstruct the sound system insofar as possible, a whole new chanson de geste emerged. I could now read the text aloud or hear it in my head when reading silently.

The standardized spellings adopted by T. Atkinson Jenkins in his edition of the *Roland* make it relatively easy to devise rules of thumb for pronouncing the words. This edition, however, is now out of print, and most scholars would prefer to give their students a less heavily edited version of the Oxford manuscript, such as the one published by Ian Short. On the CD that accompanies this volume, I have recorded eight selections from this edition (see track listing, in "Materials" section). It will be possible, however, to follow the text by looking at any edition of the Oxford manuscript. (The text of five of the eight selections appears in the appendix to Burgess's translation.) The listener will notice that the sounds do not automatically correspond to the spellings used by the twelfth-century Anglo-Norman scribe, who was copying a text written in northern France. Given the likelihood that the poem was originally composed in Normandy in the late eleventh century, I have opted for the sound system of the western region in that period. Pope provides a concise summary of this system (500–03).

The pronunciation of the words is very important, but so is the rhythm of the verse. The decasyllabic lines of the *Roland* are grouped in stanzas of varying length, usually referred to as laisses. In each line, there is a regular pause called a caesura after the fourth syllable, which is accented. If this fourth syllable is followed in the same word by a syllable containing an unaccented *e*, we have what is known as a feminine caesura, because final *e* is so often used in Modern French to distinguish the feminine from the masculine. Like a feminine *e* in a syllable at the end of a line, this *e* does not count as one of the required ten syllables, and the pause at the caesura is long enough to enable a reader to pronounce the *e* without disturbing the rhythm. There is no elision at the caesura, but elsewhere within a line a feminine *e* at the end of a word is silent before a word that begins with a vowel. The lines of each laisse of the *Roland* are linked to one another acoustically by assonance rather than rhyme. In other words, the last accented vowel or diphthong is repeated throughout the laisse with one possible variation: a simple vowel may assonate with the accented part of a diphthong. Whether a caesura, a laisse, or an assonance is masculine or feminine depends on the absence or presence of the feminine *e*.

The recorded passages consist of the introduction, the conclusion, and some of the more dramatic sections. In passage 2 (lines 814–25), the many feminine caesuras followed by masculine assonances give the impression that the riders, during their ill-advised crossing of the Pyrenees, are reining in their horses after galloping through these lines. Passages 3, 4, and 5 all contain "similar" laisses, that is, successive laisses in which the same themes are repeated in the same order (those laisses compose lines 1049–81, 1702–21, 1753–95, 2297–354, 2355–96). Jean Rychner has described such laisses as lyric pauses in the narration that allow the characters to express their feelings in some detail (*Chanson* 93). The reuse of the same themes encourages the incantatory repetition of phrases in the same metrical position such as "Cumpainz Rollant" (1051, 1059, 1070), "Felun paien" (1057, 1068), "Jo vos plevis" (1058, 1069, 1072), "Ço dist Rollant" (1702, 1713), "Jo l'en cunquis" (2322, 2324, 2327), and "Si l'en cunquis" (2323, 2325). In passage 6, after the two introductory laisses (lines 2855–80), the two similar laisses at the beginning of Charlemagne's formal lament (2881–908) are developed in the remaining three laisses of the lament (2909–44), and the apostrophe "Amis Rollant" is repeated at the beginning of a line in each of the five laisses (lines 2887, 2898, 2909, 2916, 2933). The seven phrases mentioned here each occupy the first hemistich of the line and are thus given special emphasis by the stressed syllable and the pause at the caesura.

We regularly teach our students the basic facts of epic prosody, but Old French had a strong expiratory word accent (Pope 99–119) that native speakers of both English and French have trouble reproducing. The result is very monotonous renditions of Old French texts. To remedy this situation, I composed a chantlike tune for the laisses of the *Roland* with note values that help students feel the rhythm of the verse. The tune is made up of three melodic units, the last of which is used only for the final line of the laisse. The other two can be repeated as often as necessary, and all three units can be adapted to accommodate the word accents. The version that fits laisse 1 (1–9) is reproduced in "Musical Examples," in the "Materials" section of this volume.

We know little about the music of the chansons de geste (Beissinger 98–100; Stevens, "Reflections" 233–38), but Andrew Taylor has shown that chant and reading aloud are both plausible modes of performance for an epic that has been copied into a manuscript (*Textual Situations* 59–63, 229–30). It is hoped that the musical examples and the recording of selected passages will enable both teachers and students to enjoy more fully the beauty of the *Roland* as oral poetry.

# The Art of Echo

## Edward A. Heinemann

Repetitions and choppiness, perceptible even in translation, are likely to strike every reader of the *Song of Roland*. This seeming awkwardness in the flow of language and story is, however, a setting that highlights subtleties; this essay examines some of what goes into both setting and subtleties. Language is a remarkable instrument, and the *Song of Roland* plays it extraordinarily well. Although most students bring to their first encounter with the *Song of Roland* little or no knowledge of Old French, not only is it possible to work back from the translation to the original, but the effort sharpens perception and appreciation of the poetry. Read the translation, as necessary, for the story; turn to the original to enjoy it.

Whether or not we know that *si* is a conjunction and *jo* a pronoun, the recurrence of these words emphasizes for us Roland's pride in his conquests (lines 2322–34), and, whether we know or not to count four syllables in *vostre olifan*, we recognize the mounting tension between Roland and Oliver in laisses 83–85. The dry technicalities of versification and grammar help us understand poetic and narrative effects and thereby open our eyes to an increasing range of such effects.

The stop-and-go language and fragmented narrative are a kind of repetition in themselves. Short sentences line up one after another with very little connecting them and produce a fairly small set of repeating grammatical patterns. (See the appendix to this essay for a summary of grammatical types.) Meter too is a recurrence of a syllabic pattern: the line of verse divides into four syllables, a pause, six syllables, and a stop. (The strophe, called a laisse, is a metric unit too, with its own complex effects of repetition.)

The most obvious repetitions, of course, are clusters of phrases several verses long, and we shall begin examining what goes into echo by looking at one such passage, the horn scene. Having climbed a hill in laisses 80–81 and seen the pagan army about to fall on the rear guard, in laisse 83 Oliver asks Roland to sound his olifant:

Cumpaign Rollant    kar sunez vostre corn    (line 1051)

Roland refuses, and in laisse 84 Oliver asks again:

Cumpainz Rollant    l'olifan car sunez    (line 1059)

Again Roland refuses, and in laisse 85 Oliver asks for a third time:

Cumpainz Rollant    sunez vostre olifan    (line 1070)

Note the near identity of the phrasing: Oliver's frustration mounts as he repeats himself, and then repeats himself again. That the bare fact of repetition suffices to express his growing irritation shows that occurrences are never identical: we have rather a first, and then a second and a third, each one building on the others.

Roland's obsession with his own and his family's good name manifests itself in the increasing length of that particular part of his refusal, two lines in laisse 83,

> Respunt Rollant    jo fereie que fols
> En dulce France    en perdreie mun los    (lines 1053–54)

three in 84,

> Respont Rollant    ne placet Damnedeu
> Que mi parent    pur mei seient blasmét
> Ne France dulce    ja chëet en viltét    (lines 1062–64)

and four in 85,

> Ne placet Deu    ço li respunt Rollant
> Que ço seit dit    pur nul hume vivant
> Ne pur paien    que ja seie cornant
> Ja n'en avrunt    reproece mi parent    (lines 1073–76)

(For a progression in the excuses that Roland advances, see Burger 116; Paquette; Carton.)

A deceptively obvious point is in order. Each occurrence of the echo fills its laisse, as happens in a number of passages: Blancandrin plots with Ganelon (laisses 28–30), the pagans boast (69–78), Roland offers to sound the horn (129–30), Roland tries to break his sword (171–73), Charlemagne laments Roland's death (Short, laisses 207–10; Burgess, laisses 207–11), Charlemagne (Short 216–25; Burgess 218–27) and Baligant (Short 232–34; Burgess 236–40) draw up their battle formations.[1]

In the first wave of the battle at Rencesvals, laisses 93–102, when the pagans go down in the same order as they uttered their boasts (Martin and Lignereux 82–84), the laisses line up parallel to one another, and the second wave, in which French and pagan deaths alternate, is a series of parallel pairs of laisses.

Parallelism of laisses is emphasized as well where introductions echo one another, as in Oliver's death:

> Oliver sent    quë a mort est ferut    (laisse 146, line 1952)

> Oliver sent    qu'il est a mort nasfrét    (laisse 147, line 1965)

> Oliver sent    que la mort mult l'angoisset    (laisse 150, line 2010)

Roland's death scene (laisses 168–76) is more intricate, the hemistich "Ço sent Rollant" opening laisses 168, 170, 171, 174, and 175, and a subset (168, 174, 175) evoking his approaching death in the second hemistich.

At a still greater distance, lines 2609–11, opening laisse 189, recall the first lines of the poem and mark the beginning of a new episode.

Echo is, however, far from limited to emphasizing the shape of the laisse. Enumerations, for example, build echoes out of word length, grammatical and lexical categories, and word order. In laisse 12, the list of men in Charlemagne's council (lines 170–76) is a minor lyric gem building up to Ganelon's appearance in line 178. The schematization in figure 1 shows the rhythms created in lines 170–76 by the presence or absence, the position, and the length of three components: the man's name, the expression given to parallelism (underlined), and the verb (italicized).

Fig. 1. Rhythms in lines 170–76.

| | 1 | 2 | 3 | 4 | 5 | 6 | 7 | 8 | 9 | 10 |
|---|---|---|---|---|---|---|---|---|---|---|
| 170 | | | Oger | | | | | | Turpin | |
| 171 | Richart | | | | e | | | | Henri | |
| 172 | e | | | | | | | Acelin | | |
| 173 | Tedbalt | | | | e | Milun | | | | |
| 174 | e si | | | *furent* | e | Gerers | | et | Gerin | |
| 175 | Ensembl'od els | | | | | | Rollant | | | *vint* |
| 176 | E | Oliver | | | | | e | | | |

Note the amplification accorded to Roland and Oliver, who each merit a full verse in contrast to the other characters. Roland receives special emphasis, first in a full hemistich expressing parallelism, and then in the only verb of action up to this point in the enumeration (a verb that will be echoed at the caesura of line 178 introducing the traitor).

Similarly, the list of conquests in lines 2322–34 makes poetry out of the length and position of place names, and, in laisse 232 (Short's edition), a framing rhythm in lines 3220–23 and 3229–31 highlights the hypnotic impact of Baligant's battle formations in lines 3224–28. (Burgess's translation gives three laisses in this passage, emphasizing still further the starkness of the enumeration.)

Immediate recurrences like these have an incantatory quality. The rhythm of language predominates while the actual meaning of the words fades to background coloring: because the men in laisse 12 are our heroes, the chant rouses pride and hope, and because they are the enemies in laisse 232, the rhythms stir dread.

The two components, length and position, bring us to the next step in our analysis. In laisses 83–85, each time Roland refuses to blow the olifant, his reason becomes longer. At the beginning of the battle at Rencesvals (laisses 93–102; see fig. 2), the three leaders receive detailed attention as they charge into combat, and the followers correspondingly less.

Fig. 2. Rhythms in Laisses 93–102.

| Laisse Number | Name of French Knight | Number of Lines in the Laisse | |
|---|---|---|---|
| 93 | Roland | 25 | ○○○○○○○○○○○○○○○○○○○○○○○○○ |
| 94 | Oliver | 22 | ○○○○○○○○○○○○○○○○○○○○○○ |
| 95 | Turpin | 26 | ○○○○○○○○○○○○○○○○○○○○○○○○○○ |
| 96 | Gerin | 8 | ○○○○○○○○ |
| 97 | Gerer | 6 | ○○○○○○ |
| 98 | Sansun | 6 | ○○○○○○ |
| 99 | Anseïs | 8 | ○○○○○○○○ |
| 100 | Engeler | 8 | ○○○○○○○○ |
| 101 | Otes | 7 | ○○○○○○○ |
| 102 | Berenger | 7 | ○○○○○○○ |

As a general rule, amplification corresponds to greater importance and compression to lesser, but a look back at the full verse accorded to Acelin at line 172, equal in length to Roland in line 175, makes it clear that many things go into the expression of importance.

The second hemistichs of lines 1051, 1059, and 1070, quoted above, illustrate a particularly delicate use of the number of syllables in a word. The three-syllable *olifan* alternates with the one-syllable *corn* by means of compensating changes: the article *l'* (no syllable), the one-syllable particle *car*, and the one- or two-syllable adjective *vostre*. I would not recommend looking for meaning in this bit of syllabic play, but, in anticipation of a point about importance that we shall take up below, I do suggest trying to feel just the slightest tickle of musical pleasure in the disappearance and reappearance of the possessive adjective and the length of the noun referring to the horn. To increase the enjoyment of that tickle, notice that the noun shifts from final position in the hemistich to initial and then back.

Initial and final positions are fairly clear, both in the verse and in the laisse. Most laisses begin with a marked introduction, many of them, as at line 2488, reviewing the situation as it stood at the end of the previous laisse, a device that confers a concluding tone to the final position of the previous laisse:

> Li emperere   ad prise sa herberge

Note here how the subject, filling the first hemistich, delays the beginning of the action until the second hemistich.

The verse has two very clear positions, the two hemistichs. Since a first hemistich never occurs without a second one following, the pause at the caesura always carries an element of suspense. In contrast, the pause at the assonance always implies a full stop. Pushing still further into abstraction, let us say that the first hemistich announces a topic and the second makes a statement about it, an effect made concrete when the subject fills the first hemistich and the predicate occupies the second:

> Li amiraill   chevalchet par cez oz   (line 3214)

Line 89 offers an instructively subtle contrast. Although few people are likely to remark that the first hemistich of this verse is the direct object of *amener* in the second hemistich, most will feel at the cesura that the sentence begins slowly, just as it does in line 3214, at the same time that they feel by the end of the line that the slow beginning evokes the recipient of the action rather than the performer.

> Dis blanches mules   fist amener Marsilies   (line 89)

We are dealing with subtleties, but the reader who has followed me this far may perhaps have felt, without looking at an edition of the poem, that line 89 opens a laisse.

In the horn scene, the three verses in which Roland rejects Oliver's suggestion (lines 1053, 1062, 1073, quoted above) make delicate use of position by reversing, in the final occurrence, the order of speech presentation and refusal. Is line 1073 the strongest refusal of the three?

These considerations bring us to what may be the essence of the poetry in the chanson de geste. The choppy, fragmented rhythms, the strongly marked interruptions at caesura and assonance, the paratactic construction, make hemistichs, verses, and laisses into wholes so that disruptions within and connections between them are the very heartbeat of the story, where we feel the action ebb and flow.

At its most abstract, the flow of language or narrative from one metric unit to the next has the feel of a complete stop, of an anticipation, or (after the fact) of a reopening. Concrete sentences and incidents bring endless modulations, subtle or striking, to this flow, reinforcing or undermining the grammatical suspense at the cesura, the grammatical stop at the line end, and the narrative halt at the end of the laisse. This intricate ebb and flow lies at the heart of an intense lyricism, not only in the *Song of Roland* but also in many Old French epics.

To begin with the unabashedly grammatical in the cohesion of hemistichs and verses, the grammatical suspense at the caesura is strong in line 2934, because at that point the sentence is clearly incomplete:

L'anme de tei     seit en pareïs mise

In 2943 the grammatical suspense is weaker because the clause is complete at the caesura:

Ploret des oilz     sa blanche barbe tiret

In line 1974, the clause seems complete at the caesura, but the second hemistich reopens and finishes it:

Munjoie escrïet     e haltement e cler

The second hemistich of 1974 confirms the metrical anticipation of the caesura while that of 2943 weakens it.

One particular grammatical type (Type III verses; see app.) plays grammar against the feeling of completion at the assonance, whether the verses reopen a seemingly complete sentence,

Franceis descendent     si adubent lor cors

D'osbercs e d'elmes     e d'espees a or     (line 1797–98)

or anticipate completion in a following verse:

Par granz batailles     e par mult bels sermons

Cuntre paiens     fut tuz tens campïuns     (lines 2243–44)

For examples of the impact of anticipation and reopening, look at how the delays in lines 2207–13 (Roland's lament for Oliver) build to a climax in 2214, a line that makes its point in understatement. Look at lines 222–27, where Ganelon's tortuousness manifests itself in an elaborate piling of subordinate clauses that contrasts with the general use of coordination and juxtaposition in the poem. Look at the slowing of action in lines 281–84, when Ganelon throws off his cloak in anger and everyone looks at him in wonder.

Although I would not go so far as to assert that every occurrence of the conjunction *e* introduces a repetition and, with it, some little poetic or narrative trick, coordination and juxtaposition are often a step toward echo. In 2811,

Puis sunt muntez     es chevals e es muls,

the conjunction divides the second hemistich into two echoing parts (nouns designating the mounts) and barely slows the narrative. In 2834,

>  Mei ai perdut   e trestute ma gent,

it coordinates the second hemistich to the pronoun at the beginning of the first, marks a pause, and insists eloquently on the extent of Marsile's losses. As one last example of the flow within the verse, notice how the grammatical function of the underlined words in 2840 echoes that of the first hemistich:

>  Par les degrez   <u>jus del paleis</u> descent

Between laisses, cohesion is a matter of narrative rather than grammatical flow. Ordinarily the relation is a simple chronological succession, and often a laisse opens with a review, from a slightly different perspective, of the situation at the end of the previous one:

>  L'anme del cunte   portent en pareïs   (laisse 176, line 2396)
>
>  Morz est Rollant   Deus en ad l'anme es cels   (laisse 177, line 2397)

But how are we to understand Roland's reaction when Ganelon names him to the rear guard? In laisse 59 he thanks his stepfather with biting sarcasm, and in 60 he turns on him with fury. It is not particularly difficult to accommodate the one set of words to the other, for the tone of the thanks is as sharp as the subsequent verbal assault, and we can see the two laisses as a kind of instant replay from different angles, revealing different sides to the action. It is less clear, however, that the action of laisse 60 follows that of 59; both seem to begin at the same point in time:

>  Li quens Rollant   quant il s'oït juger
>  Dunc ad parlét   a lei de chevaler   (laisse 59, lines 751–52)
>
>  Quant ot Rollant   qu'il ert en rereguarde
>  Irëement   parlat a sun parastre   (laisse 60, lines 761–62)

The mere sequence from 59 to 60 implies that the one occurs after the other and that 60 is a reaction to Ganelon's irony in line 760. The parallelism of lines 751 and 761, however, seems to point to the same moment in time, when Roland hears his nomination. Which is it: chronological succession or psychological complexity?

Understated or unstated, the thrusts found at caesura, assonance, and laisse boundaries bring us to recognize the fundamental importance of the silences between metric units.

And now I ask the reader to remember that tickle of pleasure in the disappearance and reappearance of the possessive adjective in lines 1051, 1059, and 1070 of the horn scene. The emotion expressed by those variations intensifies as Oliver builds to understatement in his final request. The first request observes straightforward word order: the intensifying particle *kar*, then the verb and its direct object. The second time, Oliver emphasizes the direct object by putting it first. In his final request he resorts to the ultimate eloquence: simplicity, verb followed by direct object. Coming at the end of the series, the simplest request is the strongest of all.

No small part of the poem's intensity derives from understatement and the unstated. Complete ideas being juxtaposed rather than linked by explicit connections, we see the acts but must work to understand how one act leads to the next, and multiple understandings apply.

Who is to carry Charlemagne's reply to Marsile? In laisse 17 Naimes offers to go, and Charles rejects his offer with the words "Vos estes saives hom" (248). Just what does he mean? Roland, Oliver, and Turpin offer, and Charlemagne tells them to be quiet. What is different when in laisse 20 Roland names Ganelon and a murmur of approval runs through the council? How is the decision made? Charlemagne does not open his mouth until the last two verses of laisse 23. We ponder the connections.

Which is the "real" *Song of Roland*, the text translated by Glyn S. Burgess (299 laisses, laisse 125a throwing the count off) or the one edited by Ian Short (which totals 291 laisses and which transposes the second wave at Rencesvals, lines 1467–670, from the order in the manuscript)? In the transmission of the text, whether through inadvertent scribal error or deliberate editorial intervention (modern or medieval), changes at the connecting points—caesura, assonance, and laisse boundary—happen easily and with considerable effect on meaning. Just as we ponder the quarrel between Roland and Ganelon, we ponder two rhythms to the second wave of battle and the rhythms of differing laisse counts.

The *Song of Roland* was and is "une poésie qui vit de variantes" (Menéndez-Pidal, Chanson 51), and the variants themselves bring home to us the tug of rhythm in meaning and narrative, a powerful incentive to read the poem in the original, where tight constraints highlight subtleties and give depth and ambiguity to the story. With the help of a little dry syllable counting and grammatical analysis, the intelligent reader today can enjoy the living poetry, just as the intelligent listener did over eight hundred years ago.

## APPENDIX
### Grammatical Types

As a general rule, many, if not most, verses contain a single clause in which a noun phrase fills one or the other of the hemistichs. The following schematization of the most common grammatical patterns summarizes my adjustments to a system laid out by Jean Rychner ("Observations").

**Type I:** The verse contains two clauses, each one filling a hemistich.

Tant chevalchat    qu'en Saraguce fut    (line 2818)

**Type II:** The clause fills the verse.

IIn: A noun phrase (n) fills, more or less, one or the other hemistich (IIn1 [first hemistich] or IIn2 [second hemistich]). The principal noun functions are subject, direct or indirect object, and modifier of a noun or of a verb. Line 2816 is Type IIn2, and 2817 is Type IIn1.

Puis est munté    en un sun destrer brun
Ensembl'od lui    em meinet quatre dux    (lines 2816–17)

IIv: The verb (v) is divided between the first and second hemistichs.

Baligant ad    ses cumpaignes passees    (line 3324)

**Type III:** The verb appears in either a preceding or a following verse.

Carles li reis    nostre emperere magnes
Set anz tuz pleins    ad estét en Espaigne    (lines 1–2)

NOTE

[1]See Kibler's "Editions and Translations," in the "Materials" section, for equivalencies between editions.

# The *Song of Roland* across the Curriculum

## Michelle R. Warren

The foundational status of the *Song of Roland* for French medieval studies has long been noted. Bernard Cerquiglini has gone so far as to claim that to be a French medievalist means to take a position on the epic poem ("Roland" 40). In other words, successive generations of scholars have defined themselves and their field by studying France's oldest surviving epic. They have, moreover, ensured that successive generations of students enter the medieval field via Rencesvals. In the nineteenth century, teaching the *Song of Roland* meant purveying an overtly nationalist pedagogy—from Gaston Paris's 1870 course at the Collège de France during the Prussian Siege of Paris to the first of Léon Gautier's many editions for classroom use in 1880 (e.g., Cerquiglini, "Roland" 41; Duggan, "Franco-German Conflict"). If the twentieth century saw a gradual dilution of such teaching (Guillaume Machaut is now more likely to appear on French university reading lists in literature), the *Song of Roland* has nonetheless remained a classroom staple, as this volume attests. In fact, as the only volume so far in the MLA series on a medieval French topic, this collection both witnesses and sustains the *Song of Roland*'s unique status in the pedagogy of French culture in the United States.

Teaching the *Song of Roland* in the United States in the twenty-first century entails a confrontation with the poem's history as a product and instrument of French nationalism. How can it be taught without also adopting the ideological prejudices that brought it into the general-literature classroom in the first place and that its teaching long supported? Can it be taught without perpetuating the values of "great origins" that attach to foundational works? In these days of revisionist literary history, should the *Song of Roland* be taught at all? It would be easy enough to sidestep the inheritance of the nationalist canon by teaching more congenial works. And yet teachers with widely varying goals, values, and contexts continue to teach the *Song of Roland*. I would suggest that the enduring viability of the oldest French epic rests at least partly on a formulation somewhat different from Cerquiglini's: whatever position one takes, it can be taken on the *Song of Roland*. Identifying as a French medievalist, moreover, may even be optional.

Like many professors, I have mainly taught courses that usually serve as students' only exposure to the Middle Ages. I have therefore felt a certain responsibility to include the most widely referenced works. In this sense, I maintain a notion of canonicity as a means of enabling shared reading experiences and encouraging thoughtful dialogue across generations of students and teachers. At the same time, I feel responsible (to my students and to myself) to offer interesting and varied topics. In the case of the *Song of Roland*, these two efforts have so far never been in conflict. The poem thus enters the curriculum not only as "France's oldest surviving epic" (and therefore a must-read) but also as an exemplary point of departure for explorations of particular themes and questions. The examples described in this essay demonstrate the *Song of Roland*'s flexibility and the possibilities for including the poem in any number of teaching contexts—not as a perpetuation of Francocentric glorification, but as an intervention in resistant reading. By reading and rereading the *Song of Roland* in various curricular settings, I teach an approach to literary history that, I hope, equips students to read the canon critically and to engage the past with enthusiasm.

One of the most frequent contexts for teaching at least portions of the *Song of Roland* is the introductory survey of French literature, often beginning with the Middle Ages and ending with the eighteenth century. The version I have taught most often covers the twelfth through the sixteenth centuries. Students in this course have widely divergent goals, from studying the French language to fulfilling general humanities credits in literature to choosing a class that fits conveniently into their course schedule; rarely if ever are students initially interested in medieval literature per se. Given this diverse group, I teach the survey as an exploration of personal themes that subsequently take on literary and historical dimensions. The *Song of Roland* is the first text we read and our first opportunity to put into practice this critical methodology, "le passé face au futur" ("the past facing the future"). My strategy is inspired in part by Virginia Scott's article outlining her approach, as a linguist teaching a general literature course, to engaging students who have initially little interest in literary study. During the first class meeting, each student identifies and explains a single topic of current personal concern (e.g., family, love relationships, faith, violence). We use these topics to structure our first readings of each new text. Once the familiar themes have been discussed, we move to historically specific issues (distinct definitions of family, love, faith, violence, etc.) and to differences between current ideas and those found in the texts and their historical periods. Students are also able to analyze the meaning of the greater or lesser presence of their preferred themes in particular works. In most cases, the themes they identify as personal concerns are broadly humanistic and have preoccupied writers for centuries. Yet that they begin their readings from this personal standpoint diminishes the barriers that can stand between today's students and historical literatures. The *Song of Roland*, then, seems immediately meaningful because students find in it what they already consider meaningful. Instead of learning only that the *Song of Roland* is one of France's oldest poems, students also experience some of the reasons why it remains an important and relevant site of reflection.

Many choose to write on the *Song of Roland* when given the opportunity to select topics and are most articulate in arguing for the poem's literary and cultural qualities. In some cases, I have assigned students to write papers in groups of two or three as a way of further interrogating the differences between medieval and modern notions of authorship. The dynamics of collective composition are unsettling for students trained to value individuality and originality, but the process leads to a vivid understanding of the complexities of the composition, narration, and reception of the anonymous *Song of Roland*.

The survey of French culture and civilization, another common course in the upper-level curriculum, can also engage the *Song of Roland* as one of "France's oldest poems" and as the story of a hero whose name has continued to reverberate through French history (as a figure of romantic chivalry, as a model for the Resistance, etc.). Here, teaching the images of Roland and Charlemagne alongside those of other iconic figures (Vercingétorix, Joan of Arc, Louis XIV, Napoleon) affords an opportunity to study how successive generations have used the past. This approach is structured into the popular textbook *La civilisation française en évolution, I*; studies by Harry Redman, Jr., and Robert Morrissey are excellent sources of further ideas for expanding the study of Roland and Charlemagne in the modern periods. Although a course like this covers a lot of ground in a short amount of time, the sessions spent with extracts from the *Song of Roland* usefully bridge several historical moments and rescue the course from its potential to proceed with misleading linearity. Instead of leaving the Middle Ages behind after the first two forgettable weeks of the term, students repeatedly have the opportunity to connect the past with more contemporary concerns. In this vein, the *Song of Roland* might also make a valuable contribution to courses on contemporary France, where Roland continues to make periodic appearances in political rhetoric (and Jean-Marie Le Pen has a penchant for invoking Ganelon).

Beyond historical surveys, courses focused on thematic topics offer numerous opportunities for work with the *Song of Roland*. The possibilities are limitless, as this volume and its readers will surely demonstrate. I have had successful experiences with several courses that I will describe here, and that may be of interest to others. In a course on objects and the literary representation of material culture, the *Song of Roland* offered a rich point of departure.

While underscoring the construction of our textual objects of study (manuscripts edited into print, Old French translated into modern), the course interrogated how, on the one hand, objects can come to organize human relations and, on the other, undergo their own kind of biographical trajectory. Objects of study included rings, relics, cloth, swords, and the grail. With the *Song of Roland*, we focused especially on the trajectory of the olifant (analysis of its material history can be found in my "The Noise of Roland") and of course on the famous named swords Durendal, Hauteclaire, and Joyeuse. The naming not only personifies the swords but also invites a discussion of the differences between metonymy and synecdoche in the swords' relations to their heroes. Overall, students in this course concluded that the idea of history itself arises in part from collective human investments in materials that endure beyond the human body. The dynamics of memory, and the strategic recovery of the past—indeed, the designing of objects (including poems) for posterity—suffuse the *Song of Roland*. This observation shaped a lively introduction to subsequent readings that included lais from Marie de France, *Le roman de Merlin*, *La quête du saint graal*, and *Le roman de la rose*. The *Song of Roland* provided definitions of chivalry, valor, and Christianity that enabled students to understand more thoroughly the subsequent interactions of these ideas in later literary objects.

In a course on exile and exclusion in the Middle Ages, the *Song of Roland* once again provided a productive point of departure. The typical traits of exile as understood in the modern sense of forced geographic relocation play a relatively minor role in the poem (Bramimonde's move to Aix is perhaps the closest to this kind of exile). However, the poem contains one of the earliest uses of the word *exill* in Old French (line 1862), in a phrase that dramatically underscores the common vernacular understanding of the term for much of the medieval period—ruination, often with agricultural overtones of devastated productivity. Beginning in the twelfth century and lasting into the seventeenth, this meaning coexisted with the connotation of expulsion. By beginning with the *Song of Roland*, students were able to find the expected theme of political banishment while also breaking with this expectation to understand the various historical connotations of the word *exile*. The lexical and thematic treatment of exile and exclusion in the *Song of Roland* set the framework of conversation for subsequent readings that included troubadour lyric, *Le jeu d'Adam*, Wace's *Roman de Brut*, and Chrétien de Troyes's *Erec et Enide*. As banishment seemed to become the dominant form of exile, the *Song of Roland* served as a reminder of the term's agricultural overtones—tones that also echo through later texts when one tunes in to their lexical subtlety.

*Exill* also raises a revelatory point about editorial practice. Ian Short, in the most widely used current French edition, states that he has edited the Oxford manuscript with more corrections than Joseph Bédier but less than an interventionist like Cesare Segre ([1990] 21). And indeed, Short renders line 2935 "dulce France ad hunie" ("has shamed sweet France"), whereas Bédier writes,

"France ad mis en exill" ("has placed France in 'exil'")—precisely the phrase preserved in the manuscript (Laborde, folio 53). Students can easily see the line themselves on the Bodleian Library Web site (*Bodleian*). Short's choice reflects a long tradition of emendation based on later manuscripts that goes back to Gautier's 1880 edition. Segre summarizes this evidence in his critical edition, going so far as to declare even the *exill* of line 1861 "suspect" ([1989] 1: 240, 2: 246). Interestingly, Glyn S. Burgess's English translation renders the sense of Old French *exill* in both lines, such that students studying the poem in English encounter, in this instance, a version closer to the Oxford manuscript than those studying Old French or Modern French. Teaching and reflecting on disagreements like this can remind students of the incessant vagaries of textual evidence. One must finally ask whether or not exile actually exists in the *Song of Roland* and must consider how to interpret variation in a poem that occupies such a seemingly stable place in literary history. Textual comparisons of this sort may seem overly technical for undergraduates, but I have found students most receptive to this kind of issue when they are presented with visual materials and clear guidelines for interpreting what they see.

Orientalism is another topic for which the *Song of Roland* proves illuminating. The poem is of course famous for the stark declaration, attributed to Roland, that "[t]he pagans are wrong and the Christians are right" (1015). This oft-cited line encapsulates a number of features that emphasize the oppositional relation between the French and their enemies, one that intensifies with the arrival of Baligant from the geographic east. Yet the *Song of Roland* also presents numerous parallels between the opposing groups and suggests in many ways that they are just as similar as they are different. It thus portrays a complex combination of both "othering" and "saming" that opens productive considerations of the historical permutations of European imaginings of the East. Emphasis can be given to the descriptions of pagan chivalry, the circulation of Arabic goods in Frankish society, the characterization of Bramimonde, and the Baligant episode. These discussions, especially if conjoined with critical or theoretical readings from modern studies of Orientalism, yield a number of insights that provide the groundwork for subsequent readings. In my course, these included *La prise d'Orange*, selections from the Crusade accounts of Robert de Clari and Geoffroi de Villehardouin, *Aucassin et Nicolette*, *Le jeu de saint Nicholas*, *Le roman de Mahomet*, and selections from the French versions of the narratives of Marco Polo and John Mandeville. The *Song of Roland* vividly portrays the complexity of Orientalist discourse in even the oldest texts and sensitizes students from the beginning to adjust their expectations of simple, or even simplistic, oppositional tactics.

These themes all arise from the *Song of Roland*'s overt and well-known topical engagements. Apart from these kinds of perhaps obvious themes, the *Song of Roland* might seem to have little or not enough to offer when so many other texts address one's concerns more directly. Yet for students who will study little medieval literature, the *Song of Roland* is, I would argue, a vital reading experience. And in fact, it can be well worth the effort to teach the poem in courses with seemingly more oblique thematic relations. An upper-level course on the representation of marriage from the Middle Ages to the eighteenth century, for example, prompted a highly productive reconception of the *Song of Roland*. Kinship bonds frame the initial conflict between Roland and Ganelon over the designation of who will carry Charles's message to Marsile, with Ganelon insisting on the obligations that marriage has created for both Roland and Charles (lines 277, 287, 312). When Roland and Oliver begin their own dispute, the status of Roland's anticipated marriage to Oliver's sister figures prominently (1719–21). Aude's dramatic refusal of a new marriage is of course one of the most commented on aspects of the epic's conclusion. Arguably, the poem's central debates concern the appropriate role of family in political decision making. The putatively small role of women in the epic should not blind us, as Sharon Kinoshita has also argued, to the strength of gender in forming the chivalric ethos ("Romance"). Other works in this course included several lais from Marie de France, several fabliaux, selections from Marguerite de Navarre's *Heptaméron*, and Madame de La Fayette's *La princesse de Clèves*. In this context, the *Song of Roland* taught us that the marriage plot is hardly the only source of kinship drama and that women writers are not the only ones concerned with the social effects of marriage and the status of women (an assumption that many students bring to a course dealing with issues of gender).

These examples may be of direct use to other teachers seeking to integrate the *Song of Roland* into similar kinds of courses. More important, though, they may inspire others to seek their own reflections in the poem and to bend it continually toward new understandings and innovative contexts. In this way, future generations of students may come to understand the *Song of Roland*'s vital place in literary history while continuing to reshape that history through their own insights and interrogations.

# Lord of the Valleys:
# History Students Meet Roland and Friends

## Joel T. Rosenthal

In the standard introductory survey of medieval Europe, as offered by countless history departments to countless undergraduates, the *Song of Roland* appears on the syllabus somewhere around the middle of the academic year. It comes as a welcome rest stop or way station on a pilgrimage that began back in the lonely and crepuscular world of *Beowulf* and that will eventually wind up on a crowded landscape occupied and claimed by the literature of courtly love, an endless string of Arthurian tales, and Chaucer.

Situated in this position, the *Song of Roland* is a treasure trove of material for our old classroom companions, compare and contrast. The *Song of Roland*'s world of big numbers—a feature usually of some interest to students who think of the Middle Ages as anumeric—is in stark contrast to the small-scale setting of the Old English poem, whereas its world of male bonding and locker-room towel snapping stands out boldly against the explicitly sexualized world of Chaucer and of courtly and Arthurian literature (as well as of those assigned to read them). The *Song of Roland* is a Cecil B. DeMille production, brimming over with swash and buckle and a cast of hundreds of thousands. As such, we can set it somewhere between our brooding Old English disquisition about fame, fate, and the meaning of life and death—a black-and-white affair directed by Ingmar Bergman—and that vast stable of semiserious sex comedies from the studio of a young (and Christian!) Woody Allen.

But beyond its broad sweep of boasting, bashing, and anathematizing, what is there in the *Song of Roland* for the social historian of the Middle Ages to lay on the table? Working from the reasonable premise that historians read and teach literature for its value as a window into the society whence it emanated, three themes—integral to the undergraduate survey and deeply embedded in the culture of eleventh- and twelfth-century Europe—come to mind. They are feudalism, militant (and racist and chauvinistic) Christianity, and the historicized and mythopoeic depiction of Charlemagne. Much of the interest the epic holds for students seems to rest on the way these powerful themes—familiar, we trust, from the textbook and the lectures—are inextricably woven into a single whole. They loop back on each other and constantly intertwine—literary counterparts to the carpet pages of the *Book of Kells* or to the coiled and twisted patterns supposedly familiar from the buckles and brooches of the Sutton Hoo treasure.

Let's begin with *feudalism*, a troublesome "ism" word that begs to be reified. As an explanatory device, feudalism has taken some hard knocks in recent years (see also Beech's "Feudalism in the *Song of Roland*," in this volume).

The warnings of Elizabeth A. R. Brown about "the tyranny of a construct" and the elaborate assault launched by Susan Reynolds have made many of us more circumspect about our exposition of "the system" than we were in the good old days when Marc Bloch's *Feudal Society* was the unchallenged and hegemonic text. But an old discipline, like an old dog, does not take all that kindly to too many new tricks. If we can say that the *Song of Roland* is a conservative text, offering a conservative view of social norms, values, and relationships, we can also argue that teaching it, at least in the survey course, still takes us back to an older and more conventional depiction of medieval society. Though we are aware of the pitfalls of putting too much stock in feudalism as an integrated structural-functional system, rather than as a heuristic anachronism shaped and cut for classroom explication, there is some solace in the idea that no one seems to have informed Turoldus or whomever, let alone his main characters—be they Christian or Muslim, good guys or bad—about the problem. Maybe they just don't know any better, stuck as they were (and will continue to be) in the late eleventh or early twelfth century.

If the two main ligatures of the feudal system are the personal bond—the lord-vassal relationship and all the affect that goes with it—and the fief, the poem does indeed seem to bespeak a world of ur-feudalism. In its earliest lines the poem resounds with the credo of reciprocal lord-vassal ties, ties that underlie the social and political system and that likewise encompass such cultural constructs as honor and shame. In a military epic, zeal and headstrong devotion are cardinal virtues on which all the rest depends. "For his lord a vassal must suffer hardships / And endure great heat and great cold; / And he must lose both hair and hide" (lines 1010–12), as Roland tells his fellows, though admittedly speaking while mired in the midst of a worse-case scenario. Archbishop Turpin echoes this all-or-nothing level of commitment: "A good vassal will never give up whilst still alive" (2088). But in keeping with the Roland-Oliver pairing of bravery as against wisdom, a little discretion, or common sense, does not always go amiss: "a true vassal's act, in its wisdom, avoids folly; / Caution is better than great zeal" (1724–25). Nor does the reciprocity on which the whole system supposedly rested go unnoticed, as Roland declares when the end is near: "I have never seen better vassals than you; / You have given me long and faithful service / And conquered such great lands for Charles's use" (1857–59).

While poetry, virtually by definition, tilts toward interpersonal relationships rather than toward a concern with the mode of material exchange, our friend the fief is also hanging around, eager to be called on stage. Compared with the heavy emphasis on the honorific and symbolic values of rings, boar-crested helmets, and bejeweled bridles that we read of in *Beowulf* or with a fair maiden's hand and what would follow thereafter in the high medieval material, the *Song of Roland* is candidly materialistic—perhaps only a bit this side of the venal. The fief may be depicted as following from personal loyalties, rather than as the force that creates such bonds. Nevertheless, land, or what came with or on it, was never a matter for diffidence or deference. The poem may not be as straightforward as the foundation charter of the Abbey of Cluny about the worldly wealth transmitted by William of Aquitaine: "the town . . . with the court and demesne manor, and the church, the villa, the chapels, the serfs of both sexes, the vines, the fields, the meadows, the woods, the water, the mills, the incomes and revenue, what is cultivated and what is not" (Henderson 329–32). But if not as explicitly as in this charter of 910, we have come a long way in the *Song of Roland* from that earlier and more poetic "Dark Age" world wherein gift giving and treasure were primarily assessed for their symbolic significance.

In addition, the sacrosanct descent of the fief from father to son, as the Carolingians acknowledged in the Capitulary of Quierzy in 870, was very much on the table. In Ganelon's rather testy farewell address to Charlemagne's court, he reminded those whom he did not expect to see again: "I have a son / . . . and he will become a valiant man. / To him I bequeath my honours and my lands" (313–15). And as the social fabric was but one large and seamless garment, a king's realm was simply the fief writ large; no qualitative distinction between its vast scope and a mere knight's fee: "Lord king, emir, / I hereby place all Spain in your hands / And Saragossa and the fief which goes with it" (2831–33), as the wounded Marsile says when turning things over to Baligant. For all their lofty talk of honor and death-defying loyalty, neither our Christian heroes nor their mirror-image adversaries of Islam are depicted as unworldly men. Whatever spiritual agenda drove them, we should note that the early negotiations regarding Charlemagne's withdrawal from Spain were expressed, in good part, in a vernacular not only of conspicuous accumulation but also of religious conversion. The old emperor's heart was warmed by a tribute that took the form of bears, lions, trained hounds, seven hundred camels, a thousand moulted hawks, and four hundred mules laden with Arabian gold, plus five additional carts filled with a miscellany of goodies, now being transferred from infidel hands and coffers to those of his chosen people. It seems that a tilt in the balance of trade was also part of God's plan.

If feudalism virtually jumps off the page, so does what I characterize as militant Christianity. Whatever the mystery of its date, the manner of its composition, and its putative journey from oral to written form, the *Song of Roland* is a poem of a crusading era and a crusading ethos. No student who has stayed awake into the tenth week of the survey course should still have any illusions about a Christianity of turn the other cheek, especially if he or she has done the assigned reading about Charlemagne's wars against the Saxons. And yet even against that background the *Song of Roland*'s depiction of the Islamic world—a near neighbor for over three centuries—displays a willful ignorance that is both revealing and disturbing. This myopic perspective or interpretation runs from those opening lines that couple the worship of Muhammad with Apollo, since they are revered in Marsile's false pantheon (he "who does not love God"; 7), to the Saracen denunciation of their various failed and false gods, a repudiation acted out in both word and deed after those gods had proven useless in their shoot-out with the forces of Christ. Apollo and Tervagant's carbuncle is denounced and vandalized ("Anyone who serves you well received a poor reward"; 2584), and Muhammad (presumably in some statuary form) winds up in the ditch, "where pigs and dogs bite and trample on him" (2591).

The epic battlefield scenes, first of Roland and the Twelve Peers, and then of Charlemagne himself, are virtually unqualified and unreflecting in terms of right versus wrong: they depict (white) Christian good guys against a variety of evil emperors, empires, minions, and allies. This theme almost never waivers or loses a beat, and all the while our poet remains blandly or blindly indifferent to the irony of an Islam presented as a dark-side image of Christendom: feudalized, fief-centered, all-embracing in ambition and reach, and presumably every bit as narrow-minded and intolerant. The *Song of Roland* wallows in the language of imperialism and virtuous alterity, of culture clash and the god of battles. Involving and invoking God in the most martial of all his aspects, not to mention the partisan appearances of Gabriel on occasion, these passages serve as a constant reminder of the cosmic aspects of the war of us against them, as does the Good Friday–like darkness that accompanies the death and ascension of Roland. What would be an instance of naked aggression in a more dispassionate tale and what would be Roland's unquenchable and hawkish appetite for war and conquest in a less partisan vehicle are but menu items on Christendom's long-range agenda—a poeticized but unquestioned agenda of mass conversion, genocide, and imposed spiritual uniformity (on those who did survive). In the *Song of Roland* there is "no vocabulary of compromise" (Vance 1). In the destruction of Saragossa the iron hammers and hatchets of the thousand Franks, turned loose as a wrecking crew, suffice to bring down "[t]he synagogues and the mosques as well / . . . They shatter the statues and all the idols. / Neither sorcery nor falseness will be left there" (3662–64). Clearly, neither the poet nor the audience had much idea of what the inside of either a mosque or a synagogue looked like, let alone what went on during the prayer services.

The demonization of Islam is occasionally softened by the realization that mirror-image worlds do allow for the odd touch of virtue and heroism on the part of those born on the wrong side of the spiritual, cultural, and racial blanket. But while no Christian warrior fell short of the expected standard—except for Ganelon and those yoked to him by kinship—the good guys on the Muslim side were rare exceptions, flashed before us from time to time as though to drive home the prevailing rule. We do have a few lines about the emir from Balaguer, who, "[h]ad he been a Christian, he would have been a worthy baron" (899) and about the archenemy Baligant, with curly hair "as white as a flower in summer" (3162), about whom the poet writes, "O God, what a noble baron, if only he were a Christian!" (3164).

However, these anomalies were but small matters when set against the grand design, and both poet and audience were more at home with a stock fare of denunciation, bold assertions regarding good and evil, and comforting reminders of the sacred nature of "our" side. As Turpin put it, "This Saracen appears to me a great heretic; / It is far better for me to strike him dead" (1484–85). And as that message is vindicated by the flow of fortune and events, it proves infectious: "The emir thereby begins to realize / That he is wrong and Charlemagne right" (3553–54). Nor, in an effort to probe the worldview of crusading Europe, should we overlook the deeply embedded racism that runs throughout, a racism used to justify the most brutal aspects of the Christian cause and the creation of medieval "Jim Crow" laws. A champion who might have been one of ours, in a different setting, is an implacable enemy: "He does not believe in God, the son of the Virgin Mary; / And is as black as molten pitch" (1473–74). The theme is reiterated: "He has the black race in his power; / They have large noses and broad ears / And together they number more than fifty thousand men" (1917–19).

Archbishop Turpin, as we have seen, offers a case study in militant Christianity, a perfect blend of cross and sword. He is a role model for all those militant padres and chaplains of World War II movies, swinging away with his cheerful pronouncement: "It is far better for me to strike him dead. / I have never been fond of cowards or cowardice" (1485–86). He also, to stick to the metaphors of the screen, provides a sneak preview of the indulgences Urban II spelled out at Clermont in 1095 for those who would take the cross for the Holy Land: "Moreover, the sins of those who set out thither, if they lose their lives on the journey . . . in fighting against the heathen, shall be remitted in that hour; this I grant to all who go" (Foulcher, "Urban"). Turpin enjoins his lay companions: "Confess your sins, pray for the grace of God; / To save your souls I shall absolve you all. / If you die, you will be blessed martyrs / And take your place in paradise on high" (1132–35; cf. 1521–23). It is no wonder that the soldiers of this world, men who tapped their feet as they listened to the *Song of Roland*, scrupled neither to spare the Jews of the Rhineland nor the noncombatants of Jerusalem on that fateful day in July 1099 when their armies breached the walls of the Holy City in what is arguably the all-time grand climax of militant Christianity.

The last of the three themes, of course, is Charles himself, our noble emperor—he who "[h]as been in Spain for seven long years, / And conquered that proud land as far as the sea" (2–3). The *Song of Roland* opens with Charles and it closes with Charles, who is weary by now and who must get out of his warm if lonely bed and once more take up the sacred cause. Roland's death, along with the events leading up to and then following from it, turns out to be but one case study, one story out of so many—told or untold, preserved or lost—that help us uncover the medieval interest in mining and creating a vigorous and faith-affirming present out of the myth-history of the past.

We can say that there were three particularly striking characteristics of Charlemagne as the poet depicts him. One, which always catches student interest, is his open emotionalism: weeping, fainting, leading a mass faint, tearing his hair, and so forth. Here we have Achilles mourning Patroclus rather than the stiff upper lip we might expect from this hoary veteran of so many battles for Christ (and for himself). The second characteristic is his larger-than-life status: two hundred years of service stripes for the cause, an empire embracing men of some eleven realms and provinces of France and drawing its leaders from even farther afield, the conquest of England, and more of this divinely endorsed hyperactivity. What we wind up with is a résumé or wish list of heroic Christian leadership; that Charlemagne had friends in high places who might halt the sun's course in the sky on his behalf hardly detracted from his special aura. Moreover, the way the poem can enlarge so widely from one particular episode, based on fleeting historical references to a disaster of 778, reveals how the medieval imagination fused history, legend, and fantasy. Since students are often steered to the Rencesvals passage in Einhard's *Life of Charlemagne* (Thorpe 64–65), they realize how a murky event—and hardly one to brag about—is being stroked and inflated to give us the open-ended glories of a later day.

The last characteristic of Charlemagne to note is his passive-aggressive role as king and emperor. In some passages he makes clear that he runs the show: he states, "Go and be seated on that white silk cloth; / Do not say another word, unless I bid you to" (272–73) to his archbishop and, "You will certainly go, since it is my command," (328) to a reluctant Ganelon. Here we have eleventh-century kingship at its most dominant, something akin to *The Anglo-Saxon Chronicle*'s entry for 1086 on William the Conqueror (Garmonsway 219–21)—a poetic counterpart of a real-life model. But in other passages and situations Charles is but the retiring chairman of the feudal executive committee or board of directors, seeking advice, weighing diverse counsels, assessing the reliability of counselors, tossing votes into the air to see which would blow away and which settle at his feet: "He wishes to be guided entirely by the men of France" (167).

Moreover, in the most critical test that confronts him—the trial of Ganelon—Charlemagne waivers in a most distressing fashion. We know that Ganelon committed treason. Why is the emperor so indecisive? We know that Ganelon makes a pledge of loyalty to Charles and that his claim to a right to personal vengeance against Roland is mere sophistry. Why doesn't Charles see this? We see the peers' acceptance of the idea that Roland dead was lost and gone but that Ganelon alive might prove a useful ally as specious, contrary to the whole thrust of the poem's dramatic structure. Why does Charles seem inclined to buy this canard (even though he is unhappy with it: " 'You are traitors to me' . . . everyone has failed him"; 3814–15). And finally, when it all rests on a knife's edge, we know how risky it was to leave the final call to the god of battles, especially given the seemingly uneven match between Pinabel and Thierry. Why couldn't Charles figure this out?

But it all ends well, or at least well enough. Thirty of Ganelon's kinsmen get the noose, which is the flip side to kinship bonding. Our Judas leaves the scene in a fashion befitting a Merovingian royal who lost his (or her) throw of the dice. Bramimonde accepts the "true religion." Charles gets at least a few hours sleep before Gabriel arrives to brief him on his next assignment. Does the *Song of Roland* have a happy ending?

Like a gadget or appliance assembled at home, there are always parts left over; some will have to be discarded. References to our tale appear in old chronicles—the droll use of the ritual insult on the battlefield, the symbolism of the right hand (to swear allegiance; to bind in false allegiance; and literally to be lost as a symbol of failure, of divine disfavor, and of impotence), half-informed Christian views of the scope and range of Islam, among others.

But perhaps the most striking omission in our eyes is women: women, girls, maidens, virgins, widows, wives, sex, gender, male-female relations, and all the other aspects and permutations of the topic. Not even politically instrumental marriages are mentioned much, whereas in *Beowulf* such marriages were often alluded to, whatever Beowulf's own skepticism about the value of the marriage bed as the site for feud healing. If we accept that the role of poor Aude, Roland's fiancée, is almost laughable in its formulaic brevity and maidenly decorum, we have Queen Bramimonde and little more. She, at least, is as rounded a character as we find, male or female, Christian or Muslim; advising her husband, venting against her false or useless gods, accepting her fate (to be reborn as Juliana, "convinced of the truth"; 3987). I always hope—though in vain—for some flickering hint of romance between this doughty woman and Charlemagne (for the historical Charlemagne's liaisons, see Thorpe 73). We knew, long before *Montaillou* became a best seller, that spiritual sponsorship could be "the beginning of a beautiful friendship" (Le Roy Ladurie). Perhaps this promising topic was taken up in a poem no longer extant, one of those missing links in the chain between the chansons de geste and the romances yet to come. The historic Charlemagne was not nearly as abstemious as the epic one. According to Einhard, who tracks Charles's partners, though he misses some of the children who died very young, our hero's marital career covered an early marriage to a daughter of Desiderius, king of the Lombards; then marriage to Hildigard, of a noble Swabian family; then to Fastrada, an East Frank or German; and finally to Luitgard, of the Alamanni. Beyond this, there was a daughter by a concubine "whose name I cannot remember," and children by Madelgard; by Gersvinda, a Saxon; by Regina; and by Adallinda (Thorpe 73).

If a more sober summary is needed, we can conclude by affirming that the *Song of Roland* hits the mark in terms of using material we now consider literary to help us explore medieval society from the historian's perspective.

The poem has a fleeting basis in a real event, the creation and exploitation of tradition, which is a good thing in terms of how the past is used, reused, and built on. The poem seems to be in line with what other contemporary sources, plus the mainstream of modern scholarship, say about the zeitgeist of the world it depicts. The poem offers a credible level of tension between an ethos of individual choice and the burden of being saddled from on high with a larger and more enduring sociocultural agenda. Finally, reading the *Song of Roland* reminds us that dividing the world into good guys and bad guys has a venerable, if not necessarily a praiseworthy, ancestry. Though I have serious reservations about using either the classroom or the assigned tests to harp on such themes as tolerance and multiculturalism, there are lessons to be learned from the *Song of Roland* about our zeal to kill the other—whoever he, she, or they might be—that I like to think may linger long after the final exam in the survey course is but a distant memory.

# Teaching the *Song of Roland* in Upper-Level Courses

## Margaret Switten

Since New Critical or formalist approaches, emphasizing aesthetic apprecia-
tion of literature to the exclusion of social engagement, have retreated from
the classroom in recent years, the most attractive way of presenting the *Song
of Roland*, particularly in upper-level courses where some basic knowledge of
how to read a literary text may be presumed,[1] is through the contexts the
*Song of Roland* both presents and represents. These contexts are rich and
varied; many of them are discussed in this volume. Amidst such an abundance
of riches, the first problem is what to choose, and choice, of course, depends
on the approaches and requirements of any given course. It will be my pur-
pose here to suggest a few tactics I have found effective. I will focus specif-
ically on music and musical performance, Crusade and pilgrimage, and Ro-
manesque art represented both in pilgrimage churches and in the Bayeux
Tapestry. I will use the opening laisse and the theme of betrayal to relate
these contexts to the study of the *Roland*.

## Setting the Stage: The First Laisse

I like to begin study of the *Roland* with a close analysis of the first laisse. This
analysis allows me to introduce what I consider important concepts: the notion
of genre as applied to the *Roland* (medieval men and women would not rec-
ognize the division between literature [belles lettres] and history we take for
granted today), the language of the *Roland* and the structure and the prop-
erties of the laisse (see Bennett, "Orality"; Colby-Hall; Heinemann, in this
volume). The first of my concerns is the object students usually have in front
of them: a book, an edition, perhaps with a facing translation or maybe just a
translation, in any case a single text. No one living in the Middle Ages would
ever have seen such an object. How then might medieval audiences have come
to know the *Song of Roland*? As specialists have often observed, we don't
know the exact answer to that question, but seeking an answer leads me first
to a brief examination of manuscript culture, often using manuscript pages
that can be found on the Web (such as *Bodleian*), then to the notion of oral
poetry and the meaning of chanson de geste (see Colby-Hall and Bennett,
"Orality," in this volume).

The word *chanson* suggests musical performance. The *Song of Roland* does
not begin with direct reference to this designation, as, for instance, does the
*Charroi de Nîmes*: "Oëz, segnor . . . Bone chançon plest vos a escouter / Del
meillor home qui ainz creüst en Dé?" ("Hear ye, my lords . . . Will it please
you to listen to a good song / About the best man who ever believed in God?";
McMillan, lines 1, 3–4; my trans.; for other examples, see Stevens, *Words*

222–23). There are only two references to *chanson* in the *Roland*, both preceding the main Rencesvals conflict. Lines 1014 and 1466, the first pronounced by Oliver, the second by Roland, make reference to "male cançun." Here, both Oliver and Roland state that by their bravery in battle, they must make sure that no "male cançun" ("shameful song") will be sung about them ("Male cançun de nus chantét ne seit"; 1014). These references connect *chanson* to singing and demonstrate the power of song to make or break reputations (for further discussion on the "male cançun," see Warren, "Noise"). There is sufficient evidence to warrant the assumption that the *Roland* was sung, although one should not forget that for this period, singing and saying could be almost interchangeable (Stevens, *Words* 200). No manuscript, however, has music. How then might the *Song of Roland* have been performed, and where, for, and by whom?

To imagine how the *Roland* might have been sung, one must look to several musical contexts. The first context comes immediately to mind: Gregorian chant. The chant was an essential part of the medieval sonorous universe. It can usefully be emphasized in the classroom without great detail, through a short description of its main characteristics: monophonic unison chant of the Christian church, that is, unaccompanied melodies set to the Latin texts of the liturgy—liturgy broadly defined as the formal services of the official rites of the church, such as Mass or Offices (see Kerman for the introductory level but do not confuse this edition with subsequent brief editions; Crocker; Hoppin; Yudkin; Stevens, *Words*; *New Grove*; *Harvard Dictionary*; *Oxford Companion*). It is difficult to imagine a jongleur who would not have been familiar with the chant repertory. Although the church opposed the introduction of nonofficial material, various additions or accretions nonetheless crept into the repertory. Poets and musicians needed fresh outlets for their talents, and so they added to or structured around the chant, or even composed themselves new forms of expression, such as sequences or tropes (the trope is a textual or musical addition to an existing chant) or new hymns. At the same time, changes in Latin poetry led to lines that were determined by rhyme, by syllable count and accent rather than by quantity. This new Latin poetry, not directly connected to the liturgy but cultivated in monasteries, was set to music. Such developments, only briefly alluded to here, led not only to the development of polyphony but also to the creation of many types of monophonic song, sacred and secular, initially in Latin, later in the vernaculars (Stevens, *Words*; Yudkin, ch. 6). This outburst of musical and poetic activity, of which we have record, characterized the period during which we can place the earliest performances of the *Roland*. We have no record of a different area of music that one might loosely call popular, yet features of this popular music might well have inspired jongleurs. And later, into the thirteenth and fourteenth centuries, a number of mostly literary works refer to chansons de geste, offering hints of performance practice.

Which aspects of these rich musical contexts can help us understand how the *Roland* might have been performed? The *Roland* is narrative poetry; strophic forms are thus not suitable, nor would the highly ornamented melodies that characterize some chants be appropriate. One important category of chant, however, would lend itself to narration: liturgical recitative, as illustrated by the singing of prayers, lessons, and psalms. Psalmody offers simple declarative musical structures that convey words with supple and varied inflections. Outside the chant, in the secular realm, we can find several examples of uncomplicated, repetitive melodies in vernacular works, notably in the thirteenth-century *chantefable*, *Aucassin et Nicolette*, a work in which singing and saying alternate and in which the parts marked for singing have the laisse structure of a chanson de geste (see further examples in Stevens, *Words* 222; Hoppin 290). Available musical evidence allows us to hypothesize that music for the *Roland* would likely have been of simple construction and largely repetitive, would have lacked the regularity of strophic song but rather would have followed a looser laisse structure. Possible melodic reconstructions to demonstrate how the *Roland* might have been performed on the basis of these assumptions are provided by examples 1–5 in the "Musical Examples" section of this volume. The recordings on the accompanying compact disc, tracks 9–14, enable students to hear these reconstructions. Further details about the melodic reconstructions may be found in the essay by Alice M. Colby-Hall and in the "Notes to the Compact Disc."

Literary texts can direct us to possible place and manner of performance (Page, *Voices*; *Owl*). Several venues can be proposed: the great hall of a castle after feasts of various sorts, outdoor settings in public places, churches along the pilgrimage routes, possibly even the battlefield. Wace in his *Roman de Rou* (Holden, lines 8013–18), for example, states that one Taillefer sang of Roland's deeds to inflame the men before the Battle of Hastings, the chronicler William of Malmesbury makes reference to the *Roland* as a stimulus to courage, and a twelfth-century fresco shows a jongleur singing and playing for crusaders in battle dress (Gitton 9). Although the chansons de geste represent aristocratic values of the knightly class, the audiences were likely mixed, depending somewhat on the place of performance. One thinks most readily of a male performer for a genre that so thoroughly represents masculinity. However, there are references to female performers, such as the passage in Jean Renart's *Roman de la Rose*, where the sister of a jongleur is represented as singing a passage from what is likely a chanson de geste in a castle to entertain the emperor Conrad (Lecoy, lines 1332–67; Boynton; Coldwell). Wherever the performance and whoever the performer, one feature would seem to have been constant: the jongleur had to reach the audience and maintain interest in the story, whether for entertainment or for encouraging the values to be conveyed. Thus one may assume that the jongleur modified his work (possibly both tune and text) to suit the audience and carry the listeners through the sweep of dramatic unfolding. The notion of variability that characterizes a manuscript culture is, for performance, essential.

Having established important features of poetic structure, musical contexts, and performance, I like to ask students to read the first laisse, usually imitating me, in order to gain some understanding of the sounds of the language. Especially useful for teachers with little knowledge of the language but a fine resource for all teachers, the compact disc accompanying this volume provides excellent readings of a generous selection of laisses. Once students have attained a rudimentary understanding of language sounds, I ask them to try singing the first laisse, usually after listening to me or to other musical reconstructions. Here again, the accompanying compact disc furnishes examples of singing that can facilitate such an exercise. (Although I do not specifically address that issue here, comparative listening can also be enlightening. For example, if it is available, the 1961 Folkways Records version of *La chanson de Roland* illustrates a very different approach to musical performance. No consistent attempt is made to sing, but instruments, mostly modern and chiefly trumpets and horns, are called on to provide "atmosphere." The Folkways recording usually produces hilarity in my classes, but analysis of why it produces hilarity, on what assumptions the hilarity is based, can be very instructive.) The exercise of reading and singing provides what might be called hands-on experience, giving students a better feel for the text and a better understanding of the sonorous nature of the *Roland*, so aptly described by Michel Zink:

> La chanson de geste fait . . . appel à ce qu'on pourrait appeler les effets physiques du langage: la fascination et presque l'hypnose de la répétition; le vertige de la même assonance résonnant vers après vers tout au long de la laisse et celui né d'une mélodie très simple, d'une psalmodie répétée, toujours identique, vers après vers, avec tout juste la variation d'une cadence sur l'hémistiche finale de la laisse    (Zink, *Littérature* 75)

> The chanson de geste . . . makes use of what one might term the physical effects of language: the almost hypnotic fascination exerted by repetition; the dizzying effect of the same assonance resonating line after line throughout the entire *laisse* as well as that of a very simple melody, repeated as in psalm singing, always the same, line after line, with just the variation of a cadence on the final hemistich of the *laisse*.[2]

Like any good introduction (and this is a superb one), the first laisse also states main themes of the work. I like to emphasize the staged clash of cultures and of characters, the stark portrayals of good and evil in which the enemy to be defeated functions as a negative image of the eventual winners. To address the various aspects of this clash, I like to use some manuscript images and refer to crusade and pilgrimage, and especially to the Spanish theatre. A favorite technique for examining the vexed question of the other is to place beside the opening laisse of the *Song of Roland* a miniature from the *Grandes chroniques* where one can see Charlemagne confronting Saracens disguised as devils, the speech of Urban II calling for the Crusade in 1095, and a letter from the Pope Calixtus II on the Crusade in Spain that forms an appendix to the *Pseudo Turpin* (see the sample assignment "The First Laisse," below).

If one wishes to play out more fully relations between the *Song of Roland* and pilgrimage, one may explore the road to Santiago, a rich nexus of religious and artistic values. Early in the twelfth century, it became apparent that the call to Jerusalem was draining man power to hold off the enemy in Spain, thus new efforts were launched to protect Christianity's western flank against the Arabs. The promotion of the pilgrimage to Santiago grew out of these efforts, and the *Song of Roland* may well have some relation to them (Gicquel, *Légende* ch. 3). My preferred technique for studying the pilgrimage road is to start with a good map (such as www.humnet.ucla.edu/santiago/spancmno .html) and then to choose one place to visit among the celebrated sites on the road. The choice would depend on what one wishes to emphasize: Romanesque architecture or sculpture through the pilgrimage churches (Seidel; Brault, Song; Shaver-Crandell, *Middle Ages*; Shaver-Crandell and Gerson, *Pilgrim's Guide*; Lejeune and Stiennon, *Légende*; Farnham), music to be heard along the route, and so forth. Students can be asked to pick a site and report on it in class. I like to stop at Limoges, perhaps spend the night at the Abbey of Saint Martial (Shaver-Crandell and Gerson, *Pilgrim's Guide* 223–30). Although the abbey no longer exists, it was a flourishing monastic community in the eleventh and early twelfth centuries, particularly renowned for its library of musical manuscripts, and boasted a flourishing school of poets and composers (Treitler). There, one could hear the latest musical compositions, among them Latin monastic songs moving out into the secular realm, such as *Tu autem*, in Old Occitan, performed on the compact disc accompanying this volume. (For recordings that can help expand the role of music for the pilgrimage routes, see the list below.)

Further explorations of the pilgrimage road can be carried out by dipping into the prestigious manuscript known as the Codex Calixtinus (c. 1170) because its composition was attributed to Pope Calixtus II (1119–24), although it was likely the work of a northern French scribe or compiler. This compilation, somewhat heterogeneous in nature, contains a wealth of information: the justly celebrated *Pilgrim's Guide* (Vielliard; Melczer), the *Pseudo Turpin* (*Historia Karoli Magni et Rotholandi* [Gicquel, *Légende* 523]), as well as musical compositions (Moisan). A letter appended to the *Pseudo Turpin* was mentioned above. The *Pseudo Turpin* was one of the most popular works in the Middle Ages; following the version in the Codex Calixtinus, there were innumerable manuscript versions in Latin and in vernacular translations. The author of the *Pseudo Turpin* seems to have been inspired by the chansons de geste, notably the *Roland*. The *Pseudo Turpin* influenced the *Grandes chroniques* as well as the Charlemagne window at Chartres. One may read the complete *Pseudo Turpin* (which is not long) beside the *Song of Roland* for a comparative study of themes and political motivations (Spiegel).

## The Theme of Betrayal

The first laisse introduces the main dramatic opposition, religious and political, and tells us how the work will inevitably end, but it does not lay out what one might call the internal conflict between the knights surrounding Charlemagne. I like to approach this internal conflict through the theme of betrayal. In the end, the two conflicts join: if Ganelon has committed treason against Charlemagne, he has also committed treason against God (see also Mickel, "The Implications of the Trial of Ganelon," in this volume). Juxtaposing the *Song of Roland* and the Bayeux Tapestry provides a rich comparative context for examining the notion of betrayal and its central importance to what Fredric Cheyette has called the "Culture of Fidelity" (185–247). Moreover, the tapestry opens the way to exploration of political and linguistic relations between France and England, initiated by the conquest it describes, if one wishes to push further in that direction in the context of a course in French literature. The theme of betrayal engages the centermost features of feudal relations, which are described elsewhere in this volume. Betrayal leads, ultimately, to the battle of Rencesvals and to the death of Roland; to the trial and death of Ganelon; and, for the tapestry, to the death of Harold. The tapestry is also a good source of images of battle, the medieval spectator sport par excellence. It helps students understand prechivalric knights, erasing the visual image of the "knight in shining armor" that haunts student imaginations (for a way of studying the conception of the prechivalric knight in the *Roland*, see Switten, "Chevalier" 405–10).

Studies of the Bayeux Tapestry are too numerous to mention; each instructor will have his or her favorite (Wilson is standard; see Musset for a recent detailed study in French). To open the tapestry is to enter the world of the late eleventh century as it was perceived and interpreted by the creator of the work (Parisse). I say "to open" because I like to use for teaching the foldout that can be obtained from the Centre Guillaume le Conquérant (ordering information provided below). The tapestry is available also on Web sites and a CD-ROM (see resources for the tapestry below), but these representations do not, for me, convey the narrative experience of the tapestry as vividly as the foldout, which students can set up in their rooms so they can literally walk through the story. Comparisons with the *Song of Roland* are numerous; many have been proposed by Shirley Ann Brown ("Bayeux Tapestry"). Careful analysis of Harold and Ganelon brings into focus important questions surrounding the theme of betrayal and how it is played out in both narratives, the one textual, the other visual. (Such analysis also can raise the issue of narrative techniques in different media.) For specific suggestions, see the sample assignment "Betrayal," below.

In this essay, I have explored artistic, religious, and political contexts that can help students understand the universe, particularly its sonorous and visual dimensions, in which the *Song of Roland* came to be and from which it took its meaning. Some of these contexts are less familiar than others. All can, it is hoped, suggest intriguing ways of approaching the *Song of Roland* in advanced courses.

## Sample Assignments for Teachers

### The First Laisse

1. Two worlds: Charlemagne and Marsile. Who is Charlemagne and what is he doing in Spain? Who is Marsile? Study accents and rhythms in lines 1 and 7 and the position of the names: What is the effect of these poetic features? Why is there a conflict between the two men? What larger conflict do they represent? (This question could be nuanced to allow for the possibility of some recent interpretations viewing the Frank-Saracen confrontation as a mask for something else; see, for example, Kinoshita, "Pagans.")
2. How are the Saracens compared with Christians? Do you think the author of the *Roland* knew—or even wanted to know—about real Saracens? Explain your answer.
3. Compare the attitudes of the *Roland* poet, Pope Urban II preaching the First Crusade, Pope Calixtus II promoting the Spanish crusade, and an image from a fourteenth-century manuscript of the *Grandes Chroniques de France*. What similarities and differences do you find? Can one reach any general conclusions about attitudes of the West toward the East? Are such attitudes still with us? (See Maalouf.) The French text of Urban's speech is in Foulcher de Chartres ("Appel"; *Historia* 323–24; *Histoire* 7–9). The text of Calixtus's letter in Modern French translation is in Gicquel (*Légende* 591–92). For the miniature showing Charlemagne and the Saracens from the *Grandes Chroniques de France*, Bibliothèque nationale de France, fonds français 2813 (14th century), folio 119, see www.mtholyoke.edu/~mswitten/roland/.
4. Do you know already by the end of the first laisse how the conflict between Charlemagne and those who serve Muhammad will end? What literary technique is involved? In what genres do we find this technique particularly prominent? What do you think might have been the intended effect of its use here?

### Betrayal: *Roland* and the Bayeux Tapestry Compared

1. Establish (or review) the main story lines and compare the goals of each work.
2. Within these frameworks, identify the main characters and the relationships between them.
3. Focus on Harold and Ganelon: Who is betrayed by Ganelon (no neat an-

swers!)? Why? How is the betrayal played out textually. Who is betrayed by Harold? Why? How is the betrayal represented visually? (Assess, for example, the crowning of Harold as betrayal and its visual representation, the distortion of the main figure, etc.)

4. What are the results of the betrayal? Does your comparative study suggest any general conclusions about perceptions of fidelity and betrayal in the late eleventh and early twelfth centuries?

5. Is there a religious dimension in the tapestry?

6. Consider the artistry of the tapestry (if one wishes to go in that direction): how do the sequence of images, the linking of images, and inscriptions work together? Consider borders and fables: What is their function? Analyze, for example, the specific fables selected and their relation to the main story; relate the borders in the battle scenes to the main story of the battle.

7. Does viewing the Bayeux Tapestry enrich the imagined visual experience of reading the *Song of Roland*? Does it invite you to revise the vision of knighthood you previously had? Explain your answer (this can lead to a debate about the effect of visual representations of literary works; students frequently have sharply different opinions).

## Resources for the Bayeux Tapestry

*The Full Bayeux Tapestry*, http://hastings1066.com/bayeux1.shtml (with translations)

Martin K. Foys, *The Bayeux Tapestry*, CD-ROM

To order foldouts of the *Tapisserie de Bayeux* from the Centre Guillaume le Conquérant, use the following contact information: Web address: www.bayeux-tourism.com/decouvrir/deecouvrir.html; e-mail address: tapisserie@mairie-bayeux.fr (the response may be slow); telephone: 02 31 51 25 50 (011 33 2 31 51 25 50 from the United States); fax: 02 31 51 25 59; regular mail: Tapisserie de Bayeux, Centre Guillaume le Conquérant, Rue de Nesmond, 14400 Bayeux, France. In all cases ask for "dépliants complets." Inscriptions for the foldouts are in English, French, and German.

# Selected Discography for Music on the Pilgrimage Road

(Titles cross-reference entries in the works-cited list.)

*Jerusalem: Vision of Peace*
*Compostelle: Le chant de l'étoile*
*The Pilgrimage to Santiago*
*Medieval Pilgrimage to Santiago: Auf Jakobs Wegen*
*Nova Cantica: Latin Songs of the High Middle Ages*
*Aquitania: Christmas Music from Aquitanian Monasteries*
*The Medieval Lyric: A Project Supported by the National Endowment
    for the Humanities and Mount Holyoke College.* CD 1, anthology 1:
    Monastic Song, Troubadour Song, German Song.

NOTES

[1]I am here thinking of courses in French literature taught in French, but most of my suggestions are also valid for courses taught in English. The suggested readings are, for the most part, in French.

[2]Translation by Jeff Rider in Zink (*Medieval French Literature* 20), modified by Margaret Switten to fit Zink (*Littérature*).

# French Medieval Literature in Modern English Translation

## Deborah M. Sinnreich-Levi

The *Song of Roland* presents an assortment of difficulties to students who read it in translation. Some of these difficulties are inherent in reading all literature of a far-off place, time, culture; some are specific to this epic—results of its poetic form, the kind of heroes and heroic action it depicts, and its religious chauvinism. All of these cruxes can be multiplied by the many hands that have translated the epic over time. How does an instructor address these concerns, especially for the nonmedieval major?

I always begin teaching the *Song of Roland* the same way: I recollect an anecdote of Frederick Goldin's. He would tell his graduate students (I was fortunate to be one in the late 1970s) about having recently finished his translation of the *Song of Roland* and about the long suffering of his family as he toiled over it. To celebrate the translation's publication, his family took him to see a new film version of the epic (dir. Cassenti). Under the opening credits, a magnificently clad knight rode down a slope, pennons streaming behind him as he smoothly descended to Charlemagne's camp. And Fred knew in that moment that the film adaptation would have nothing in common with the epic he had come to know so intimately (and that he'd have to suffer through it anyway so as not to disappoint his family). Why? As students who read even the first few laisses know, narrative fluidity is not one of the epic's characteristics. The contrast between what modern readers assume good narrative structure to be and what the epic offers is a good point of departure for the student reading in translation—assuming that the instructor has chosen a translation that preserves the *Roland*'s characteristic episodic choppiness, such as Glyn S. Burgess's or Goldin's.

In the introduction to his translation, Goldin discusses the episodic nature of the laisses and the poetic devices that adorn the action, and his observation bears repeating:

> Every reader of *The Song of Roland* is struck by its distinctive and unforgettable style: the flat declarativeness of its lines, the dizzying shifts in tense, the absence of an explicit connection between one statement and another, the wholesale repetition of many passages, the frequent restatement of the same idea and retelling of the same event, the thinness of the vocabulary (consisting of fewer than 1800 words) and the rare use of figurative language, the powerful conclusiveness of each *laisse* . . . , which gives one the feeling that the narrative repeatedly comes to an end and then resumes. (28)

Students, especially on their first encounters, are put off by these devices. Demystifying how they work is critical, but all of them can be made accessible. The flat nature of the writing may be compared with some kinds of music whose apparent monotony is the bane of middle-aged parents. Put more positively, the repeated use of simple vocabulary coupled with the frequent repetitions of the fundamental information many laisses contain evokes the venerable classical trope of *repetitio*. Beyond classical rhetoric and pop culture, one can easily appeal to the numerous studies of folklore that explain the language use of what Albert Lord called "the singer of tales."

The switching of tenses is best addressed as an aspect of the *Roland*'s having been recited before a live audience. The immediacy expressed by a shift to the present tense gives primacy to certain utterances in the same way that students today might say, "So I *went* to my professor, and she *goes*, 'Blah, blah, blah.'" The tense shift transforms "listeners into witnesses" (Goldin, "Time" 131). Not all translations capture these verb tense shifts, but they are central to understanding the epic:

> [T]ense is not used exclusively for the designation of time. Different tenses are used to distinguish different aspects of an action, or different points of view; to differentiate inevitability from eventuality, or to establish moral categories. . . .                    (Goldin, "Time" 136)

> [O]nce we have renounced our lineal, eye-minded, reader's expectations—once we have freed our notion of sequence from our notion of time—we are able to see that the distribution of tenses in the . . . *Roland* is not haphazard at all, that it reflects a coherent pattern of history and necessity in which every event—every act, every gesture—finds its inevitable place.                                             (130)

The formulaic repetition and tense shifts also find their explanation in the oral/aural needs of both reciter and audience. We see each scene from slightly staggered perspectives, rather like the new panoramic photography in which hundreds of shots from multiple perspectives taken simultaneously yield an apparently moving image that tracks around a central, stationary spot or figure. That is, the person, for example, is immobile but seen from 360 degrees as the background shifts behind him. In the *Song of Roland*, as consecutive laisses add information, the reader sees the same scene, but slightly differently. For example, laisses 80–86 yield different views of the same moments—those crucial moments before Oliver urges the sounding of the olifant. In laisse 80, we learn

> Oliver is on a lofty hilltop.
> He looks down to the right over a grassy vale

And he sees the approach of the pagan army.
He called to Roland, his companion    (1017–20)

a description of the massed enemy and also voiced his suspicion of Ganelon's
having betrayed the French. Roland replies simply that he will not listen to
badmouthing of his stepfather. In laisse 81, "Oliver has climbed a hill. / Now
he has a clear view of" the assembled enemy, too numerous to count (1028–
29). Troubled, he descends the hill to share the news. This pair of laisses pres-
ents the enemy in increasingly ominous terms and sets up the conflict that is
about to arise between Roland and Oliver. The shift in verb tenses marks Oli-
ver's progression up the hill, and his moment of looking around before ad-
dressing Roland. Roland makes no reply. In laisse 82, Oliver again describes
the arms of the enemy, and he warns the French that the impending battle will
be like nothing they have ever experienced. In reply, the French soldiers state
their intention to stand their ground: "A curse on him who flees!" (1047). In
these three laisses, Oliver's trip up and down the hill is shown from different
angles, and little cogent riposte is offered. Laisses 83–85 include the three
times Oliver urges Roland to sound the olifant. Oliver's arguments grow in
force, from strictly logical (the pagans outnumber the French, and Charles will
return with help if he hears the horn) to hortatory (sound the olifant, and
Charles will return with all the barons) to desperate (sound your olifant now;
"I swear" [1072] Charles will hear it and return). Roland's replies are more of
one cloth; he meets Oliver's mounting desperation with impatient expressions
of ego and self-assurance. First, Roland would be a fool and shamed if he
sounded the horn. Then, Roland's kin and all of France would be shamed if he
sounded the olifant. Finally, Roland asserts that no man should ever be able to
say that mere pagans made him call for help. In each laisse, Roland expresses
his certainty that the enemy will die at his hands, that he will wreak havoc with
Durendal, and that the Spanish are fey. In laisse 86, Oliver finally replies to
Roland's reiterated argument: there is no shame in calling for help in the face
of such overwhelming odds. Roland retorts that the uneven field inspires him
and repeats his oath by "God and his angels and saints" not to shame France
(1089). His refrain about the doomed pagans is, however, replaced with the as-
sertion that Charles loves his men when they fight well. These carefully crafted
laisses lead up to the pivotal laisse 87 contrasting the *preux* Roland with the
*sage* Oliver. Each warrior's characteristics have now been set up: the valiant,
good, worthy Roland and the wise, careful, thoughtful Oliver.

   Perhaps the most important aspect of discussion for teaching the *Song of
Roland* is the point of view of the narrator. Students quickly discern that the
very first laisse positions the reader with the French: Charles the king is "our"
emperor. "We" are aligned with a powerful Christian warrior-king. His last op-
position lies in the hands of "King Marsile who does not love God" (7). By the
end of the first laisse, Marsile's inescapable doom is declared. Modern readers
unfamiliar with a medieval audience's literary aesthetic are sometimes put off

by this early announcement of the apparent denouement of the work. Their po-
litical radar is also set off by the clearly articulated, ignorant bigotry of the nar-
rator, who doesn't even know that Muslims do not worship Apollo (laisse 1).
"Why keep reading?" some ask. "We know the ending, and we don't like the pol-
itics." It is useful to discuss how earlier audiences found originality as we per-
ceive it today to be the hallmark of lesser works (see also Duggan's "Beyond the
Oxford Text: the Songs of Roland," in this volume). The reinvention of familiar
stories and the imitation of existing forms drew the praise of the medieval au-
dience. Knowing the ending is trivial; the route to the end is compelling. It is
also useful to remind students of the religious-political point of view of the
times. To that end, referring students to the works of Einhard and William of
Malmesbury is a good start. Also useful is contemporary Islamic material (see
also Stevenson, "The Postcolonial Classroom: Teaching the *Song of Roland*
and 'Saracen' Literature," in this volume). Both Christian and Islamic accounts
are conveniently found in Paul Halsall's *Internet Medieval Sourcebook*.

Most college students are familiar with other epics. The reader focuses on
an idealized, sometimes flawed, hero and on his extraordinary deeds—heroic
feats that advance stories of national, historical, or legendary significance.
There are standard parts to the epic, including the (usually lone) hero, the
journey (often to the otherworld), and the decisive battle. By the end of the
epic, the reader is filled with awe or pity for the hero and his people. Some
examples suffice. The geopolitical struggles of the Greeks and Trojans served
as a backdrop to Achilles's ruinous, personal wrath against his commander; by
the end of the *Iliad*, the reader is forced to contrast forever-immoderate Achil-
les to Hector, the pious son, loving husband and father, and loyal warrior.
Achilles's and Hector's personal journeys define the *Iliad*. Wily Odysseus,
whose odyssey is also set against the Trojan War, traveled in space and time;
overcame all obstacles, including those produced by his overbearing pride;
and returned to set his own house in order by means of a decisive battle. In
the *Aeneid*, pious father Aeneas led the ragtag survivors of the Trojan War to
their new home, confronted most of the challenges faced by Odysseus (in a
Roman way, of course), and almost reluctantly defeated Turnus in a battle
necessitated by the jealous bickering of the gods. And Beowulf, a hero about
whom the reader knows the least, destroyed three monsters that attacked
human civilization. All these epic heroes are showcased in lengthy poems
whose narrative structure is linear and continuous. The fates of these heroes
make sense to the reader. The same cannot be said of Roland.

A poem of French nationalism, the *Song of Roland* is the ultimate "us versus
them" epic. Unlike the authors of the *Iliad*, the *Odyssey*, the *Aeneid*, or *Be-
owulf*, the author of the *Song of Roland* sees only one perspective: "we" are
good, and "they" are evil and must—and will—be destroyed. "We" need know
nothing of "them" beyond the most surface information: they are dark-
skinned, mendacious infidels whose only perversely positive quality lies in the
misplaced valor of some of their warriors. But what sense can readers make

of Roland, who doesn't survive past the midpoint of his epic and who is welcomed to heaven by angels after slaughtering thousands of his demonized enemies? "Only absolute fidelity to an ideal can account for Roland's behavior throughout the poem, and especially for the manner of his death" (Terry, "Roland" 157). The narrator's love for France and Christianity—to the exclusion of all other points of view—informs and drives this hero. Again, historical contexts for the poem help the reader. Few undergraduates know how advanced the civilization of Muslim Spain was. Contemporary Muslim views on conflicts with Christians provide the most interesting counterpoints to those verifiable kernels that underpin the epic: Einhard's mention of Roland during the slaughter of Charlemagne's rear guard at Rencesvals, and William of Malmesbury's assertion that the *Song of Roland* was used to inspire warriors on the eve of battle.[1]

However, historical context is insufficient. It even can be limiting for the nonmajor, who may have only one encounter with this difficult text. Reader response can yield more-fruitful avenues for class discussion. After 9/11, some students—and some faculty members—have a reservoir of emotions that relate painfully to the conflict of a Western culture with the Islamic world. Some readers have perhaps experienced fear of and impotent fury against an unknown enemy, as well as the desire to wipe a dark threat from their world. Others have been the victims of the bigotry that arose out of that same fear and fury that wished ill on an enemy. The medieval epic's rhetoric does not differ significantly from the saber rattling of late 2001, so faculty members can avail themselves of a powerful teaching slant in that it is easier for students to discuss why blind hatred of another people or their religion is abhorrent and wrong when safely distanced by centuries. And the perspectives gained from this discussion of a long-distant battle can help process the difference between a war on terrorists masquerading in a cloak of religious fanaticism and the persecution of whole peoples.

Student readers fall into two main categories. There are students who side with Roland and the French because that is what the narrator does; that is, they accept the epic's point of view uncritically. And there are students who see immediately the rank nature of the polemic. Addressing the first set of readers is easier if more disturbing: instructors have to resist the urge to rail, Can't you just see the bigotry? Teachers can point to numerous examples of blatant racial stereotyping. Three examples will serve: laisse 3's assertion that the Muslims would rather sacrifice their sons than lose their dignity; laisse 78's description of the country of one Muslim leader, the land where

> The sun does not shine and grain cannot grow,
> Rain does not fall nor dew collect.
> There is no stone which is not completely black.
> Some say that devils live there;         (980–83)

and laisse 114's description of "a Saracen, Abisme," who "is black as molten pitch" and "loves treachery and murder" (1474–75). Clearly, for the French warriors, "War against a pagan enemy would be a gift from God" (Terry, "Roland" 158). Hagiography from this time period is replete with martyrs who viewed their suffering and deaths as gifts from God. The French warriors—granted absolution from their sins in return for death in battle against the Saracens—shared this view (laisse 89). Furthermore, in the second major section of the *Song of Roland*, the story of the betrayals of Roland and Charlemagne by Ganelon is overshadowed by the narrator's contemporary anti-Muslim vitriol, linked to the Crusades of his own era. "Roland, Oliver, and the others of the rear guard are irreproachably courageous" (Terry, "Roland" 159), but is their behavior commendable or even understandable? Why should Roland believe firmly that asking for help is shameful? The answer lies in the Christian filter of their moral vision. "Roland acts out of a faith so much a part of himself that he does not even allude to it" (Terry, "Roland" 161). But the sheer numbers of the dead, the odds of each confrontation, the decisiveness of the battles, and the completeness of the French victory are "travesties of proportion" (Vance 58) that are difficult for modern readers to accept. The most useful modern parallel is the unrealistic scale of action-adventure films. But such films generally lack the religious conviction that is the driving force for Roland and his peers—and his enemies, however allegedly misguided. In some ways, the westerns of the 1950s provide a better parallel: the white man's westward expansion, fueled by the philosophy of eminent domain, with its total disdain for the native peoples and their cultures that it displaced, is closer to the nationalist fervor and single-minded animus of the French.

Addressing the students who see the narrator's bigotry is more complex and rewarding. On 12 September, 2001, I taught the *Song of Roland* to a freshman Western literature survey in a classroom from which we could see, smell, and taste the smoke from the plume that marked the fallen World Trade Center. The very same students who wanted to "nuke 'em back to the Stone Age" had to admit that they had no idea whom it was they wanted to fight and that their desire for absolute destruction of an unknown enemy was painfully, embarrassingly equivalent to the French warriors' motives for destroying Muslim Spain. The narrator allows no room for a range of opinion. Indeed, the final disposition of Ganelon and his supporters and family shows that the author believes even mere contact with nonorthodox beliefs is a possible contamination to society. Other epics view conflict with more ambivalence, tolerate a range of readings. But the *Song of Roland* does not allow for such a range: its purpose—promoting French nationalism—does not permit it to.

NOTE

[1]See the section "Spanish Expedition" in Einhard. See also William of Malmesbury, "Battle" and *Gesta* 455.

# Teaching the *Song of Roland* in General and Survey Courses in World and Medieval Literature

*Ann W. Engar*

I teach a semester course for honors students entitled Intellectual Traditions, in which students read major literary, philosophical, and religious texts of the Middle Ages. In particular, students look at the feudal relationship between lord and vassal, the importance of male friendship in warrior societies, and the multivoiced judgments of medieval heroes. The *Song of Roland* plays a pivotal role in the discussion of the hero between the early Germanic *Beowulf* and the late-Renaissance *Hamlet*: his self-confidence expressed verbally before the court; his dedication to his king; his strength as a fighter; his friendship with other warriors; his belief in divine powers; his longing for renown, gold, and goodness; and the dangers to which his loss exposes his society.

Reading *Beowulf* establishes for students the medieval relationship between a lord and his thanes. Beowulf, the nephew and thane to Hygelac, does not fight directly for his lord in the major adventures of the poem but gives him the richest treasures he acquires and announces his loyalty and subordination (lines 1830–35). Though Beowulf had been considered a laggard in his youth (lines 2183–89), as a young adult he exhibits the bravado and strength of a hero. Arriving on the Danish shore, Beowulf announces to the watchman that any respite for Hrothgar from Grendel's attacks will come from him: "I can calm the turmoil and terror in his mind" (282). Beowulf has no lord-thane bond to Hrothgar, but he bravely comes to Denmark and announces he will fight weaponless with Grendel "to heighten Hygelac's fame / and gladden his heart" (435–36). He clearly values renown. As he later tells Hrothgar, "Let whoever can / win glory before death. When a warrior is gone, / that will be his best and only bulwark" (1387–89). His motivation is thus personal reputation as a form of immortality and fame for his lord.

Because these tribes were warrior societies with men fighting beside one another, depending on one another, and protecting one another, it is inevitable that male friendship would become an important theme of medieval literature. One of Hrothgar's greatest losses in the fights with Grendel and his mother is that of his "soul-mate," "true mentor," and "right-hand man," Aeschere (1325–26). To some extent Beowulf begins to assuage Hrothgar's sorrow, as Hrothgar tells him, "My liking for you / deepens with time, dear Beowulf" (1853–54), praises him for bringing about a pact of friendship between the Geats and the Danes, and warns him to beware of pride (1760).

With the themes of the hero, the lord-thane relationship, and friendship in mind, students are now prepared to confront the second part of the poem, when Beowulf finds himself in Hrothgar's position as an old king, once a powerful protector but now shrunken in strength. With a mind "in turmoil" and brain confused by "unaccustomed anxiety and gloom" (2331), Beowulf prepares once again to fight single-handedly, "too proud / to line up with a large army / against the sky-plague" (2346–47). Accompanied by twelve warriors, he excuses them from battle by saying that it is only up to him to prove his worth as king and win gold. Though his words emphasize honor and riches, his actions defend his people and take vengeance for the burning of his home and kingdom. The poet praises Beowulf for not taking the "coward path" (2541). Beowulf fulfills his kingly obligation though is unwise to fight alone.

Betrayed by his shield, which does not hold long against the dragon's flames, and his sword, which fails "as it never should have" (2586), Beowulf is further abandoned by his "high-born," "hand-picked" followers, who take the coward's path in running for the wood's safety (2597). Only Wiglaf lives up to his duty. He reminds his associates of their pledges of loyalty to their lord in the mead hall and promises to repay the gifts of swords and helmets. He inspires the wounded Beowulf with thoughts of glory so that he deals the dragon a death wound. The poet praises Beowulf and Wiglaf for living up to their commitments to each other (2706–09). The last duties Wiglaf performs for Beowulf are gathering the treasure and building a burial barrow to be seen by all ships.

John Niles, in his book *Beowulf*, formulates good questions about the ending of *Beowulf* for students to discuss and to adapt when they read the *Song of Roland* (238–44):

> Is Beowulf's decision to fight the dragon imprudent? (238)
>
> Should the hero have accepted help? (240)
>
> Does the hero act for his own glory, out of pride? (241)
>
> Is the hero defeated, and does he die in vain? (243)

Beowulf prides himself on leaving a legacy of gold and fame. The poem does close with funereal praise of his graciousness, fair-mindedness, kindness, and keenness to win glory. But I ask my students if they as readers feel any tension at the end of the poem, any questioning of the values of these warrior societies. They find evidence of tension, since Beowulf's death has left his people exposed. News of the cowardliness of his followers will spread; Hygelac's attacks on the Franks will be remembered; the feud between the Geats and Swedes will revive; and, by Wiglaf's order, the sought-after treasure will melt in Beowulf's funeral pyre and be buried along with him. The "wise" Wiglaf predicts feuding, wars, and exile for the Geats. Though Beowulf's longing for treasure was not selfish, Wiglaf comments, "Often, when one man follows his own will / many are hurt" (3077). Obviously the dragon's rampages had to be stopped, but Wiglaf claims Beowulf could not be convinced to leave the custodian of the gold hoard alone. Beowulf's heroism and the cowardice of the Geat warriors leave the kingdom in chaos.

After reading selections from the Koran and Islamic philosophy, my students read major portions of the *Song of Roland*. One immediate response they have is to criticize the poem as a biased piece of Christian propaganda, given that the poet turns Muslims into worshipers of idols, Muhammad, and multiple gods. Another immediate response is to judge Roland as a cartoonish superhero who is too prideful to blow his horn in time to save his men. In their eyes Oliver is the greater hero, since he demands that Roland blow the horn to bring Charles's troops and save their forces.

My first reaction to their comments is to ask them why the poem is entitled the *Song of Roland* and why Charles and the other nobles do not criticize Roland for not blowing his horn earlier. Furthermore, if pride is the major sin of medieval thought, why do saints and angels bear Roland's soul to paradise?

These questions obviously call for a reexamination of the feudal code and Roland as a hero. Like Beowulf, he is the nephew and vassal of the king. He enters the poem with Oliver, and the poet terms them both "proz" ("valiant"; 176) and "gentilz" ("noble"; 1093). Roland's first speech correctly advises Charles to avoid trusting Marsile and to live up to the feudal code by avenging the deaths of his murdered ambassadors. When Charles asks for a volunteer to go to Marsile, Roland is the second to volunteer. When Charles rejects his offer, Roland nominates Ganelon and says, "it must be a wise man who delivers the message" (294). Like Beowulf, Roland speaks fearlessly of the deeds he is willing to perform. In this first scene he reveals himself as a wise and committed adviser to his lord and a willing ambassador.

Roland and Oliver's friendship is one of the greatest in Western literature, comparable to those of Achilles and Patroclus or David and Jonathan. Unlike Hrothgar and Beowulf or Beowulf and Wiglaf, Roland and Oliver are peers and similar in age. Oliver repeatedly refers to Roland as "sire cumpainz" ("lord companion"). As readers, we first see them together as Oliver tries to get himself nominated as ambassador: he competitively denigrates his friend as being too quarrelsome, hostile, and fierce (though Roland in the next few laisses will merely smile or laugh as Ganelon wrathfully attacks him). Charles silences Roland and Oliver as he would boisterous brothers. When Ganelon nominates Roland to be in the rear guard, Oliver loyally accompanies him.

I ask students to characterize Oliver and Roland and to examine their relationship. Why is Roland, not Oliver, the hero? Oliver is the watchdog: he first comments on hearing the Saracens and is first to climb a hill to see their approach. He is first to blame Ganelon for treachery. He calculates the disparity between Saracen and French forces and tells Roland to blow his horn. He sees no dishonor in asking for aid when the French are so outnumbered. The poet then praises both men as marvelous vassals, brave, wise men with lofty words. Oliver blames Roland for not deigning to blow the horn and says that if Charles were here, the troops would suffer no harm. Oliver is pragmatic, but self-preservation has never been the hallmark of a hero.

Roland does not upbraid Oliver for cowardice or for failure to live up to the heroic code. He reminds his "Lord companion, friend" (1113):

> For his lord a vassal must suffer great hardship
> And endure both great heat and great cold;
> He must also part with flesh and blood.   (1117–19)

Archbishop Turpin next rides forth, does not criticize Roland, and reminds the Franks, as Roland had, of their commitment to Charles. Roland then summons Oliver, praises him for his perspicacity in recognizing Ganelon's betrayal, and assures him that it is the emperor's duty to avenge them. He upholds both the feudal code and his love of his friend.

When students in the precursor to this course, Intellectual Traditions: The Ancient World, read the *Odyssey*, they frequently criticize Odysseus for shouting his name after he had blinded the Cyclops, especially because the Cyclops then throws rocks at the ship causing it to be drawn back toward shore. They accuse Odysseus of hubris and only reluctantly begin to see that, because of the importance of reputation and excellence in his culture, Odysseus *must* shout out his name, regardless of the danger. Similarly, students accuse Roland of pride and disregard for his troops and misunderstand the cultural context (for more on the pride question, see Jones's essay, "Roland versus Oliver," in this volume). Because of Roland's commitment to the feudal code, he must carry out his responsibility as leader of the rear guard. Only after he has done so can he blow the horn and summon Charles to vengeance. Otherwise, "throughout the fair land of France" he should "lose" his "good name" (1054).

Fame and reputation thus motivate Roland as well as Beowulf. Roland too worries about more than personal fame: he does not want either his kinsmen or fair France to incur reproach. His love for France has far more strength than Beowulf's sentiments about Geatland. Likewise, gold is not a large consideration for Roland, though he does claim he and his sword have made Charles mighty and rich (2354). Another important element in Roland's story is loyalty to God, the liege lord of Charles. Whereas Beowulf and Hrothgar spoke vaguely of "halig God," the "Almighty Judge / of good deeds and bad, the Lord God, / Head of the Heavens and High King of the World" was unknown to their people (180–83). But in the *Song of Roland* duty to God becomes a primary element. In his last acts Roland confesses his sins, prays for God's grace, and proffers "his right glove to God" (2389).

I next ask students whether there is tension in the *Song of Roland*'s version of the feudal code similar to the tensions in *Beowulf*. The tension between Oliver and Roland is resolved as Oliver dies blessing Roland above all men. Within the poem the deaths of Roland, the Twelve Peers, and twenty thousand Franks are blamed on Ganelon, not Roland, and Roland is credited with defeating Marsile, killing thousands of Saracens including Marsile's heir, and protecting Charles. Yet modern readers still feel that the feudal code itself has large deficiencies because Charles could have aided the rear guard and saved lives. In addition, though the poem does not attack feudal mentality, it does end on a strong note of battle weariness as Charles once more prepares to fight pagans and "weeps and tugs at his white beard" (4001–02). If there is order and stability in this world, it is bought at tremendous personal cost.

The final work students read in the semester is *Hamlet*, which provides a last look at the medieval hero, his feudal world, and friendship. The story of Hamlet, probably as ancient as that of Beowulf, is nevertheless cast in the world of Renaissance humanism and politics. Like Beowulf and Roland, Hamlet is the nephew of the ruler, though he exhibits distrust of Claudius rather than fealty. He enters the poem not boasting of his ability, advising his king, and volunteering for a dangerous mission but in an aside. His remarks to the queen and king are angry and mournful, but he does assert himself as an honest man and promises to obey the queen's wishes.

However, Hamlet's father represents the medieval hero and lives by the feudal code more than Hamlet does. Hamlet's father's spirit is dressed in warrior's clothing and tells Hamlet he is bound to revenge. The spirit speaks in traditional Christian terms of tormenting flames and a need for purgation. He will not dictate how Hamlet is to carry out the revenge, but Hamlet is to cleanse the house of Denmark.

Hamlet, however, is not a typical medieval hero. He has been a scholar, poet, lover of theater, and lover of Ophelia (no woman is mentioned in connection with Beowulf, and Aude appears in the *Song of Roland* only to fall dead at news of Roland's death). Though he has practiced fencing, Hamlet is no warrior. Whether his lord is considered to be Claudius or his father, neither man's commands are immediately carried out: their truth and morality must be analyzed and tested. Before Hamlet can kill Claudius while Claudius is praying in the chapel, before he can "drink hot blood / And do such bitter business as the day / Would quake to look on" (3.2.398–400), he must consider whether killing Claudius at that point would effect the revenge he has sworn to seek. Hamlet believes humans have "capability and godlike reason," which should not "grow moldy from lack of use" (4.4.38–39).

Though Hamlet is more hero as intellectual than hero as warrior, friendship still appears as a strong theme in the play. Rosencrantz and Guildenstern, like the retainers who desert Beowulf and like Ganelon who betrays Charles, represent false friendship: more important to them is the favor of those who wield power, so much so that they are willing to escort Hamlet to his death.

More in the role of a true friend like Oliver is Horatio. Though he does not have the social status of Hamlet, he too is a scholar at Wittenberg. Like Oliver, he is the watchdog: he is called on to see the ghost, begs it to speak, feels his duty to report its presence to Hamlet, and informs the watchmen of the designs of Fortinbras. Like Oliver, he is pragmatic: he warns Hamlet not to follow the ghost lest it lead him into danger or madness. He calls Hamlet "sweet lord" (3.2.55) and Hamlet praises him as a "just" (line 74) man "who is not passion's slave" (line 75) whom he will wear in his "heart's core" (line 76). But when Hamlet jubilantly calls on him to confirm Claudius's behavior at the play, Horatio says he did "perceive" and "note" the king's behavior but does not pronounce his guilt (3.2.293, 296). Horatio is the dependable man who can tell the truth of the tragedy of the Danish court and defend Hamlet's honor; but the man who is not passion's slave cannot be an avenger, cannot brutalize himself to kill.

The final problem students consider is the ending of *Hamlet*. I ask students if they feel any tension or perceive a multiplicity of views, as in *Beowulf* or the *Song of Roland*. Is Claudius alone responsible for the seven deaths in the play? Does Hamlet, although moral and admirable like Roland, bear some responsibility? Or is the tragedy a result of the moral turpitude of the time?

Hamlet does not act for personal fame or for gold, though he is willing to fight Laertes for his honor, to have Rosencrantz and Guildenstern killed for betraying him, and to kill Claudius because he "hath killed my king, and whored my mother, / Popped in between th' election and my hopes, / Thrown out his angle for my proper life" (5.2.64–66) in short, to prevent "this canker of our nature come / In further evil" (69–70). Hamlet himself admits his longing for power, but his major reason for revenge is moral disgust. Like Roland in stopping the Saracens or Beowulf in killing the dragon, he acts valiantly in ridding Denmark of the contagion of Claudius. Like Beowulf, Hamlet has his funereal praise in the lines of Horatio—"Now cracks a noble heart. Good night, sweet Prince"—who wishes him a heavenly cortege like that of Roland, "And flights of angels sing thee to thy rest" (5.2.360–61).

But this play has no surety in a liege-lord God and in ultimate justice, since death is an "undiscover'd country" (3.1.76). Also, just as Beowulf's death has left his kingdom vulnerable and in disarray and just as the death of Roland, Charles's greatest warrior, has left Charles weakened emotionally and militarily, so too Hamlet's death leaves Denmark open for Fortinbras, the man who inadequately pays tribute to Hamlet as a potential warrior and the profligate who for "a little patch" of unprofitable ground has spent enormous money and troops (4.4.18). As with the reader's reaction to Roland's death, the response to Hamlet's death is not only sorrow over the loss of a noble and irreplaceable man but also weariness in the knowledge that the battle against evil will not end.

Studying the *Song of Roland* in tandem with *Beowulf* and *Hamlet* can thus highlight the strengths of the poem. Reading *Beowulf* and the *Song of Roland* can help students understand the reciprocal elements of the lord-vassal relationship and the consequences of its breakdown. They can see the addition of service to God and love of land as parts of the hero's responsibilities in the *Song of Roland*. They can also learn to appreciate the significant achievement of the portrayal of male friendship. In juxtaposing Roland with Hamlet, students can contrast a hero whose strength comes from absolute, self-sacrificing devotion to the values of his society with a hero whose strength comes from questioning the moral underpinnings of his society. The character and role of Horatio can make clearer the sensibility and secondary nature of Oliver.

Finally, through reading and writing about all three works, students can examine the whole notion of heroism—the struggle to achieve or uphold some moral principle, the sense of honor, the self-confidence, the desire for glory, the courage, the violence, the anxiety, the recklessness, the instinct for self-preservation, and the threat of social disintegration that Beowulf, Roland, and Hamlet all confront.

# Roland versus Oliver

### Catherine M. Jones

The celebrated quarrel between Roland and Oliver has, in the words of Ge-
rard J. Brault, "caused more ink to be spilled than any other single episode
in Turoldus's epic" (Song 1: 179). The companions' heated exchanges over the
sounding of the olifant figure prominently in discussions of the song's history
and poetics. Joseph Bédier considered the conflict to be the brainchild of the
Oxford *Roland* poet, conceived in a "sacred minute" that inspired the com-
position of the entire masterpiece (*Légendes* 3: 448). The episode's importance
is clearly marked in the economy of the poem by its formal virtuosity. Re-
counted in two separate but echoing series of similar laisses, the dispute arises
on the threshold of battle and resurfaces at the realization of imminent defeat,
providing a lyrical and rhetorical frame for the disaster of Rencesvals.

Above all, the two horn scenes are frequently extracted from the whole for
the purpose of character study, since they are crucial to the interpretation of
the hero's behavior. According to one school of thought dating back to Gaston
Paris, Roland refuses initially to sound the horn because of the tragic flaw of
hubris, expressed in Old French as *desmesure*; bellicose and confident of vic-
tory, he is responsible for the defeat of the rear guard but ultimately repents
and thereby merits his apotheosis (see Burger; Hall; Jonin "Deux langages";
Le Gentil, "Propos"; Paris, *Histoire* [1974]; and van Emden, "Reception").
Another group of scholars has sought to debunk the *desmesure* hypothesis,
claiming that Roland's decision is based on his earlier promise to lead the rear
guard and resist Saracen attack; faithful to the feudal values binding him to
Charlemagne, he recalls his lord only to exact vengeance and ensure proper

burial for his knights (see Brault, Song; Cook; Crist; Foulet; Guiette; and Kibler, "Roland's Pride").

The horn scenes present two opposing but defensible views of the meaning of Rencesvals and as such are highly conducive to lively classroom discussion. The absence of any explicit judgment by the narrator should, in theory, constitute a genuine interpretive challenge. I have found, however, that when students read the episode without advance preparation, they generally characterize the debate as a "no-brainer" in favor of Oliver's position. Indeed, Roland's choice may be placed alongside other moments of decision in early French literature (for example, the ending of La princesse de Clèves) that students misconstrue from a lack of contextual knowledge, a failure to read closely, and a set of cultural values alien to those expressed in the text. Since I expect students to make a reasoned and informed judgment, whether for or against the desmesure hypothesis, I try to compensate for the fundamental alterity of Roland's stance by highlighting in advance the textual and contextual cues that justify it. In this way, students are led to reflect critically on the "surprising otherness" of Roland's worldview before contrasting it with their own horizon of expectations (see Jauss 182).

I would like to acknowledge my debt to Robert Francis Cook's The Sense of the Song of Roland, which long ago prompted me to revise in a significant way my pedagogical approach to this work. Regardless of one's own position on the problem of desmesure, Cook's impeccable scholarship and careful reading illuminate those aspects of the poem that students find most puzzling. Drawing on his commentary, I set up the "Roland versus Oliver" conflict on the day before students read the episode by presenting an introductory lecture and discussion; I then distribute a series of pointed questions to orient their reading. This initial phase is unabashedly biased in favor of Roland's position, since it anticipates and counterbalances students' inclination to dismiss manifestations of the feudal ethos that are in fact indispensable to the understanding of the hero's discourse. It is, however, only a prelude to further consideration of the merits of each argument.

In my introductory remarks, I explain the obligations inherent in the lord-vassal relationship, including the lord's responsibility to avenge his vassal's wrongful death. Other pertinent feudal values are the importance of lineage and the vital role of oral promises. I also find it useful to elicit from students the definition of a rear guard, and I ask them to speculate on the function of such a unit in the retreat of a vast army through the treacherous mountain passes of enemy territory. This commonplace of military strategy is obvious but often overlooked: a rear guard constitutes only a fraction of the force (generally no more than one-fifth), and it is designed to protect the main force from enemy attack. All of this contextual knowledge is essential to the understanding of not only the two horn scenes but also the nomination scene, which forms the basis of Roland's decision not to recall Charlemagne (see Guiette 850; Cook 56).

My questions direct students first to the specific language used in the nomination scene, in which Roland accepts the charge of the rear guard. What does Roland promise in laisse 59, and how does he qualify that promise?

La rereguarde avez sur mei jugiét.
N'i perdrat Carles, li reis ki France tient,
Men escïentre, palefreid ne destrer,
Ne mul ne mule que deiet chevalcher;
Nen i perdrat ne runcin ne sumer
Quë as espees ne seit einz eslegiét.     (754–59)

You have appointed me to the rearguard.
Charles, the king who holds France, will not lose,
I warrant, a single palfrey or war-horse,
Nor mule or jenny, which is fit to ride,
And he will not lose a single pack-horse or sumpter
Without its first being purchased by the sword.

Roland's declaration is confident but precise. He does not guarantee the rear guard's absolute safety. Rather, in a rare hypotactic construction, he promises that Charles will lose nothing that is not first vigorously defended (see Cook 46–47). Later, in laisse 63, he promises the principal army safe passage across the perilous mountain passes (line 790). He thus promises nothing that he does not eventually accomplish (Cook 137). Mindful of the conventional composition of a rear guard and proud of his family's tradition of service, he refuses Charles's strange offer of half the army, accepting only 20,000 men to protect the approximately 100,000 troops accompanying the emperor (lines 784–89). These lines establish the parameters of Roland's role as leader of the rear guard, as he himself envisions it.

In analyzing the two-part horn conflict, I focus on both the lyrical and the polemical dimensions of the episode. The first horn scene is composed of a series of five exchanges, each initiated by Oliver in response to the growing certainty of battle. The episode may be subdivided into an initial set of four laisses preparing the dispute (79–82) and the three *laisses similaires* (83–85) in which Oliver urges his companion to sound the olifant. First, I ask students to appreciate the subtle play between repetition and narrative or rhetorical development in each section: what gestures and utterances are repeated, and with what nuances? How does the argument progress? Students quickly become attuned to the masterful techniques of oral-formulaic style that account for the "beautiful architecture" of the Oxford *Roland* (Rychner, *Chanson* 100). Repeated elements in the first series of laisses (Oliver's vantage point atop a lofty hill; the formidable display of Saracen armor) convey essential narrative information and highlight the formal contours of each stanza. The *laisses similaires* present a well-calibrated reiteration of Oliver's anguished exhortation and Roland's refusal, as Roland offers slightly varying reasons with each retelling.

Students are next asked to analyze the vocabulary used to characterize each knight's reaction to the prospect of battle. In the first four laisses, Oliver is associated with verbs of sensory perception. His first pronouncement is prompted by the sound of a thousand enemy trumpets: "Granz est la noise, si l'*oïrent* Franceis. / Dist Oliver: 'Sire cumpainz, ce crei, / De Sarrazins purum bataille aveir' " ("The noise is great and the Franks *heard* it. / Oliver said: 'Lord companion, I think / We may have a battle with the Saracens' "; 1005–07). The verb *veoir* ("to see") echoes throughout laisses 80–82: "Si *veit* venir cele gent paienur" ("And he *sees* the approach of the pagan army"; 1019); "Devers Espaigne *vei* venir tel brunur" ("Over towards Spain I can *see* the glint of burnished steel"; 1021); "Or *veit* il ben d'Espaigne le regnét" ("Now he has a clear *view* of the kingdom of Spain"; 1029); "Dist Oliver: 'Jo ai paiens *veüz*' " ("Oliver said: 'I have *seen* pagans' "; 1039). Oliver's gaze is directed at the sheer quantity of enemy troops, figured metonymically by their armor: "*Tanz* blancs osbercs, *tanz* elmes flambëus" ("*So many* shining hauberks and [*so many*] gleaming helmets"; 1022). He is intent on estimating their numbers: "Sul les escheles ne poet il *acunter*: / Tant en i ad que *mesure n'en set*" ("On his own he cannot *count* the divisions; / They are too numerous for him to *measure their extent*"; 1034–35). In the three *laisses similaires*, Oliver draws his strategic conclusion: alarmed by the ratio of Saracens to Christians (five to one), he urges his companion to sound the horn and summon Charles's army.

Whereas Oliver's discourse is rooted in the perception of immediate circumstances, Roland responds in terms of general principles. He utters his famous feudal credo: "Ben devuns ci estre pur nostre rei: / Pur sun seignor deit hom susfrir destreiz / E endurer e granz chalz e granz freiz" ("It is our duty to be here for our king: / For his lord a vassal must suffer hardships / And endure great heat and great cold"; 1009–11). In refusing to sound the olifant, he envisages the unacceptable consequences in conditional and subjunctive clauses (1053–54, 1062–64, 1073–75). He offers three successive reasons for his decision, all of which reflect transcendent values: his *los* ("good name"; 1054), which is not personal glory, but rather "the opinion of those whose responsibility it is to judge trustworthiness on the basis of knowledge"(Cook 66); France's reputation (1064); and his family's honor (1064, 1076). Each of the *laisses similaires* concludes with future clauses in which Roland announces the fierce blows he will strike with his sword Durendal and the eventual defeat of the pagan forces. All of these declarations will prove true.

The first horn scene concludes with the oft-quoted and controversial line 1093, "Rollant est proz e Oliver est sage" ("Roland is brave and Oliver is wise"), which must be weighed in conjunction with the following narratorial pronouncement: "Ambedui unt merveillus vasselage" ("Both are marvellous vassals"; 1094). It has been argued that these particular lines point to the classic opposition between *fortitudo* and *sapientia*, or "warrior temperament" and "prudence" (Curtius 176). Once again, however, I alert students to word choice.

"E" and "ambedui" suggest that the passage attests to the companions' joint worthiness (see Brault, *"Sapientia"* 104–07). In those classes using an Old French or bilingual edition, students may be asked how the words *proz* and *sage* are used elsewhere in the text. Of course, scholars have undertaken exhaustive lexical studies of the two epithets. Evidence shows a great deal of semantic overlap. *Proz* designates general knightly excellence and may be used in the context of bravery or even intelligence; it is used elsewhere to describe Oliver (line 576). *Sage* in the Oxford *Roland* is usually linked to general discernment and military or diplomatic savvy but is also associated with courage (see Brault, *"Sapientia"* 105–13; Misrahi and Hendrickson 361–67; Cook 70–71). In any case, line 1093 is neutral with respect to the companions' quarrel: it constitutes neither an endorsement of Oliver's advice nor a condemnation of Roland's boldness.

I ask students to read the second horn scene against the first, noting similarities in structure and differences in narrative circumstances. The ironic reversal is immediately apparent. In the lines preceding the dispute, it is now Roland who perceives immediate circumstances (*"Tanz* bons vassals *vëez* gesir par tere!"* ["You see so many fine knights lying on the ground"; 1694). Likewise, the series of *laisses similaires* highlights the reversal of roles, as Roland's decision to sound the olifant reverberates against Oliver's furious appeals to family honor and knightly reputation. Laisse 131 is typically cited as evidence of Roland's tragic flaw, as it opposes *mesure* ("caution"; 1725) to Roland's supposed *folie* ("folly"; 1724) and *legerie* ("recklessness"; 1726). I ask students to consider the source of these charges (Oliver) and whether Oliver's angry accusations may be considered authoritative. After all, only one other voice in the text reproaches the hero for excessive pride: that of Ganelon (389, 474; see Kibler, "Roland's Pride" 148–49).

Finally, I note that Roland does not express remorse with regard to his previous decision, and I ask students to explain what has changed since the first horn scene. How does Turpin's intervention help to explain Roland's bewildering change of heart? The archbishop acknowledges that Charlemagne cannot save the rear guard but agrees that Roland should sound the olifant: "Venget li reis, si nus purrat venger" ("Let the king come, then he can avenge our deaths"; 1744). Turpin, whose authority we may reasonably accept, understands Roland's reasoning. The leader of the rear guard has kept his promise; the troops have stood their ground but are now sustaining grievous losses. Their deaths must be avenged (see Guiette 850–51; Cook 88).

Once students have completed this close reading, they are prepared to engage in an informed discussion of the quarrel. To what extent is each knight justified? Does the text ultimately condemn or vindicate Roland's decision? Are we being asked to admire Oliver's pragmatism or Roland's fierce submission to duty? Or do their irreconcilable differences reveal weaknesses in the feudal system (Vance 51)? As they debate these questions, students are interested to discover that scholars continue to debate them as well. I introduce for their consideration arguments from both sides of the fence, several of which I summarize here.

In support of the *desmesure* hypothesis, Pierre Jonin presents a detailed linguistic analysis of the first horn scene. He demonstrates that Roland's discourse is characterized by heavy use of the first person singular, verbs of will and action (most of the latter promising violence), and the absence of demonstratives. Oliver, on the other hand, uses the more inclusive first person plural, verbs of perception, and demonstratives that gesture outward. Roland invokes the sword, a symbol of rupture and violence, whereas Oliver champions the horn, a symbol of communication and defense. Jonin concludes that Roland is self-centered and fanatically aggressive, as opposed to the more reflective and social Oliver ("Deux langages" 98).

Jody Enders examines the horn scenes in the context of medieval logic. Shifting the discussion away from character traits, she studies instead "correctness of thought, logical progression of ideas, and relevancy of opinions expressed" (83). For her, Roland does not exhibit *desmesure*. Roland's mode of reasoning is deductive: he proceeds from established feudal principles to legitimate conclusions. Oliver, however, reasons inductively, proceeding from observation of the physical world to general conclusions about the appropriate course of action. Enders observes that deduction and induction are complementary forms of reasoning but that deduction is always considered superior (91–92). Moreover, she detects serious flaws in Oliver's argument, notably his failure to consider two enthymemic (that is, unstated but self-evident) premises: Roland's promise to Charles and the rear guard's function (90–93). She concludes that Roland "acts with loyalty, logic, and reason, thus representing the cause of Christianity with the best possible means" (100).

Intertextual evidence may also be adduced to assess the medieval reception of the conflict. This sort of comparative analysis is best suited to a graduate course in the epic, but undergraduates should at least be aware that Roland and Oliver reappear in a number of chansons de geste. Wolfgang van Emden finds that, despite some positive portrayals of Roland's character, most later epics depict him as excessively prideful ("Reception" 30). Robert Guiette compares the horn scenes in the Oxford *Roland* to their counterparts in the fifteenth-century prose *Conquestes de Charlemagne*. The prose adaptation substantially modifies the second horn scene, since Roland admits that he was wrong in refusing the wise counsel of his friend Oliver (848). Guiette asserts, however, that the later reworking is more clerical in tone and betrays the spirit of heroic sacrifice glorified by the Oxford *Roland* (854). Clearly, medieval poets were no more unified than modern scholars in their appreciation of Roland's behavior.

# Coping with the Death of Roland

*Gerard J. Brault*

If one asks any class to comment on the scene in which Roland dies in the Oxford poem, chances are someone will bring up "the five stages of dying," namely denial, anger, bargaining, depression, and acceptance. Popularized by the psychiatrist Elisabeth Kübler-Ross in 1969, this sequence may shed light on the process many people today undergo trying to cope with death, one's own or a loved one's. But when used to describe Roland's death it almost invariably leads to a forced interpretation that finds little or no support in the text. For example, the hero of the *Song of Roland* does not bargain or become depressed as he prepares to die.

Actually, the way Roland meets his death in this epic is told from two different points of view, that of the omniscient narrator and that of Charlemagne, who arrives on the scene with his men after Roland's passing. The author says that he is able to provide his version of what transpires at Rencesvals—which, it turns out, includes supernatural occurrences—thanks to a saintly eyewitness's account. The emperor reconstructs Roland's dying moments by recollecting his nephew's words at Aix and by describing what he sees at Rencesvals.

What Charles already knows and what he learns at Rencesvals are more fragmentary than the poet's earlier and more detailed story of what actually happened. However, in addition to arousing anew the audience's emotional response to the death of Roland, the poet's recounting of the emperor's moving experience enables one better to distinguish what in the earlier passage is of this world as opposed to what is not.

## The Long Farewell

The lengthy battle of Rencesvals has two phases. The first part, the encounter between Charlemagne's rear guard and Marsile's army, begins with the poet's exclamation: "See now, Franks and pagans joined in battle" (1187), which immediately precedes the clash between Roland and Marsile's nephew, Aelroth (1188). After defeating Marsile in a desperate and costly struggle, Roland and the remainder of his men immediately and unexpectedly confront a whole new Saracen army led by Marganice, the caliph (1913–14). This new phase ends when Roland finally drives the enemy from the field, leaving him completely victorious (2162–63). Only the mortally wounded archbishop remains with him now.

About halfway through the initial encounter, just before Engeler is slain—he is the first of the Twelve Peers to perish—the poet describes a great storm in France (1423–37). Things are plainly beginning to go very badly for the

Franks and their leader, for the poet interprets the tempest prophetically as "the great sorrow for the death of Roland" (1437).

When does Roland become convinced that he is about to die? As the first phase of the battle is about to begin, Roland twice suggests that he may meet his end in this conflict (1091, 1122), but he utters these words while rousing his men to fury, and the reference is simply forceful speech. At this point, the likelihood of his actually dying is clearly not on his mind (see also 1867: "I shall die of grief, if nothing else kills me"). When the second phase commences, Roland realizes that, this time, he cannot escape alive (1922–23, 1935–36). But once again, he does not dwell on his impending death; characteristically, he redoubles his efforts instead.

Even after he bursts his temple sounding the olifant (1764, 1786, 2102), accidentally inflicting a fatal wound and excruciating pain upon himself (1761–62, 1787, 2101, 2260)—the hero never suffers any injury from the *enemy* (2159)—and even after he faints from loss of blood while riding on his horse and then while falling to the ground as he walks, Roland still shows no concern about being in extremis. It is only after all his men have perished and after he has personally attended to the Twelve Peers and to Turpin that Roland begins to retire within himself (2259). Even so, he first performs a number of penultimate acts—discussed below—before he finally succumbs (2392).

## Getting the Complete Picture: The Poet's Perspective

It is generally assumed that eyewitnesses are more reliable sources than persons who arrive on the scene after the fact and who must deduce what happened from available evidence. That is why the "lone survivor" device is sometimes used in literature to give credibility to a narrative (Rosenberg 73–84, 242–43). In the *Song of Roland*, the witness is Saint Giles, who is said to have been present at the battle and to have set down his recollections in a chronicle preserved at Laon (2095–97). As it happens, no further particulars are provided about this alleged witness, but, as Joseph Bédier pointed out, "sans doute il y a été ravi en vision" ("undoubtedly he was transported there in a vision"; *Commentée* 27; my trans.). In the Middle Ages, as in the Bible, a holy man's vision offered incontrovertible reasons for being believed.

The poet's description of Roland's agony (2259–2396) involves a cascade of particulars. Roland is surrounded by landscape evocative of his Christian faith as he begins his fervent last prayers, but he is also intent on signaling Charlemagne that he has kept his promise to die a hero's death. What follows is a summary of the passage in question and a few explanations of important elements in this scene.

Roland prays for the happy repose of his men's souls and for his own salvation (2261–62). He advances toward Spain (2265–66), being careful to carry the olifant and Durendal with him to avoid reproach (2263–64). He is in a fallow field ("un guarét," 2266). He climbs a steep hill (2267, 2367). There are two trees (2267; some editors emend to read one tree). He faints on the grass (2269–70, 2273). There are four shiny marble blocks nearby (2268, 2272). A Saracen attempts to steal Durendal (2274–83); Roland slays him with his olifant (2284–96). The hero tries in vain to damage Durendal beyond repair by repeatedly striking a dark stone (2300–02, 2312–14, 2338–41). He prays to the Virgin Mary (2303) and to God the Father (2337). He praises Durendal (2304–11, 2316–37, 2344–54). He runs to a pine (2357, 2375). He lies on the grass (2358). He covers his sword and olifant with his body (2359). He turns his face toward the enemy so Charles will say that he died victoriously (2360–63; also, at 2367, 2376, he faces Spain). He confesses his sins (2369–72, 2382–83), raising his glove to God and beating his breast (2364–65, 2368, 2373, 2383–89). Angels descend from heaven (2374). Roland reflects on his past triumphs and on the things he loves best (2377–81). He recites the prayer in the hour of greatest need (2384–88; see Brault, Song 1: 460, commentary 36n1). The archangel Gabriel accepts his glove (2390). Roland rests his head on his arm (2391). He dies, hands joined together (2392). Archangels bear his soul away (2393–96); his soul is now with God in heaven (2397).

Religion manifests itself here chiefly in the form of prayers, confession, and the presence of angels, but additional religious symbolism has been conjectured, too. For instance, climbing a hill to be nearer God is a widespread custom, and trees, of course, are reminiscent of the cross.

The hero's supplications are accompanied by related bodily movements (beating his breast, joining his hands, and bowing his head) that can easily be understood, but also by the less recognizable proffer of a gauntlet. Roland's raising of his glove, much debated by scholars, has most convincingly been interpreted as a gesture of propitiation, expressing the hero's desire to obtain forgiveness for his sins; what he is offering in return is remorse (Hackett; Lyons; Brault, Song 1: 254–60; van Emden, *Chanson* 73).

The four mysterious marble blocks ("Quatre perruns i ad de marbre, faiz," 2268; "Quatre perruns i ad luisant de marbre," 2272) constitute another difficult problem. Bédier considered them "un emplacement carré ou rectangulaire, où la main de l'homme avait planté deux beaux arbres et disposé des marbres bien taillés" ("a square or rectangular site where someone had planted two beautiful trees and placed skillfully sculpted marble blocks"), which he interpreted as "des bornes pour marquer la limite entre la chrétienté et la païenie,—la frontière" ("boundary-stones to mark the border between Christianity and Heathendom,—the frontier"; *Commentée* 308–10; my trans.). However, the French medievalist confused the dark stone Roland repeatedly struck with his sword with the marble blocks (308). More than likely, these man-made ("faiz") objects form a symbolic gateway to paradise, the hero being about to pass from this world into the next (Brault, Song 1: 71, 246–50).

Roland's lengthy and emotional praise of "fair and sacred" Durendal (2344), whose golden hilt contains many holy relics, is an indirect way of recapitulating his own stunning military career and of implying that his deeds were accomplished in God's name. Consequently, when a rash Saracen attempts to steal the sword, Roland views this act as not only shocking but also sacrilegious. Indeed, the Saracen is the incarnation of Satan, who, at the last minute, attempts to wrest Roland's most precious possession, his sword/soul, from Saint Michael. When Durendal cannot be broken, although the undamaged weapon reflects the hero's élan and tenacity, it mainly symbolizes his extraordinary integrity (close here to its etymological sense, unimpaired [Brault, Song 1: 250–53]).

Roland's determination to position himself facing Spain and ahead of his men, and his painstaking attention to his olifant and to Durendal, are intended to bolster his reputation among men, but the overall religious context of the scene impinges on these acts. For Roland, the line between the *lei de chevalers* (752, 1143) and the *lei de chrestïens* (38) is blurred (Brault, *Chanson* xxiv–xxv). Dying courageously and triumphing over pagan enemies (2867) clearly epitomize knightly *and* Christian values, regarded by the poet as one and the same. This positioning echoes, then, Roland's alignment of the bodies of his fellow peers before the dying Turpin (2184–205), since both positionings communicate the deceased counts' righteousness to Charles, who is their earthly judge and who symbolizes their heavenly judge (Brault, Song 1: 238–40).

The fatal wound Roland suffers is an excellent topic for class discussion. Mentioned above, for example, is the idea that no enemy is capable of even touching the hero, much less injuring him. Therefore, one of the great ironies of this poem is that the invincible Roland unintentionally causes his own death.

There are other interesting aspects to this wound. Here as elsewhere, studying the etymology of key words (see Curtius 600–06) or scrutinizing Romanesque art for clues as to how contemporaries imagined narrative scenes can lead to insights into the processes of the poet's mind. Among the many subjects one might investigate, for example, is the possibility that Roland's temple, that is, the side of his forehead (Old French *temple*), was confused with the religious edifice of the same name. Perhaps, to the poet's way of thinking, this part of the human anatomy was the locus of the soul. Hence, serious injury to the temple would almost necessarily have resulted in the soul leaving the body. In medieval art, the departure of the soul was often depicted as a doll-like figure emerging from the dying person's mouth (Brault, Song 1: 260).

## Getting the Complete Picture: Charlemagne's Perspective

Disregarding for the moment the outrageous anachronism involved, the following exercise enables one to make an important observation about the manner in which Charles and his men view the scene when they return to Rencesvals. Imagine how an embedded CNN correspondent might have reported the disaster at Rencesvals on live television. (The reporter would have had to be with the main body of the emperor's army because the rear guard was completely annihilated.)

The anguished emperor, who has already concluded—in a synoptic scene akin to the split-screen technique used in cinematography—that Ganelon was implicated in the disaster (1816–29), is shocked by the utter carnage he sees on his arrival (2398–401). The ground is strewn with Frankish and Saracen cadavers that are so intermingled and mangled that it is difficult to tell them apart. Worst of all, the emperor cannot find the Twelve Peers and Roland (2402–10). After Charles and his men have destroyed the fleeing remnants of Marsile's army and rested overnight (2443–569, 2845–54), the emperor, advancing alone (2858), is guided in his search by his recollection of a proud declaration made earlier by Roland at Aix that he would die "conquerrant-ment" ("as a conqueror"; 2867).

Charles locates his nephew with relative ease because, as anticipated, Roland lies ahead of his men (2865; cf. 2868–69), facing the enemy (2866). The blows struck by the hero on three stones ("treis perruns," 2875) also point the way. Charles does not appear to see any particular significance in the hill (2869), the two trees (2874), the grassy meadow (2871, 2876), and the nearby pine (2884), but the poet presumably does not mention these same landscape features without good reason.

In any event, a new and obviously symbolic element is introduced here, the flowers, "Each stained red with the blood of our barons" (2871–72). Their effect on the emperor is immediate and overwhelming: "Beset with grief, he cannot hold back his tears" (2873). Arguably, the mere thought of the slaughter of his men could account for Charles's distress, but it is apparent that, in this context, the bloody flowers are emblematic of martyrdom, a connection made explicit in two earlier passages (1856, 2197). As such, then, they constitute the sole landscape feature in this section that harks back to the readily understood religious imagery discussed above.

The CNN correspondent would certainly have insisted on making a live report at this point to provide his listeners with an account of the distressing state of the battlefield and the recovery of the hero and his companions. There is every reason to believe, too, that he would have noted a few significant items mentioned earlier by the poet. For example, Roland no doubt has a frightful trauma at his temple; blood stains on his lips; and, possibly, some residue in his ears from the lesion to his brain (1763, 1785, 2260). The reporter would doubtless also have remarked on the hero's battered helmet (1995), his pious dying attitude (hands joined together, head resting on his arm), Durendal and the damaged (2295–96) olifant lying under Roland's body, and the alignment of the bodies of the Twelve Peers before Turpin, all of which cry out for reportage and speculation.

These details are missing from Charles's survey and were probably omitted by the poet for narrative economy. However, what is one to make of the curious silence in this passage regarding the four marble blocks and the body of the Saracen who attempted to steal Durendal? Surely these objects and the cadaver, the former strange, the latter particularly vile (2276), would have been very noticeable near Roland.

By omitting them from this scene, the poet probably meant to suggest that the marble blocks/portal and the Saracen/Satan were apparitions, perceivable only to a person at death's door, much the same as the angels sent from on high. For that matter, there is no mention of Roland's right glove here either (cf. 2390: "Saint Gabriel took it from his hand"). Is it missing now, actually taken up to heaven, or was the angelic transfer, like the marble blocks and the encounter with the ill-fated Saracen, a mystical experience for Roland and an event undetectable later on by Charlemagne and his men?

The episode depicting Roland's death includes imagery and occurrences that are either natural or supernatural, but the poet does not always keep the two phenomena distinct. Charlemagne's initial halt at Rencesvals is brief and frustrating for him (2398–442). His second, less hurried visit to the scene of Roland's passing, with its glaring omission of any reference to the four marble objects, the diabolical Saracen, and the gauntlet, marks a return to narration devoted to the actual world, or rather to what passes for the actual world in this epic poem.

Numerous other supernatural events occur earlier and later in this poem, for example Charlemagne's first dreams involving an angel's presence (719–36, 836–37); the miraculous sun-stopping episode (beginning at 2458); the emperor's second dreams, presided over by Gabriel (2526–68); God's intervention to save Thierry in his duel with Pinabel at Aix (3923); and Gabriel's summons in the poem's memorable closing scene (3994–98).

These occurrences, awesome and marvelous though they may be, are more or less conventional in the chansons de geste and do not quite reach the level of transcendence evoked by the happenings involving Roland shortly before he passes away. Juxtaposing this sublime episode at Rencesvals and the passage describing Charlemagne's anguished visits to the same locale helps the modern reader appreciate more fully the poet's exceptional artistry and his profound reverence for what transpired there.

# The Baligant Episode

## Mary Jane Schenck

The portion of the *Song of Roland* referred to as the Baligant episode represents about one quarter of the whole text, or approximately one thousand lines. It recounts Charlemagne's revenge and triumph over the emir Baligant, who arrives in Spain just after Marsile's troops drown in the Ebro. The events surrounding this spectacular second battle are included in the Oxford Digby 23 manuscript and in other French versions of the poem, with the exception of Lyon (for an edition of Lyon, see Duggan et al., vol. 3). This battle is not, however, part of the Latin legends and fragmentary texts. Whether it is considered a later interpolation that violates the spirit of an older poem focused on Roland or an authentic part of the vision of a poet writing in the late eleventh or early twelfth century, there is no doubt that the episode has characteristics that make it an identifiable subsection of the whole.

After Roland's death and Charlemagne's return to Rencesvals, God intervenes, as he did for Joshua at Jericho, to provide enough daylight for Charlemagne's pursuit of the Saracens. Once they have been slaughtered or drowned, Charlemagne offers thanks and falls asleep. At approximately this point, the Baligant episode begins. The precise opening is debated; Joseph J. Duggan calculates the length and parameters of the episode in two different ways that are instructive (Song [1973]). Building on the groundbreaking work by Jean Rychner on the "séances," or sittings, of the oral performances (Rychner, *Chanson* 38–39), Duggan identifies a recitation sequence concerning Baligant (lines 2609–3704) that is signaled by an "articulation motif," a brief recapitulation (2609–12) to bring the audience up to speed (Song [1973] 64). He finds only four of these "articulation motifs" in the entire poem, the third being this one, the fourth introducing the trial of Ganelon. For him, this is evidence that the late-eleventh-century singer/poet who composed the Oxford *Roland* conceived of it as divided into four, rather than three or five, sections as has been proposed by Gerard Brault (Song) and Fern Farnham.

The other way to define the Baligant episode is not as the straightforward narrative or recitation sequence but as two separate passages concerning Baligant, interrupted by a passage focused on Charlemagne. Duggan considers lines 2555–844 and 2974–3682 of the Oxford text in his careful study of the formulaic diction (see below). The intervening passage, lines 2845–973, depict Charlemagne returning to Rencesvals after his pursuit of the Saracens; burying the dead; and preparing the bodies of Roland, Oliver, and Turpin for repatriation. This scene is considered older because it is found in other versions of the poem that do not include the arrival of the emir.

The first passage of the Baligant episode (2555–844) begins with Charlemagne's second dream, which prefigures the trial of Ganelon at Aix. Then the scene switches to events that occurred before this dream: the flight of Marsile

to Saragossa; Bramimonde's cursing of the pagan deities; and the arrival of
Baligant, emir of Babylon, who dispatches men to Saragossa, where the
wounded Marsile tells the emissaries of his desperate situation. Baligant comes
immediately to Marsile, who relinquishes his fiefdom to enlist Baligant's help.
The emir mounts up and calls on his men to pursue Charlemagne (2844).
The non-Baligant material (2845–973) switches back geographically to Ren-
cesvals for the burial scene, which ends as Charlemagne has placed silk cloth
on the three carts bearing the bodies of Turpin, Oliver, and Roland.

A new laisse starts the second Baligant passage rather abruptly: "The em-
peror Charles is set to depart" (2974) but is surprised by two heralds an-
nouncing Baligant's arrival. A long sequence follows where Charlemagne
names new leaders, the divisions are amassed, the battle joined, and ultimately
a single combat is fought between the powerful heads of Christendom and
Islam. Once Charlemagne has cut down Baligant, the Saracens flee. Charle-
magne then enters Saragossa, where Marsile has just died of grief, and Bra-
mimonde turns over the city to the emperor. He and his men demolish both
synagogues and mosques, convert at sword point 100,000 Saracens, and bring
Bramimonde out of the city so that she can be brought to France and
converted.

If the contested Baligant passages were removed, the Song of Roland would
be focused on the hero, Roland, and the only revenge for his death would
consist of God's intervention in stopping the sun so Charlemagne can push
the Saracens to their watery grave. In the end, we would be left with several
images of Charlemagne. First, he sleeps under Gabriel's care and dreams of
a future battle. Then, after his return to Rencesvals, he proclaims in his lament
over Roland's body, "My grief is so great that I no longer wish to live" (2936).
Finally, he returns to France, convenes Ganelon's trial, and witnesses Bra-
mimonde's baptism.

The Oxford text, the oldest and best, includes the Baligant episode, so why
is there a controversy over whether it is authentic? The question stems not
only from its absence in some other versions but also from its own character-
istic features. The sudden appearance of the emir Baligant, whose name has
not been mentioned previously, seems strange in a text that foreshadows and
forewarns about all major characters and events. In the laisse that precedes
Baligant's attack, Charlemagne is clearly preparing to leave Spain with little
spirit for a fight (2936). It is odd, as Jules Horrent points out, for Charlemagne
to return from the Ebro River instead of pursuing the original goal of the
campaign in Spain and pushing on to Saragossa, where he would chase the
pagan forces, not vice versa.

There are also ten previously unmentioned characters in this segment, in-
cluding Jozeran, who helps Naimon assemble the new divisions, as well as
Rabel and Guinemant, who are named by Charlemagne to replace Oliver and
Roland. They are only briefly described in laisses 240–43 and 251 and scarcely
compare with their heroic predecessors. There are inconsistencies that may

be only cases of "Homer nodding," such as the olifant that was split by Roland at Rencesvals but nonetheless sounds loudly in the Baligant section (3119) or the keys to Saragossa that are brought to Charlemagne by Ganelon (677) and then given to Baligant's emissaries by Marsile (2762).

Critics have pointed out various thematic and stylistic questions: the flat repetitiousness of the massing of the troops that overwhelms the rather brief single combat between Charlemagne and Baligant; the absence in the Baligant episode of *laisses similaires*, a significant lyrical device of the *Roland*; and, most especially, the clerical (didactic) tone of the battle between Charlemagne and Baligant, which is drawn in stark terms of good versus evil without the psychological subtleties of the confrontations between Roland and Ganelon and between Roland and Oliver.

Gustave Lanson thought Baligant a "shabby addition, designed to flatter national vanity at the expense of the poetry" (qtd. in D. Sayers 23). Others find the long passages of the episode "lack the inspired touch" of the preceding section (Owen 19). The marked contrast between the battles led Ramón Menéndez-Pidal to describe the second one as an example of "mauvais goût," ("bad taste"; Chanson 125). It is as if it was not enough that God made the sun stand still so that Charlemagne could chase down the remaining Saracens and drive them into the Ebro.

Detailed linguistic studies have failed to find marked differences at the level of lexicon, and differences in phrasing for battle scenes can be attributed to the demands of assonance, not different—later or earlier—usage (Delbouille). As part of his seminal study of the formulaic diction in the poem, Duggan reviews the theories on its unity, agreeing with Menéndez-Pidal but calling Charlemagne's vengeance simply "overblown" rather than in poor taste (Song [1973] 76). Since the episode is neither logically nor symbolically necessary (Charlemagne's vengeance being already complete), he believes it was not part of the plot during oral formulation (82). His contribution to the debate is through the detailed analysis of formulas. A first calculation reveals that there is not a significant difference in density of formulaic hemistichs, so "Baligant" (he encloses the sections in quotation marks to distinguish "Roland" sections from the name of the whole poem) is part of *an* oral tradition. But whether it is the same oral tradition is not proven (83). Duggan also tabulates all formula types to demonstrate that, of the total 907 types in the *Song of Roland*, 526 are exclusive to "Roland," only 81 to "Baligant," and 300 are in common. Because so many more are shared than are exclusive to "Baligant," Duggan concludes that this section does not have a formulaic repertory of its own (Song [1973] 84), which is borne out by his further study. He also compares occurrences of specific formulas, such as "l'estreu li tint," (348, 3156). Turning from formulas to laisse structure, however, Duggan draws on Rychner's pioneering study *La chanson de geste* to point out that linked laisses are more common in "Roland" (54 percent of the section) than in "Baligant" (34 percent of the section). This alone is not enough to decide on the question of unity, but what is more informative is that there are no *laisses similaires* in "Baligant," which indicates its more recent composition and a "poetic poverty" (100). As Rychner maintained, the older lyrical style, organized in laisses, is characteristic of the *Song of Roland* but not of later epics where narrative overtakes strophic structure. Duggan points out that "Baligant" lacks this more archaic technique, so it was composed no earlier than the eleventh century.

Elsewhere Duggan has shown that the presence of Turks, Persians, and Armenians in the emir's troops connects the episode to the battle of Manzikert (which occurred in 1071), where influential Normans joined the forces of the first Byzantine ruler to be defeated by Turks. This battle created such a memory for the Norman chroniclers that it was credited with the rise of crusading fervor. Thus "Baligant" represents the danger of military conquest by the Islamic East that must be countered by the head of Christendom, Charlemagne (Duggan, "Generation"). In sum, formulaic diction is more consistent than different between the two parts of the poem, but the marked distinction in laisse structure, proper names, and provenance of Baligant's troops do suggest that this episode comes from the late eleventh century.

Duggan puts the issue into perspective by saying that to ask whether the episode is authentic is to pose the wrong question. The poem was elaborated in song, and "Baligant" has been introduced into the poem just as other fictional characters were introduced into the slim historical record. "Whether 'Baligant' improved the poem or not is a matter of taste and conjecture: we have no choice but to accept the episode as an example of the ordinary process of mythical expansion carried out by the oral tradition upon Roland's poetic legend" (Song [1973] 104).

So, how has the episode been justified aesthetically? One of the most influential critics, Joseph Bédier, thought the Baligant episode an integral part of Turoldus's poem. This is consistent with his formalist position against the traditionalists, for whom the poem was a reweaving of old lyrico-epic oral songs. The *Song of Roland* is the inspired vision of the individual poet, who understands that Charlemagne must not only chase Marsile's men to their deaths but also put the lie to Ganelon's statements that Charlemagne would be destroyed if Roland died. Thus Charlemagne must be shown to defeat an even greater horde of pagans led by the supreme leader of the Muslim world (*Légendes* 3: 444).

Most justifications for the episode follow Bédier's lead in suggesting that the religious theme of the poem reaches its fullest expression here. Dorothy Sayers sees the Roland-Ganelon confrontation as a private war within a national war, continued in the final portion as a war between belief and unbelief (26). For her, it is wrong to suggest that Charlemagne's enactment of the confrontation between cross and crescent is just an episode. For Sayers, the change of pace, the rapid succession of events, and absence of debate or psychological questionings are appropriate because the new events are "God's hammer-blows" (27), fulfilling a medieval, Christian vision of the world. Brault gives the most elaborate religious reading of the details (Song 1: 268–314) by connecting the dreams to various Biblical visions and spectacles of Saracen wealth to lessons against envy, avarice, and the fascination with evil. The battle prefigures Armageddon with vast hordes covering the plains, and Charles is not a mere crusader, but positively "messianic" in his role because Turoldus "conceived of the conflict between Charles and Baligant in terms of Christ's struggle against Anti-Christ" (312). Brault is not alone in calling the second battle cosmic (Song); Robert F. Cook adds that, although Roland's death may be the apogee of the literary text, the Baligant episode shows that Christianity is not entirely dependent on an individual warrior.

The religious significance of Baligant's defeat does not eclipse, however, political and social issues. Paul Aebischer makes the case that from a legal point of view, Baligant is a logical consequence of feudal relationships. He points to all the feudal legal terminology in the poem and maintains that Charlemagne's numerous calls for vengeance are not Christian or patriotic sentiments but feudal obligations. That Marsile is a vassal of Baligant also "fait rebondir l'action" ("rekindles the action"; my trans.) ("Pour la défense" 215). In answer to those who protest that Charlemagne becomes the hero displacing Roland, Aebischer says that Charlemagne is only there for Roland because Roland has the right to be avenged. The help a lord owes his vassal is as binding as the loyalty a vassal owes his lord.

John Halverson gives a slightly different reading of the same political themes. He contends that the battle is not between cross and crescent since the emir does not shout "Allah akbar." He compares the great heroism of Roland with that of Beowulf, whose faithfulness and service to a lord are part of an old order. The heroism of Charlemagne is something new—downward loyalty—because Charlemagne thinks of what his men need and calls in all the troops. This is an international brigade fighting without Roland in a communal effort where individual heroes are not as important as the common good. Thus the poem capably promotes the Capetian drive for royal centralization in the twelfth century.

Other studies further the suggestions that Baligant shifts to a new model of kingship. For Eugene Vance, the legend of Charlemagne is enhanced because Baligant is a worthy antagonist, even though the single combat is "a narrative flop" (76). The poet suffers a poverty of invention by simply listing the battalions; however, complexity enters the poem through contradictions incorporated into one character, Charlemagne, rather than through the conflict between characters, such as Roland and Ganelon. The conflict is between Charlemagne's wish to die and his mission to be God's champion. If, as Vance says, weak spots in poetry reveal vexed questions, then the curiosity shown about Saracen riches and beauty betrays an uncertainty that a crusading poem cannot express directly. Worldliness cannot be openly admired, but, in the

Baligant episode, "moral triumph becomes unrewarding and dull, and pretended depravity vibrates with all the colors of life" (Vance 80).

Peter Haidu also links the cosmic qualities of the second battle to the establishment of a new political order. It "universalizes" the conflict, showing the whole world is at stake and moving away from feudalism, a regime of the many, to monarchy (*Violence* 146). New characters, new narrative programs are needed to point toward a dimly imagined future. The problems with the old, feudal regime expressed in the conflict between Ganelon and Roland are somewhat obscured, Haidu thinks, by Roland's epic heroism, so the second sequence of events, new men in the Baligant episode, as well as Thierry in the trial scene are required to support the evolving image of the monarch.

Our own times present us with issues and confrontations eerily similar to those in the *Song of Roland*. Reading the poem has new relevance, and, thanks to the long interpretive history provided by scholars, it can be appreciated as the rich and complex text it is. Precisely because the *Roland*'s portrayal of the other is so relevant to our times, it is ideal for bringing a historical-literary perspective into a current political debate that appeals to all students; and, for our literature majors, it can illustrate how different critical assumptions lead to different interpretations.

The fundamental questions surrounding the Baligant episode have been answered in a variety of ways by the consideration of form and meaning and by shifting assumptions about medieval textuality. The questions about Baligant were once caught up in controversies between the "traditionalists" and the "individualists" over the origins of the poem itself, and interpretations offered more recently provide excellent examples of oral composition theory, reception theory, and a variety of new historical approaches. For example, given the presence of Bramimonde in this episode, students could be encouraged to read as feminists, asking why Bramimonde has a prominent role and whether her characterization reflects knowledge of the Saracen world or an image of eleventh-century Anglo-Norman women. Therefore, among many good reasons for teaching the Baligant episode as part of reading the *Song of Roland*, two stand out—the presentation of a global confrontation fueled by religious fundamentalism and the presence of women at the fault lines, and increasingly the frontlines, of those conflicts.

## APPENDIX
## Class Exercises

### Small-Group Work

Assign groups to represent the Christian or Saracen/Muslim side and have students calculate the number of divisions and total number of troops for each side. Groups prepare a response to the following questions for full group discussion: What is the effect of the poet's citing numbers for each division instead of totals? What impression is made by the imbalance? What is the significance of the geographic origins?

Set up a debate between groups on whether the Baligant episode seems to fit with the Roland section. First, ask groups to define what *fit* or *authenticity* might mean. Have them find specific elements to support their judgments. Different groups could focus on a specific aspect, comparing the pairs Roland/Oliver with Rabel/Guinemant, Charlemagne's behavior in the two parts, emotional tone, battle preparations or scenes, emphasis on religious figures or rituals, comparing laisses 136 and 137 with 226, 227, and 228.

## Discussion Questions

Do you believe that the Baligant episode raises the question of whether Roland or Charlemagne is the hero of the *Song of Roland*?

Is the episode necessary? Does Charlemagne seem to want further vengeance after he returns from the Ebro River?

Do you think that the poem makes better sense with or without the Baligant episode?

Compare descriptions of Charlemagne, Baligant, and their troops. Are they mirror images or clearly differentiated? Depending on your answer, how does this color your view of confrontation?

What do we learn about Saracen life through the scenes with Marsile?

What sort of person is Bramimonde? What is the significance of her role in this episode?

How is the religious life of the Saracens presented? What do the inaccuracies in the depiction of Islam tell us?

What picture do we get of Christian life and values?

Discuss laisses 245 and 246. Are Baligant's words designed to corrupt and Charlemagne's to inspire, or do similar things motivate the troops on both sides?

What is your reaction to Charlemagne's actions when he enters Saragossa (laisse 266)?

What details would you use to support the view that Roland's battle against Marsile is private (in the feudal sense) and national, whereas Charlemagne's against Baligant is "cosmic" (good vs. evil), expressed as the opposition West/East.

# The Implications of the Trial of Ganelon

## Emanuel Mickel

From the moment the Oxford Digby 23 manuscript of the *Song of Roland* was found in the early nineteenth century, scholars have tried to establish when the poem was written or first sung. Because written literature in the vernacular did not become commonplace until the twelfth century, scholars hypothesized that songs about Roland and Charlemagne sprang up shortly after the historical events they portray. In his *König und Vasall* Karl Heinz Bender argued that the baronial turmoil and the struggle between aristocracy and royal family is reflected in the chanson de geste as a genre. Bender argued that this conflict is present in *Roland* (despite its glorification of Charlemagne) in the treason and trial of Ganelon. Ultimately this argument goes back to an earlier conflict between German and French scholars concerning the origins of the French epic. In Germanic eyes Charlemagne is indeed a Germanic emperor, and what has come to be called France merely represents the westernmost part of the Frankish conquest. German scholars also claimed that the epic impulse in Western vernacular literature is manifestly a Germanic cultural characteristic (see the *Nibelungenlied* and Old Norse sagas). Although these narrative poems appear in the twelfth and thirteenth centuries in Old French, their historical and social *matière*, they argue, is purely Germanic in spirit and character. Prominently cited in proof of this thesis were the legal features of the Ganelon trial (Ruggieri) and the social-warrior ethic that underlies Roland's character (Jones). In these works the Christian ethos of *Roland* is seen as a thin veneer placed on this deeply Germanic, pagan work originating in a distant past. This idea, though not accepted in its more chauvinistic features, has won support from a number of scholars both in Europe and North America. It is reflected in the common attack on Roland as a flawed hero whose pride causes his downfall and the death of all his comrades. This view stops short of justifying Ganelon, but it accepts that Ganelon was wronged by Roland's answers and attitude. Those who see the twelfth-century redaction of the poem as a later Christian rewriting point to the trial and its issues, among other aspects, as reflecting not only older Germanic law but also a conflict between this older Germanic tradition, which was upheld by the baronial aristocracy, and the growing royal authority, which was bolstered by the influence of the Roman law that was gaining importance in the twelfth century. The barons represent the old traditions of custom law in a decentralized state where the king is really *primus inter pares* (the first among equals), a baron like themselves serving as king among them and with their approval.

Those who see an underlying Germanic tradition in conflict with the new order point to the trial of Ganelon. It is noted that Ganelon rejects the charge of treason in arguing that Roland harmed him, that he made the required formal defiance of Roland, and that he was only exercising his right of vengeance in the ancient Germanic practice of the feud when he arranged Roland's death. Furthermore, scholars point to the fact that the barons return from their deliberation urging that Ganelon be pardoned, as if they agreed with his defense that he was not guilty of treason:

> They say to the king: "Lord, we beseech you
> To absolve Count Ganelon,
> Then let him serve you in faith and love.
> Let him live, for he is a very noble man." (3808–11)

Ruggero M. Ruggieri goes so far with the Germanic thesis that he imagines that the early version of the *Song of Roland*, our modern name for the text, was really a kind of tragedy centered on Ganelon, a knight whose desire for vengeance ruined an otherwise great reputation as a warrior and led to his own demise.

If one is to know whether this understanding of the trial proceedings and Ganelon's rejection of the charge of treason might have been accepted by readers or listeners at the time (sometime in the ninth, tenth, eleventh, or twelfth centuries), one must look at the plausibility of this interpretation in the light of the law of the period. Since there are arguments that allege that *Roland* might have been an oral epic from the ninth or tenth century and only written down in the twelfth, one must face the possibility that the legal understanding of treason might reflect the law from Charlemagne's time or that it might reflect the later redactor's understanding of treason from his own time. Moreover, not only might a twelfth-century redactor merely set the trial anachronistically in the law of his own time as he knew it, he might just as easily be framing the trial in what he thought was an archaic legal context appropriate for some long-ago period. One might also ask how other manuscripts of the *Song of Roland* presented the trial. Did they give Ganelon some justification in their reading of the charge?

First, it is interesting that the other versions do not provide the trial of Ganelon as it is found in the Oxford manuscript (for more on the differences between the various versions, see Duggan's "Beyond the Oxford Text: The Songs of Roland," in this volume). The Venice 4, Châteauroux, Paris, Cambridge, Venice 7, and Lyon manuscripts all have a similar version of the trial that is very different from that in Oxford. In the expanded Châteauroux trial one can see an interpretation of the trial that makes the motives and attitudes explicit. Here the texts emphasize Ganelon's acceptance of money from the Saracens. Greed becomes his primary motive (for a detailed discussion of greed, see Mickel, *Ganelon*; see also Brault, *Song*; Cook). Moreover, Ganelon is clearly afraid to face Roland in single combat because he knows that he is wrong and would thus be opposing God and the right. Even Pinabel does not put his lips to the relics in the ceremony before the combat and shows his fear in fighting for Ganelon. Various Latin versions, the *Historia Karoli Magni et Rotholandi,* the *Carmen de prodicione Guenonis,* and the Anglo-Norman version of Willem de Briane associate Ganelon with Judas, emphasize his greed, and underscore his deceit and clever tongue (see Meredith-Jones; Paris, Carmen; Smyser). These texts and others one might cite certainly do not reflect any sympathetic reading of Ganelon's position.

An aspect of Ganelon's trial often cited as a vestige of early Germanic law is Ganelon's use of the feud as his defense against the charge of treason. Ganelon denies the charge of treason against Charlemagne, arguing that he did not betray Charlemagne or the Franks. He merely exercised his right of vengeance against Roland, Oliver, and their companions:

> Ganelon said: "A curse on me, if I conceal this!
> Roland wronged me in respect of gold and wealth;
> For which reason I sought his death and his woe.
> But I admit to no treason in this act."    (3757–60)

Ganelon refers to the council scene when Roland and he disagreed about what the Franks' response should be to the Saracen proposal delivered by Blancandrin. When Roland suggested Ganelon be named as emissary to the Saracens bearing Charlemagne's reply, Ganelon became angry and accused Roland of deliberately trying to do him harm. The dispute quickly leads to Ganelon's defiance of Roland and all those who love him (lines 286–91; 322–26).

Later Ganelon appeals to the barons that he merely took vengeance against Roland (after defying him openly) and that this should not be considered treason. Subsequently, when the barons deliberate, they hesitate to condemn Ganelon despite Charlemagne's anger. Scholars have argued that the baronial response secretly favors Ganelon's argument because his appeal is to an older Germanic custom law, which allowed the settlement of feud through vengeance. Moreover, the barons favor the old code and the clannish power and order it represents rather than the law of central authority.

Following the description of Tacitus in the *Germania,* scholars have imagined a time in early Germanic history when there was no central authority and disputes between families were settled by conflict and composition (Murray). The older Germanic codes, extant in texts written down in the sixth through the ninth century, are filled with tariffs, monetary penalties established to compensate for the family's loss of limb or even person. In these earliest codes the feud is recognized as something that occurs between families whose members come into conflict, but the feud is never accepted as a legal remedy; always the legal remedy is through the king's justice and laws that seek to compensate the family adequately enough to end the private warfare.

But there is an even more serious flaw in thinking that an older Germanic ethical code explains the conflict in Ganelon's favor. Ganelon's defense rests on the long-standing medieval idea that public defiance can justify subsequent open combat between adversaries. Essentially Ganelon asserts that his defiance of Roland in the council scene gave him the right to take vengeance on Roland at the next opportunity. There is this truth in what Ganelon says: had the French not been engaged in a military campaign against the Saracens, Ganelon could have fought a duel against Roland at any time. But old Germanic law and the later Norman and Anglo-Norman law of the twelfth century are both explicit in forbidding private conflict during military campaigns. Such an action is deemed treason. There is a serious breach of law here that goes to the core of the Germanic code of honor, one might even say civilization. It is true that Ganelon had defied Roland and, according to the custom and law of the period, whether ninth century or twelfth, could have challenged him to public combat to settle his dispute. But what Ganelon did was not legal in any period; his open defiance did not authorize him to set up an ambush against Roland and twenty thousand members of Charlemagne's army.

The idea that the barons' attempt to reconcile Charlemagne with Ganelon (by urging Charlemagne to forgive the offense and permit Ganelon to return to his former faithful service) is motivated by their belief that Ganelon's actions might have a legal basis in law does not stand up well under scrutiny. A closer look at the law allows another perspective of their action. Ganelon comes from a powerful family that poses a serious threat to peace (as the rebellious vassal cycle of chansons de geste demonstrates). In early Germanic medieval law codes, judges could be challenged—as well as witnesses and compurgators. Even as late as Glanville and Bracton judges could be required to defend their judgment (see Mickel, *Ganelon* 63n115). This means that any of the judges who refused to grant reconciliation had to face possible reprisal from the powerful Pinabel, the warrior who has offered to defend Ganelon. Because it is the king himself who brings the charge, there can be no *judicium dei* combat between the accuser and the accused. For obvious reasons medieval law did not allow challenge of the king to single combat. The code of Henry de Bracton is explicit: the king has the entire nation for champion (Bracton 2: 402; for a detailed discussion of this point, see Mickel, *Ganelon* 67–72). That is, to challenge the king is to declare war. Otherwise, rebels might easily usurp the throne by killing the king in single combat. This makes it easier to understand the intimidation factor that a champion like Pinabel posed and it casts another light on the council's timidity and their weak argument that Roland cannot be brought back to life in any event:

> Because of Pinabel they are inclined to peace.
> They said to each other: "It is best to let matters drop.
> Let us abandon the trial and beseech the king
> To absolve Ganelon this time;
> Let him then serve him in love and faith.
> Roland is dead, never will you see him again.
> He will not be recovered for gold or any sum of money;
> Anyone who fought over this would be a fool." (3797–804)

Note how explicit the text is once one understands the threat: "Pur Pinabel se cuntienent plus quei" (3797). The self-justification that Roland cannot be brought back to life anyway is then followed by the real reason: "Mult sereit fols ki . . . se cumbatreit" (3798). It also makes clear the significance and consequences of Thierry's action in refusing to go along with the rest of the council and in prosecuting Charlemagne's charge of treason. Thierry's action stops the council's judgment not to punish Ganelon and places the decision of Ganelon's guilt or innocence before God, to be revealed in the outcome of the duel.

As for the manner of Ganelon's punishment, scholars such as Ruggieri insisted that dragging and quartering represented an old Germanic custom, but Joseph Bédier, Léon Gautier, and others denied it. A review of all extant Germanic codes from the earliest Continental versions of the Middle Ages to the later *coutumiers* and the twelfth- and thirteenth-century law books of England does not confirm a stipulated form of punishment. Over and over one can see the provision that the person guilty of treason is to lose his life (unless specifically pardoned by the king) and that his property escheats to the crown, but the manner of death is not stipulated. Those who argue that hanging and dragging is an established tradition point to the death of Brunhild in Fredegarius's chronicle (*Chronicarum*, ch. 42). There is no proof that quartering was a feature of punishment for treason nor is there even a hint of it. In fact, where the punishment becomes severest, where loss of limbs is mentioned, is in the Englishman Ranulf de Glanville's discussion of *lese maiestatis*: "The crime of *lese maiestatis* in the laws . . . [is] by the ultimate penalty or by cutting off of limbs" (Glanville 3). Even here one must note that the loss of limbs is not attached to the death penalty but offered as an alternate solution. In any case, it is noteworthy, as S. H. Cuttler and others note, that treatment of treason becomes much severer in the twelfth, thirteenth, and fourteenth centuries, where harsh treatment and intransigence were the rule. In the earlier periods, where conflicts were often between blood relatives, mercy was granted at times, unless the offense represented a relapse from a previous conviction of treason.

One of the curious findings of the study of the law, Germanic and Roman, from the sixth century to the fourteenth, is that the features found in Ganelon's trial, if they reflect any time period, seem to evoke later, twelfth-century law rather than the earlier codes. Not only does the manner and harshness of punishment tend in that direction, but so too does the use of single combat on horseback, a feature that cannot be established in Carolingian times (Mickel, *Ganelon* 155).

Frequently in studies of the *Song of Roland*, Roland's character is discussed in terms of the Germanic ideal of the warrior. George Fenwick Jones treats Roland and Oliver as a contrastive pair of warriors. Roland represents the values of the old Germanic warrior, the other-oriented man who sees his reputation and honor in terms of how others see him. He is the less rational, more primitive man whose sense of honor resides in the fixed code of the clan. He is not an inner-oriented, reflective man who has his own internal values but lives up to an external code of honor. Oliver is the inner-oriented, modern man of the twelfth and thirteenth century. He is reflective and capable of making a decision that would satisfy him and his own conscience rather than hold to the values of the group.

There is an interesting point here not made often enough: Roland is conscious throughout the poem of his reputation. On more than one occasion he expresses that he will never give a bad example, that his relatives will never be shamed by his conduct, and that never will a bad song be sung about him and the Franks. Because of the tendency to view Roland's expressions in terms of his personal reputation, readers miss the importance of this attitude in an oral society. How the song was sung determined what the hearer knew as history. Roland is determined that the tale that is told will follow the truth of the Franks' unflinchingly courageous combat. His last acts as the only survivor, pagan or Christian, left on the battlefield prove that it is important to him that the Franks be given their due. Before his final prayer begging absolution, Roland traverses the battlefield turning the warriors' faces toward Spain in front of Archbishop Turpin, a fitting tribute to his companions lest any backs toward Spain might leave a false impression of flight and inspire a "malveise chanson" that did not reflect the truth about their deaths (1014).

It should be noted that Roland correctly anticipates how his own society would judge his blowing of the horn. After he blows the horn, allowing Charlemagne to take vengeance and to finish conquering the Saracens, we see clearly the reaction of the Franks. Ganelon feigns that Roland is a frivolous man who jokes by blowing the horn in jest, pretending danger. The Franks, in contrast do not even consider that Roland would blow the horn unless he were in deep trouble and, in fact, dying. They do not think that he is stubborn and prideful but know his devotion to duty and his fearless loyalty. They are confident that he will carry out the mission as it was designed without thought for his own life. Once again, in the argument between Roland and Oliver knowledge of the law helps one understand the point of view of the writer and his Christian audience. Roland and Oliver argue about blowing the horn; toward the conclusion of the battle, Oliver, wounded and dying, blood streaming down his face, encounters Roland, who is riding to help him. Oliver strikes Roland without warning. Roland is stunned by this act of treachery, to strike without warning, and asks if Oliver had indeed struck him "de gred" ("on purpose"; 2000): "Ja est ç' Rollant ki tant vos soelt amer? / Par nule guise ne m'avez desfiét" ("This is Roland who loves you so dearly; / You had not challenged me in any way"; 2001–02). Oliver immediately assures him. "Jo ne vos vei, veied vus Damnedeu!" ("I do not see you, may God watch over you"; 2004). He asks for Roland's pardon and Roland forgives him "ici e devant Deu" ("here and before God"; 2007). It should be noted here that in the final meeting of the two heroes, there are no recriminations, and no animosity exists between the two. Roland shows no remorse for his decision, and Oliver does not mention it; it is Roland who forgives Oliver for his inadvertent blow.

Roland is not a flawed hero who needs God's forgiveness for a terrible error in judgment. In Roland's epic prayer there is no reference to his decision as a mistake or fault. Moreover, Roland's heroic death and life gain him the special grace of being taken up to heaven by angels, something not granted Oliver or Archbishop Turpin. It has been noted on many occasions that the poet's description of earthquake, darkness, and storm on earth at the time of Roland's death is a clear reference to Christ's Crucifixion. This typological reading of Roland and his sacrifice sees death not as a victory for the Saracens (the theological parallel with Satan and Christ is unmistakable) but as utter defeat (Folz; Nichols, *Romanesque*).

To understand the trial of Ganelon one must realize, as mentioned above, that Charlemagne is the accuser in a charge of treason that everyone accepts. Ordinarily the person who made the accusation had to be ready to defend his accusation by duel if the case was not provable by witness or some evident means of proof. In this case, however, the king can never be subjected to duel. When Charlemagne turns to his judges, he does not look for a verdict of guilty or not guilty; instead, he expects them to name the punishment due for treason. In Germanic law judges were often obliged to uphold their verdict, if it were challenged, by single combat. Here the judges are not prepared to prescribe Ganelon's punishment for treason, rather they wish to urge that he be pardoned and return to his former faithful service.

Those who might have wished to condemn Ganelon were too afraid of Pinabel, except for Thierry, who comes forth on behalf of Charlemagne and the deceased Roland. When Thierry speaks about his judgment, it is interesting that he answers Ganelon's self-justification, whereas the other judges would mention nothing about treason:

> Bels sire reis, ne vos dementez si!
> Ja savez vos que mult vos ai servit;
> Par anceisurs dei jo tel plait tenir:
> Que que Rollant Guenelun forsfesist,
> Vostre servise l'en doüst bien guarir.
> Guenes est fels d'iço qu'il le traït,
> Vers vos s'en est parjurez e malmis.
> Pur ço le juz a pendre e a murir,
> E sun cors metre en peine e en exil
> Si cume fel ki felonie fist.
> S'or ad parent m'en voeille desmentir,
> A ceste espee, que jo ai ceinte ici,
> Mun jugement voel sempres guarantir

Fair lord king, do not distress yourself so.
You know that I have served you very well;
By virtue of my ancestors I must make this case:
Whatever Roland may have done to Ganelon,
The act of serving you should have protected him.
Ganelon is a traitor in that he betrayed him;
He committed perjury against you and wronged you.
For this I judge that he be hanged and put to death
And his body should be placed . . .
As befits a man who has committed treason.
If he now has a kinsman who would give me the lie,
With this sword I have girded on
I am willing to uphold my verdict at once.    (3824–36)

Thierry dismisses Ganelon's assertion that Roland had done him harm earlier (and thus gave him the right to vengeance) by pointing out one of the oldest and most consistent Germanic features: personal feuds and private vendettas were especially prohibited during military campaigns. As Thierry notes, Roland falls under this protection. Any action against him constitutes treason. Ganelon's crime was against the emperor and his army. The writer cuts to the quick of the matter by having Thierry critique so precisely both of Ganelon's arguments. He has Thierry use the conjunction "que" and the subjunctive "forsfesist" to indicate that the accusation is not a fact (3827). Even if the offense did take place, the subjunctive tells us, it would have no bearing on the case for treason against Ganelon. This much would have been clear to the audience, but the difficult part must yet be faced—upholding what was legally correct against the formidable champion, Pinabel.

Why Pinabel should be permitted to act as a champion for Ganelon is not certain. Although normally women, minors, the infirm, and those over sixty could employ a champion, Ganelon does not fall into any of these categories. In the ancient laws where compurgators (those who vouched for one's version of the events without really being able to testify as a witness) and witnesses are involved, it was permitted to challenge the witness or compurgator in combat to lift his testimony, that is, to establish that it was not true or of no value. In this case Pinabel may be defending his role as one of the thirty pledges Ganelon is required to provide (Mickel, "Thirty *Pleges*"). However, it does appear that Pinabel fights for Ganelon and not for himself.

That the writer perceived the presence of Pinabel as primarily an intimidating factor is clear from his contrastive description of the two men. Pinabel "is tall and strong, brave and swift; / The man he strikes has come to the end of his days" (3839–40). Thierry is described otherwise: "His body was spare and slim and slender, / His hair black and his face somewhat tanned. / He is not big, but nor is he too small" (3820–22). The David and Goliath motif, so often used in the chansons de geste, is present throughout this combat. Here Thierry dares to face Pinabel (3870–72). Although the onlookers see the disparity in size, they cannot see the unknown factor. The two men refuse offers of settlement during combat. When the combat resumes, the writer gives Pinabel the seeming upper hand (3915–23).

One is immediately reminded of the writer's earlier warning that the person whom Pinabel strikes is no more. The writer makes God's protection of Thierry clear. In his wounded condition Thierry gives the death blow (3924–29). Although the church never acknowledged single combat or any form of *judicium dei* as a reasonable appeal to God for decision in men's affairs, the practice was widespread. Not until the Fourth Lateran Council in 1215 were clergyman ordered not to participate in such ordeals by blessing the elements of the trial. However, the practice of ordeal—and especially single combat—continued throughout the thirteenth and fourteenth centuries as a way to solve conflicting accusations and denials that could not be established otherwise (Nottarp). In effect Thierry's victory signals that Ganelon was indeed a traitor to the Franks and Charlemagne despite his disingenuous protest.

As one can see, questions of law become very important when one tries to interpret what is meant by the language in key scenes of the poem. But the use of the *judicium dei* was so prevalent in the philosophical and popular theological perspective of the period that it permeates the *Song of Roland* as an organizing motif and as a rhetorical device in constructing the poem.

For more than a hundred years scholars have argued whether the Baligant episode belongs in the poem or not. One can point to both French and Latin versions of the poem that have no Baligant episode. One might indeed argue whether the "original" *Roland* had this episode. But this does not seem to me a particularly interesting question anymore because a negative or positive answer changes nothing. We have come to see each version as the product of a redactor, working at a given time, who puts together the elements of the narrative that fit his design. In this light it is interesting to note that the redactor who "added" Baligant perceived that the rest of the *Song of Roland* was structured on the *judicium dei* motif. In fact, the final combat between Baligant and Charlemagne resembles the Thierry-Pinabel conflict in more than just having the same motif. Both actually follow the format of the judicial trial and can be said to provide a model on which the entire poem is constructed (Mickel, "*Judicium Dei*").

In the largest sense this conflict is not only a worldwide struggle for dominance on this earth between the Christians and pagans but also a battle in the sense of Prudentius's *Psychomachia* for the souls of mankind. In effect, the entire poem is a *judicium dei* that will test the conflicting pagan and Christian claims. Here there is no middle ground. If Charlemagne and the Christians are right in asserting that there is but one God who sees and has power over all things, indeed who made all things, then the basis of the Saracens' faith and their material claims are without foundation. The land indeed belongs to Charlemagne, as God's representative, by right, and all souls should worship one God.

That the text is modeled on the medieval idea of the trial can be seen in the two major conflicts pitting Saracens against Christians. In the first, Roland and his rear guard of twenty thousand soldiers stand against the vastly superior Saracen force. After the defeat Saracens recognize that they have been involved in a kind of trial, evident from their actions in returning to their camp. Marsile, Bramimonde his wife, and twenty thousand men attack their gods (2580–91). It should be noted that the Saracens do not draw the conclusion from the turn of events that their gods do not exist, only that they have no power to affect events—an attitude prevalent both in the Old Testament and in early medieval chronicles and histories. The defeat of the Saracen force, despite its strength and numbers, means only one thing: judgment has been rendered against their gods and their false presumption to power.

With Baligant's arrival the poem takes on a kind of new beginning. The issues will be the same, and the model of the trial will be ever present as the framing structure of the narrative. Baligant reverses the situation found at the beginning of the poem. He makes it clear that it is he who comes to challenge Charlemagne's faith and right to hold land. Baligant claims that he will force Charlemagne to renounce his faith and that, if Charlemagne does not, he will take the crown from the emperor. Baligant now comes to make a claim not just for Spain but for France as well. The two armies confront each other, but the issue will again be settled by a *judicium dei* combat, this time a single combat between the two emperors. In this combat one sees again the elements of the trial. Charlemagne's epic prayer (Short, laisse 226; Burgess, laisse 228) invokes God as *guarant*. Charlemagne does not presume to call on his own strength to gain victory but turns to God. Baligant argues that Charlemagne should hold Spain from him since he, Baligant, is its overlord. Charlemagne rejects this argument by drawing the fundamental line between pagans and Christians. Baligant must accept Christianity and serve the omnipotent God before there can be any "pais ne amor" between them. In the conclusion to the combat, Charlemagne's religious perspective will be shown to be right, since God gives him the vital aid necessary for victory.

If the poet presents the larger episodes of the poem in the form of a trial where judgment is rendered through the agency of single combat, it is probably because it represents a model for his understanding of the nature and resolution of man's conflicts. However, it is fascinating to see the extent to which this model is used in the inner structure of *Roland*. In the Rencesvals section, the poet shapes the narration of the combat by focusing on the Twelve Peers and their Saracen counterparts selected to accompany Marsile's nephew, Aelroth, into combat. In this larger structure the poet focuses the listener-reader's attention on the three principal French heroes, Roland, Oliver, and Turpin. In each laisse there is a single-combat confrontation between one of the Saracen and one of the French peers. In this carefully crafted structure, it is important to note that each of the laisses presents a miniature trial with a *judicium dei* as the required proof. In a medieval trial the accuser brought his charge before the court. The accused then denied the charge word for word to avoid any chance of misunderstanding. Next, the court set a day for trial and named an appropriate proof that the accused must perform to support his denial. If he succeeded in the proof, the accusation was overcome. In each of these laisses the individual combat is presented as if it were a miniature trial. Aelroth rides up to Roland and makes accusations against Charlemagne and the Franks (1191–95). After Roland has defeated Aelroth, who is lying dead at Roland's feet, he answers Aelroth's accusation point by point, emphasizing the fact that his death proves the charge was erroneous (1207–10). Afterwards Roland encourages his men and points out the significance of his victory over Aelroth: "Ferez i, Francs; nostre est li premers colps! / Nos avum dreit, mais cist glutun unt tort" ("Strike, Franks, the first blow is ours! / We are right, but these wretches are wrong"; 1211–12).

The poet reduces these individual encounters in subsequent laisses while still giving each peer his due. In laisses 96–102, each laisse ranging from six to eight lines in length, the preliminary description of the pagan and his challenge are eliminated. All lines but the last five, six, or seven are devoted to the brief description of the Frank killing a Saracen peer. To end this first combat sequence, the poet brings Oliver and Roland back in laisses 103 and 104 to confront the last two Saracen peers. After Roland has dispatched Chernubles in laisse 104, he turns to him in scorn and reiterates what the combat has just demonstrated: "Then he said to him: 'Villain, you set out to meet your doom; / You will receive no help from Muhammad / A wretch like you will not win today's battle' " (1335–37). This sequence is a miniature structure of the entire poem. Just as in these laisses, Roland's force is initially victorious and then gradually worn down by the numerically superior Saracens; this is followed by Charlemagne's vengeance and justification of the French position.

Here one can see how the poet's understanding of history and the nature of the Christian confrontation with the Saracens perceived in the context of the medieval trial could shape not only the larger organization of the narrative but also the personal confrontations that make up the whole. If the Christian-pagan conflict involved entire nations, the struggle was nonetheless an individual one. Each person had to face the challenge individually. This is why the perception of the text seen through the model of the *Psychomachia* works so well (Mickel, "Parallels"). Medieval combat involved movement of foot soldiers in coordination with the mounted chevaliers. But the medieval poet presents this melee as individual confrontations, each one a trial resolving the spiritual conflict that divides the two combatants. It is a conflict between ideologically separate nations and the individuals who make up the whole. But it is perceived as a never-ending conflict, one that occurs within as well as between men. Ganelon, a Christian warrior, is the enemy within, just as Discordia rises up among the Virtues in the *Psychomachia* even when all warfare seems ended. And when Charlemagne is awakened by Gabriel to go fight yet more Saracens in Italy, he is the image of a beleaguered mankind in an unending struggle, just as the weary soul of the *Psychomachia* will face future temptations. This understanding of reality and the image of each conflict as a trial shaped the poet's ordering of the narrative.

# The Death of Aude and the Conversion of Bramimonde: Border Pedagogy and Medieval Feminist Criticism

*Lynn T. Ramey*

The *Song of Roland* is a quintessentially border epic, situated in a frontier land. Its locale moves between France and Spain, and its climactic moment takes place in a pass in the Pyrenees that is figured as the literal passage between France and Spain. In this contested space, as with many borderlands, the tale that emerges is a master narrative, bending to the ideological imperatives of the stronger force, the French army. An instructor teaching this text as one that crosses and recrosses boundaries will find that border pedagogy, a teaching approach outlined and developed by Paulo Freire (*Education*) and Henry Giroux (*Border Crossings*; "Living"), helps readers confront those transitional moments in the text where one gender and culture meets another and both cede to the greater power of the metanarrative. The death of Aude, the Christian fiancée to the hero Roland, and the conversion of Bramimonde, the wife of the Saracen king, Marsile, are both located within the nexus of power, ethnicity, and gender that border pedagogy aims to address.

This essay does not attempt to resolve the importance of Aude and Bramimonde to the text, though recent work in medieval feminist scholarship certainly indicates that the role of women in epic is more central than one might have originally thought in this "masculine" genre (e.g., Kinoshita, "Pagans"; Kay, "Représentation"). Just as it seems impossible and even undesirable to resolve the question of whether Roland acted appropriately or not—after all, the real interest is in the debate of the question and not its resolution—the ambiguity of the female characters in the *Song of Roland* provides the impetus for discussion about core values and critical choices that define human existence.

When we teach the *Song of Roland*, we never know what backgrounds and identities may come with students who enter the borderland of the classroom. Most of the classes where I have introduced my students to this classic of French literature have been composed solely of women, who came from widely divergent ethnic and social circles. Much of the earliest criticism, from Paulin Paris and Gaston Paris to Joseph Bédier focuses on the *Song of Roland* as a seminal text in the formation of masculine French national identity. For these critics, the *Song of Roland* treats questions of male honor and power relationships among noble men; based on their readings of the text, the *Song of Roland* became the first work (chronologically and symbolically) of French literature. Turning this classic text, which for decades has been a cornerstone of the "dead white male" canon, into a meaningful text for today's multi-gendered, multiracial classroom is a call that must be heeded. The *Song of Roland* includes two women characters in its cast of thousands. The reduced role of women in the story, notable even for a genre that is often male-centered, means that the two women characters, Aude and Bramimonde, deserve and must receive careful critical consideration.

Feminist strategies of reading have taught us much about ways that women access and appropriate subject positions in texts that are resistant to female readers. Critics including Shoshana Felman and Patrocinio P. Schweickart have revisited reader-reception theory to think of ways that women can read autobiographically and still occupy subject positions in male-centered texts. Roberta Krueger warns of the danger of positing any single type of medieval woman reader or audience, even for the generally laudable purpose of constructing a female subject (16), but despite this warning, feminist readings often do construct a monolithic female reading, placing their readings in opposition to a male perspective. Opposed to a deconstructive reading that would suggest that the male-centered text is inaccessible to women, Schweickart asserts, "At this stage I think it behooves us to choose the dialectical over the deconstructive plot. It is dangerous for feminists to be overly enamored with the theme of impossibility" (56). While the feminist project remains essential—women students must be able to create empowering reading strategies—creating a dialectic that excludes some students (even, or particularly, if they are in the minority) does not satisfy the democratic ideal of reaching all students. In addition, classes apparently composed only of women cannot be imagined as uniform in their expression of gender, class, and racial identity. Postcolonial theory has in part attended to this impasse, proposing a merger between the feminist ideal of autobiographical readings and the deconstructive denial of any fixed subject position. Proposed as a postcolonial theoretical approach to teaching, border pedagogy addresses this epistemological impasse and opens up feminist reading strategies to all students.

When students consider the two female characters, Aude and Bramimonde, three essential elements of border pedagogy pertain (Giroux, "Living" 48–49):

All representations are unmasked as historically contingent.
Class discussion must address the ethical and political purposes of any representation.
A variety of critical approaches should be used, and students should be aware of the power of pedagogical approaches over representations.

These three goals are not necessarily independent; pedagogical practice can deal with more than one of these at the same time. The remainder of this essay will examine ways that these strategies can be productively used to concentrate on two challenging moments in the *Song of Roland*: Aude's death and Bramimonde's conversion.

## Aude's Death

When Aude makes her appearance before Charlemagne after the massacre at Rencesvals, she refuses the substitution the king proffers: his own son in the place of the unfortunate Roland.

> "Sister, dear friend, you ask me about a dead man.
> I shall give you a very fine replacement:
> That is Louis, I do not know of better.
> He is my son and he will rule my kingdom."
> Aude replies: "These are terrible words.
> May it not please God or his saints or his angels,
> That I live on after Roland's death!"
> Drained of colour she falls at Charlemagne's feet.
> She died at once, may God have mercy on her soul!
> (3713–21)

As with the feminist project, students must consider how they read, thinking of how different audiences might respond to the text and then reading "against, within, and outside [its] established boundaries" (Giroux, *Border Crossings* 30). The question of audience in the medieval text is always tricky, since scant evidence remains concerning audiences for specific genres or works. Instead of hiding this uncertainty, teachers must encourage students to imagine different audiences and postulate their reactions to Aude's death. What would an all-male audience belonging to the nobility think of Aude's refusal to take Charlemagne's son as husband? How would women react? What difference would it make if the women were members of a privileged class or peasants? The story is set in Carolingian times but was put in manuscript form much later. What are some differences in women's roles between these two eras? Inviting students to occupy another subject position transforms Aude from a bit player to a central character. Aude embodies in many ways the typical, Christian, female character of twelfth- to fourteenth-century French epic, but historical grounding on women's roles helps unmask the politics behind her representation; a sourcebook such as Emily Amt's can provide primary material for, by, and about women who may have been in the audience when the epic was performed.

Discussion of Aude's death in the *Song of Roland* responds well to the use of varied critical approaches. Her relationship with men, and men's relationships with one another, dictate her position in society. The first mention of Aude is made in the most privileged of masculine spaces, the battlefield, where she becomes a pawn in the power struggle between the *preux* Roland and the *sage* Oliver. "Oliver said: 'By this beard of mine; / If ever I see my noble sister Aude, / You will not lie in her arms' " (1719–21). She has been a gift between noble men, destined to be the wife of Roland, her brother's best friend, as explained by Claude Lévi-Strauss's work on kinship. But when the two men argue, it is clear that she is a gift that can be revoked should the homosocial relationship sour.

Aude's collapse is a highly ambivalent moment for women. It can be read as Aude's exercise of her only option—suicide—to control her destiny or, alternatively, as an illustration of the death-or-submission bind that renders female power and agency a self-annihilating act. Is her death a suicide, or the expiration of a stereotypical, overly fragile being at the announcement of life-changing news? Gayle Rubin notes in her critique of structural anthropology and psychoanalysis that feminists have seen female suicide as a self-affirming act. Rubin quotes Monique Wittig's tirade in *Les guérillères* against Lévi-Strauss:

> He writes that you are currency, an item of exchange. . . . Better for you to see your guts in the sun and utter the death rattle than to live a life that anyone can appropriate. What belongs to you on this earth? Only death.                              (Wittig qtd. in Rubin 200)

The poetics of heroism, already explored through the Oliver-Roland debate and Aude's suicide, are reiterated in the court drama of Aude's death. Aude's death does not enjoy the same explicit textual debate that its masculine counterpart does. It thus forces us to examine not only the historical options for medieval women but also our own ideas about what constitutes heroism and agency for those who are not part of the dominant power structure.

## Bramimonde's Conversion

Aude's Muslim counterpart, Bramimonde, sets the model for the eventual stereotype of the "Saracen princess" that was so prevalent in romance epic. If Aude invites the student to step into the subject position of a twelfth-century woman, Bramimonde offers an even more complex viewpoint. While Aude is a woman written into a male-authored story entrenched in patriarchal modes of power, at least she participates in the dominant religious structure: Christianity. Bramimonde is both woman and Muslim, what we would expect to be a doubly denigrated being.

In fact, Bramimonde acts in ways that Aude never seems to consider. Bramimonde's appearance in the *Song of Roland* is more developed, since she figures prominently in eight different laisses, whereas Aude is mentioned in one and is physically present in two others. The Muslim queen performs a female version of the gift exchange, offering jewelry to Ganelon's wife (laisse 50). When the tide turns against Marsile after Roland's death, Bramimonde questions the power of the gods of Islam, joining a mob of twenty thousand men to trample and smash images of Apollo, Tervagant, and Muhammad (laisse 187). Portending the downfall of the Muslim armies, Bramimonde sees clearly the assiduity and superiority of Charlemagne and his troops (laisses 189, 195, and 196). Arguably, she comes to the rational conclusion that Christianity must be superior to Islam because God clearly aligns himself with Charlemagne over her husband's forces. She, alone of all the Muslims, is converted through love, "par amur," rather than by force (line 3674). As students imagine various audiences, the image of Bramimonde becomes more complicated. While the men in the audience may have found victory or desire in a final "taming of the shrew," I suggest elsewhere that women may have reacted with less enthusiasm as Bramimonde, like other "Saracen princesses," is effectively silenced and controlled by her assimilation (see Ramey 139).

Bramimonde's character serves the political purpose of uniting the French and Christian forces against the Muslim, but how does her image compare with medieval sources about Muslim women? A fascinating foil to the French view of the brazen Muslim and the feminine Aude can be found in an excerpt from the twelfth-century Arab historian ʿImad ad-Din entitled "Frankish Women of Peace and War" (Gabrieli 204–07). The link between sexuality and the feminine other, central to Edward Said's orientalism but here inverted from the East toward the West, provides a counterpoint to the absence of Christian women and the lack of cultural context for women in this period. For the Muslim historian, Christian women are the mirror of Bramimonde and the literary Saracen princesses who follow her. The women described by ʿImad ad-Din, who are warriors, sexually promiscuous, and outspoken, provide yet another perspective for reading Bramimonde and Aude.

Recent work on women in medieval Islam reveals the roles some Arab women played. Nadia Maria El-Cheikh finds examples of Arab women wielding considerable power in secular anthologies of the tenth century (140–44). Chronicles from Andalusia indicate that only rarely did women exercise public roles, but an intriguing exception to this rule was the eleventh-century Berber warrior woman Jamila, who appears in a genealogical treatise by Ibn Hazm (Molíns 167).

The instruction of Bramimonde serves as a cautionary tale for the teacher of the *Song of Roland*:

> "In my house there is a noble captive;
> She has heard so many sermons and parables
> That, wishing to believe in God, she seeks Christianity.
> Baptize her, so that God may have her soul."
> They reply to her: "May it be done through godmothers,
> Very loyal and noble ladies."
> In the baths at Aix there is a vast gathering;
> There they baptize the Queen of Spain.

They found for her the name of Juliana;
She is a Christian, convinced of the truth.   (3978–87)

The Saracen queen who appears several times as an opinionated, outspoken visionary ends the tale in brainwashed silence. Charlemagne speaks Bramimonde's will in a way that Marsile never did. Giroux questions a pedagogy that results in silence: "The first question is: Can learning take place if in fact it silences the voices of the people it is supposed to teach? And the answer is: Yes. People learn that they don't count" (Giroux, *Border Crossings* 15).

Does Bramimonde count? Bramimonde has learned that her religion and culture are to be annihilated. As a final act of appropriation, her very identity is removed and Christianized. The renaming of Bramimonde to Juliana exerts further control over the former queen, an act that Trinh T. Minh-Ha postulates as essential to removing the threat of otherness and making the colonial subject desire to be "like us" (Trinh 52–54).

A class that looks to the historical background that gave rise to the representations of Aude and Bramimonde and that employs diverse critical methods, including anthropological, reader reception, postcolonial and feminist, satisfies two of the three tenets of border pedagogy. Perhaps the most important element of Freire and Giroux's approach, however, is the meaning that students construct for themselves and their own lives. As students examine the political and ethical nature of the representations of Aude and Bramimonde, they should be encouraged to draw parallels to their experiences. By occupying in turn the perspectives of those endowed with power and those with little or no agency, students may find stories that resonate with their own lives. If Robert Scholes is correct in suggesting that "a major function of the teacher of fiction should be to help students identify their own collectivities, their group or class interests, by means of the representation of typical figures and situations in fictional texts" (23), then the figures of Aude and Bramimonde provide a pedagogical space in which to try on identities that can help students understand themselves and the political forces that shape their own identities.

# An Alternative Reading of the *Song of Roland*

## *Robert Francis Cook*

From the time it was first studied and taught, the *Song of Roland* has, with few exceptions, been interpreted in print according to a single scheme. The earliest medievalists established the canonical paraphrase of the work, a paraphrase based on the theme of Roland's unheeding pride. His flaw is the cause of the disaster of Rencesvals. Though the reading predicated on Roland's *desmesure* did not derive from systematic narrative analysis of the full text, its repeated use in both history and criticism since the late nineteenth century has led critics to make the hypothesis itself a primary explanatory device, often treating elements of the text as they relate to the idea of Roland's pride and fall, rather than as they relate to each other or to themes we associate with early medieval ways of organizing society.

This essay offers an alternative way of presenting the contents of the *Song of Roland* and of bringing out some of the ideas that shape it. This nontraditional reading is based on a traditional way of exploring narrative texts, through examination of events, their sequence, and their outcomes. Though I attempt to show the coherence and some of the explanatory value of this presentation, space does not allow full development of the arguments behind it.[1] What follows is a summary, or précis, not unlike those encountered in reference works, textbooks, the introductions to editions, and survey courses. It is meant, among other things, to suggest that the work is too well knit to be understood through the citing of isolated lines or scenes. Nonetheless, although my paraphrase sometimes emphasizes events that are rarely referred to, it cannot evoke every significant element. It is not intended as a complete analysis of the type one might do in a seminar.

The reader may adopt this nontraditional interpretation or may reject it, but, whatever the choice, the pedagogical value of a second reading, whose procedure and textual credentials can be compared and contrasted with the traditional one, is obviously considerable. After the paraphrase that follows, I conclude with a few words on some of the many potential classroom uses of the reading.

King Marsile has invaded Spain, but he cannot defeat Charlemagne, who has come to drive him out. Marsile calls on his council for advice in his desperation. The solution is simple: Blancandrin tells him to lie. Charles will trust not Marsile's words but an offer of hostages, and, once the emperor's army has been dispersed and winter has nearly begun, Marsile's failure to submit will necessarily go unpunished. The hostages will be sacrificed to this plan; they are not meant as a guarantee but as part of the deception.

The poem thus begins with what is sometimes thought of as a dramatic device. It lets the reader (or, at the time of its making, the hearer) have crucial information that it does not explicitly make available to all the characters. In the earliest scenes, we see, among other things, feudal leaders responding to a crisis. Charlemagne and his men have no immediate proof of treason, though they fear it and the audience expects it. When Blancandrin brings the offer to Charles, his council is not fooled. Roland, who is Charles's field commander, the first knight named in the work (line 104, cf. 671), and the first to speak in council, points out at once that the offer is not new. Marsile sent this very message before, and the only outcome was the sacrifice of Charles's ambassadors, men who have never been avenged (193–213).

Vengeance is one of those concepts that were less obviously repugnant to the early medieval mentality than in later times. We can grasp its potential practical value with some reflection. The term refers not to vendetta but rather to a duty of lordship. Failure to punish a treasonous killing leaves the enemy free to kill one's men again. That this principle of government is open to flagrant abuse does not disqualify it as a principle. The poem will show that peace, shaky as ever, returns only once Charles has finally avenged Basan and Basile, and Roland as well.

It is important also to recognize that in the first council, as elsewhere, Roland's arguments are valid and his conclusions are correct—if we keep in mind the contents of the poem. We may find his proposal distasteful in the abstract. We may decide that war is never the right response to treachery; we may reason as Naimes does and consider the offer of hostages decisive; or we may sympathize with Ganelon's desire to accept Marsile's offer without any regard to the circumstances. But we already know Roland is right to say that the offer is a lie. It is not Roland's response that creates the danger.

The offer of hostages carries the day, and the Frankish barons vote to accept Marsile's proposal. Yet Charles is not willing to allow Roland, who volunteers first to risk his life as ambassador, or Oliver or any member of his household to go to the enemy camp. Given such limitations, Roland finally suggests

Ganelon for the mission, and his choice is immediately ratified by the vote of the group. Ganelon argued from the outset in favor of the false offer, but he knows the story of Basan and Basile as well as anyone. He flies into a rage, accusing Roland of having singled him out (Charles is obliged to correct Ganelon's claim), swearing enmity to his own comrades, and promising dire consequences for Roland and the peers (296–336).

Ganelon pursues his personal ends, not those of the Franks (and certainly not those of the Saracens), when he arrives in the enemy camp. He taunts Marsile and states harsh conditions for surrender that are in conflict with the conditions given in the written document he carries, a letter from Charles. This is the first element of Ganelon's treason. Then Ganelon insists the enemy king can save himself by destroying Roland, the only cause of the war (538–79); in fact, the poem will show Charles's energetic vengeance after Rencesvals has run its course. Ganelon promises to arrange Roland's death, and, when he returns to the Frankish camp, he lies to Charles. He makes two claims: first, that Marsile is ready to submit—this implies success in the mission Ganelon was given—and, second, that, despite this success, he was unable to bring the one credible hostage (cf. 680–97 with 492–94).

Charles nonetheless proceeds as though the transaction were honest. This may appear naive or rash, but it is not; instead, it shows the limits on Charles's power, part of the homage bond between the king and his men. The king cannot act arbitrarily with respect to Ganelon, a vassal with whom he has exchanged the promises of support that are part of the homage rite. Reflection leads us to the realization that until solid proof is somehow made available to all those whose support he needs, Charles will only weaken the structure of mutual trust by allowing his suspicions to take over. This is true even after Charles has had his foreshadowing dreams of loss and disaster on the eve of his departure from Spain.

The nature of Ganelon's treason and the threat to the Frankish army become evident as the men prepare to withdraw from the country they have not yet wholly retaken. To reach their lands, they must cross the Pyrenees—a task as formidable for the medieval army as many a battle. The Franks will have to make a great effort in order to climb the high passes that to this day are an obstacle to movement. Traveling unarmed, they are leaving an undefeated and unsubmissive enemy in the rear. An effective rear guard is vital. Ganelon has promised harm to his fellow knights, Marsile is not to be trusted, and the time and place are favorable for an ambush. It is not a surprise that when Ganelon suggests Roland as commander of the rear guard, Roland at once accepts the duty, saying that Charles will not lose a single chattel that has not been fought for. Charles's frustration and anger are no surprise either, for he knows, yet cannot prove, what the risk is.

This is the moment at which Roland's fate is sealed. The public promises he makes in lines 751–59 are simple and straightforward. He promises to resist if attacked and to make the attacker pay dearly. Charles needs to fear no man as long as Roland is alive. He does not say anything about a victory—that is not the function of a small detachment, and, as he points out in lines 783–91, rear guards are axiomatically detachments, not armies. Or, as we might put it, they buy time in case of a sudden attack at a vulnerable point, allowing the main body of the army to recognize the threat and prepare for it. The poem carries out—to the letter—the promises Roland makes here, and, as he implies it might, it will cost him his life.

Like the narration, the speeches of the characters suggest drama. First of all, the poem was delivered orally to an audience by a performer. In addition, it describes the acts that embodied public policy and the public good in its time, and these acts were also in a sense performances. Knights sealed their engagements by gestures such as the kneeling and touching of homage and spoke aloud to assemblies that were expected to remember the words and to hold the speakers to their promises.

From this point, the poem moves to the working out, in action, of Roland's promises. He calls for volunteers, and they join him; he prudently sends one of his men, Gautier del Hum, to occupy the high ground. Probably Gautier knows the risk as well; at any rate, he does not depart without making his own statement of principle: "I am Roland's vassal, I must not fail him" (801, cf. 807). Gautier will fight at the head of his detachment as long as he can, thus mirroring the fight Roland carries out in the larger battle. Then, rather than flee, he will come to Rencesvals and die by Roland's side.

As the army struggles to reach the borders of home, Marsile comes to Rencesvals. Preparing for their ambush, the enemy peers make boasting promises: they will kill Roland, occupy France, and seize Charles's crown. When Oliver sees Marsile's huge force approaching, he is greatly disturbed (1036). He pleads with Roland to call for help. Roland responds vigorously: if he were to do as Oliver asks, he would lose his standing. Instead, he makes further promises of his own. He will strike great blows; it is the knight's duty to suffer for his lord. Roland swears not that he himself will kill the enemy but that the pagans are marked or fated for death (1058, 1069, 1081).

It is necessary to insist on the nearly immediate juxtaposition of two sets of vows, the ones the Saracens make and the ones Roland makes soon afterward. Events show that the Saracens' vows are exaggerated and false. Roland's speeches match the remainder of the poem. The way to judge these promises and Oliver's reactions is, once again, to put them into context. The poem frames both words and action, near the outset, by setting up expectations in the council scene where Roland accepts the rear guard. Later the framing device consists of showing how, during his argument with Oliver, Roland's precise statements (consistent with the earlier scene) contrast with the symmetrically structured but rhetorically opposed bombast of the enemy peers. There are several example's of their vain boasts in the scene where the Saracens prepare to attack. One occurs when Marsile's nephew says he will kill Roland, drive the Franks out of Spain, and win peace for his uncle (866–72).

But his pagan deity Muhammad cannot save him: instead, he is the first Saracen Roland kills (1188–212). Then the emir of Balaguer promises that once he has killed Roland, Oliver, and the Twelve Peers, Charles will lose heart (so said Ganelon in lines 537–600) and Spain will be free. He too dies in the first clash. Finally, the diabolical Chernubles swears to attack Roland and kill the Franks; it is he who is split in two by Roland's most famous sword stroke. Such are the "great blows" Roland promises in line 1055; furthermore, as he says, the enemy has no protection from death (this is the literal sense of line 1081). Marsile's men will not survive the day.

Of course the rear guard cannot resist the waves of attackers forever. At the end, when only a few are left, Roland suggests blowing the olifant, asking, "How shall we let [Charles] know?" (the literal sense of line 1699). Oliver tries to prevent it and (perhaps thinking Roland expects rescue) accuses Roland of wrongdoing and wrongheadedness. These accusations are at the heart of the traditional interpretation of the poem. But Archbishop Turpin points out that the horn call will indeed bring Charles, not to save the detachment (it is too late for that), but to avenge it. When Charles and all his men hear the call of the horn over a great distance, they at last are able to act. Ganelon can prolong his treason no further, his objections are spurned, and the army prepares to return and fight Marsile. Meanwhile, Oliver has been fatally wounded, literally blinded, in an attack from behind. Before he falls, he assaults Roland in confusion, but (like his earlier accusations) the blind stroke does no harm, and Oliver receives Roland's forgiveness (1989–2007). Gautier, Turpin, and Roland make their last stand. The last to die is Roland, sword in hand, untouched by his foes, as the enemy flees the field. Only a miracle allows Charles to catch up with the enemy and take his exemplary vengeance.

The poem we know goes on to show Charlemagne in combat against the supreme Saracen ruler, the emir Baligant, who now arrives with an even more powerful army. This new battle is a victory for the emperor, who fights the emir hand to hand and defeats him with the help of an angel. It occupies a fair amount of space but seems to express primarily the superiority of Christian beliefs and of Christian warriors over the invaders, who are described not as Muslims but as idolaters and polytheists. This judgment of God, reminiscent of Crusade preaching, deserves fuller consideration than I can give it here, as does the death of Aude, who refuses to live after she learns of her sworn fiancé's death. The narrative sequence ends with Ganelon's trial and the duel between Thierry and Pinabel, made necessary by the Frankish barons' failure to carry out their duty to render justice. Pinabel is an imposing fighter, and Thierry is an ordinary man, but (despite what the pagans said, and despite Oliver's accusation in lines 1727 and 1732) the emperor and the system he represents do not need a Roland to defend them. With divine help, Thierry strikes Ganelon's champion down, and the traitor is at last put to death. Charlemagne's life is a burden to him, but he will fight on, as his last angel bids him to do in lines 3993–98. In other words—the grim words of the narrator,

sentential in form and perhaps the nearest thing to a moral in the work—
"Mult ad apris ki bien cunuist ahan" ("He who knows true pain has learned
a great deal"; 2524).

Ganelon's lies to the enemy and to his overlord, the boasts the enemy peers
make in juxtaposition with Roland's limited and accurate promises, or the
symbolic pardon Roland gives Oliver: these and other events work in tandem
with textual pointers like Roland's literal triumph at Rencesvals, Gautier's
plunge into the battle that will mean his death, or Thierry's unlikely victory
in his duel with Pinabel. The result is a picture of a mental world not unlike
that known to us from other sources. It is a world where martyrdom is not
defeat, loyalty is the cement of social structure, and the given word is binding
in detail. The poem is not about the psychology of an individual, which is not
a surprising thing to suggest about an epic from the twelfth century, or even
the eleventh, if we agree the poem or its antecedants are that old. It is an
exemplary work about how society is to be organized and defended in harsh
times. It evokes, of course, not a formal system of the sort traditionally called
feudal (though the term has been challenged) but habitual ways of talking
about relationships between one person and another and between persons
and power.[2]

This summary is, of course, far from complete. Still, it leads to questions
about long-standing claims. Roland is not presented as a youth (the characters'
ages are not stated in the poem). He does not disobey orders (Charles is not
in a position to give him any). Oliver's prudence is not consistent (he takes
the opportunity to espouse prudence not in the council scenes but only when
he sees the vast host approaching). Similarly, both heroes have been assigned
opposing traits of character on the basis of line 1093. The shades of early
interpretations of this line will perhaps float over the poem for as long as it
is read. And yet there are arguments for taking the line, in conjunction with
the following lines that extend it, to be a description of the two men as alike.
Once the early hypothesis about the poem's global meaning is set aside, even
experimentally, the teacher and the student will find in the work other ele-
ments like the ones I have just listed—elements capable of arousing curiosity
and inspiring discussion. The narrator's comments in particular need to be
integrated into the interpretation of the work; here I will quote only the state-
ment he makes on Roland's ethos, which situates the hero in the mainstream
of early knighthood: "Li quens Rollant unkes n'amat cuard, / N'orguillos hume,
malvais de male part" ("Count Roland never loved a coward, / Nor arrogant
men nor those of evil character"; 2134–35).

Despite the omissions to which I have referred, and of which I am acutely
conscious, the summary I have given of the poem in the preceding pages
should suffice as a first motivation for reading the *Song* in a way that is not
dependent on the traditional one yet offers strong textual credentials. It may
also imply at least temporary acceptance of the notion that feudal principles,
however alien at first glance, were nominally coherent. What Joseph Strayer

called "public power in private hands" (*Feudalism* 12) implies personal re-
sponsibility, unless we assume our ancestors never cared for stable government
at all.

Questions of relevance, or immediately applicable ethical and political les-
sons to be drawn from the work, will almost certainly arise in twenty-first-
century classrooms. The religious and ethnic attitudes exhibited by the nar-
rator and the speakers must be taken into account, and that is no small
challenge. In mixed classes (Middle Eastern, American and European Mus-
lims, Orthodox and Eastern Christians, secular Turks, Africans, anthropolo-
gists, religion majors, members of the active military and ROTC, French ma-
jors) I have thought it best to maintain a reportorial stance. There is more to
be drawn from problematic interpretations, however, than just timeliness. The
existence today of a positive reading of Roland's acts and words also allows us
to introduce the contrasts that are the empirical basis of critical thinking.
Anyone, teacher or student, who wants to settle on an interpretation of the
*Song* must sift the evidence and read the text closely, in a historical frame of
mind. Anyone who wants to insist instead on the fragility of the act of reading
may dwell on the different outcomes proposed by scholars using what appears
to be the same method.

In theory, of course, it is possible to claim that both interpretations are valid
and correct, or that no interpretation is. Such claims can furnish the starting
point for investigation of developments in reading theory and in response
theory over the past three decades or so. In practice, many teachers and
students will want to make at least a provisional choice. Making the choice in
turn means choosing criteria of validity (internal? historical? ethnic? psycho-
logical? moral?) and justifying one's choices to other readers who may not
agree. Like other texts with more than one explanation (*Hamlet*, Genesis,
Romantic poems), *Roland* may inspire students to go beyond the materials
used in the classroom. Some will be interested in the potentially surprising
uses of key terms in the time of the original audience: *proz, los, honor, desfier,
venger*, and other words are as far from their classical, early modern, and
Modern French cognates as are commonly glossed words like *brogne, destrier*,
or *museraz* from the vocabulary we know (see, e.g., Burgess, *Contribution*;
Flori, *Idéologie*). The work's terminology may then point to the culture that
used the terms, as language study usually does. Beyond the necessary caveats,
such study may lead not only to a clearer picture of early feudal times, even
in their physicality, but also to a better idea of the evidence and arguments
that apply to historical and structural readings of old and complex works. And
I have been restricting myself to the work's compelling sequences with barely
a word for its unique power of expression.

Indeed, as I come to the end of these remarks, I find myself returning to
a reaction that never quite left me over thirty-four years of teaching this text
in a wide variety of settings. I am tempted to repudiate the expository strategy
I announced at the outset and to declare that in its richness *Roland* always

deserves a seminar at the very least. Still, summary is inevitable in an academic world that limits strictly the time given to medieval studies, whatever their pedagogical value. In most courses there will not even be enough time to read such a lengthy work as a whole. I hope the summary given here, though a poor substitute, will invite close attention to aspects of the text that might not seem vital without it.

## NOTES

[1]Those arguments are given in detail in Cook; for the origins of this reading see Crist; Foulet. Brault's highly detailed commentary is also a nontraditional reading, focusing as much on religion as on social structures (Song).

[2]Among the numerous recent studies of feudal ideas are Bournazel; Duby, *Féodalité*; Flori, *Chevalerie*; Henneman; Strayer's older remarks in *Feudalism* remain useful.

# Three Epic Swords and
# the Stories They Tell

## Eugene Vance

The *Song of Roland* is the most admired of medieval French epics. However, its disjointed story of relentless violence and its unreflective, formulaic eloquence make its tragic meaning obtuse. Surely the obtuse aspect of the poem kept its story alive in the emerging consciousness of French premodern culture. As modern readers of this epic, perhaps we can identify in its story some of the ethical and spiritual crosscurrents that propelled the quest for political and spiritual order characteristic of the the Capetian royal dynasty's reign.

Although archaic elements of *Roland* date back to AD 778, the year Charlemagne's army was ambushed in the Pyrenees, the poem as we know it mainly matured in the late eleventh and early twelfth centuries (Menéndez-Pidal, *Chanson*). Later details could have been interpolated into the story right up to its transcription in the mid–twelfth century. Therefore, if the poem's archaism is partly authentic, it was also regularly embellished over several centuries to renew its truth value as legend or fiction. As an epic hero, Charlemagne himself personifies—and vivifies—the archaism of his own story: his white beard flows in the wind, we are told, and he is two hundred years old!

As emperor and king, Charlemagne is at once the poetic emissary of an imagined, lost heroic age and the sovereign of a new world: that of a nascent French culture marked by two deeply ideological controversies. The first was the Holy War, which culminated in the exalting (yet genocidal) conquest of Jerusalem in the First Crusade (during 1096–99). It was to be severely undermined, though, by the disastrous defeat of the crusading armies during the Second Crusade (1145–49). The second was the struggle over the expansion of royal power by Capetian kings of France in the twelfth and thirteenth centuries at the expense of the high nobles.

One way of probing the message of this dark and restless tale is to consider the succession of three starkly differing heroes, each central to a distinct section of the epic: Roland, Charlemagne, and Thierry. I do so by asking the following: how do the swords that these heroes wield define, each in its own way, the hero's meaning in a fictional world where action itself is more eloquent than mere words?

Obviously, in a Christian military culture such as that of the Middle Ages, an epic sword was more than an instrument of war. It was a figure of its bearer's very soul and his destiny in the mortal combat against God's enemies. Thus, the arming of a young knight with a sword was a rite of passage into manhood; so too the sword's success in battle would stand as a defining emblem of a knight's honor and fame.

To evoke the perfection of a heroic sword and its exploits was a test of an epic poet's own mettle. An exemplary sword could give its provenance, service to political and spiritual causes, and honor to a young knight who came to possess it or to a new king when it was conferred on him along with the regalia of the crown and scepter. Finally, a sword that served both God and France could be venerated as a holy and national relic—no matter how much its authenticity was in doubt. Even today, a sword called Durendal is enshrined in the Chapel of the Black Virgin at the fortress of Rocamadour, in the south of France.

By definition, an epic hero's sword summoned great stories about its invincibility—even in defeat—and not stories of shame. As a concept, however, victory is always ethically variable and at times contradictory: only much later did the legacy of what was lost in the Christian conquest of Jerusalem during the First Crusade become apparent. So too, in the conflicted historical vision of this poem, each of these sword's victories is equivocal—and tragically so— as we see below.

## Roland and Durendal

In this epic, Roland's and Durendal's prestige are undissociable: to defeat the knight and capture his sword is the supreme prize to which any pagan warrior aspires. Thus, during the final moments of Roland's last stand in the pass at Rencesvals, the dying hero wants to preserve Durendal from the shame of falling into the hands of some pagan "who might flee before another" (2309), and so he tries to break its blade on a rock. Three times, however, Durendal (whose very name connotes endurance) rebounds into the sunlight, a clear sign of Roland's triumph, even in defeat, as a martyr for his "Lord" (whether Charlemagne or Christ). Its rebound is perhaps also an augury of Roland's resurrection. Only at the climax of the death scene do we learn of Durendal's provenance and why the mighty force behind it was far more than the martyr's own. Durendal, he exults, had been sent to him by God himself:

> O, Durendal, how fair and clear and white you are!
> How you shimmer and sparkle in the sun!
> Charles was in the Vales of Maurienne,
> When through his angel God on high told him
> To give you to a captain count.
> Then the noble and mighty king girded it on me.   (2316–22)

The chronicle of the sword's conquests that ensues evokes legendary regions of France and Europe (and even Constantinople!) that reflect historical myths of the Carolingian Empire as it was later imagined to have been carved out by Durendal. The relics of four great saints are embedded in the sword's pommel (2344–48). Together, they signify that Roland's mission has been predestined by God; separately, each helps define his sacred mission: Saint Peter's tooth assures us that Roland's cause is the true apostolic one, certainly a welcome political claim at a time when the French and German sovereigns supported rival popes. Saint Basil's blood is the relic of the most prestigious early Byzantine theologian, so it assures a Western audience vexed by schisms that Durendal has served the whole of Christendom. The hair of Saint Denis, the legendary patron saint of France, signifies that Roland's service to Charlemagne embodies a distinctly French sacred history—a prominent theme during and after the First Crusade. The piece of Saint Mary's clothing is a token of her pledge to intercede for Roland at the Last Judgment. Despite his intemperate nature, Roland—and by extension Durendal—exemplifies (though imperfectly) the Christian soldier who has perfected himself as the vassal of his earthly emperor and as an image of the militant Christ.

## Charlemagne and Joyeuse

With the death of Roland in the poem's middle, the emperor's own "right arm" (697, 727) has also perished. Bereft of his best soldiers and left to deal with the messy aftermath of defeat, how can this stricken old emperor possibly serve as the poem's "new" hero?

It is relevant to recall, first, that the founding motive of the crusading ideal was pilgrimage undertaken not only in a spirit of penitence but also with the goal of directing Christian belligerence against God's enemies instead of against other Christians. Christian warriors of the First and Second Crusades were assured by the clergy of their future redemption when they took up the sword for Christ—and for France. By the same logic, the defeat of the French army at Damascus during the Second Crusade in 1149 was interpreted by Saint Bernard (who had preached the Crusade) as God's just punishment for their sins of impurity in the Holy Land. Roland's triumph as a martyr obviously reflects the ideal of Holy War, whose outcome was the First Crusade. However, Charlemagne will be humiliated both as a holy warrior and as the sovereign of an empire where Christians are killing each other and whose high nobles are in rebellion against him.

Charlemagne and his sword Joyeuse express a paradigm of Christian heroism that is more complex than Roland's own. Charlemagne not only is Roland's uncle (and perhaps even his father by incest, as legend held) but also, in many ways, is himself a "Roland" who has not died but grown old. Charles has lived to see his worldly empire as a desolate wasteland abandoned by God: "O, fair land of France, how bereft you are!" (2928), he laments after the defeat at Rencesvals. In other words, with the death of his nephew, a part of Charlemagne himself has perished. True, Charlemagne (but not Joyeuse) will exact vengeance from the Saracen army that destroyed his best men. However, his vengeance is evoked in a mere seventeen verses of epic shorthand (2458–

75), in which—to the glory of none—God's enemies drown ignominiously in the Ebro River, and those who wear armor sink conveniently right to the bottom. At this point, is epic poetry itself perhaps not flagging?

Not exactly: rather, its discourse reaches for a new and very different understanding of heroic action. Now, we read of an emperor and a weary army given over to abject grief. Charlemagne and his army collapse in an eerie moonlight, too exhausted to disarm or unsaddle their horses, who cannot even stand up to graze. At this still point of epic action, we encounter a moving and different kind of epic eloquence, one that summons in us a sentiment of compassion instead of awe. In stark contrast with Roland's jubilant and painless fight to the death, Charlemagne's exemplary role is now that of a grieving and penitent leader (recalling, of course, the penitences of King David and of the Christian Roman emperor Theodosius) for whom Christ's suffering on the cross will redeem his own. With Charlemagne, suffering becomes action in its own right.

Like Durendal, Joyeuse is also a reliquary sword, but it contains only a single relic: the tip of the spear with which the legendary Roman soldier Longinus pierced the side of the crucified Christ and captured his blood in a vessel. This legend came into greater prominence in the Grail literature of the late twelfth century that Chrétien de Troyes inaugurated in his *Perceval; or, The Story of the Grail*. In the historical culture of the *Song of Roland*, though, the spear was more immediately associated with the turning point of the First Crusade, when the Christian army was hopelessly besieged by the Turks in the city of Antioch. Their despair ends when a miraculous vision informs the French that the spear awaits them in a nearby church. This discovery restores their faith that God will sustain them, whereupon they break the siege and go on to conquer Jerusalem.

In the *Song of Roland*, however, we are told that the tip of this lance has caused Charlemagne's sword to be called Joyeuse and that "Munjoie" (evoking, perhaps, the mountain of Calvary and Christ's victory over death) is the battle cry of the invincible French at Rencesvals. However, since the French have just been defeated, the significance of Joyeuse in this poem is contradicted by the new circumstances. As Charlemagne lies grieving and still armed in the moonlit field after the battle at Rencesvals, the poet says:

> [He] girt about him his sword *Joiuse*, which had no peer.
> And whose colour changes thirty times a day.
> We could speak for a long time about the lance
> With which our Lord was wounded on the cross:
> Charles has its point, thanks be to God,
> Which he has had mounted in his golden pommel.
> Through this honour and this excellence
> The name Joiuse was given to the sword.
> Frankish barons should not forget it;

From it they derive their battle cry "Monjoie."
For this reason no race on earth can withstand them.   (2501–11)

Have the French not just been badly beaten? Clearly, the relic embedded in Charlemagne's sword radically displaces the notion of Christian victory away from the immanent struggle against God's enemies on earth. Its realm is a spiritual one whose hero struggles privately with his despair in the night. The mysterious, changing colors of Joyeuse are no longer those of the natural or historical sunlight in which Roland triumphed, even in death. Rather, the "joy" of Joyeuse is that of spiritual illumination born in suffering, modeled on Christ, the suffering hero of Calvary. Despite the prophetic dreams that warn Charlemagne of the forthcoming war with the pagan emperor Baligant—which all critics agree is a late interpolation into the poem's story—Charlemagne's own motivation has now veered away from that of a heroic knight yearning for the final fight and toward that of a heroic pilgrim setting out (as Charlemagne had previously resolved) for Rencesvals on one of the very roads that innumerable twelfth-century French pilgrims traveled to reach the shrine of Saint James of Compostela, in Spain. In this context, the whole army's weapons of war are to be laid down by crusaders now serving the so-called pilgrim-God instead of the militant Christ:

> In the morning, at the first light of dawn,
> The emperor Charles awoke from his sleep.
> Saint Gabriel, who watches over him on God's behalf,
> Raises his hand and makes the sign of the cross over him.
> The king rises and laid aside his armour;
> And throughout the host the others disarm themselves;
> Then they mounted their horses and ride at top speed
> Following the long roads and the broad highways.
> They make their way to see the terrible destruction
> At Rencesvals.                            (2845–54)

In other words, the sword Joyeuse has been laid aside, and a penitent Charlemagne will set out to consecrate the triumphant martyrdom of his vassals at Rencesvals, whose relics he will have enshrined.

In the hollow interpolation of the ensuing battle with an old and bearded emir Baligant, who is Charlemagne's own pagan mirror image, French pride triumphs again as the emperor prevails—but just barely. Now the name Joyeuse and its spiritual meaning have been replaced by a far shallower ideological epithet: "the Sword of France" (3615). This indeed is the meaning that later prevailed in Charlemagne's legend, to the point where the monks of Saint Denis manufactured this very sword to serve in the coronation of the young King Philip Augustus in 1180. The sword continued to serve that same purpose for successive French kings throughout the Middle Ages, and to this day the Sword of France lies prominently on display in the Louvre Museum.

## Thierry and Cortain

The final episode of the *Song of Roland* deals with the trial of Ganelon, Roland's stepfather, whom Charlemagne has accused of treason for having conspired with King Marsile to avenge his stepson for nominating him for the dangerous mission to the pagan court. At the poem's opening, all Charlemagne's vassals were united in their resolve to defeat God's enemies, but now French Christians are intractably divided against each other. Insoluble political controversies have supplanted spiritual ones. Like the Capetian kings who wanted to govern their realm in the manner of emperors, Charlemagne will invoke God as the judge of his political cause. That judgment will be based on a judicial duel between Thierry and Pinabel, the respective champions of the emperor and of Ganelon. Earlier, Thierry and his brother Geoffrey of Anjou had distinguished themselves as two of the emperor's closest vassals; so too in other versions of the poem Thierry had been Roland's squire, and he had been armed with Cortain ("short blade"), the famous sword of the great epic hero Ogier the Dane. None of this aura remains in this now puny knight, for we see him at the Oxford poem's end as thin, black-haired, somewhat dark-skinned, and neither very big nor small—anything but the heroic vassal of before (3820–23). He is conspicuously mismatched with the more splendid knight Pinabel. The champion of imperial authority is weak; that of the high barony is strong. Nothing, moreover, is said about either of the champions' nameless swords, except that the pommels are made of gold (3866). Neither of the swords is heroic or invincible, nor is this even a time in the poem when heroism itself is to be prized over subservience—which will indeed be seen as a new virtue in its own right (Haidu, *Violence*).

The outcome of this grim judicial duel is inglorious and marks the eclipse of chivalric virtues that had stirred the Christian warriors of the poem's first half: Pinabel's mortal blow to Thierry is suddenly deflected by God himself, whereas Thierry's little sword (and not Cortain) cleaves Pinabel's helmet, causing his brain to spill out: "God has performed a miracle," the barons cry out (3931). Thus the unpopular cause of monarchial supremacy has prevailed.

There are no heroes at the poem's end. With the death of the splendid Pinabel, the quartering of the proud Ganelon, and the hanging of the thirty loyal clansmen who had served as his pledges, Charlemagne becomes, to be sure, an absolute sovereign. But he is also a tired and desperate leader whose empire is all but destitute of heroes yet who will be immediately summoned in a dream by Saint Gabriel to undertake another expedition in the service of God to rescue Christians in the remote East (3994–95). In one sense, the poem's story ends as it had begun, though this new call to war is unwelcome. What remains of the world of exultant warriors of before, except a depleted army and conspicuously mediocre hero who has usurped the place of Roland? Who, we may ask, is now the enemy of those great barons who fought in the names of God and Charlemagne? It is none other than Charlemagne himself. The abject emperor of France will now strip his best soldiers of their independence and pride and press them to pursue a new and perhaps interminable holy war. At the poem's bitter end, the once invincible and joyous conqueror of the poem's outset lies alone in the night, worn out, lonely and in despair. He has outlived his legend yet is not free to die: " 'God,' said the king, 'how wearisome my life is!' / He weeps and tugs at his white beard" (4000–01).

Clearly, no twelfth-century epic poet would have taken it on himself to finish off the very emperor whose legend the Capetian kings of France were now actively reinventing as a foundation of their own tenuous power. This greatest of French epics has not found narrative closure, yet the semantic power of the consecrated formulas of the poem's earlier heroic language has become all but obsolete and is at odds with a changed world, where weakness is prized over prowess and subservience over loyalty, intimidation has replaced leadership, and political motives have supplanted spiritual ones. Of course, other songs of Roland continued to be composed during more than a century after the Oxford version of the poem was written. Modern readers probably agree, though, that the feigned oral epic discourse of those later poems rings hollow in comparison to the Oxford version, whose tragedy eclipses them all. May I suggest, however, that the *Song of Roland*, sublime even in its obsolescence, helped galvanize a new generation of great French poets who would find different paths to poetic distinction? Especially during the long reign of King Philip Augustus (1180–223), the so-called epics of revolt disclosed, with devastating thoroughness, the hopeless cause of the oppressed French barony against their ambitious sovereigns. The most disturbing of these is surely *Raoul de Cambrai*. In contrast, the more optimistic genre of courtly romance quickly came into its own at the hands of its greatest and most original early poet, Chrétien de Troyes. One of his most famous heroes, Yvain, or the Knight of the Lion, fights for the cause of love even better, we are told (lines 3233–37), than Roland fought for God and empire with his sword Durendal at Rencesvals! In short, the greatness of the *Song of Roland* is borne out less by its imitators than by innovators who looked back at it as a tragic threshold into a new and distinctly French culture, which some thinkers of the time considered modern. So too, Aristotle looked back at Homer's *Iliad* as the foundation of Athenian tragedy. Like the *Iliad* in ancient times, the *Song of Roland* has endured as a provocation for later modernities, including those of the Italian Renaissance and of nineteenth-century French culture. Charlemagne's sword, "the sword of France" was among the regalia of the emperor Napoleon's coronation (1804) in the cathedral of Notre Dame. In 1835, the Oxford manuscript of the poem was "discovered," exactly where it had lain for over a century, in the Bodleian Library.

So too, in our own new century, some readers will glimpse in the contradictions of this magnificent poem a revealing but cracked mirror of our time.

# Violence and *Desmesure*
# in the *Song of Roland*

*Patricia E. Black*

This foundational French epic always holds potential interest for the modern reading audience, especially in the guise of its representation of violence. Two events make this epic poem more relevant. The destruction of September 11, 2001 has brought the United States into conflict with persons and entities of the Islamic world, echoing the opposition between the Franks and the Saracens in the *Song of Roland*. In addition, Peter Jackson's film trilogy of *Lord of the Rings* offers an image of violence in a world recalling the Middle Ages (though the novel by J. R. R. Tolkien differs somewhat from the films). The miraculous nature of the victory over Sauron offers visual cues to the imagination of the reader of *Roland*. Thus, although this work is distant from us, it is not completely inaccessible because the representation of violence opposing two irreconcilable forces has parallels in our own time. However, the celebration and description of warfare in medieval texts can jar the modern reader. And the *Song of Roland* devotes a central portion of the text to warfare.

Histories of the medieval army (in chronological order) include Charles Oman's *Art of War in the Middle Ages*, Ferdinand Lot's *L'art militaire et les armées au moyen âge en Europe et dans le Proche Orient*, John Beeler's *Warfare in Feudal Europe*, and J. F. Verbruggen's *The Art of Warfare in Western Europe during the Middle Ages*, as well as Philippe Contamine's *La guerre au moyen âge*. They are still the most complete general histories for this subject. René Girard's *Violence and the Sacred* is a foundational study on the genesis and "management" of violence in society. In *The Subject of Violence: The* Song of Roland *and the Birth of the State*, Peter Haidu reads the poem as an allegory of the violence stemming from the change from a feudal to a monarchical state. Finally, Regina M. Schwartz in *The Curse of Cain* examines the violent nature of monotheism.

The topic of Roland's *desmesure* was introduced early in the scholarship on this poem; in *The Sense of the* Song of Roland, Robert F. Cook gives an overview of the arguments concerning this theme as well as many references (148–52); though clearly in a minority, he himself does not subscribe to the opinion that Roland's pride led to disaster. He points out (as do others) that *desmesure* "is a concept not named" in this poem (149). Yet many readers have had the impression that notwithstanding the poem's celebration of war there is a surplus of eagerness for violence on Roland's part. I test the question of *desmesure* against the context of the poem's representation of violence. How, if at all, does Roland exceed the norms of warfare established by the poem?

This essay addresses primarily those portions of the poem where blood is shed in war. These representations of violence usually receive short shrift, and even Edmond Faral in La chanson de Roland: *Étude et analyse,* Cook in *The Sense of the* Song of Roland, and Gerard J. Brault in The Song of Roland: *An Analytical Edition,* who all closely interpret the entire poem, do not dwell on the violence of the battles. For example, Cook says that the battle scenes "have a specifically epic function of displaying action at length and for present purposes require little detailed analysis" (79). When he returns to them, he discusses them in general (ch. 8).

In the opening lines of the poem we learn that a Frankish army occupies Spain and that even their opponents are very good knights (lines 24–25; this idea is repeated throughout the poem). *Roland* shows two feudal societies with armies composed of mounted knights (Oman 103–04; Davis 12–13). Another reality greets us in the first laisse: Charlemagne has stayed in Spain seven years and needed that entire time to conquer all of its towns but one, Saragossa. Though unrealistically lengthy, this process of warfare is logical in the narrative as well as in historical fact, because in the Middle Ages war was a process of sieges.

Much of the representation of violence in *Roland* concerns military action, the pitched battles that in reality medieval armies avoided (Verbruggen 288, 300; see also in this volume DeVries, "Military History and Technology in the *Song of Roland*"). It is thus worthwhile to compare how much space the text devotes to describing combat versus the preparations for war and the aftermath of battle. Ninety-two laisses lead into the battle charge of Rencesvals; the mopping up operation ends at laisse 185. Thus there are ninety-three laisses of battle description. The next phase of war is another direct confrontation lasting from laisses 239 to 264, culminating in the sack of Saragossa (264–66). This second operation concludes in a total of twenty-eight laisses. There are 121 laisses showing violent, direct combat and 170 laisses surround these scenes. The battle of Rencesvals occupies almost exactly the laisses that form the second third of the poem in the Oxford version; therefore, the first third forms a prelude to the battle, and the last third the postlude. The confrontation at Rencesvals has a privileged position in the poem, whereas the battle in the Baligant episode (laisses 189–265) forms an echo of the earlier engagement.

The battle of Rencesvals begins with a Frankish cavalry charge (laisse 92). During the general melee the poem highlights tremendous feats with the lance; these laisses unrealistically show warfare as a series of individual engagements (Bliese 203). For example, Roland kills Aelroth, the nephew of Marsile. Using the lance, Roland breaks Aelroth's shield; splits his hauberk; slices his chest; breaks the bones; severs the spine from his back; throws out his soul; thrusts the weapon into the enemy and causes his body to shake; and then, with the full length of the lance, throws him down dead with his neck broken in two (laisse 93). Despite the attention focused first on Roland, then on Oliver and Turpin, both armies are engaged: "Francs e paiens, as les vos ajustez" ("Franks and pagans; behold them in battle"; line 1187; my trans.).

Oliver strikes Falsaron (a symbolic name) in a valiant manner recalling Roland's feat with the lance. Turpin slays Corsablix with his lance. The effect of repetition focuses attention on the valor and skill of these three knights in particular, and on the Franks in general as they charge with their lances. The poem describes the attack by Roland on his opponent in such horrific detail that each subsequent scene becomes shorter. In foregrounding Roland, the text gives him the opportunity to back up with deeds what he earlier said: "Cist paien vont grant martirie querant" ("These pagans are looking for martyrdom"; line 1166; my trans.). Over and over, the spotlight illuminates another Christian knight fighting an important Saracen warrior. However, at the end of this series of attacks, the text reminds us that "La bataille est merveilluse e cumune" ("The battle is wondrous and widespread"; line 1320; my trans.).

This technique slows the action so that the audience or reader can appreciate the damage the blow wreaks. The characters and the audience even have time to look down on the enemy's body and gloat at his defeat (e.g., lines 230–31, 1251–52), as if notching their swords. By doing the opposite of the Saracens, who first talk and then fight, the Franks have the last word. The pauses for monologues in the enumeration of violent acts in the *Song of Roland* serve the same purpose as that identified by Girard: "violence itself offers a sort of respite, the fresh beginning of a cycle of ritual after a cycle of violence" (135).

In the battle of Rencesvals, once the lances break, swords come out to hack until the enemy's blood pools on the ground. Oliver uses the last bit of his lance to hit Malsarun (another symbolic name with the root *mal*, evil), so that his eyes pop out and his brains fall on his feet (1353). Then Oliver provides the first example of the favorite epic sword stroke: he splits an enemy knight in two from the head down through his horse (laisse 107).

Here the poem leaves the domain of verisimilitude to enter that of idealization. It seems logical to change from lance to sword in order to continue the fight; however, evidence of the tactics of medieval armies shows that the knights formed up for charges again because the use of cavalry was designed to break enemy formations (see De Vries, "Military History and Technology in the *Song of Roland*," in this volume). At the very least, they remained in groups because fighting individually often led to defeat or worse (Verbruggen 81).

As for the splitting downward sword stroke, it appealed to the medieval audience, which could imagine itself as skilled with a sword as these literary heroes. In the audience for the Oxford version, there would have been seasoned knights and a general public, all either dreaming of the future or recalling the glorious past. There must have been an aesthetics of the violence depicted in poems like this; otherwise, the great variety of the descriptions of mayhem would not have been included. This desire for action scenes was long-lived. Linguistic evidence shows that some of these passages were gradually amplified from the tenth century to the twelfth (Hall 114). Moreover, such depictions of bloody violence bypass the usual level of conscious analysis and appeal directly to the emotions; the audience members thrill vicariously in response to the violence presented. "Nothing, perhaps, could be more banal than the role of violence in awakening desire" (Girard 144). Nor could anything be more banal in warfare than bloodshed, hence the desire for ever-more-graphic details.

The ostensible enemy, target, and companion in spilling blood are the Saracens. They do not differ from the Christians in their armor (hauberks and helmets), their weapons (swords, shields, and lances), or in their preparations for battle (laisse 79). The poem praises Saracen warriors for their courage and valor (see lines 8959–60 or 1593) with exactly the same terms used for Christians (see, for examples, lines 118, 314, and 3074).

Were it not for the poem's assurances concerning nationality and religion, the audience member or reader might be confused about who is who during the description of these battles. The poem trains a leveling gaze on the diversity of this world yet distinguishes among characters who have everything in common. Historically, the feudal system depended on knights to oppress the peasantry and exact what was owed the lord, yet knight and peasant often shared the same social background (Haidu, *Violence* 51, 61). Just as the crusaders marched on other Christians during the Albigensian Crusade, Charlemagne often made war against other Christians. Similarly, although the Saxons against whom Charlemagne strove for more than thirty years were not of the same religion as the Franks, they were of the same ethnicity. In fact, Basques, not Saracens overran his rear guard as he left Spain. Each of these historical events recalls the originary violence preceding the splitting of the group, after which this violence is ritualized, that is, repeated in the same way (Girard 249). In this poem, the Franks repeatedly fight the Saracens as a way to gain land and spoils. Yet Ganelon, a Frank, proves as much an enemy as any Saracen. The idea of a foreign threat is certainly motivated by historical coincidences; nevertheless, the foreign also stands for one's own group, the most threatening of all. Certainly, it is not accidental that the *Song of Roland*'s representation of violence is bound up in religion, the agent that transforms violence into ritual and suppresses war inside the group (Girard 8).

The Middle Ages was a time of a scarcity economy because technological innovations did not keep pace with population nor permit abundance. The historical Franks and those in the *Roland* struggled to acquire lands and goods. The seven-year campaign against the Saracens does not seem to have led to the spoils the Franks were seeking, since Marsile still has vast economic strength, to judge from the accoutrements of the messengers to Charlemagne (laisse 7) and his marshaling of forces (laisse 79). However, there is hope of gaining spoils on both sides. Armies do not gather to fight if there is no likelihood of tangible rewards.

Even a knight's disappearance from the ranks is not necessarily bad. In case of death, the fief remains and can be repossessed. Ganelon discovers that he is not essential to the army when he is sent as messenger to Marsile; he well understands that his lands are of interest to other Franks. The poem predicates an economy of scarcity for the Franks and symbolically represents scenes of rivalry in the group as war (Schwartz 115).

Since Roland is a favored member of the army, his court and familial relations bear examination insofar as they contribute to his becoming leader of the rear guard. Nephew of the king through his mother (line 216) and stepson to Ganelon (277), he is the "ami" of Oliver, in Old French meaning ally and even kinsman (2024). According to the poem, Oliver meant to give his sister to Roland to cement their alliance (1720). Thus Roland has powerful relations in both generations; he himself is one of the Twelve Peers whose advice Charlemagne seeks (262), and he will ally himself by marriage to yet another of those peers. The Twelve Peers contain other family groups: "Richard li velz e sun nevuld Henri" ("Richard the old and his nephew Henri"; 171; my trans.) and "Tedblad de Reins e Milun, sun cusin" ("Tedbald of Reims and Milun, his cousin"; 173; my trans.). Families as well as military experience define the Twelve Peers and give them status.

Roland clearly outranks Ganelon, his mother's second husband, and could cause trouble for Baldwin, Ganelon's son (363–64). As his mother's firstborn Roland would logically have claim on lands she inherited as well as other fiefs awarded to her by her brother's family. Despite his sister, the king enigmatically does not deign to protect Baldwin's rights (laisse 23); thus he prefers one nephew over the other. Charlemagne also does not mention that Ganelon has spent a lot of time at the court and has a good reputation (lines 351–52). At camp Ganelon keeps gold spurs (a portion of his spoils?) and enjoys the fellowship of a group of followers, some, or all, of whom could be family members (348–49). When Ganelon clarifies to Roland and the other peers that "[t]u n'ies mes hom ne jo ne sui tis sire" ("you are not my vassal and I am not your lord"; 297), he shows the depth of this discord. The army is clearly divided between groups jockeying for position. Ganelon's lack of standing with the emperor is exemplified by his dropping the glove (333) or staff (770). That lack of standing may also come from Ganelon's predilection toward talking instead of volunteering to take action (laisse 15), which would make Ganelon a real courtier indeed.

The text mentions nothing about Roland being at court. Although he speaks his mind (laisse 14), he has more courage to act than Ganelon since he volunteers for the mission to Marsile. Nominated by Ganelon to the rear guard, Roland requests of Charlemagne a token related to war, the bow (766), thus reinforcing the difference between his stepfather and himself. Oliver declares that Roland cannot be counted on for diplomacy (256–57). However, the Franks say that Ganelon is "saive" (279), a word the text also uses for the Saracen messenger Blancandrin (24). Both Blancandrin and Ganelon fill the courtier's ultimate role, negotiating an advantage (for themselves) while also preserving their own lives during their visit to enemy territory. Ganelon negotiates military life as court politics, but Roland notes that politics is best accomplished by war (laisse 14).

The poem adheres entirely to Roland's position. Roland, the only Christian combatant in the rear guard not to die of wounds, plays a role that simply outweighs any interest the poem can muster in court politics; warfare is where he and it find fullest meaning. That fullness of meaning, though often expressed critically by modern commentators as a form of *desmesure*, gives the *Song of Roland* its shape and Roland his essence. His feats and fate, not his words, set him apart from the other peers and knights. By the homage words pay to deeds, the battle of Rencesvals does not fade away with the fallen. The poem is up to the task of demonstrating the force of arms, the meaning of blood, and the warrior ethos Roland exemplifies. Ganelon suffers the poem's final act of violence because, paradoxically, the representation of violence required one skilled with words, one whose echoes are captured by the Oxford *Roland*.

Though singled out by both Charlemagne and Ganelon, Roland does not initially exceed the norms of his group and show *desmesure*. He demonstrates that he is one of the knights in several ways. He advises Charlemagne not to fall for Marsile's offer and, instead, to besiege Saragossa in order to avenge the envoys murdered by the Saracens (laisse 14). Nevertheless, he volunteers for this assignment, second after Naimon (laisse 18). As for the rear guard, Ganelon assigns Roland to it. Charlemagne offers half an army as rear guard, but Roland, not having foreknowledge of his stepfather's plot, refuses his offer as unfitting for the family tradition out of which he came (laisse 63). Prudently, he sends one thousand men to guard the high ground (laisse 65). These are not foolhardy actions, as Ganelon would have it (line 229). Only in view of his stepfather's plan for revenge do Roland's actions take on the air of *desmesure*. It is ironic that as Ganelon's worldview prevails, wisdom turns into foolishness and vice versa. Unfortunately for the rear guard, Roland's *desmesure* does not lie in his attitude toward violence or love of war. Again, many passages demonstrate that he is like other warriors (see laisses 107, 115, 117, 127). His *desmesure* results from what Oliver pointed out earlier: "Vostre curages est mult pesmes e fiers / Jo me crendreie que vos vos melisez" ("Your disposition is very fierce and violent / I would fear that you get into a fight"; lines 256–57; my trans.). In the context in which Oliver makes this statement, he means that Roland is undiplomatic and likely to insult Marsile. However, Roland's attitude goes with him to the battlefield. There his lack of discernment and hard-charging attitude come to the foreground. Though he knew what Marsile could do, he did not foresee a concerted plan for the rear guard's destruction. These twenty thousand Franks, of which Roland is the leader, can be beaten only by two large forces of Saracens. Roland outlasts the others only to die calling Charlemagne to avenge all their deaths. In the end, Roland's *desmesure* allows the warrior's reason to triumph.

# The *Song of Roland*:
## Structuralism and Beyond
### *Ellen Peel*

A "shaping spirit" permeates the *Song of Roland*, for this epic lies much closer to imagination than reality.[1] Readers today may not initially care to look for this shaping spirit; in fact, improbable images such as that of a hundred thousand soldiers swooning at once may at first cause students to snicker (2907). Structuralism, however, provides a surprisingly powerful lens through which to discern the shaping spirit.[2] As Gérard Genette suggests, structuralism may be more appropriate than hermeneutics for studying literature that is "distant and difficult to decipher" (14).

I use this approach in a course that is an introduction to graduate study for master's students in comparative literature. Studying *Roland* together with structuralist theory helps the class understand both. The combination can encourage students interested in theory to appreciate medieval literature and the epic genre, and it can assist student medievalists in learning about theory, rethinking old observations on this text from an uncommon angle. (In a class that does not focus on theory, a professor who has some familiarity with structuralism can no doubt enhance presentation of the *Roland* without needing to teach the theory itself.) Structuralism, with its emphasis on how system and patterns shape a text, can show students how to take pleasure in the stylized aesthetic of a medieval epic, which is far different from more recent, familiar realism and psychologism. In particular, the structuralist emphasis on binarism can sharpen students' awareness of the visceral feeling of balance and imbalance characteristically experienced when reading the *Song of Roland*. Although unconventional, linking structuralism in this way with aesthetics and reader response has worked well in my class.

The course is designed to function on several levels: in addition to introducing students to graduate study and various notions of comparative literature, I present several theories—both textual and contextual ones—that are used in literary study, and we apply these theories to a few literary texts chosen from the department's list of options for the master's oral exam. No course of this nature could hope for comprehensiveness in its choice of theories and literary texts; instead the goal is to give students a taste of possibilities. I choose literature that ranges widely in genre, period, and nationality: along with *Roland*, I typically include Johann Wolfgang Goethe's *Faust* (1833) and Murasaki Shikibu's *The Tale of Genji* (c. 1000).

The students vary greatly in their familiarity with theory. For the novices the theoretical portion is as much a general introduction to a new way of thinking and speaking as it is the transmission of a specific method, whereas for the experienced this portion serves more as a way to investigate and evaluate a method that they may decide to add to their repertoire. I believe that teaching theory without applying it is like poring over a map without ever traveling to the intriguing places it represents. Each unit therefore consists of one week on a theory, one week on a literary text, and one week pairing the two, in hopes that the theory will make possible a richer encounter with the literature, and that the literature will both clarify the theory and help students decide how useful it is for their individual purposes.

Although structuralism is no longer fashionable, it continues to prove its usefulness, especially in fields such as narrative theory and film studies. More generally, structuralism has fostered two of the most dominant and long-lasting theoretical developments in recent decades: the linguistic turn (the movement of scrutiny away from things themselves and toward the discourse about them) and the critique of essentialism (questioning the validity of defining something by inherent, unchanging properties).

Furthermore, I stress to my students that a grasp of structuralism is crucial to a grasp of deconstruction. Both attend to structure; deconstruction is not, after all, destruction. Deconstruction not only reacts against structuralism but also builds on it, as one finds in Jacques Derrida's seminal, and somewhat Oedipal, essay, "Structure, Sign, and Play in the Discourse of the Human Sciences," which I assign during the unit on deconstruction. Much current theory in turn builds on deconstruction. Fields such as cultural studies can hardly be understood satisfactorily without concepts such as the margin and the questioning of binary oppositions, ideas that stem from deconstruction and, in turn, from its ambivalent relation to structuralism. When applied to the *Roland*, structuralism shows its value, both on its own and as a springboard to deconstruction.

## *Structuralism*

I would like now to sketch out how I introduce the basic components of structuralism to my students.[3] In a lecture accompanied liberally by diagrams and charts on the board, I begin by explaining that the term *structuralism* does not simply mean any approach involving attention to structure; instead, the term is more specific and offers a rigorous method for studying structure. I then describe the origins of structuralism in the early twentieth century, going back to Ferdinand de Saussure, often considered the father of modern linguistics. Whereas the nineteenth-century study of language had been dominated by a diachronic (historical) method, Saussure had the insight that language could also be studied synchronically (in its state at a given moment), for at any one time language forms a system. He revolutionized linguistics by focusing on patterns and relations, on the way that structure functions in a dynamic system. Taken up by Claude Lévi-Strauss, such concepts spread to anthropology and, from there, to a range of other fields, including literature.

Structuralism has much in common with semiotics (the study of signs), to which Saussure also made major contributions. Instead of regarding the sign as the signifier for the object it signifies, he considered the sign to be the relation between the signifier and the signified, between, for example, the sound pattern "horse" and the concept of a horse. When structuralism rippled outward from linguistics, it often stressed the signifier over the signified, bringing the linguistic turn to a number of disciplines. In literary study this tendency sparked increased attention to self-referentiality—to the way that literature can refer to itself and to language instead of simply to the world outside the text. In fact, in "Linguistics and Poetics," Roman Jakobson says the main function of verbal art is to "focus on the message for its own sake" (36).

Underlying much of structuralism is the distinction between langue (the basic rules describing a language or other system) and parole (manifestations of the system, such as individual utterances [Culler 8–10]). In chess, for example, the langue describes how each piece can move, and the moves in a particular game are the paroles. In literature, one can consider the conventions of a genre, such as epic, to be a langue and individual texts, such as *Roland*, to be paroles.

Another key notion in structuralism is that elements in a system are defined not by some inner, timeless essence but rather by their relations with other elements. A classic example is the relation between right and left. Another way to explain this antiessentialism is to observe that, in a connect-the-dots picture, structuralism would emphasize the connections more than the dots. I point out that a structuralist would describe me not by some salient personality trait but as a node in a web: I am the teacher of some people, the daughter of others, the customer of still others, and so on.

Structuralists often put relations in terms of difference. I draw a simple map of modern-day France and its neighbors on the board and explain that a structuralist would characterize it not in an essentialist way as, say, "the land of love," but instead as not England, not Spain, not Italy, and so on. On the literary level, scholars have found such ideas useful in thinking about how one genre defines itself in relation to another: Realism, for instance, develops dialectically as not Romanticism. On the social or political level, structuralist antiessentialism can downplay individual selfhood, instead locating the individual in a web of relationships, at the intersection of numberless societal forces.

The best-known kind of relation identified by structuralists has been the binary opposition. In its original linguistic context, the term *binary opposition* was applied to pairs of phonemes, two different sounds that, in the same environment, distinguish different words—such as *light* versus *right*. Each phoneme is defined not by some essence but by its relation within a specific language to other sounds, by its similarities to and differences from others. Consider /b/ versus /p/, which distinguish *bet* from *pet* (see fig. 1).

Fig. 1. Mild Binary Opposition

|  | /b/ | /p/ |
|---|---|---|
| Consonantal? | Yes | Yes |
| Dental? | No | No |
| Labial? | Yes | Yes |
| Voiced? | Yes | No |

For concision, this figure omits several
criteria that follow a similar pattern.

Note that these two phonemes differ in only one way and thus form what I
call a mild binary opposition.

Now that the notion of binaries has spread beyond linguistics, it more often
takes the form of what I call a strong binary opposition. Since I teach in San
Francisco, it can be amusing to use the example of that city's relation to its
rival in Southern California (see fig. 2).

Fig. 2. Strong Binary Opposition

|  | San Francisco | Los Angeles |
|---|---|---|
| Is it foggy? | Yes | No |
| Is it glitzy? | No | Yes |
| Is it bookish? | Yes | No |
| Is everyone required to wear black at least once a week? | Yes | No |

While this example is meant to be smiled at, it does bring to the fore the fact
that people frequently think in binaries and sometimes define themselves or
their group in opposition to another person or group, consciously or uncon-
sciously striving to accentuate the differences.

## A *Structuralist Reading of the* Roland

Given this brief sketch of structuralism, we can now move to the *Roland*.
Employing the theory can enrich students' reading of the epic, and seeing the
theory in action can prepare them to use it elsewhere. The theory can be
applied to the text in a number of ways; below appear just a few examples.

When I ask students what structuralism helps them discern in this epic,
they often mention binary oppositions first. Most fundamentally, the *Roland*
opposes the Christians to the Muslims (or rather an almost comically distorted
version of Muslims). This conflict—between what the *Roland* defines as Chris-
tianity and paganism, heroes and villains, good and evil—energizes the entire

epic. As one might expect, the resulting binary opposition often takes the strong form, in which the two poles have nothing in common:

> Out in front rides a Saracen, Abisme;
> He [Marsile] had no greater villain in his company,
> A man of evil traits and mighty treachery.
> He does not believe in God, the son of the Virgin Mary;
> And is as black as molten pitch.
> He loves treachery and murder
> More than he would love all the gold in Galicia.
> No one has ever seen him play or laugh.    (1470–77)

The Christians' enemies are not only evil; some of them look or sound like animals (e.g., lines 3221–23, 3526–27), and they treat their gods with childish disrespect after losing a battle (lines 2580–91). Observing how *Roland* places Christians and Muslims in a strong opposition brings the structuralist notion to life and can prompt a discussion about how in our own society one group may define itself in strong opposition to another, as self versus other.

Although the epic usually structures its fundamental Christian-Muslim conflict as a strong opposition, I point out that, interestingly, the conflict at times takes the form of only a mild opposition, in which the two sides resemble each other in all ways except religion. These resemblances lead to structural parallels in characters, such as the twelve Muslim lords who correspond to the twelve Christian peers (laisse 70), and in plot, such as the councils held by Charlemagne and Marsile. Most striking are Muslim warriors like the courageous, handsome emir Baligant: "O God, what a noble baron, if only he were a Christian!" (line 3164). I ask the class what such surprisingly mild oppositions are doing in an epic about mortal enemies. The question guides students to realize that a mild opposition can illustrate the strength and seductiveness of evil. Moreover, the Muslims need to be represented as worthy opponents for the Christians, enemies against whom the Christians can prove their courage and skill, since an easy victory would have little meaning (D. Sayers 21). Even the villainous Abisme "is a man of courage and great zeal" (line 1478). Finally, as potential converts to Christianity, the Muslims must be somewhat diverse, for they cannot all be portrayed as utterly alien.

Another mild opposition can be found in the relationship between Roland and his companion Oliver: they resemble each other in a number of traits (such as valor; prowess in battle; and, if the enemy attacks fairly, an almost supernatural invulnerability to death). Yet they differ in one crucial respect: "Roland is brave and Oliver is wise" (line 1093). This opposition results in a chiasmus when insightful Oliver is literally blinded by the blood streaming down his face, whereas metaphorically blind Roland retains his literal ability to see (laisse 149). I help students observe that, in this scene, the two friends almost reverse behavior. On the one hand, Oliver's blindness causes him to attack his friend—an act reminiscent of Roland's rashness. On the other, Roland's sight enables him to understand and forgive his friend's mistake—an act one might expect from thoughtful Oliver. A similar chiasmus occurs after Roland's refusal, despite Oliver's pleas, to sound the olifant, for Roland later decides to blow it, this time over Oliver's objections.

The epic also offers examples of oppositions that are bridged, or mediated. The opposition between the Frankish and Saracen camps, for instance, is mediated by the envoys who carry messages between them and by the hostages sent as sureties. The mortal danger faced by these go-betweens can give students a vivid understanding of how mediation not only can bridge a gap but also can emphasize the very existence of that gap (Altman 43). A stronger opposition, between heaven and earth, is mediated by the angel Gabriel's visits to Charlemagne. We spend a little time in speculating on how mediation can occur between two such disparate realms and how it can be represented in literature. I suggest that, given the *Roland*'s Christian message, this particular literary text might itself be interpreted as a form of mediation between heaven and earth.

Once students have found some of the individual binary oppositions, I urge them to seek broader patterns, for structuralism often seeks to integrate levels within a system. We can start by observing that a number of the oppositions combine into one overarching system, ranging from microcosm to macrocosm. To elaborate on a comment made by Dorothy L. Sayers (25), the small-scale joust that Thierry and Pinabel fight to decide Ganelon's fate corresponds to the battle between Charlemagne and the emir Baligant, which in turn corresponds to the clash between God and gods and ultimately between Christianity and Islam.

Furthermore, the binary oppositions are part of this epic's tendency toward binarism in general: the text contains a variety of pairs, in only some of which the elements are opposed.[4] Binarism crops up frequently, for instance, in details such as certain companions' names (e.g., laisse 177 lists Gerin and Gerer, Yvon and Yvoire).

At the other extreme, binarism gives an overall structure to the plot. Students at times wonder how unity is possible in a text whose eponymous hero dies in the middle, a text that famously divides into two halves. It helps to regard the split as part of a binary pattern—action and reaction, the Rencesvals plot and the revenge plot, Roland's struggle and Charlemagne's struggle—that is akin to what Robert Harrison calls the "folding mirror" structure (46). One can regard this division as reflecting the Christian-Muslim opposition: in the first half of the epic, one group is slaughtered, in the second half, the other. In addition, the overall binarism of the revenge structure echoes the references to payment that pervade the text (e.g., "a curse on the man who does not first sell himself dear" [line 1924]). When I first assign the *Roland*, I ask the class to be on the lookout for the payment metaphor; when we come to examine the plot pattern of revenge, we understand it as the dark context in which repayment means payback.

Drawing on narrative theory, I mention the dynamics that animate the dualistic plot system: the second half restores the equilibrium that was disrupted in the first half. It is then fruitful to ask where we should locate the cause of the disequilibrium. Some of our most lively discussions of the *Roland* have explored why the Rencesvals disaster occurs—because of Ganelon? Roland's rashness or pride? the Muslims? evil? fate? God? More generally, noticing the pervasive binary patterns can aid students in appreciating the epic's artistry and in accounting for the rhythm that swings its readers back and forth between imbalance and balance, asymmetry and symmetry.

This epic is systematic in other ways as well, most clearly in the sets of repetitive laisses, such as those recounting Roland's death, and in the verse patterns throughout, especially the formulaic nature of verse intended for oral performance (on formulas in the *Roland*, see Nichols, *Formulaic Diction*). The world represented in the text also has a systematic quality, as manifested in the stylized rituals at court and particularly on the battlefield. The langue (the chivalric rules of combat) prescribes a certain sequence of events, from initial threat to final boast, which occur in paroles (individual combats)—even, or especially, the goriest ones. System shapes the text in still other ways. The plot demands that Roland die, and yet, as the ultimate warrior, he cannot be killed by an enemy; hence, he in effect kills himself by blowing his horn (D. Sayers 23n1; see also Mickel's "The Implications of the Trial of Ganelon," in this volume). Similarly, Oliver, too skillful to be bested in a fair fight, can be killed only by a treacherous blow from behind.

System also contributes to the representation of characters in the *Roland*. Many are constituted by their functions or their relationships to other characters (relations that may or may not be binary), for, as Ian Short says, medieval epics focus more on the community than on the individual (*Chanson* [1990] 17). Charlemagne, for instance, is not a three-dimensional character who happens to be a ruler; rather, he is constituted by his function as emperor, having no life outside it. He is the central node in a web that ties him to his subjects. Lords are defined by having vassals and vice versa. And the members of each pair of peers exist in terms of their function as warriors and their relationship to each other.

The most striking example of a figure characterized by a relationship is Roland, who in modern parlance would be called Charlemagne's right-hand man: Ganelon says, "If anyone could bring about Roland's death, / Then Charles would lose the right arm from his body" (lines 596–97). To help students perceive the full import of this metaphor, I suggest in advance that they be alert to mentions of hands—especially right hands—and of related objects, such as arms and gloves. After they have read the text, I ask what sorts of functions define the hand, a question that evokes observations about how hands are used to kill an enemy or about how a literal hand can perform a metaphorical function, as when it entrusts someone with a token of authority, such as a staff or glove (e.g., lines 319–20). Similarly, the literal loss of a hand plays a metaphorical role when Roland cuts off King Marsile's right hand, at which point the king and a hundred thousand of his men flee (laisses 142–43). What is more, the subsequent loss of Roland, Charlemagne's metaphorical right hand, suggests payback for the loss of Marsile's literal right hand.

I remind the class that structuralism highlights not only system but also signification. Students may be surprised to find that, in a fast-moving martial epic filled with such gory details as "slicing through his eyes and his face" (line 1328), the sign can count for as much as the sword. An example that brings this issue to life is Roland's horn, the olifant, a major means of signifying. To begin with, Roland's decisions about when to blow it or not play a key role in the events of the Rencesvals battle (he also uses it as a weapon [lines 2287–88]). And, as noted above, it is by blowing the olifant—not, as one might expect, by fighting—that Roland brings about his death. Interestingly, the horn, like the epic itself, outlasts Roland and is used by others after his death (e.g., line 3302). Mentioning the text's emphasis on the signifier can also give students a fresh way to think about the value that epics accord to reputation—a concept that seems almost inconceivable today, when people confuse fame with notoriety. In the *Roland*, it is important not only to perform great deeds but also to earn fame for them. Roland says:

> Now let each man take care to strike great blows,
> So that no one can sing a shameful song about us.
> The pagans are wrong and the Christians are right.
> No dishonourable tale will ever be told about me.    (1013–16)

## Deconstruction

While structuralist analysis can, in all the ways just explained, help students uncover system and signification in the *Song of Roland*, it goes without saying that no single theory can account fully for an entire text. The quirkiness of literature always foils the structuralist effort at completeness. Students themselves may well comment on such anomalies; this offers an appropriate moment to bring in deconstruction, which focuses on the leaks in the system. Deconstructionists, for instance, typically comment on the difficulty of pinning down a definitive origin—a point particularly apt when studying an anonymous oral epic. In fact, the *Roland* serves well as a path into deconstruction, for several of its structures deconstruct themselves.

For instance, although men occupy the center of the narrative and women the margins, a deconstructive (and feminist) reading reveals that the women exercise the power of the Derridean *supplément*, that which seems extra or unnecessary and yet is relied on by what seems dominant.[5] In the *Roland*'s masculine, martial world, women serve as potential rewards for valor (e.g., lines 1720–21) and as recipients of reports from the battlefield who help seal a soldier's all-important reputation. Oliver says to an opponent:

> . . . to no woman or lady you may have seen
> Will you boast . . .
> That you have robbed me of a single penny
> Or inflicted any damage on me or anyone else.    (1960–63)

As a subject, Marsile's queen, Bramimonde, has the function of commentator on the entire system; as an object that is captured, renamed, and converted to Christianity, she functions as proof of the completeness of Charlemagne's victory. The male picture needs the female frame (see too Ramey's "The Death of Aude," in this volume).

The epic's most deconstructive element—and the one that most often provokes discussion—is Ganelon, who, for reasons never fully given, goes from the Christian pole of the main binary opposition to the Muslim one, thereby revealing a blot in the purity of the Christian side. His treachery might stem from legitimate resentment of an offense by Roland, which would cast a shadow on the hero's virtue. Alternatively, the betrayal might stem from a flaw in Ganelon himself, which would mean evil could exist in a high-ranking Christian. Either way, his move raises questions akin to the eternally vexed conundrum: If Eden was perfect, how could evil enter it? Ganelon's ambiguous, disruptive status persists until his death. One might expect Charlemagne's revenge, the closure of the neat disequilibrium-equilibrium design, to be completed on enemy soil. The traitor, however, not being a Muslim, is in a sense left over and must be brought back to Aix, where only with his execution is equilibrium restored. And even this closure is disrupted at the very end, when the angel Gabriel again commands Charlemagne to fight, to start a new narrative. Thus, drawing attention to structures and then examining the moments at which they break down can aid students in comprehending how a structuralist analysis can lead to a deconstructive one.

In these ways, structuralism—followed by deconstruction—helps students appreciate the *Song of Roland*, which in turn helps them comprehend and appreciate theory. Readers who come to the *Roland* expecting realism are like viewers who come to a stained glass window in a medieval cathedral expecting the linear perspective of a Renaissance painting. Maybe disappointed or puzzled at first, they can learn to see that a work of art with a bold shaping spirit and jewel-like details can shine with its own beauty.

NOTES

I am grateful to Pamela Gehrke and Elizabeth Wright for their comments on this essay.

[1]Northrop Frye applies the term "shaping spirit" to the romance tradition in general (35). Although the *Roland* is not a romance in the strict sense of genre, it has a number of elements that place it in the broad category of romance as opposed to realism. Ian Short contrasts the medieval epic with the realistic novel of Balzac (Introduction 15).

[2]Eugene Dorfman also applies structuralism to the *Roland*, though very differently.

[3]The best single reference for instructors interested in learning more about structuralism is Jonathan Culler's *Structuralist Poetics: Structuralism, Linguistics, and the Study of Literature*, which includes an extensive bibliography. Most anthologies of literary theory have essays on structuralism that can be assigned to students. For example, I use *Modern Criticism and Theory: A Reader*, edited by David Lodge and Nigel Wood, in which I assign "The Object of Study," by Ferdinand de Saussure; "Linguistics and Poetics," by Roman Jakobson; and "The Typology of Detective Fiction," by Tzvetan Todorov. I also assign Gérard Genette's "Structuralism and Literary Criticism."

[4]Short, for example, has observed "tout un réseau de bipolarités" ("a whole network of bipolarities"; 19; my trans.) and "[l]e souci de la répétition et de la symétrie, du parallélisme et de l'antithèse" ("the concern for repetition and symmetry, parallelism and antithesis"; 15–16; my trans.). Describing early medieval art, Robert Harrison refers to "a stylized universe of abstraction" and "the cult of symmetry and balance" (45).

[5]See "Structure, Sign, and Play" (99–100) and " . . . That Dangerous Supplement . . . ," in *Of Grammatology* (141–64).

# Political Uses and Responses: Orientalism, Postcolonial Theory, and Cultural Studies

*Sharon Kinoshita*

In 1978, Edward Said defined *orientalism* as, among other things, "a Western style for dominating, restructuring, and having authority over the Orient" (3). From the late eighteenth century onward, he writes, Europeans rationalized and naturalized their colonial ventures by positing a radical difference between themselves and the peoples they were colonizing. Europe, or the West, was constructed as modern, rational, vigorous, and enlightened, in opposition to an Oriental other represented as static, decadent, and despotic. One remarkable feature of orientalism is its "sheer knitted-together strength" as a discourse, which has remained "unchanged as teachable wisdom (in academies, books, congresses, universities, foreign-service institutes)" from the 1840s to his present (Said 6).

Though focusing primarily on the age of nineteenth-century colonialism, Said repeatedly alludes to orientalism's very long history, with the European Middle Ages as a central moment. Drawing on the Belgian historian Henri Pirenne, Said sees Islam as "the very epitome of an outsider against which the whole of European civilization from the Middle Ages on was founded" (70), its emergence in the seventh century marking a watershed in the history of Mediterranean Europe. In this standpoint, it is easy to read portrayals of "pagans" in the *Song of Roland* as paradigmatic of medieval Europe's ignorance of and hostility toward the Islamic other. Stigmatizing the Franks' enemies as those who do not love God; glorifying the titular hero who rouses his men with the battlefield exhortation, "pagans are wrong and the Christians are right!" (1015); and culminating in Charlemagne's apocalyptic victory against the pagan emir of Babylon, the poem lends itself perfectly to readings inspired by Said's unmasking of the mechanisms of orientalist discourse.

The new questions that orientalism and, more recently, postcolonial theory have placed on the critical agenda serve as a useful corrective to certain blindnesses and erasures in the long history of *Roland* scholarship. Nineteenth-century French readings of the *Roland* were strongly conditioned by issues of nationalism and national identity. In the same way, recent analyses by North American critics of the poem's representations of race and cultural difference speak to the preoccupations of the present moment. While providing salutary insights, however, such postcolonial medievalism runs the risk of reducing *Roland* to a catalog of numbingly repetitive tropes demonizing the racial and religious other. In teaching the *Roland*, I encourage my students to resist this reading of least resistance and to notice instead the variety and complexity of concerns teeming just below the poem's apparently simple surface. Introducing just a few aspects of the *Roland*'s historical context—the northern French engagement with Islamic Iberia in the late eleventh and early twelfth centuries—allows me to present the poem in a different light, making it come alive as the site of multiple, occasionally conflicting values on the one hand and taking it as a window onto a surprisingly turbulent and counterintuitively multicultural Middle Ages on the other.

As the discipline of medieval studies took shape in the late nineteenth century, reading the *Song of Roland* was, from the beginning, defined as a political act. In December 1870, during the third month of the siege of Paris in the Franco-Prussian war, the celebrated medievalist Gaston Paris delivered a lecture at the Collège de France entitled "*The Song of Roland* and French Nationality" ("*La chanson de Roland* et la nationalité française"). Working from the premise that "literature is the expression of national life" that gives form to the "vague and indeterminate" feeling shared by all the citizens of a nation, he identified the *Song of Roland* as the repository of a precocious French national sentiment (Duggan, "Franco-German Conflict" 99; 100):

> Yes, gentlemen: eight centuries ago, when none of the nations of Europe had yet truly achieved self-consciousness, when several of them—like England—were still awaiting elements essential to their formation, the French fatherland [patrie] was established: national sentiment existed in its most intimate, noble, and tender form. It is in the *Song of Roland* that that divine expression, "sweet France" [douce France] appears, expressing with such grace and depth the love that this lovable land [terre] already inspired in its children. Sweet France! The Germans envied us this word, and tried in vain to find its counterpart in their national poetry (Paris, "*Chanson*" 107–08)[1]

Medieval literature, and the *Roland* in particular, were cast as the place where (beleaguered) Frenchmen could take the measure of their own long history and national identity:

> We will recognize that our national life was dominated, from that point on, by the two great ideas that have animated it ever since and that have given it such richness and power at different moments of our history: the tendency toward unity, and the tendency toward expansion. . . . From that moment, the unitary tendency has taken as its ideal the perpetual and voluntary collaboration of all the country's forces (led by the royalty) toward a common goal, a goal it places outside the nation itself, in its action on neighboring peoples. (Paris, "*Chanson*" 103–04)[2]

In context, the "unitary tendency" Paris extols was undoubtedly aimed at healing the political and social breaches created by the Paris Commune and its violent suppression during the summer of that year; furthermore, the external force against whom this unity is to be directed is obviously the emergent

German state. Yet considering the conflict between Christian and Saracen at the heart of the *Roland*, the notion that national self-realization is achieved through actions on "neighboring peoples" inevitably evokes the third signifi-cant political event of 1870: the French annexation of Algeria. Algeria had been held under military rule since the French conquest of Algiers in 1830. In 1870, however, the political turmoil destabilizing Paris led the European settler community to call for the country's official annexation, formalized in a series of decrees passed between October and December of that year. In March 1871, a revolt of native Berber Kabyles was quickly suppressed (the French governor-general, Gueydon, compared the insurgents to the Com-munards) but became both the motive and the pretext for seizing tribal lands and dismantling traditional forms of indigenous society. French politicians and colonists aimed at nothing less, in the words of Louis-Henri, comte de Guey-don, than "crushing the native population, reducing it, I dare say, to servitude" ("l'écrasement, j'ose dire le servage, de la population indigène"; Thobie and Meynier 11–12; my trans.). In Algeria, the educational system put in place during these years was "designed to submerge the Arab-Islamic identity" (Abun-Nasr 268). Meanwhile, in the wake of Paris's lecture, the *Song of Ro-land*—incorporated into the *agrégation* in 1877 and the standard secondary school curriculum in 1880—became the canonical text of the French Middle Ages. In other words, though Paris had made no overt mention of France's domination over Algeria, it would be hard to think of a more coherent example of the way in which "the Orient and Islam" were, as Said puts it, "represented as outsiders having a special role to play *inside* Europe" (71). The "incom-parable monument" of an age in which "the French nation" established the "hardy roots" ("racines vivaces") still attaching it to the soil ("sol"), *Roland* was well on its way to being institutionalized as the French national epic (Paris, *Poésie* 111, 117).

Despite a long tradition of scholarly attention to medieval representations of Islam (Tolan 312n9), the critical tradition derived from *Orientalism* and postcolonial theory has heightened our awareness of the ways medieval Mus-lims and nineteenth-century Algerians alike have largely been erased from our critical consciousness (on *Orientalism*, see Loomba 43–51; Young 383–84). In this, medieval postcolonialism provides a useful corrective to our tendency to read past the way a text like the *Roland* constructs its others (Cohen, *Post-colonial*; Dagenais and Greer; Hahn, "The Difference"; Holsinger, "Medieval Studies"; Ingham and Warren; Warren, *History*). As John Tolan notes, Bali-gant's forces include

> monstrous semihumans: the Micenes have large heads and spines on their back; the soldiers from Occian have skin as hard as steel armor; those from Malprose are giants ([lines] 3214–64). The individual soldiers have names that express their evilness and deformity or that associate them with biblical enemies of God. They include such colorful figures

as "Siglorel, / The enchanter who once visited hell; / Jupiter led him there by sorcery" ([lines] 1390–92), the kind of enemy whose slaughter calls for no justification. The same is true for Chernuble de Munigre, who comes from a land inhabited by demons, where the sun never shines and rain never falls ([lines] 979–83). When Archbishop Turpin sees Abisme, "black as molten pitch," approach carrying a banner with a dragon on it, he proclaims: "This Saracen appears to me a great heretic; / It is far better for me to strike him dead" ([lines] 1484–85; Tolan 125–26)

In the book from which this analysis is taken, Tolan demonstrates how strongly the medieval representation of "Saracens" drew on conventional images of idolatrous pagans forged before the rise of Islam, in the early centuries of Christianity. In addition, Tolan notes, the *Roland*'s depiction of pagans reflects a literary as well as a political paradox: the adversary must be dehumanized so that the poem's audience might "enjoy the violence [and] revel in the blood and killing" without remorse. And yet, "he cannot be made too other, for it is not valorous to slaughter mere beasts." Thus "alongside the monstrous creatures are virtuous knights" of whom the poet can proclaim, "O God, what a noble baron, if only he were a Christian!" (3164) (Tolan 26; *Roland* quotation modified to correspond to Burgess's translation.)

While Tolan's account, then, is sensitively contextualized, it shares with other recent studies the tendency to single out some of the poem's most highly demonizing portraits for quotation. Such representations, in which physical and moral ugliness or deformity are assumed to go hand in hand, are easy to find in the epic tradition and undoubtedly make for dramatic reading. Significantly, however, such representations of the *Roland* are most common in studies on other topics that refer to the Old French tradition only in passing. A study of Bernard of Clairvaux's sermons on the Song of Songs, for example, calls the *Roland* "one of the most violent and widely diffused pieces of anti-Muslim literature in the years surrounding the First Crusade" and goes on to cite its representation of Abisme, "black as molten pitch," and Roland's view of the "accursed men" who are "blacker than ink" (Holsinger, "Color" 170; *Roland*, lines 1474 and 1932–33, conform to Burgess's trans.). In another example, the introduction to a recent volume on medieval Iberia characterizes Saracens in the *Roland* as "a lusty, black-skinned people" who brought "the darkness of Africa" as well as "the temptations of the soul's darker side" dangerously close (Blackmore and Hutcheson 1). In their vividness and quotability, such characterizations—in which somatic blackness shades into a moral and metaphorical darkness—take on a life of their own. Spreading from one essay to another by the logic of scholarly citation (see, for example, Cohen, "On Saracen" 120), they risk coalescing into a kind of metaorientalist discourse with a "sheer knitted-together strength" all its own.

One potentially troubling aspect of such analyses is their focus on the representation of race. In our own racially conscious moment, such an emphasis may seem inevitable. Yet this persistent attention to skin color runs against the grain of recent work demonstrating the lack of a biological notion of race in the high Middle Ages. Robert Bartlett, for example, argues that peoples were distinguished not by biological essence but by language, law, "dress, domestic rituals, dietary habits, hair-styles and a host of other habitual practices" (197–98) that, unlike race, could be changed "not only from one generation to the next, but even within an individual lifetime" (197). This is not to say that medieval people were oblivious to somatic variation: they simply did not automatically equate skin color or other racial features with significant difference. In the Iberian peninsula in particular, physical appearance was a notoriously unreliable sign of identity (Kinoshita, *Medieval Boundaries* 184). Yet if the essays cited above are any indication, in recent work in postcolonial medievalism, the *Song of Roland* is well on its way to becoming a locus classicus of the racialized demonization of religious difference.[3]

The ease with which we accept such characterizations reveals how reflexively we take medieval intolerance as a given. Building alternate genealogies is difficult, in part because of the "sheer knitted-together strength" of commonplace wisdom, and in part because of the specialized knowledge required for such corrective visions. Yet if we look beyond the poem's representation of the physically deformed and morally monstrous—the "simple, radical" alterity staging "an 'us *vs.* them' as purely categorical as that between the cowboys and the Indians in the old westerns" (Haidu, *Violence* 36)—what strikes us about the pagans is precisely their astonishing variety. Despite the impression created by selective quotation, most of the *Roland*'s Saracens are in fact unmarked for somatic difference. Marsile's inner circle (that is, his *maisnie*, or feudal household) in many ways parallels that of the Franks. The king is attended by his wife, Bramimonde; his son, Jurfaleu the Blond; his nephew, Aelroth; his uncle, the "algarife"; and his wise counselor, Blancandrin. Baligant, the emir of Babylon who first appears two-thirds of the way through the text, is represented as "a man of great age" (2615), a tributary ruler who commands a great naval force and disembarks in Saragossa attended by seventeen kings and innumerable dukes and counts (laisses 189–92). As critics invariably point out, such mirror-image representations directly serve the *Roland*'s ideological purpose: the Saracens must be worthy and commensurate adversaries in order for the Franks' victory over them to be valorous. Yet given the poem's interest in, if not to say obsession with, definitions of good vassalhood, the representation of certain pagans as stout vassals must be read, I think, as more than mere structural convenience.

How are we to get beyond this critical impasse? One way is to question the assumed continuity between clerical discourses and lay vernacular forms. Where Tolan, for example, takes the *Roland*'s ideology to be "the same as that of the crusading chronicles with which it is roughly contemporary" (125), Peter Haidu urges us to distinguish between official, usually Latinate discourse and vernacular literature, which functioned as "a major ideological workspace of medieval society":

> Lay, vernacular culture developed practices of fictional representation that possessed a great tactical benefit: the virtue of deniability. . . . Although men of the church disliked [poetry, epic, romance, vernacular history, and chronicle], the danger they posed to the church's monopoly on ideological discourse did not appear until the beginning of the thirteenth century. Lay, vernacular culture developed for nearly a century, eluding dominant opponents before being subjected to concerted pressures that warranted changes in the way it transacted its ideological business.    (*Medieval/Modern* 77–78)

One way to put this insight into practice is to distinguish between medieval Christian attitudes toward Islam, on the one hand, and Old French representations of Muslims, on the other. The two are far from identical. In the Middle Ages, the Latin Christian conception of Islam was undeniably rife with misunderstandings (Tolan). Even medieval thinkers like Peter the Venerable and Ramon Llull, often favorably cited for their interest in Islam, were driven by the desire to persuade Muslims of the error of their doctrinal ways. At the same time, the modern focus on medieval popes and polemicists obscures how strongly the secular nobility, for whom poems like the *Roland* were presumably composed, frequently embraced concerns that were political and feudal rather than theological. In the *Roland*, for example, to be Christian means less to adhere to a certain theology than to conform to a set of cultural beliefs and practices, including accepting Charlemagne as one's lord. At the beginning of the poem, Marsile's duplicitous offer to "receive the Christian faith" ("recevrai la chrestïene lei"; 85) is inseparable from his promise to become Charlemagne's vassal "in love and faith" ("Serai ses hom par amur e par feid"; 86)—with the words "love" and "faith" evoking a feudal context at least as strongly as a spiritual one (Jones, ch. 2).

At this point, it is useful to alert students to the discrepancies between literary representation and historical reality, not to impugn the poem's "inaccuracy" but to emphasize the extent of the cultural manipulation in play. It is well known that when Charlemagne's army was decimated in the Pyrenees in 778—the event constituting the historical kernel of the *Roland*—the aggressors were not Muslims but Basques, who were fellow Christians (Burgess, *Song*, 9–10, and Kibler, "Rencesvals: The Event," in this volume). In the eighth century, in other words, the Carolingian empire and Latin Christendom were nearly but not completely identical; the *Roland*'s representational program may be seen as an effort to bring the two into more perfect alignment.

A different kind of perspective may be gleaned from excavating the role of the city of Saragossa—site of the *Roland*'s fictional siege—in late-eleventh- and early-twelfth-century history. One of the many *taifa* ("party") kingdoms to emerge out of the disintegration of the caliphate of Córdoba (1031), Saragossa was ruled by a dynasty of Muslim kings, the Banu Hud (1039–110), known for authoring mathematical treatises and lavishly patronizing the arts. As was so common in the history of medieval Iberia, they frequently made alliances across religious lines, seeking help from Christian kings and mercenaries against fellow Muslims; the historical Cid, for example, spent the years of his first exile (1081–85) fighting for al-Mutamin against a coalition consisting of al-Mutamin's brother al-Mundhir (ruler of Lérida and Tortosa) and al-Mundhir's Christian allies, Sancho I of Aragon and Ramon Berenguer II of Barcelona (O'Callaghan 205). In 1118, Saragossa (controlled by the North African Almoravids, who had overthrown the Banu Hud in 1110) was conquered by Alfonso I, king of Aragon. In contrast to the fictional Charlemagne, who clears the town's mosques and synagogues and orders the forced conversion of "[m]ore than a hundred thousand" pagans (3671), Alfonso guaranteed his new Muslim subjects their lives, property, and freedom of worship in order to encourage them to remain under his rule (Lacarra 67–72). However surprising to us, this policy was consistent with long-standing Iberian practices (Barton). These practices, moreover, would have been familiar to at least some of the Frenchmen constituting the *Roland*'s likely audience: on his mother's side, King Alfonso was related to the Champenois family of Roucy; his cousins Bertrand de Laon and Rotrou II de Perche played a prominent role in his campaigns—Rotrou, for example, served as governor of Tudela after its conquest in 1119.

This recognition that, in the Middle Ages, relations between Latin Christians and Muslims were rarely as stark and simple as it is our wont to suppose goes a long way in contesting the traditional view of "a medieval Europe of simple paternity and unambiguous truths and meanings" (Menocal 499). Being more attentive to internal periodization—taking the long twelfth century as an age *before* European hegemony, when the racializing and totalizing taxonomies that emerge in the later Middle Ages are still inchoate—allows us to perceive the *Roland* less as the repetition of a fully formed ideological pronouncement and more as a complex exploration of and negotiation between potentially incommensurate attitudes and practices. In restoring the *Song of Roland* to its historical and cultural context, we ask our students to interrogate the meaning, the stakes, and the political use of Roland's assertion that "[t]he pagans are wrong and the Christians are right" (1015).

NOTES

[1]All translations are mine unless otherwise indicated. Paris writes, "Oui, messieurs, il y a huit siècles, alors qu'aucune des nations de l'Europe n'avait encore pris véritablement conscience d'elle-même, quand plusieurs d'entre elles, comme l'Angleterre, attendaient encore pour leur formation des éléments essentiels, la patrie française était

fondée: le sentiment national existait dans ce qu'il y a de plus intime, de plus noble et de plus tendre. C'est dans la *Chanson de Roland* qu'apparaît cette divine expression de 'douce France,' dans laquelle s'est exprimé avec tant de grâce et de profondeur l'amour que cette terre aimable entre toutes inspirait déjà à ses enfants. Douce France! Les Allemands nous ont envié ce mot, et ont vainement cherché à en retrouver le pendant dans leur poésie nationale."

[2]"Nous reconnaîtrons que notre vie nationale était dominée, dès lors, par les deux grandes idées qui l'ont depuis animée et qui lui ont donné tant de richesse et de puissance à différents moments de notre histoire: la tendance à l'unité et la tendance à l'expansion . . . dès lors la tendance unitaire devient prépondérante dans la nation; elle se donne pour idéal la collaboration perpétuelle et volontaire de toutes les forces du pays vers un but commun, sous la direction de la royauté, et ce but, elle le place en dehors de la nation même, dans son action sur les peuples voisins."

[3]See Bartlett chs. 8–9, esp. 197–98; cf. Goldberg on the construction of race as perhaps *the* defining feature of modernity (24). Hahn lists a number of visual artifacts depicting "black physiognomies" (11), but his examples all date from the fourteenth century or later.

## APPENDIX
### Reading Guide and Study Questions

*Laisses*　　*Episode*

**1**　　**Introduction**

What is the role of counsel (*consilium*)? How does it work (lines 20, 166)?

Note the use of the terms *vassal* (lines 39, 84, 86, 231, 297, 352, 696) and *love* (lines 7, 86, 306, 323, 325).

**2–7**　　**Saracen Council**

What do the pagans decide to offer Charles (line 3)? Why?

Who is Blancandrin? How is he represented? Note the parallelism between this and the following scene.

**8–27**　　**Frankish Council**

Note the role of *repetition*, for example, of Marsile's offer (laisse 13, reprising 3).

What arguments are put forward in laisses 14, 15, 16?

Note the importance of group opinion (lines 243; cf. 61, 77).

Note the structure of each nomination scene (laisses 17, 18, 19).

How does Ganelon react to Roland's nomination of him (laisses 20–24)?

Note the representation of Ganelon (laisses 20, 27).

**28–54     Ganelon's Embassy**

What figure does Ganelon cut at the pagan court (laisses 33, 34, 35)?

Note both the repetition and progression in the similar laisses (laisses 40–42).

What is Ganelon's plan (laisses 43, 44, 45)?

Note the role of objects and gifts in sealing the pact (laisses 46–50).

**55–68     Nomination of Roland and Departure of the Franks**

Note the way laisse 55 partially reprises laisse 1 (cf. laisses 164, 187).

In Charlemagne's dream, note the role of the Pass of Cize (line 719; cf. line 583).

Nomination of Roland (laisse 58): how does this scene unfold?

Analyze Roland's reactions to being nominated by Ganelon (laisses 59–60).

Note evocations of the mountainous landscape (lines 805, 809, 814).

**69–78     The Pagans Prepare for Battle**

Note the parallelism between the twelve Franks and twelve pagans (lines 858, 878).

Catalog of Pagans (Laisses 70–78)
Note the variety of pagans; what traits characterize them?

Note the importance of verbal boasts.

Note evocation of Roland *and* Oliver (lines 902–03, 935–36, 947, 963–64).

Note evocation of Roland's sword Durendal (lines 926, 988).

**79–92     The Franks Prepare for Battle**

Note Roland's speech on the duties of a good vassal (laisse 79).

Compare the mention of "vassal" in lines 887 and 939.

What is Oliver's concern, and what is it based on (laisses 80–83)?

Note the similar laisses 84–85: what is the argument about?

Laisse 87: note the first two lines (1093–94); see the Old French (p. 194).

Note Roland's speech on a good vassal (laisse 88; cf. laisse 79).

What does Archbishop Turpin promise the Franks (laisse 89)?

Note Roland's declaration of Ganelon's betrayal (laisse 90; contrast laisse 80).

### 93–113    First Battle at Rencesvals

Parallel laisses: Pagans strike Franks (laisses 93–95), and Franks strike pagans (laisses 96–102).

In laisses 93–95, analyze the pairings of pagans and Franks.

How does Aelroth taunt Roland? (laisse 93; cf. with laisse 92, lines 1171–74 and with laisse 95)

What elements unite the parallel laisses 96–102?

Note the cuts between the battle and Charles/France (laisses 109–11).

Compare the two modes of memory evoked in laisse 112 (line 1443) and laisse 113 (line 1466; cf. laisse 79, line 1014).

### 114–76    Second Battle at Rencesvals

Compare the description of Abisme (laisse 114) with that of other pagans.

Note the parallelism between the pairs of laisses in this episode (117–18, 119–20, etc.).

What's different in the second olifant scene (laisses 129–30; contrast 84–85)?

Roland sounds the olifant: note the similar laisses 133–35.

Note the representation of Marsile's uncle and his men (143–44).

Observe the death of Oliver in laisses, 147, 148, 149, 150. What values are privileged?

In Turpin's last stand (laisse 155), note the evocation of "the annals" and the charter of Saint Giles. Compare lines 1684–85; contrast line 1517.

Note that Roland assembles the dead before Turpin (laisses 161–63).

Death of Roland: note the apostophe to Durendal (laisses 171, 172, 173). Where and how does he die (laisses 174–76)? What kills him (see laisse 156)?

### 177–88    Charlemagne's Revenge

Compare Charlemagne's prayer with the pagans' prayer (laisses 179–80); what's at stake?

Compare Charlemagne's two "visions" (laisses 185–86) with earlier ones (laisses 56–57)

Note Bramimonde's reaction to Marsile's return (laisses 187–88).

**189–273**     **Baligant Episode**

Compare laisse 189 to laisse 1.

How is Baligant's power portrayed?

Note Bramimonde's role in speaking to Baligant's envoys (laisses 195–96).

Note Charlemagne's lament over Roland (laisses 206–11); what effect will his death have on Charlemagne and his empire?

PREPARATIONS AND BATTLE

Note the role assigned to Rabel and Guineman (laisse 219; see laisses 246–48, 257).

Note parallel laisses 220–27. How does this catalog of Charlemagne's troops differ from that in the first battle of Rencesvals?

Note the descriptions of Baligant (laisses 231–32) and his troops (laisses 236–40).

Compare Baligant's and Charlemagne's exhortations to their men (laisses 251–52).

Note the confrontation between Baligant and Charles (laisses 264–68, esp. 266).

Note the stages in Charlemagne's capture of Saragossa (laisses 270–71, 272).

Note what happens to heroes' bodies (laisse 273; cf. laisses 213–14).

**274–75**     **Belle Aude** (cf. lines 1720–21).

**276–96**     **Trial of Ganelon**

Who is to judge Ganelon (lines 3699–704, 3742–743; cf. 3793–96)?

What is Charlemagne's accusation? Ganelon's defense (laisses 278–79)?

In the first trial, what is the peers' verdict, and why (laisses 282–283)?

In the second trial, note the description of Thierry; what is his argument (laisse 284)?

What form does the second trial take (laisses 286–94)?

What is the "miracle" God performs (line 3931)?

**297**     **Conversion of Bramimonde** (cf. lines 3671–74).

**298**     **Epilogue**

**Assignment 1** (Laisses 1–55)

What are the poem's most striking stylistic features?

Compare King Marsile's council (laisses 2–7) with Charlemagne's (laisses 12–26). How do decisions get made? What is the relationship between each king and his barons?

How do material objects function in the society represented in this poem?

What is the relationship between Charles, Roland, and Ganelon?

Pay special attention to Roland's speech in laisse 14.

**Assignment 2** (Laisses 56–176)

In the scene where Roland is nominated to lead the rear guard, try to figure out what is going on in laisses 59–60.

Compare Roland and Oliver's first (laisses 80–87) and second (laisses 129–32) disputes over whether to sound the olifant. What position does each one take, and why does each change his mind?

In the catalog of pagans (laisses 69–78) and elsewhere, pay attention to both the form and content of the way the pagans are represented. What physical, moral, and political features are attributed to them? How do they or don't they differ from Charlemagne's side?

Pay special attention to Roland's speech in laisse 79, the invocations of the archbishop and Roland (laisses 112–113), and the protracted death of Roland (laisses 168–76).

# NOTES ON CONTRIBUTORS

**Matthew Bailey** is associate professor in the Department of Spanish and Portuguese at the University of Texas, Austin. His publications include Las mocedades de Rodrigo: *Estudios críticos, manuscrito y edición*, and a Web site dedicated to the *Cantar de Mio Cid:* (www.laits.utexas.edu/cid/). Currently he is studying the expression of thirteenth-century Spanish narrative poetry in relation to speech.

**George T. Beech** is professor emeritus in the Department of History at Western Michigan University. Among his publications are *Le conventum d'Aquitaine (vers 1030): Précurseur des premières épopées* with coauthors Yves Chauvin and Georges Pon; *Une société rurale dans la France du moyen âge: La Gatine poitevine aux XIe et XIIe siècle*; and *Was the Bayeux Tapestry Made in France? The Case for St. Florent of Saumur.* His research and teaching interests are the history of Muslim Saragossa (Spain) in the eleventh century and the production site of the Bayeux Tapestry. He is working on a biography of William IX, duke of Aquitaine, the troubadour.

**Philip E. Bennett** is reader in French at the University of Edinburgh. Among his recent publications are a translation of Paul Zumthor's *Toward a Medieval Poetics*; *Reading around the Epic, a Festschrift in Honour of Professor Wolfgang van Emden*, which he edited with Marianne Ailes and Karen Pratt; *La chanson de Guillaume*, which he edited and translated; a thematic study of *La chanson de Guillaume* and *La prise d'Orange*; and a general study of the William cycle, *Carnaval héroïque et écriture cyclique dans la geste de Guillaume d'Orange.*

**Patricia E. Black** is professor of French at California State University, Chico. Her publications include the essays "The Gendered World of the *Chanson de Guillaume*," and "Guillaume de Lorris, Jean de Meun and the *Roman de la Rose*" in *The Dictionary of Literary Biography*. Her current project is on music and poetry in the Middle Ages in Thibaut de Champagne.

**Gerard J. Brault** is Edwin Erle Sparks Professor Emeritus of French and Medieval Studies at Pennsylvania State University. His publications include *Early Blazon* and *The Song of Roland: An Analytical Edition*. His current projects concern coats of arms of Charlemagne and his Twelve Peers and the influence of Adenet le Roi on medieval heraldry.

**Mark Burde** has served on the faculties of Ithaca College, Yale University, and the University of Michigan. He has published articles on satire and parody in the medieval French tradition and on nineteenth- and twentieth-century reception of the *Roland* in France. He is interested in the French comic tradition, the alimentary imaginary, the history of the French language, and the history of medieval studies, especially in the nineteenth century.

**Kimberlee A. Campbell** is professor of romance languages at Harvard University. Her publications include *The Protean Text: A Study of Versions of the Medieval Legend of Doon and Olive*, as well as articles on the representation of women and minorities in medieval epic, on Rabelais, and on the history of printing in the Renaissance. Her most recent book is titled *Echos: Cultural Discussions for Students of French*. Her research interests include Renaissance travel journals and computer-assisted language learning as well as the Old French epic.

**Alice M. Colby-Hall** is professor emerita of Romance studies at Cornell University. She has published *The Portrait in Twelfth-Century French Literature: An Example of the Stylistic Originality of Chrétien de Troyes*, as well as articles on the epics of the William of Orange cycle. Her research interests include the Occitan origins of material in the William cycle epics. She is currently completing a book entitled "Guillaume d'Orange et les légendes épiques de la basse vallée du Rhône."

**Robert Francis Cook** is professor emeritus of French at the University of Virginia. His publications include *Le Bâtard de Bouillon*; *Le deuxième cycle de la Croisade* (with Larry S. Crist); *Chanson d'Antioche, chanson de geste*; *The Sense of* The Song of Roland; and *Baudouin de Sebourc*, edited with Larry S. Crist. His current projects include a new edition of the Franco-Italian *Song of Roland*.

**Kelly DeVries** is professor in the Department of History at Loyola College. He has published *A History of Gunpowder Weaponry in the Middle Ages: The Artillery of the Valois Dukes of Burgundy, 1363–1477* (coauthored with Robert D. Smith); *Guns and Men in Medieval Europe, 1200–1500: Studies in Military History and Technology*; *A Cumulative Bibliography of Medieval Military History and Technology*; *Joan of Arc: A Military History*; *The Norwegian Invasion of England in 1066. Infantry Warfare in the Early Fourteenth Century: Discipline, Tactics, and Technology*; and *Medieval Military Technology*. Currently he is writing a book on the Hundred Years' War and another on Eastern Mediterranean warfare from Troy to the twentieth century.

**Joseph J. Duggan** is professor of French and comparative literature and associate dean, graduate division, at the University of California, Berkeley. His publications include *A Concordance of the* Chanson de Roland; *The Song of Roland: Formulaic Style and Poetic Craft*; *A Guide to Studies on the* Chanson de Roland; *A New Fragment of 'Les Enfances Vivien'*; *The* Cantar de mio Cid: *Poetic Creation in Its Economic and Social Contexts*; and *The Romances of Chrétien de Troyes*. Currently he is general editor of a new edition of all the French texts of the *Chanson de Roland* and is working on an edition of *Garin le Loherain*.

**Ann W. Engar** is assistant professor and lecturer in LEAP and Honors Programs at the University of Utah. She contributed to *Approaches to Teaching Vergil's* Aeneid and to *Approaches to Teaching* Hamlet. She has published articles on teaching methods and the practice of biography. She is currently a senior bibliographer for the *MLA International Bibliography*.

**Jane E. Everson** is professor of Italian literature at Royal Holloway, University of London. She is author of *The Italian Romance Epic in the Age of Humanism: The Matter of Italy and the World of Rome* and *Bibliografia delle edizioni del* Mambriano *di Francesco Cieco da Ferrara*, as well as articles about chivalric epic from Boccaccio to Ariosto, and about the bibliography of early printed texts of Italian literature. She is currently working on an edition of *Il Mambriano*, by Cieco da Ferrara.

**Edward A. Heinemann** is professor emeritus in the Department of French at the University of Toronto. He is the author of *L'art métrique de la chanson de geste: Essai* *sur la musicalité du récit* and articles about the aesthetics of echo in the chansons de geste. He is currently working on a book-length study of the metric art of the *Charroi de Nîmes.*

**Catherine M. Jones** is associate professor of French and Provençal in the Department of Romance Languages at the University of Georgia. She has published *The Noble Merchant: Problems of Genre and Lineage in* Hervis de Mes; *"Por la soie amisté": Essays in Honor of Norris J. Lacy* (edited with Keith Busby); as well as articles on Old French epic, Philippe de Vigneulles, romance, and allegory. Her research interests include the later chansons de geste and modern adaptations of medieval texts. Her current project is a book entitled "Philippe de Vigneulles and the Prosaics of Translatio."

**William W. Kibler** was the Linward Shivers–Superior Oil Centennial Professor of Medieval Studies in the Department of French and Italian at the University of Texas, Austin. He has worked extensively on Chrétien de Troyes, Guillaume de Machaut, and the French chansons de geste. He recently completed an edition of the Lyon manuscript of the *Song of Roland* and has published editions of *Lion de Bourges* (with Jean-Louis Picherit and Thelma Fenster) and *Huon de Bordeaux* (with François Suard), as well as a translation of *Raoul de Cambrai.* He is the author of *An Introduction to Old French.*

**Sharon Kinoshita** is professor in the Literature Department at the University of California, Santa Cruz. She is the author of *Medieval Boundaries: Rethinking Difference in Old French Literature* and essays on medieval French epic and romance of the twelfth and early thirteenth centuries, including articles on *La fille du comte de Pontieu, Raoul de Cambrai,* and the *Roman de Silence.* Her research and teaching interests include Old French representations of the medieval culture of empire, Mediterranean studies, and postcolonial medievalism.

**Emanuel Mickel** is professor of French literature in the Department of French and Italian at Indiana University. Among his publications are *Marie de France; Ganelon, Treason, and the* Chanson de Roland; *Enfances Godefroi;* and *Le retour de Cornumarant.* His research and teaching interests include chanson de geste, romance, and personified dream narrative. He is currently working on two book-length projects, one on the history of persona and another on history and romance.

**Leslie Zarker Morgan** is associate professor of modern languages and literatures at Loyola College. She has published an English translation of Ariosto's *Cinque canti;* edited *The Foreign Language Classroom: Bridging Theory and Practice,* with M. A. Haggstrom and J. A. Wieczorek; edited *Dante: Summa Medioevalis,* with Charles Franco; written articles on Franco-Italian texts; and edited the *Geste Francor,* which is forthcoming.

**Ellen Peel** is professor in the Departments of Comparative and World Literature and of English at San Francisco State University. Among her publications are *Politics, Persuasion, and Pragmatism: A Rhetoric of Feminist Utopian Fiction;* an essay in *Approaches to Teaching Murasaki Shikibu's* The Tale of Genji; and articles on women and narrative in English and French. She is currently working on a book, "The Text of The Body / The Body of The Text," on the constructed body in literature and film.

**Lynn T. Ramey** is associate professor of French at Vanderbilt University. Among her publications are the book, *Christian, Saracen, and Genre in Medieval French Literature*, and articles on the *Jeu de Saint Nicolas* and on representations of women in epic and lyric. Her research and teaching interests are historical and literary relationships between Christians, Jews, and Muslims and women and power in the Middle Ages. She is currently working on a study of the role of the Middle Ages in the formation of modern ideas on racial consciousness.

**Joel T. Rosenthal** is Distinguished Professor in the Department of History at the State University of New York, Stony Brook. Among his recent publications are *Late Medieval England (1377–1485): A Bibliography of Historical Scholarship, 1990–1999* and *Telling Tales: Sources and Narration in Late Medieval England.* His teaching interests run from general medieval (especially the use of primary materials and literature) to a focus on the Germanic invasions, popular religion, and women and family life. He is currently working on an exploration of secular piety, with a focus on Margaret Paston.

**Mary Jane Schenck** is professor of English at the University of Tampa. She is the author of *The Fabliaux: Tales of Wit and Deception*; *Read, Write, Revise*; as well as coeditor of the collection *Echoes of the Epic.* She has published on the *Song of Roland* and *Le roman de Renart*, is currently working on a book on medieval trials and customary law, and has completed a study on the Charlemagne window at Chartres.

**Ian Short** is professor of French at Birkbeck College, University of London. He is the editor and translator of the Modern French translation cited in this volume, *La chanson de Roland.* He has published widely in his areas of teaching and research interest, medieval French and Anglo-Norman.

**Deborah M. Sinnreich-Levi** is associate professor of English and comparative literature; director, writing programs; and director, Humanities Resource Center and Graduate Certificate Program in Professional Communications at Stevens Institute of Technology. She cotranslated *Selected Poetry of Eustache Deschamps*; coedited *Reconstructive Polyphony: Studies in the Rhetorical Poetics of the Middle Ages*; and published *Eustache Deschamps, L'art de dictier.* She has edited and translated, with R. Barton Palmer and Ian Laurie, an edition of Deschamps's *Miroir de mariage*, which will be published by Pegasus Press in 2007.

**Barbara Stevenson** is professor of English at Kennesaw State University. Her publications include *Crossing the Bridge: Comparative Essays on Medieval European and Heian Japanese Women Writers*, edited with Cynthia Ho. Her teaching and research interests are Chaucer and other Middle English writers, medieval women writers, and cross-cultural approaches to medieval literature.

**Margaret Switten** is Class of 1926 Professor of French at Mount Holyoke College. Among her publications are *The Cansos of Raimon de Miraval: A Study of Poems and Melodies* and *Music and Poetry in the Middle Ages: A Guide to Research on French and Occitan Song.* She has directed two multimedia teaching projects, both supported by the National Endowment for the Humanities and Mount Holyoke College: *The Medieval Lyric* and *Teaching Medieval Lyric with Modern Technology.* She is currently working on Aquitanian *versus* and their relation to troubadour songs.

**Patricia Terry** is adjunct professor of literature (retired) at the University of California, San Diego. Among her publications are translations of the *Song of Roland* and *Renard the Fox*; *The Honeysuckle and The Hazel Tree*; *Poems of the Elder Edda*; and *The Romance of the Rose or Guillaume de Dole* (with Nancy Vine Durling). *Lancelot and the Lord of the Distant Isles*, a retelling with Samuel N. Rosenberg, is forthcoming.

**Eugene Vance** is professor of French and comparative literature at the University of Washington. Among his publications are *Reading* The Song of Roland; *Mervelous Signals: Poetics and Sign Theory in the Middle Ages*; and *From Topos to Tale: Logic and Narrativity in the Middle Ages*. He is interested in the patristic foundations of medieval culture; rhetoric and discourse analysis; methods of historical criticism; and relics, images, and models of spirituality. His current project is a book on the poetics of literature, ritual spaces, and monumental forms in the Middle Ages.

**Michelle R. Warren** is associate professor of comparative literature at Dartmouth College. She has published *History on the Edge: Excalibur and the Borders of Britain (1100–1300)* and coedited the volumes *Postcolonial Moves: Medieval through Modern* and *Arts of Calculation: Numerical Thought in Early Modern Europe*. Current projects include a postcolonial history of medieval French studies and studies of late medieval English translations of French romance.

# SURVEY PARTICIPANTS

John Baldwin, *Johns Hopkins University*
Jeanette Beer, *Purdue University*
Patricia E. Black, *California State University, Chico*
Gerard J. Brault, *University of Pennsylvania*
Mark Burde, *Yale University*
Margaret Burland, *Dartmouth College*
Salvatore Calomino, *University of Wisconsin, Madison*
Kimberlee Campbell, *New York University*
Nicole Clifton, *Northern Illinois University De Kalb*
Alice M. Colby-Hall, *Cornell University*
Kelly DeVries, *Loyola College*
Joseph J. Duggan, *University of California, Berkeley*
Jody Enders, *University of California, Santa Barbara*
Ann W. Engar, *University of Utah*
Virginie Greene, *Harvard University*
Judith Haas, *Rhodes College*
Edward A. Heinemann, *University of Toronto*
Catherine M. Jones, *University of Georgia*
Sharon Kinoshita, *University of California, Santa Cruz*
Roberta Krueger, *Hamilton College*
Reinier Leushvis, *Florida State University*
Christine McWebb, *University of Alberta*
Emanuel Mickel, *Indiana University*
William D. Paden, *Northwestern University*
Ellen Peel, *San Francisco State University*
Paul Rockwell, *Amherst College*
Joel T. Rosenthal, *State University of New York, Stony Brook*
Mary A. Santina, *Lamar University*
Mary Jane Schenck, *University of Tampa*
Deborah M. Sinnreich-Levi, *Stevens Institute of Technology*
Barbara Stevenson, *Kennesaw State University*
Michelle R. Warren, *Dartmouth College*

# WORKS CITED

Abun-Naser, Jamil M. *A History of the Maghrib in the Islamic Period*. Cambridge: Cambridge UP, 1987.

Aebischer, Paul. "Les trois plus anciennes mentions du couple 'Roland-Olivier.' " *Revue Belge de philologie et d'histoire* 30 (1952): 657–75.

———. "Pour la défense et l'illustration de l'épisode de Baligant." *Rolandiana et Oliveriana: Recueil d'études sur les chansons de geste*. Paris: Belles Lettres, 1949. 173–82. Rpt. of *Mélanges de philologie romane et de littérature médiévale offerts à Ernest Hoepffner par ses élèves et ses amis*. Geneva: Droz, 1967. 211–20.

Alonso, Dámaso. "La primitiva épica francesa a la luz de una Nota Emilianense." *Revista de filología española* 37 (1953): 1–94. *La primitiva épica francesa a la luz de una Nota Emilianense*. Madrid: CSIC, Instituto Miguel de Cervantes, 1954.

Altman, Janet. *Epistolarity: Approaches to a Form*. Columbus: Ohio State UP, 1982.

Alton, Jeannine, and Brian Jeffery. *Bele Buche et Bele Parleure: A Guide to the Pronunciation of Medieval and Renaissance French for Singers and Others*. With cassette. London: Tecla, 1976.

Alvar, Manuel, ed. *Siete infantes de Lara Cantares de gesta medievales*. México: Porrúa, 1982. 31–59.

Amador de los Rios, José. *Historia crítica de la literatura española*. 7 vols. Madrid: Rodriguez, 1861.

Amalvi, Christian. *De l'art et la manière d'accommoder les héros de l'histoire de France*. Paris: Michel, 1988.

Amaya, Shane L., Fábio Moon, and Gabriel Ba. *Roland: Days of Wrath*. Santa Barbara: Terra Major, 1999.

Amiel, L. "*La chanson de Roland*." *Journal de Paris* 25 Apr. 1837. N. pag.

Amt, Emily. *Women's Lives in Medieval Europe: A Sourcebook*. London: Routledge, 1993.

*Aquitania: Christmas Music from Aquitanian Monasteries*. Perf. Sequentia. Dir. Benjamin Bagby and Barbara Thornton. DHM, 1997. DHM 05472-77383-2.

Auerbach, Erich. *Mimesis: The Representation of Reality in Western Literature*. Trans. Willard R. Trask. Princeton: Princeton UP, 1953.

Bailey, Matthew, ed. *Las mocedades de Rodrigo: Estudios críticos, manuscrito y edición*. Medieval Studies 15. London: King's Coll., London, Centre for Late Antique and Medieval Studies, 1999.

Bailey, Terence, ed. and trans. *Commemoratio brevis de tonis et psalmis modulandis*. Ottawa: U of Ottawa P, 1979.

Bartlett, Robert. *The Making of Europe: Conquest, Colonization, and Cultural Change, 950–1350*. Princeton: Princeton UP, 1993.

Barton, Simon. "Traitors to the Faith? Christian Mercenaries in al-Andalus and the Maghreb, c. 1100–1300." *Medieval Spain: Culture, Conflict, and Coexistence:*

*Studies in Honour of Angus McKay.* Ed. Roger Collins and Anthony Goodman. New York: Palgrave, 2002. 23–45.

Bartsch, Karl, ed. *Karl der Grosse von dem Stricker.* Mit einem Nachwort von Dieter Kartschoke. Berlin: W. de Gruyter, 1965 [text of the 1857 edition].

Bass, Iris. "Knights at the Opera, Part 12: Sixteenth-Century Epic Poetry." 14 Dec. 2001. 8 Aug. 2004 <http://www.suite101.com/article.cfm/opera/87617>.

Bateson, F. H., ed. *La chanson de Floovant.* Loughborough: n. p., 1938.

Baumgartner, Emmanuèle. *Moyen âge: 1050–1486.* Ed. Daniel Couty. Paris: Bordas, 1987. Vol. 1 of *Histoire de la littérature française.* 8 vols.

Bédier, Joseph, ed. and trans. La chanson de Roland, *publiée d'après le manuscrit d'Oxford et traduite par J. Bédier.* Paris: Piazza, 1921.

———, ed. La chanson de Roland *commentée par Joseph Bédier.* 1927. Paris: Champion, 1968.

———. "De l'édition princeps de la *Chanson de Roland* aux éditions les plus récentes. Nouvelles remarques sur l'art d'établir les anciens textes." *Romania* 64 (1938): 145–244; 489–521.

———. *Les légendes épiques: Recherches sur les origines des chansons de geste.* 1908. 3 vols. Paris: Champion, 1929.

Beeler, John. *Warfare in Feudal Europe, 730–1200.* Ithaca: Cornell UP, 1971.

Beissinger, Margaret H. "Creativity in Performance: Words and Music in Balkan and Old French Epic." *The Oral Epic: Performance and Music.* Ed. Karl Reichl. Intercultural Music Studies 12. Berlin: VWB, 2000. 95–113.

Bender, Karl Heinz. *König und Vasall.* Heidelberg: Winter, 1967.

Bennett, Philip E. The Chanson de Guillaume *and the* Prise d'Orange. London: Grant, 2000.

———. "Ganelon's False Message: A Critical False Perspective?" *Reading around the Epic: A Festschrift in Honour of Professor Wolfgang van Emden.* Ed. Marianne Ailes, Bennett, and Karen Pratt. London: King's Coll., London, 1998. 149–69.

———. "*Le pèlerinage de Charlemagne*: Le sens de l'aventure." *Essor et fortune de la chanson de geste dans l'Europe et l'Orient latin.* Ed. Alberto Limentani et al. Modena: Mucchi, 1984. 475–87.

Bennett, Philip E., Anne Elizabeth Cobby, and Graham A. Runnals, eds. *Charlemagne in the North: Proceedings of the Twelfth International Conference of the Société Rencesvals, Edinburgh, 4th–11th August 1991.* Edinburgh: Société Rencesvals, 1993.

Benton, John F. " 'Nostre Franceis n'unt talent de fuïr': *The Song of Roland* and the Enculturation of a Warrior Class." *Olifant* 6 (1979): 237–58.

*Beowulf: A New Verse Translation.* Trans. Seamus Heaney. New York: Farrar, 2000.

Beretta, Carlo, ed. *Il testo assonanzato franco-italiano della* Chanson de Roland*: Cod. Marciano fr. IV ( =225).* Edizione interpretativa e glossario. Testi 2. Pavia: Università degli Studi di Pavia, Dipartimento di Scienza della Letteratura e dell'Arte Medioevale e Moderna, 1995.

Berg, Robert J., and Fabrice Leroy, eds. "La chanson de Roland." *Littérature française, textes et contextes, Tome I: Du moyen âge au XVIII* *siècle*. Fort Worth: Holt, 1994–1997. 7–69.

Berthelot, Anne, and François Cornilliat. *Littérature: Textes et documents. Moyen âge–XVI*<sup>e</sup>*. Introd. Jacques LeGoff. Collection Henri Mitterand. Paris: Nathan, 1988.

Bishop, Morris. *A Survey of French Literature*. Rev. ed. Vol. 1. New York: Harcourt, 1965.

Blackmore, Josiah, and Gregory S. Hutcheson, eds. *Queer Iberia: Sexualities, Cultures, and Crossings from the Middle Ages to the Renaissance*. Durham: Duke UP, 1999.

Bliese, John R. E. "Courage and Honor, Cowardice and Shame: A Motive Appeal in Battle Orations in *The Song of Roland* and in Chronicles of the Central Middle Ages." *Olifant* 20 (1995–96): 191–212.

Bloch, Marc. *Feudal Society*. Trans. L. A. Manyon. Chicago: U of Chicago P, 1961.

Bloch, R. Howard. *Etymologies and Genealogies. A Literary Anthropology of the French Middle Ages*. Chicago: U of Chicago P, 1983.

———. "The First Document and the Birth of Medieval Studies." *A New History of French Literature*. Ed. Denis Hollier. Cambridge: Harvard UP, 1989. 6–13.

Bloch, R. Howard, and Steven G. Nichols. *Medievalism and the Modernist Temper*. Baltimore: Johns Hopkins UP, 1996.

*Bodleian Library MS Digby 23 (Pt 2)*. Oxford University, Bodleian Library MS Digby 23. 19 Dec. 2005 <http://image.ox.ac.uk/show?collection=bodleian&manuscript =msdigby23>.

Boehmer, Édouard. *Rencesval. Édition critique du texte d'Oxford de* La chanson de Roland. Halle: Niemeyer, 1872.

Bouchard, Constance Brittain. *"Strong of Body, Brave and Noble": Chivalry and Society in Medieval France*. Ithaca: Cornell UP, 1998.

Bouchor, Maurice. La Chanson de Roland *traduite en vers par Maurice Bouchor*. Paris: Hachette, 1899.

Bourciez, Édouard, and Jean Bourciez. *Phonétique française: Étude historique*. Tradition de l'humanisme 3. Paris: Klincksieck, 1967.

Bournazel, Eric. *Féodalités*. Paris: PUF, 1998.

Boutet, Dominique. *La chanson de geste: Forme et signification d'une écriture du moyen âge*. Paris: PUF, 1993.

———, ed. and trans. *Le cycle de Guillaume d'Orange, anthologie*. Lettres gothiques. Paris: Livre de Poche, 1996.

Boynton, Susan. "Women's Performance of Lyric Before 1500." *Medieval Woman's Song: Cross-Cultural Approaches*. Ed. Anne L. Klinck and Ann Marie Rasmussen. Philadelphia: U of Pennsylvania P, 2001. 47–65.

Bracton, Henry de. *De legibus et consuetudinibus Angliæ*. Ed. George E. Woodbine. Trans., with revs. and notes, Samuel E. Thorne. 3 vols. Cambridge: Harvard UP, 1968.

Brand, C. P. *Ludovico Ariosto: A Preface to the* Orlando Furioso. Edinburgh: Edinburgh UP, 1974.

Brault, Gerard J., ed. *La chanson de Roland: Student Edition.* University Park: Pennsylvania State UP, 1984.

——. "*Sapientia* dans la *Chanson de Roland.*" *French Forum* 1 (1976): 99–118.

——, ed. *The Song of Roland: An Analytical Edition.* 2 vols. University Park: Pennsylvania State UP, 1978.

Brown, Elizabeth A. R. "The Tyranny of a Construct: Feudalism and Historians of Medieval Europe." *American Historical Review* 79 (1974): 1063–88.

Brown, Shirley Ann. "The Bayeux Tapestry and the *Song of Roland.*" *Roncevaux 778–1978.* Ed. John Robin Allen. Spec. issue of *Olifant* 6 (1979): 339–50.

Burger, André. "Les deux scènes du cor dans la *Chanson de Roland.*" *Technique* 105–25.

Burgess, Glyn S. *Contribution à l'étude du vocabulaire pré-courtois.* Geneva: Droz, 1970.

——, ed. and trans. *Le pèlerinage de Charlemagne.* Edinburgh: Société Rencesvals, 1998.

——, ed. and trans. *The Song of Roland.* London: Penguin, 1990.

Burgess, Glyn S. and Anne Elizabeth Cobby, eds. and trans. The Pilgrimage of Charlemagne *and* Aucassin and Nicolette. New York: Garland, 1998.

Burton, Richard Francis, trans. *The Book of the Thousand Nights and a Night.* 6 vols. New York: Heritage, 1934. *Project Gutenberg* 14 May 2006 <http://www.promo.net/pg>.

Butterfield, Ardis. *Poetry and Music in Medieval France: From Jean Renart to Guillaume de Machaut.* Cambridge: Cambridge UP, 2002.

Calin, William. "L'épopée dite vivante: Réflexions sur le prétendu caractère oral des chansons de geste." *Olifant* 8 (1981): 227–37.

——. "Littérature médiévale et hypothèse orale: Une divergence de méthode et de philosophie." *Olifant* 8 (1981): 256–85.

Calvino, Italo. Orlando furioso *di Ludovico Ariosto raccontato da Italo Calvino, con una scelta del poema.* Turin: Einaudi, 1970.

Camille, Michael. *The Gothic Idol: Ideology and Image-Making in Medieval Art.* Cambridge: Cambridge UP, 1989.

Cardini, Franco. *Europe and Islam.* Trans. Caroline Beamis. Oxford: Blackwell, 2001.

Carton, Jean-Paul. "Aesthetic Considerations Based on 'Elaborate Style' in the *Chanson de Roland*: Patterns of Intensification and Narrative Progression in Laisses 83–85." *Olifant* 20 (1996): 63–108.

Cassenti, Frank, dir. *La chanson de Roland.* Perf. Pierre Clémenti, Klaus Kinski, Dominique Sanda, Alain Cuny. Gaumont, 1978.

Catalano, Marco, ed. La Spagna, *poema cavalleresco del secolo XIV.* 3 vols. Bologna: Commissione per i Testi di Lingua, 1939–40.

Celati, Gianni. L'Orlando innamorato *raccontato in prosa.* Turin: Einaudi, 1994.

Cerquiglini, Bernard. "Roland à Roncevaux, ou la trahison des clercs." *Littérature* 42 (1981): 40–56.

——. *Éloge de la variante: Histoire critique de la philologie.* Paris: Seuil, 1989.

Chailley, Jacques. "Du *Tu autem* de Horn à la musique des chansons de geste." *La chanson de geste et le mythe carolingien: Mélanges René Louis.* Vol. 1. Saint-Père-sous-Vézelay, Fr.: Musée Archéologique Régional, 1982. 21–32.

*La chanson de Roland.* Perf. Proscenium Studio, Montreal. Dir. Lucie de Vienne. LP. Folkways, 1961. Program notes and text with Modern French. English trans. by Dorothy Sayers.

*La chanson de Roland.* Laisses 1 and 66. *Medieval Studies.* Univ. of California, Irvine. 23 Dec. 2003 <http://eee.uci.edu/programs/medieval/ofclips.html>.

*Charlemagne.* Perf. Christian Brendel et al. Dir. Clive Donner. 5 videocassettes. Acorn, 1994.

Cheyette, Fredric L. *Ermengarde of Narbonne and the World of the Troubadours.* Ithaca: Cornell UP, 2001.

Chiri, Giuseppe. *L'epica latina medioevale e* La chanson de Roland. Genoa: Emiliano degli Orfini, 1936.

Chrétien de Troyes. *Le chevalier au lion.* Ed. and trans. David F. Hult. Paris: Livre de Poche, 1994.

*Chronicarum quae dicunter Fredegarii scholastici.* Ed. B. Krusch and W. Levison. 2nd ed. Hanover: Hahn, 1951. Vol. 2 of *Monumenta Germaniae historica, scriptores rerum Merovingicarum.* 4 vols.

*La civilisation française en évolution, I.* Ed. Ross Steel, Susan St. Onge, and Ronald St. Onge. Boston: Heinle, 1996.

Clanchy, M. T. *From Memory to Written Record: England, 1066–1307.* London: Arnold, 1979.

Cohen, Jerome Jeffrey. "Introduction: Midcolonial." Cohen, *Postcolonial Middle Ages* 1–17.

———. "On Saracen Enjoyment: Some Fantasies of Race in Late Medieval France and England." *Race and Ethnicity in the Middle Ages.* Ed. Thomas Hahn. Spec. issue of *Journal of Medieval and Early Modern Studies* 31.1 (2001): 113–46.

———, ed. *The Postcolonial Middle Ages.* New Middle Ages Series. Gen. ed. Bonnie Wheeler. New York: Palgrave, 2000.

Coldwell, Maria V. "*Jougleresses* and *Trobairitz*: Secular Musicians in Medieval France." *Women Making Music: The Western Art Tradition, 1150–1950.* Ed. Jane Bowers and Judith Tick. Urbana: U of Illinois P, 1985. 39–61.

*Compostelle: Le chant de l'étoile.* Perf. Ensemble Discantus. Dir. Brigitte Lesne. Jade, 2003. Jade 301 654-2.

Contamine, Philippe. *La guerre au moyen âge.* Nouvelle Clio: L'histoire et ses problèmes 24. Paris: PUF, 1980.

Cook, Robert F. *The Sense of the* Song of Roland. Ithaca: Cornell UP, 1987.

Crist, Larry S. "À propos de la *desmesure* dans la *Chanson de Roland*: Quelques propos (démesurés?)." *Olifant* 1 (1974): 10–20.

Crocker, Richard L. *An Introduction to Gregorian Chant.* New Haven: Yale UP, 2000.

Culler, Jonathan. *Structuralist Poetics: Structuralism, Linguistics, and the Study of Literature.* Ithaca: Cornell UP, 1975.

Curtius, Ernst Robert. *European Literature and the Latin Middle Ages*. 1948. Trans. Willard R. Trask. Princeton: Princeton UP, 1953.

Cuttler, S. H. *The Law of Treason and Treason Trials in Later Medieval France*. Cambridge: Cambridge UP, 1981.

Dagenais, John, and Margaret R. Greer, eds. *Decolonizing the Middle Ages*. Spec. issue of *Journal of Medieval and Early Modern Studies* 30 (2000).

Dakyns, Janine. *The Middle Ages in French Literature, 1851–1900*. London: Oxford UP, 1973.

Daniel, Norman. *Heroes and Saracens: An Interpretation of the Chansons de Geste*. Edinburgh: Edinburgh UP, 1984.

Danon, Samuel, and Samuel Rosenberg, trans. *Ami and Amile*. York: French Lit., 1981.

Dante Alighieri. *The Divine Comedy*. Text, trans., commentary by Charles S. Singleton. 6 vols. Princeton: Princeton UP, 1980–82.

"Darmok." *Star Trek: The Next Generation*. 30 Sept. 1991. Videocassette. Paramount, 1991. Stardate 45047.Z.

Davie, Mark. *Half-Serious Rhymes: The Narrative Poetry of Luigi Pulci*. Publications of the Foundation for Italian Studies, University Coll., Dublin. Dublin: Irish Academic, 1998.

Davis, R. H. C. *The Medieval Warhorse: Origin, Development and Redevelopment*. London: Thames, 1989.

De Hamel, Christopher. *Scribes and Illuminators*. Medieval Craftsmen. Toronto: U of Toronto P, 1992.

De Weever, Jacqueline. *Sheba's Daughters: Whitening and Demonizing the Saracen Woman in Medieval French Epic*. New York: Garland, 1998.

Delbouille, Maurice. *Sur la genèse de* La chanson de Roland *(Travaux récents-propositions nouvelles)*. Brussels: Palais des Académies, 1954.

Derrida, Jacques. *Of Grammatology*. 1967. Trans. Gayatri Chakravorty Spivak. Baltimore: Johns Hopkins UP, 1976.

———. "Structure, Sign, and Play in the Discourse of the Human Sciences." *Writing and Difference*. Trans. Alan Bass. Chicago: U Chicago P, 1978. 279–93. Rpt. in *Modern Criticism and Theory: A Reader*. 2nd ed. Ed. David Lodge and Nigel Wood. Harlow, Eng.: Longman, 2000. 89–103.

Dorfman, Eugene. *The Narreme in the Medieval Romance Epic: An Introduction to Narrative Structures*. Toronto: U of Toronto P, 1969.

Douglas, David C. "*The Song of Roland* and the Norman Conquest of England." *French Studies* 14 (1960): 99–116.

Duby, Georges. *The Age of the Cathedrals: Art and Society, 980–1420*. Trans. Eleanor Levieux and Barbara Thompson. Chicago: U of Chicago P, 1981.

———. *The Chivalrous Society*. Berkeley: U of California P, 1977.

———. *Féodalité*. Paris: Gallimard, 1996.

———. *The Knight, The Lady, and the Priest: The Making of Modern Marriage in Medieval France*. Trans. Barbara Bray. New York: Pantheon, 1983.

———. *Love and Marriage in the Middle Ages*. Trans. Jane Dunnett. Cambridge, Eng.: Polity, 1994.

———. *The Three Orders: Feudal Society Imagined.* Trans. Arthur Goldhammer. Chicago: U of Chicago P, 1980.

———. *William Marshal: The Flower of Chivalry.* Trans. Richard Howard. New York: Pantheon, 1985.

Dufournet, Jean, trans. *La chanson de Roland.* Paris: GF-Flammarion, 1993.

———, trans. *La chanson de Roland.* Présentation et dossier par Patrice Kleff. Étonnants Classiques. Paris: GF-Flammarion, 2003.

———. *Cours sur la* Chanson de Roland. Paris: Centre de Documentation Universitaire, 1972.

———, ed. and trans. *Le jeu de Robin et de Marion.* By Adam de la Halle. Paris: Flammarion, 1989.

Duggan, Joseph J. *A Concordance of the* Chanson de Roland. Columbus: Ohio State UP, 1969.

———. "The Epic." *New History of French Literature.* Ed. Denis Hollier. Cambridge: Harvard UP, 1989. 18–23.

———. "L'épisode d'Aude dans la tradition en rime de la *Chanson de Roland.*" Bennett, Cobby, and Runnals 273–79.

———. "Franco-German Conflict and the History of French Scholarship on the *Song of Roland.*" *Hermeneutics and Medieval Culture.* Ed. Patrick J. Gallagher and Helen Damico. Albany: State U of New York P, 1989. 97–106.

———. "The Generation of the Episode of Baligant: Charlemagne's Dream and the Normans at Mantzikert." *Romance Philology* 30 (1976): 59–82.

———. *Guide to Studies on the* Chanson de Roland. London: Grant, 1976.

———. "Le mode de composition des chansons de geste: Analyse statistique, jugement esthétique, modèles de transmission." *Olifant* 8 (1981): 286–316.

———. *The Song of Roland: Formulaic Style and Poetic Craft.* Berkeley: U of California P, 1973.

———. *The Song of Roland.* 14 May 2001. <http://ishi.berkeley.edu/history155/manuscripts/roland.html>.

———. "La théorie de la composition orale des chansons de geste: Les faits et les interprétations." *Olifant* 8 (1981): 238–55.

Duggan, Joseph J., et al. La Chanson de Roland: The Song of Roland: *The French Corpus.* Gen. introd. Duggan. Concordance by Karen Akiyama. 3 vols. Turnhout, Belg.: Brepols, 2005. Vol 1: *The Oxford Version*, ed. Ian Short; *The Venice 4 Version*, ed. Robert F. Cook. Vol. 2: *The Châteauroux-Venice 7 Version*, ed. Duggan. Vol. 3: *The Paris Version*, ed. Annalee C. Rejhon; *The Cambridge Version*, ed. Wolfgang G. van Emden; *The Lyon Version*, ed. William W. Kibler; *The Fragments*, ed. Kibler.

Dutton, Brian, ed. *Los milagros de nuestra Señora.* By Gonzalo de Berceo. London: Tamesis, 1971.

Einhard. *The Life of Charlemagne.* Trans. Samuel Epes Turner. New York: Harper, 1880. *Medieval Sourcebook* Ed. Paul Halsall. 24 Apr. 2006. 22 May 2006 <http://www.fordham.edu/halsall/basis/einhard.html>.

El-Cheikh, Nadia Maria. "Women's History: A Study of Al-Tanukhi." *Writing the Fem-*

*inine: Women in Arab Sources.* Ed. Manuela Marín and Randi Deguilhem. London: Tauris, 2002. 129–48.

Enders, Jody. "The Logic of the Debates in the *Chanson de Roland.*" *Olifant* 14 (1989): 83–100.

*La entrada en Espana / "El cantar de Roldan."* Facsimile of Venice, Biblioteca Nazionale Marciana, Francese Z.21 (=257). Study by Carlos Alvar. Iconographical study by Susy Marcon. 2 vols. Valencia: Ediciones Grial, 2003.

Erdmann, Carl. *The Origin of the Idea of Crusade.* Princeton: Princeton UP, 1977.

Everson, Jane E. *The Italian Romance Epic in the Age of Humanism: The Matter of Italy and the World of Rome.* Oxford: Oxford UP, 2001.

Faral, Edmond. La chanson de Roland: *Étude et analyse.* Paris: Mellotée, 1934.

Farnham, Fern. "Romanesque Design in the *Chanson de Roland.*" *Romance Philology* 18 (1964): 143–64.

Felman, Shoshana. *What Does a Woman Want? Reading and Sexual Difference.* Baltimore: Johns Hopkins UP, 1993.

Ferrante, Joan M., trans. *Guillaume d'Orange: Four Twelfth-Century Epics.* New York: Columbia UP, 1974.

Finnegan, Ruth. *Oral Poetry: Its Nature, Significance and Social Context.* Cambridge: Cambridge UP, 1977.

Fleischman, Suzanne. "A Linguistic Perspective on the *Laisses Similaires*: Orality and the Pragmatics of Narrative Discourse." *Romance Philology* 43 (1989): 70–89.

Flori, Jean. *La chevalerie en France au moyen âge.* Paris: PUF, 1995.

———. *L'idéologie du glaive: Préhistoire de la chevalerie.* Geneva: Droz, 1983.

Folz, Robert. *Le souvenir et la légende de Charlemagne dans l'empire germanique médiéval.* Paris: Belles Lettres, 1950.

Fouché, Pierre. *Phonétique historique du français.* 2nd ed. 3 vols. Paris: Klincksieck, 1966.

Foulcher de Chartres. "L'appel à la croisade du pape Urbain II." *Pays d'Islam et monde latin Xe–XIIIe siècle.* Michel Balard, Alain Demurger, and Pierre Guichard, eds. Collection l'histoire par les sources. Paris: Hachette, 2000. 64–66. <http://classes.bnf.fr/idrisi/pedago/croisades/urbain.htm>.

———. *Histoire des croisades.* Collection des mémoires relatifs à l'histoire de France. Ed. F. Guizot. Paris: Brière, 1825. <http://histoireenprimaire.free.fr/ressources/simonis3.htm>.

———. *Historia Iherosolymitana.* Recueil des historiens des croisades, historiens occidentaux. Vol. 3. Paris: Imprimerie Nationale, 1866.

———. "Urban and the Crusaders." *Translations and Reprints from the Original Sources of European History.* Vol. 1. Philadelphia: U of Pennsylvania P, 1902. 4–5.

Foulet, Alfred. "Is Roland Guilty of *Desmesure?*" *Romance Philology* 10 (1956–57): 145–48.

Foys, Martin K. *The Bayeux Tapestry.* CD-ROM. Leicester: Scholarly Digital, 2003.

Freire, Paulo. *Education for Critical Consciousness.* 1st American ed. New York: Seabury, 1973.

Frye, Northrop. *The Secular Scripture: A Study of the Structure of Romance*. Cambridge: Harvard UP, 1976.

*The Full Bayeux Tapestry*. Ed. Glen Ray Crack. 10 Jan. 1998. 21 March 2006 <http://hastings1066.com/bayeux1.shtml>.

Gabrieli, Francesco. *Arab Historians of the Crusades*. Berkeley: U of California P, 1984.

Ganshof, François Louis. *Feudalism*. Trans. Philip Grierson. 2nd English ed. New York: Harper, 1961. Trans. of *Qu'est-ce que la féodalité?* Bruxelles: Office de Publicité, 1944.

Garmonsway, G. N., trans. *The Anglo-Saxon Chronicle*. London: Dent, 1953.

Gaunt, Simon. *Gender and Genre in Medieval French Literature*. Cambridge: Cambridge UP, 1995.

———. *Retelling the Tale: An Introduction to Medieval French Literature*. London: Duckworth, 2001.

Gautier, Léon, ed. *La chanson de Roland*. 2 vols. Tours: Mame, 1872.

———, ed. *La chanson de Roland*. Tours: Mame, 1880.

———, ed. La chanson de Roland. *Édition classique à l'usage des élèves de seconde*. Tours: Mame, 1887.

———. *Les épopées françaises: Étude sur les origines et l'histoire de la littérature nationale*. 1865–68. 2nd ed. 4 vols. Paris: Welter, 1892.

Gayangos, Pascual de, ed. *Libros de caballerías*. BAE Vol. 40. Madrid: Rivadeneyra, 1857.

Genette, Gérard. "Structuralism and Literary Criticism." *Figures of Literary Discourse*. Trans. Alan Sheridan. New York: Columbia UP, 1982. 3–25.

Génin, François, ed. La chanson de Roland: *Poème de Théroulde*. Paris: Imprimerie Nationale, 1850.

Gicquel, Bernard. *Généalogie de la* Chanson de Roland *suivi de sources et modèles*. Paris: Publibook, 2003.

———. *La légende de Compostelle: Le livre de Saint Jacques*. Paris: Tallandier, 2003.

Girard, René. *Violence and the Sacred*. Trans. Patrick Gregory. Baltimore: Johns Hopkins UP, 1977.

Giroux, Henry A. *Border Crossings: Cultural Workers and the Politics of Education*. New York: Routledge, 1992.

———. "Living Dangerously: Identity Politics and the New Cultural Racism." *Between Borders: Pedagogy and the Politics of Cultural Studies*. Ed. Henry A. Giroux and Peter McLaren Giroux. New York: Routledge, 1994. 29–73.

Gitton, Bernard. "De l'emploi des chansons de geste pour entraîner les guerriers au combat." *La chanson de geste et le mythe carolingien: Mélanges René Louis*. Vol. 1. Saint-Père-sous-Vézelay, Fr.: Musée Archéologique Régional, 1982. 3–19.

Glanville, Ranulf de. *De legibus et consuetudinibus regni Angliæ*. Ed. George E[dward] Woodbine. New Haven: Yale UP, 1932.

Godefroy, Frédéric Eugène. *Dictionnaire de l'ancienne langue française et de tous ses dialectes du IX^e au XV^e siècle*. 1880–1902. 10 vols. Paris: Librairie des Sciences et des Arts, 1938.

Goldberg, David Theo. *Racist Culture: Philosophy and the Politics of Meaning*. Oxford: Blackwell, 1993.

Goldin, Frederick, trans. *The Song of Roland*. New York: Norton, 1978.

———. "Time and Performance in *The Song of Roland*." *CUNY English Forum* 1. Ed. Saul N. Brody and Harold Schechter. Introd. Allen Mandelbaum. New York: AMS, 1985. 129–53.

Gómez Redondo, Fernando, ed. "Roncesvalles." *Poesía española 1, edad media: juglaría, clerecía y romancero*. Barcelona: Crítica, 1996. 139–45.

Gouiran, Gérard, and Robert Lafont, ed. and trans. "Roncasvals." *Le Roland occitan*. Paris: C. Bourgois, 1991. 131–249.

*Grandes Chroniques de France*. Miniature. Bibliothèque nationale de France, fonds français 2813. Paris, France. <http://www.mtholyoke.edu/~mswitten/roland/>.

Gregory, Stewart, ed. and trans. *The Romance of Tristan*. Amsterdam: Rodopi, 1992.

Grigsby, John L. "Gab épique, mais gab lyrique?" *Marche Romane* 23 (1983): 109–22.

Grisward, Joël H. *Archéologie de l'épopée médiévale: Structures trifonctionnelles et mythes indo-européens dans le cycle des Narbonnais*. Paris: Payot, 1981.

Grocheo, Johannes de. *Concerning Music*. Trans. Albert Seay. Colorado Springs: Colorado Coll. Music P, 1967.

Groseclose, Barbara S. "Washington Crossing the Delaware: The Political Context." *American Art Journal* 7.2 (1975): 70–78.

Guiette, Robert. "Les deux scènes du cor dans la *Chanson de Roland* et dans *Les conquestes de Charlemagne*." *Moyen âge* 69 (1963): 845–55.

Guizot, François, ed. and trans. *La philippide*. Collection des mémoires relatifs à l'histoire de France 12. Paris: Brière, 1825.

Hackett, W. Mary. "Le gant de Roland." *Romania* 89 (1968): 253–56.

Haddawy, Husain, trans. *The Arabian Nights*. New York: Norton, 1990.

Hahn, Thomas. "The Difference the Middle Ages Makes: Color and Race before the Modern World." *Race and Ethnicity in the Middle Ages*. Ed. Thomas Hahn. Spec. issue of *Journal of Medieval and Early Modern Studies* 31.1 (2001): 1–37.

Haidu, Peter. *The Subject: Medieval/Modern: Text and Governance in the Middle Ages*. Figurae: Reading Medieval Culture. Stanford: Stanford UP, 2004.

———. *The Subject of Violence: The Song of Roland and the Birth of the State*. Bloomington: Indiana UP, 1993.

Hall, Robert A., Jr. " 'A Roland for an Oliver': Their Quarrel Again (*La chanson de Roland*, Laisses 130–31)." *Olifant* 20 (1995–96): 109–44.

Halsall, Paul, ed. and comp. *The Internet Medieval Sourcebook*. 25 Apr. 2005 <http://www.fordham.edu/halsall>.

Halverson, John. "Ganelon's Trial." *Speculum* 42 (1967): 661–69.

Handel, George Frideric. *Orlando*. Dir. Christopher Hogwood. Perf. Academy of Ancient Music. Decca-Oiseau-Lyre, 1991.

———. *Orlando*. Cond. William Christie. Perf. Les Arts Florissants. Erato, 1996.

Harington, John, trans. *Orlando Furioso*. 1591. By Ludovico Ariosto. Oxford: Clarendon, 1972.

Harrison, Robert, trans. *The Song of Roland*. New York: Mentor, 1970.

Harty, Kevin. J. *The Reel Middle Ages: American, Western and Eastern European, Middle Eastern, and Asian Films about Medieval Europe*. Jefferson: McFarland, 1999.

*The Harvard Dictionary of Music*. Ed. Don Michael Randel. 4th ed. Cambridge: Harvard UP, 2003.

Heath, Peter. *The Thirsty Sword: Sirat ʿAntar and the Arabic Popular Epic*. Salt Lake City: U of Utah P, 1996.

Heinemann, Edward A. *L'art métrique de la chanson de geste: Essai sur la musicalité du récit*. Publications romanes et françaises 205. Geneva: Droz, 1993.

Henderson, E. F. *Select Historical Documents of the Middle Ages*. 1896. New York: AMS, 1968.

Henneman, John B. "Feudalism." Kibler and Zinn, 1995.

Herrtage, Sidney J., ed. *The English Charlemagne Romances II:* The Sege off Melayne; *and* The Romance of Duke Rowland and Sir Otuel of Spayne. New York: Kraus, 1973. Rpt. of The Sege off Melayne; *and* The Romance of Duke Rowland and Sir Otuel of Spayne. *Now for the First Time Printed from the Unique Ms. of R. Thornton, in the British Museum, Ms. Addit. 31,042, Together with a Fragment of the* Song of Roland *from the Unique Ms. Lansd. 388.* Early English Text Soc., Extra Series, 35. London: Trübner, 1880.

Hieatt, Constance B., trans. *Karlamagnús Saga: The Saga of Charlemagne and His Heroes*. 3 vols. Medieval Sources in Translation 13, 17, 25. Toronto: Pontifical Inst. of Medieval Studies, 1975–80.

Hindley, Alan, Frederick B. Langley, and Brian J. Levy. *Old French–English Dictionary*. Cambridge: Cambridge UP, 2000.

Hindley, [Alan], and B. J. Levy. "Videotaping *Roland*." *Olifant* 11 (1986): 143–60.

Hjort, Poul Lindegård, ed. *Karl Magnus' Krønike*. Universitetsjubilæets Danske Samfund Skriftserie 398. Copenhagen: Schulz, 1960.

Holden, J., ed. *Roman de Rou*. By Wace 3 vols. Paris: SATF, 1970–73.

Holmes, Urban T., Jr. *A History of Old French Literature: From the Origins to 1300*. New York: Russell, 1962.

Holsinger, Bruce W. "The Color of Salvation: Desire, Death, and the Second Crusade in Bernard of Clairvaux's *Sermons on the Song of Songs*." *The Tongue of the Father: Gender and Ideology in Twelfth-Century Latin*. Ed. David Townsend and Andrew Taylor. Philadelphia: U of Pennsylvania P, 1998. 156–86.

———. "Medieval Studies, Postcolonial Studies, and the Genealogies of Critique." *Speculum* 77 (2002): 1195–227.

Holtus, Günter. *Lexikalische Untersuchungen zur Interferenz: Die franko-italienische Entrée d'Espagne*. Tübingen: Niemeyer, 1979.

Hoppin, Richard H. *Medieval Music*. New York: Norton, 1978. Trans. as *La musique au moyen âge*. Trans. Nicolas Meeus and Malou Haine. Liège: Mardaga, 1991.

Horrent, Jules. *La chanson de Roland dans les littératures française et espagnole au moyen âge*. Bibliothèque de la Faculté de Philosophie et Lettres de l'Université de Liège 120. Paris: Belles Lettres, 1951.

Howard, Kathleen, ed. *The Metropolitan Museum of Art Guide*. 2nd ed. New York: Metropolitan Museum, 1994.

Huot, Sylvia. "Voices and Instruments in Medieval French Secular Music: On the Use of Literary Texts as Evidence for Performance Practice." *Musica Disciplina* 43 (1989): 63–113.

Ingham, Patricia Clare, and Michelle R. Warren. *Postcolonial Moves: Medieval through Modern*. New York: Palgrave, 2003.

Irwin, Robert. *The Arabian Nights: A Companion*. London: Penguin, 1994.

Jakobson, Roman. "Linguistics and Poetics." *Style in Language*. Ed. T. Sebeok. Cambridge: MIT, 1960. 350–77. Rpt. in Lodge and Wood 31–55.

Jauss, Hans-Robert. "The Alterity and Modernity of Medieval Literature." *New Literary History* 10 (1978–79): 181–227.

Jenkins, T. Atkinson, ed. *La chanson de Roland*. Boston: Heath, 1924.

———, ed. *La chanson de Roland*. Rev. ed. 1929. Bibliog. Supp. Gerard J. Brault. Watkins Glen: American Life Foundation, 1977.

*Jerusalem: Vision of Peace*. Perf. Gothic Voices. Dir. Christopher Page. Hyperion, 1998. Hyperion CDA67039.

Jones, George Fenwick. *The Ethos of the* Song of Roland. Baltimore: Johns Hopkins UP, 1963.

Jonin, Pierre, ed. and trans. La chanson de Roland, *édition bilingue*. Folio classique 1150. Paris: Gallimard, 1979.

———. "Deux langages de héros épiques au cours d'une bataille suicidaire." *Olifant* 9 (1982): 83–98.

Jordan, Constance. *Pulci's* Morgante: *Poetry and History in Fifteenth-Century Florence*. London: Associated UP, 1986.

Jordan, William Chester. "Why 'Race'?" *Journal of Medieval and Early Modern Studies*. 31.1 (2001): 165–73.

Kartschoke, Dieter, ed. and trans. Das Rolandslied *des Pfaffen Konrad. Mittelhochdeutscher Text und Übertragung*. Afterword by Dieter Kartschoke. Frankfurt-am-Main, Ger.: Fischer Bücherei, 1970.

Kay, Sarah. *The Chanson de Geste in the Age of Romance: Political Fictions*. Oxford: Clarendon, 1995.

———. "The Character of Character in the *Chansons de Geste*." *The Craft of Fiction: Essays in Medieval Poetics*. Ed. Leigh A. Arrathoon. Rochester: Solaris, 1984.

———, ed. and trans. *Raoul de Cambrai*. Oxford: Clarendon, 1992.

———. "La représentation de la féminité dans les chansons de geste." Bennett, Cobby, and Runnals 223–40.

Kay, Sarah, ed., and William W. Kibler, trans. Raoul de Cambrai: *Chanson de geste du XIIᵉ siècle*. Lettres gothiques. Paris: Livre de Poche, 1996.

Keen, Maurice Hugh. *Chivalry*. New Haven: Yale UP, 1984.

Ker, W. P. *From Epic to Romance*. 1896. New York: Dover, 1957.

Kerman, Joseph. *Listen*. With Vivian Kerman. 3rd ed. New York: Worth, 1980.

Kibler, William W., trans. *Arthurian Romances*. By Chrétien de Troyes. Harmondsworth: Penguin, 1991.

———. "Roland's Pride." *Symposium* 26 (1972): 147–60.

Kibler, William W., and François Suard, eds. and trans. *Huon de Bordeaux*. Champion classiques 7. Paris: Champion, 2003.

Kibler, William W., and Grover A. Zinn, eds. *Medieval France: An Encyclopedia*. New York: Garland, 1995.

Kinoshita, Sharon. *Medieval Boundaries: Rethinking Difference in Old French Literature*. Philadelphia: U of Pennsylvania P, 2006.

———. " 'Pagans Are Wrong and Christians Are Right': Alterity, Gender, and Nation in the *Chanson de Roland*." *Race and Ethnicity in the Middle Ages*. Ed. Thomas Hahn. Spec. issue of *Journal of Medieval and Early Modern Studies* 31.1 (2001): 79–111.

———. "The Romance of MiscegeNation: Negotiating Identities in *La Fille du Comte de Pontieu*." Ingham and Warren. 111–31.

Kornhall, David, ed. *Karl Magnus enligt Codex Verelianus och Fru Elins bok*. Samlingar-Svenska Fornskriftsällskapet Häft 219. Vol. 63. Lund, Swed.: Bloms, 1957.

Krueger, Roberta L. *Women Readers and the Ideology of Gender in Old French Verse Romance*. Cambridge: Cambridge UP, 1993.

Kübler-Ross, Elisabeth. *On Death and Dying*. New York: Macmillan; 1969.

Labande-Mailfert, V. Rev. of *La légende de Roland dans l'art du moyen âge*, by Rita Lejeune and Jacques Stiennon. *Cahiers de Civilisation Médiévale* 9 (1966): 417–21.

Laborde, Comte Alexandre de, ed. La chanson de Roland: *Reproduction phototypique du manuscript Digby 23 de la Bodeleian Library d'Oxford*. Paris: Société des Anciens Textes Français, 1933.

Lacarra, José María. *Alfonso el Batallador*. Saragossa: Guara, 1978.

La Rue, Gervais de. *Essais historiques sur les bardes, les jongleurs et les trouvères normands et anglo-normands*. 3 vols. Caen: Mancel, 1834.

Lecoy, Félix, ed. *Le roman de la rose ou de Guillaume de Dole*. By Jean Renart. Paris: Champion, 1979.

Le Gentil, Pierre. *La chanson de Roland*. Connaissance des lettres 43. Paris: Hatier, 1955.

———. *La Chanson de Roland*. Trans. Frances F. Beer. Cambridge: Harvard UP, 1969.

———. "À propos de la démesure de Roland." *Cahiers de civilisation médiévale* 11 (1968): 203–09.

Le Goff, Jacques. *Un autre moyen âge*. Paris: Gallimard, 1999.

———. *Medieval Civilization, 400–1500*. Trans. Julia Barrow. Oxford: Blackwell, 1988.

———. *The Medieval Imagination*. Trans. Arthur Goldhammer. Chicago: U of Chicago P, 1988.

Lejeune, Rita, and Jacques Stiennon. "Le Héros Roland, 'Neveu de Charlemagne,' dans l'iconographie médiévale." *Karl der Grosse: Lebenswerk und Nachleben.* Ed. Wolfgang Braunfels. Vol. 4. Düsseldorf, Ger.: Schwann, 1967. 215–28.

———. *The Legend of Roland in the Middle Ages.* Trans. Christine Trollope. New York: Phaidon, 1971.

———. *La légende de Roland dans l'art du moyen âge.* Brussels: Arcade, 1967.

Le Person, Marc, ed. Fierabras, *chanson de geste du XII^e siècle.* Paris: Champion, 2003.

Le Roy Ladurie, Emmanuel. *Montaillou: The Promised Land of Error.* Trans. Barbara Bray. New York: Braziller, 1978.

Lévi-Strauss, Claude. *The Elementary Structures of Kinship.* Trans. James Harle Bell and John Richard von Sturmer. Ed. Rodney Needham. Rev. ed. Boston: Beacon, 1969.

Lewis, Charlton T., and Charles Short. *Latin Dictionary.* Oxford: Clarendon, 1900.

*Liber usualis missae et officii pro dominicis et festis I. vel II. classis.* Tournai: Desclee, 1930.

Lodge, David, and Nigel Wood, eds. *Modern Criticism and Theory: A Reader.* 2nd ed. Harlow, Eng.: Longman, 2000.

Loomba, Ania. *Colonialism/Postcolonialism.* The New Critical Idiom. London: Routledge, 1998.

López Guil, Itzíar, ed. *Poema de Fernán González.* Madrid: CSIC, 2001.

Lord, Albert B. *The Singer of Tales.* Cambridge: Harvard UP, 1960.

*Lord of the Rings: The Return of the King.* Dir. Peter Jackson. Wingnut Films, 2003.

Lot, Ferdinand. *L'art militaire et les armées au moyen âge en Europe et dans le Proche Orient.* 2 vols. Paris: Payot, 1946.

Loyn, H. R., and J. Percival. *The Reign of Charlemagne: Documents on Carolingian Government and Administration.* New York: St. Martin's, 1976.

Luquiens, Frederick Bliss. "The Reconstruction of the Original *Chanson de Roland.*" *Transactions of the Connecticut Academy of the Arts and Sciences* 15 (1909): 111–36.

Lyons, Faith. "More about Roland's Glove." *Proceedings of the Fifth Conference of the Société Rencesvals (Oxford, 1970).* Ed. G. R. Mellor. Salford: U of Salford, 1977. 156–66.

Maalouf, Amin. "Un passé qui ne passe pas." 25 Dec. 2005 <http://classes.bnf.fr/idrisi/pedago/croisades/maalouf.htm>.

MacQueen, John. *Numerology: Theory and Outline History of a Literary Mode.* Edinburgh: Edinburgh UP, 1985.

Maines, Clark. "The Charlemagne Window at Chartres Cathedral: New Considerations on Text and Image." *Speculum* 52 (1977): 801–23.

Martin, Jean-Pierre. *Les motifs dans la chanson de geste: Définition et utilisation.* Lille: U de Lille III, 1992.

Martin, Jean-Pierre, and Marielle Lignereux. *La chanson de Roland.* Clefs Concours, Lettres Médiévales. Neuilly: Atlande, 2003.

Mathieu-Castellani, Gisèle, ed. *Plaisir de l'épopée.* Saint-Denis: PU de Vincennes, 2000.

McMillan, Duncan, ed. *Le charroi de Nîmes*. Paris: Klincksieck, 1972.

*The Medieval Lyric: A Project Supported by the National Endowment for the Humanities and Mount Holyoke College*. Margaret Switten, project dir. 1988. 4 anthologies and 5 CDs. South Hadley: Mount Holyoke Coll., 2001.

*Medieval Pilgrimage to Santiago: Auf Jakobs Wegen*. Perf. Ensemble für Frühe Musik Augsburg. CHR, 2003. CHR 77264.

*Medieval Romance Poetry: A Survey of Medieval Romance Literature*. Read by Mario Pei. 2 LPs. Folkways, 1962.

Melczer, William. *The Pilgrim's Guide to Santiago de Compostela*. New York: Italica, 1993.

Menéndez-Pidal, Ramón. *La chanson de Roland et la tradition épique des Francs*. Ed. René Louis. Trans. Irénée-Marcel Cluzel. 2nd rev. ed. Paris: Picard, 1960. Trans. of *La chanson de Roland y el neotradicionalismo (origines de la epica romanica)*. Madrid: Espasa-Calpe, 1959.

———, ed. *Estoria de España: Primera crónica general*. 3rd ed. 2 vols. Madrid: Seminario Menéndez Pidal-Gredos, 1977.

———, ed. *Roncesvalles, un nuevo cantar de gesta español del siglo XIII*. Madrid: n.p., 1917.

Menéndez y Pelayo, Marcelino. *Orígenes de la novela*. NBAE 1. Madrid: Bailly-Baillière, 1905.

Menocal, María Rosa. "Signs of the Times: Self, Other, and History in *Aucassin et Nicolette*." *Romanic Review* 80 (1989): 497–511.

Meredith-Jones, C. *Historia Karoli Magni et Rothalandi ou Chronique du Pseudo-Turpin*. Geneva: Droz, 1936.

Merwin, W. S., trans. *The Song of Roland*. New York: Vintage, 1970.

Michel, Francisque, ed. *La chanson de Roland ou De Roncevaux, du XIIᵉ siècle*. Paris: Silvestre, 1837.

Mickel, Emanuel J., Jr. *Ganelon, Treason, and the* Chanson de Roland. University Park: Pennsylvania State UP, 1989.

———. "*Judicium Dei* and the Structure of the *Chanson de Roland*." *Studies in Honor of Hans-Erich Keller*. Ed. Rupert Pickens. Kalamazoo: Inst. for Medieval Studies, 1993. 28–49.

———. "Parallels in Prudentius' *Psychomachia* and *La Chanson de Roland*." *Studies in Philology* 67 (1970): 439–52.

———. "The Thirty *Pleges* for Ganelon." *Olifant* 6 (1979): 293–304.

Milá y Fontanals, Manuel. *De la poesía heróico-popular castellana*. Barcelona: Verdaguer, 1874.

Misrahi, Jean, and William Hendrickson. "Roland and Oliver: Prowess and Wisdom, the Ideal of the Epic Hero." *Romance Philology* 33 (1979–80): 357–72.

Moignet, Gérard, ed. *La chanson de Roland. Texte original et traduction*. Paris: Bordas, 1969.

———. *La chanson de Roland. Extraits*. Classiques Bordas. Paris: Bordas, 1998.

Moisan, André. *Le Livre de Saint Jacques ou Codex Calixtinus de Compostelle: Étude critique et littéraire*. Geneva: Slatkine, 1992.

Molíns, María Jesús Viguera. "A Borrowed Space: Andalusi and Maghribi Women in Chronicles." *Writing the Feminine: Women in Arab Sources.* Ed. Manuela Marín and Randi Deguilhem. London: Tauris, 2002. 165–82.

Morgan, Leslie Zarker, trans. "The Franco-Italian 'Berta and Milone' (Ms. Marc XIII)." With notes. *The ORB: On-line Reference Book for Medieval Studies.* 8 Apr. 1996. 18 May 2006 <http://www.the-orb.net/encyclop/culture/lit/italian/morgan4.html>.

———, trans. "The Franco-Italian 'Childhood of Roland' (Ms. Marc XIII)." With notes. *The ORB: On-line Reference Book for Medieval Studies.* 8 Apr. 1996. 18 May 2006 <http://www.the-orb.net/encyclop/culture/lit/italian/morgan1.html>.

———, trans. "Italian Literature: Geste Francor." With bibliog. and notes. *The ORB: On-line Reference Book for Medieval Studies.* 18 Aug. 2002. 18 May 2006 <http://www.the-orb.net/encyclop/culture/lit/italian/morganintro.html#anchor158979>.

Morrissey, Robert. *Charlemagne and France: A Thousand Years of Mythology.* Trans. Catherine Tihanyi. Notre Dame: U of Notre Dame P, 2003.

Mortier, Raoul, ed. *Les textes de la* Chanson de Roland. 10 vols. Paris: Éditions de la Geste Francor, 1940–44.

Müller, Theodor. La chanson de Roland; *nach der Oxforder handschrift.* Göttingen: Dietrich, 1863.

Murray, Alexander. *Germanic Kinship Structure: Studies in Law and Society in Antiquity and the Early Middle Ages.* Toronto: Pontifical Inst. of Mediaeval Studies, 1983.

Musset, Lucien. *La tapisserie de Bayeux.* Paris: Éditions Zodiaque, 2002.

*The New Grove Dictionary of Music and Musicians.* Ed. Stanley Sadie. 2nd ed. Oxford: Oxford UP, 2001.

Newth, Michael A., trans. *The Song of Aspremont.* New York: Garland, 1989.

———, trans. *Heroes of the French Epic: A Selection of Chansons de Geste.* Woodbridge: Boydell, 2005.

Nichols, Stephen G. *Formulaic Diction and Thematic Composition in the* Song of Roland. Chapel Hill: U of North Carolina P, 1961.

———. *Romanesque Signs: Early Medieval Narrative and Iconography.* New Haven: Yale UP, 1983.

Niles, John D., ed. *Beowulf.* Cambridge: Harvard UP, 1983.

Norris, H. T., trans. *The Adventures of Antar.* Warminster, Eng.: Aris, 1980.

———. "Arabian Folk Epic and Western *Chanson de Geste.*" *Oral Tradition.* 4.1–2 (1989): 125–50.

*Norton Anthology of World Masterpieces: The Western Tradition: Literature of Western Culture through the Renaissance.* Ed. Sarah N. Lawall and Maynard Mack. 7th ed. New York: Norton, 1999.

Nottarp, Hermann. *Gottesurteilstudien.* Munich: Kösel, 1956.

*Nova Cantica: Latin Songs of the High Middle Ages.* Perf. Dominique Vellard and Emmanuel Bonnardot. DHM, 1990. DHM 77196-2-RC.

O'Callaghan, Joseph F. *A History of Medieval Spain.* Ithaca: Cornell UP, 1975.

O'Hagan, John, trans. *The Song of Roland*. 1880. 1st Amer. ed. Boston: Lee, [c. 1887].

Oman, Charles. *A History of the Art of War in the Middle Ages*. 2nd ed. 2 vols. Burt Franklin Research and Source Works Series 360: Selected Essays in History, Economics, and Social Science 81. New York: Franklin, 1924.

Ong, Walter. *Orality and Literacy: The Technologizing of the Word*. New York: Methuen, 1982.

Owen, D. D. R, trans. *The Song of Roland*. Woodbridge, Eng.: Boydell, 1990.

*The Oxford Companion to Music*. Ed. Alison Latham. Oxford: Oxford UP, 2002.

Pächt, Otto, C. R. Dodwell, and Francis Wormald. *The Saint Albans Psalter*. Studies of the Warburg Inst. 35. London: Warburg Inst., 1960.

Paden, William D., and Patricia Harris Stäblein, eds. "*De tradicione Guenonis*: An Edition with Translation." *Traditio* 44 (1988): 201–51.

Page, Christopher. *The Owl and the Nightingale: Musical Life and Ideas in France, 1100–1300*. Berkeley: U of California P, 1989.

———. *Voices and Instruments in the Middle Ages: Instrumental Practice and Songs in France, 1100–1300*. Berkeley: U of California P, 1986.

Palisca, Claude V., ed. *Norton Anthology of Western Music*. Vol. 1. New York: Norton, 2001.

Paquette, Jean-Marcel. "Le texte en métamorphose: Contribution à une poétique des laisses similaires d'après six versions de la 'scène du cor' de la *Chanson de Roland*." *Mélanges de langue et littérature françaises du moyen âge offerts à Pierre Jonin*. Sénéfiance 7. Aix-en-Provence: CUERMA, 1979. 503–14.

Paris, Gaston. "Le *Carmen de prodicione Guenonis et la légende de Roncevaux*." *Romania* 11 (1882): 465–518.

———. "La *Chanson de Roland* et la nationalité française." Leçon d'ouverture faite au Collège de France, 8 décembre 1870. *La poésie du moyen âge, leçons et lectures*. Vol. 1. Paris: Hachette, 1885. 87–118. 2 vols.

———. *Extraits de la* Chanson de Roland. 1887. Paris: Hachette, 1919.

———. *Histoire poétique de Charlemagne*. Paris: Franck, 1865.

———. *Histoire poétique de Charlemagne*. 1905. Geneva: Slatkine, 1974.

———. *La littérature française au moyen âge*. 1888. 7th ed. Paris: Hachette, 1920.

———. *La poésie du moyen âge: Leçons et lectures*. 4th ed. Paris: Hachette, 1899.

Parisse, Michel. *La tapisserie de Bayeux: Un documentaire du XI$^e$ siècle*. Paris: Denoël, 1983.

Parry, Milman. *L'épithète traditionnelle dans Homère: Essai sur un problème de style homérique*. Paris: Belles Lettres, 1928.

———. *The Making of Homeric Verse: The Collected Papers of Milman Parry*. Ed. A. Perry. Oxford: Clarendon, 1971.

———, ed. *Serbo-Croatian Heroic Songs, Collected by Milman Parry*. Cambridge: Harvard UP, 1954.

Peckham, Robert. *Medieval French Heroic Literature*. The Globe-Gate Project. 6 Feb. 2006 <http://www.utm.edu/~globeg/heroic.shtml>.

Pernoud, Régine. *Heloise and Abelard*. Trans. Peter Wiles. London: Collins, 1973.

Picherit, Jean-Louis, trans. *The Journey of Charlemagne to Jerusalem and Constantinople*. Birmingham: Summa, 1984.

Picot, Guillaume. *La chanson de Roland*. 2 vols. Nouveaux classiques Larousse. Paris: Larousse, 1965.

*The Pilgrimage to Santiago*. Perf. New London Consort. Dir. Philip Pickett. 2 CDs. L'Oiseau-Lyre, 1991. L'Oiseau-Lyre 433 148-2.

Pope, Mildred K. *From Latin to Modern French with Especial Consideration of Anglo-Norman*. 1934. 2nd ed. Manchester: Manchester UP, 1952.

Price, Glanville, ed. Trans. Price, Lynnette Muir, and David Hogan. *William, Count of Orange: Four Old French Epics*. London: Dent, 1975.

Pulci, Luigi. *Il Morgante*. Ed. F. Ageno. Milan: Ricciardi, 1955.

Puymaigre, Théodore de. *Les vieux auteurs castillans*. 2 vols. Paris: Didier, 1861.

Radice, Betty, trans. *The Letters of Abelard and Heloise*. Harmondsworth: Penguin, 1974.

Ramey, Lynn Tarte. "Role Models? Saracen Women in Medieval French Epic." *Romance Notes* 41 (2001): 131–42.

Redman, Harry, Jr. *The Roland Legend in Nineteenth-Century French Literature*. Lexington: UP of Kentucky, 1991.

Régnier, Claude, ed. *Les rédactions en vers de la* Prise d'Orange. Paris: Klincksieck, 1966.

Reisinger, Deborah Streifford. "The Other and the Same: The Ambiguous Role of the Saracen in *La Chanson de Roland*." *RLA* 9 (1997): 94–97.

Rejhon, Annalee C., ed. and trans. Cân Rolant: *The Medieval Welsh Version of the Song of Roland*. Univ. of California Studies in Mod. Philology 113. Berkeley: U of California P, 1983.

Reynolds, Barbara, trans. Introduction. *Orlando Furioso*. By Ludovico Ariosto. 2 vols. Harmondsworth: Penguin, 1977. 11–113.

Reynolds, Susan. *Fiefs and Vassals: The Medieval Evidence Reinterpreted*. New York: Oxford UP, 1996.

Ridoux, Charles. *Évolution des études médiévales en France de 1860 à 1914*. Paris: Champion, 2001.

Rigg, A. G. *The Making of a Manuscript*. Dir. and prod. Bob Rodgers. Videocassette. Media Centre, U of Toronto, 1974.

Riquer, Martín de. *Les chansons de geste françaises*. Trans. Irenée Cluzel. 2nd ed. Paris: Nizet, 1957.

———. "Épopée jongleresque à écouter, épopée romanesque à lire." *Technique* 75–84.

Roach, Greg. *The Madness of Roland: An Interactive Novel*. CD-ROM. Hyperbole Studios, 1992.

Roche-Mahdi, Sarah, ed. and trans. Le roman de silence: *A Thirteenth-Century French Romance*. East Lansing: Colleagues, 1992.

Roncaglia, Aurelio, ed. *La chanson de Roland*. Modena: Istituto di Filologia Romanza dell'Università di Roma, 1947.

*Roncevaux: "Echos d'une bataille."* Perf. Lachrimae Consort, La Trulla de Bozes. Dir. Philippe Foulon. Narr. Alain Paris. Harmonia Mundi, 1998.

Roques, Mario, ed. Aucassin et Nicolette, *chantefable du XIII^e siecle*. 2nd ed. Paris: Champion, 1967.

Rosenberg, Bruce A. *Custer and the Epic of Defeat*. University Park: Pennsylvania State UP, 1974.

Ross, Charles S., trans. *Orlando Innamorato*. By Matteo Maria Boiardo. Oxford: Oxford UP, 1995.

Rubin, Gayle. "The Traffic in Women: Notes on the 'Political Economy' of Sex." *Toward an Anthropology of Women*. Ed. Rayna R. Reiter. New York: Monthly Review, 1975. 157–210.

Ruggieri, Ruggero M. *Il processo di Gano nella* Chanson de Roland. Florence: Sansoni, 1936.

Runciman, Steven. *A History of the Crusades*. 3 vols. Cambridge: Cambridge UP, 1951.

Rychner, Jean. *La chanson de geste: Essai sur l'art épique des jongleurs*. Société de publications romanes et françaises 53. Geneva: Droz, 1955.

———. "Observations sur la versification du *Couronnement de Louis*." *Technique* 161–78.

Said, Edward W. *Orientalism*. New York: Random, 1978.

Samaran, Charles, ed. La chanson de Roland: *Reproduction phototypique du manuscrit Digby 23 de la Bodleian Library d'Oxford. Éditée avec un avant-propos par le Comte Alexandre de Laborde*. Paris: Présentée aux membres du Roxburghe Club de Londres, 1932.

———, ed. *La chanson de Roland*. Paris: Société des anciens textes français, 1933.

Saussure, Ferdinand de. "The Object of Study." *Course in General Linguistics*. Trans. Roy Harris. Peru: Duckworth, 1983. 8–17. Rpt. in Lodge and Wood 2–9.

Sayers, Dorothy L., trans. *The Song of Roland*. Harmondsworth: Penguin, 1957.

Sayers, W. "The Jongleur Taillefer at Hastings: Antecedents and Literary Fate." *Viator* 14 (1983): 77–88.

Schmitt, Jean-Claude. *La raison des gestes dans l'occident médiéval*. Paris: Gallimard, 1990.

Scholes, Robert E. *Textual Power: Literary Theory and the Teaching of English*. New Haven: Yale UP, 1985.

Scholz, Bernhard W. *Carolingian Chronicles: Royal Frankish Annals and Nithard's Histories*. Ann Arbor: U of Michigan P, 1970.

Schwartz, Regina M. *The Curse of Cain: The Violent Legacy of Monotheism*. Chicago: U of Chicago P, 1997.

Schweickart, Patrocinio P. "Reading Ourselves: Toward a Feminist Theory of Reading." *Gender and Reading: Essays on Readers, Texts, and Contexts*. Ed. Elizabeth A. Flynn and Schweickart. Baltimore: Johns Hopkins UP, 1986. 31–62.

Scott, Virginia. "An Applied Linguist in the Literature Classroom." *French Review* 74 (2001): 538–49.

Scott-Moncrieff, Charles K., trans. *The Song of Roland*. London: Chapman, 1919.

Segre, Cesare, ed. *La chanson de Roland*. Edizione critica. Documenti di filologia 16. Milan: Ricciardi, 1971.

———, ed. *La chanson de Roland*. Trans. Madeleine Tyssens. Nouvelle édition revue. Textes littéraires français 368. 2 vols. Geneva: Droz, 1989.

————. ed. *La Chanson de Roland*. Trans. Madeleine Tyssens. Texts littéraires français 968. Geneva: Droz, 2003.

————. "Corrections mentales pour *La chanson de Roland*." *Travaux de linguistique et de littérature* 8 (1970): 277–85.

Seidel, Linda. *Songs of Glory: The Romanesque Façades of Aquitaine*. Chicago: U of Chicago P, 1981.

Setton, Kenneth M., ed. *A History of the Crusades*. 6 vols. Madison: U of Wisconsin P, 1989.

Shailor, Barbara A. *The Medieval Book*. With Illus. Medieval Academy Reprints for Teaching 28. Toronto: U of Toronto P, 1998.

Shakespeare, William. *Hamlet*. New York: Signet, 1987.

Shaver-Crandell, Anne. *The Middle Ages*. Cambridge Introduction to the History of Art. Cambridge: Cambridge UP, 1982.

Shaver-Crandell, Annie, and Paula Gerson. With the assistance of Alison Stones. *The Pilgrim's Guide to Santiago de Compostela: A Gazetteer*. London: Miller, 1995.

Shirley, Janet, trans. *Daurel and Beton*. Felinfach: Llanerch, 1997.

Short, Ian, ed. and trans. *La chanson de Roland*. 2nd ed. Lettres gothiques. Paris: Livre de Poche, 1990.

————, trans. *La chanson de Roland*. Classiques médiévaux. Paris: Livre de Poche, 1997.

Siciliano, Italo. *Les chansons de geste et l'épopée: Mythes, histoire, poèmes*. Turin: Società editrice internazionale, 1968.

Sinclair, Keith Val, ed. Tristan de Nanteuil. *Chanson de geste inédite*. Assen, Neth.: Van Gorcum, 1971.

Smeyers, Maurits, et al. *The Medieval Manuscript: Art and Function*. Videocassette. Katholik Universitet Leuven; Centre for the Study of Illuminated Manuscripts in the Low Countries; Films for the Humanities, 1993.

Smyser, H[amilton] M[artin], ed. *Pseudo-Turpin: Edited from Bibliothèque Nationale, Fonds Latin, Ms. 17656, with an Annotated Synopsis*. Cambridge: Mediaeval Acad. of Amer., 1937.

*La Société Rencesvals, American Canadian Branch*. 25 May 2006 <http://www.noctrl .edu/academics/departments/modern_and_classical_languages/department_site/ SocieteRencesvalsWeb>.

Southern, R. W. *The Making of the Middle Ages*. London: Hutchinson, 1953.

*The Song of Roland*. Prod. Katheleen Kent Watson. 2 audiocassettes. Blackstone, 1998.

*The Song of Roland*. DVD, videocassette. Films Media Group, 2005.

Spiegel, Gabrielle M. *Romancing the Past: The Rise of Vernacular Prose Historiography in Thirteenth-Century France*. Berkeley: U of California P, 1993.

Stengel, Edmund, ed. *Das altfranzösische Rolandslied*. Leipzig: Weicher, 1900.

Stephenson, Carl. *Mediaeval Feudalism*. 1942. Ithaca: Cornell UP, 1991.

Stevens, John. "Reflections on the Music of Medieval Narrative Poetry." *The Oral Epic: Performance and Music*. Ed. Karl Reichl. Intercultural Music Studies 12. Berlin: VWB, 2000. 233–48.

————. *Words and Music in the Middle Ages: Song, Narrative, Dance and Drama, 1050–1350*. Cambridge: Cambridge UP, 1986.

Stevenson, Barbara. "Antar, an Islamic Counterpoint to Roland." *Studies in Medieval and Renaissance Teaching* 10 (2003): 43–52.

Stiennon, Jacques. *Paléographie du moyen âge*. 2nd ed. Paris: Colin, 1991.

Stock, Brian. *The Implications of Literacy: Written Language and Models of Interpretation in the Eleventh and Twelfth Centuries*. Princeton: Princeton UP, 1983.

————. *Listening for the Text: On the Uses of the Past*. Philadelphia: U of Pennsylvania P, 1996.

Stone, Oliver, dir. *Platoon*. 1986. Prod. Arnold Kopelson. DVD. MGM, 2001.

Strayer, Joseph R., ed. *Dictionary of the Middle Ages*. New York: Scribner, 1982–89.

————. *Feudalism*. New York: Van Nostrand, 1965.

Suard, François. *La chanson de geste*. Que sais-je? Paris: PUF, 1993.

————. *Chanson de geste et tradition épique en France au moyen âge*. Collection Varia 14. Caen: Paradigme, 1994.

Switten, Margaret. "*Chevalier* in Twelfth-Century French and Occitan Vernacular Literature." *The Study of Chivalry*. Ed. Howell Chickering and Thomas H. Seiler. Kalamazoo: Medieval Inst., 1988. 403–47.

Tacitus, Cornelius. Dialogus, Agricola, Germania. Ed. T. E. Page, E. Capps, L. A. Post, W. H. D. Rouse, and E. H. Warmington. Cambridge: Harvard UP, 1946.

*La tapisserie de Bayeux / The Bayeux Tapestry / Wandteppich von Bayeux*. Complete reproduction. N.p.: Édition Ville de Bayeux, 2005.

Taylor, Andrew. *Textual Situations: Three Medieval Manuscripts and Their Readers*. Philadelphia: U of Pennsylvania P, 2002.

————. "Was There a *Song of Roland*?" *Speculum* 76 (2001): 28–65.

*La technique littéraire des chansons de geste. Actes du Colloque de Liège (septembre 1957)*. Bibliothèque de la Faculté de Philosophie et Lettres de l'Université de Liège 150. Paris: Belles Lettres, 1959.

Terry, Patricia. "Roland at Roncevaux: A Vote for the Angels." *Olifant* 14 (1989): 155–64.

————, trans. *The Song of Roland*. 1965. 2nd ed. New York: Macmillan, 1992.

Thobie, Jacques, and Gilbert Meynier. *Histoire de la France coloniale: L'apogée*. Vol. 2. Paris: Colin, 1991.

Thomas, Jacques, ed. *Renaut de Montauban*. Geneva: Droz, 1989.

Thomas, J. W., ed. *Priest Konrad's Song of Roland*. Columbia: Camden, 1994.

Thorpe, Lewis, trans. *Two Lives of Charlemagne*. Harmondsworth: Penguin, 1969.

Tobler, Adolf, and Erhard Lommatzsch, eds. *Altfranzösisches Wörterbuch*. 11 vols. Berlin: Weidmannsche Buchhandlung, 1925–2002.

Todorov, Tzvetan. "The Typology of Detective Fiction." 1966. *Poetics of Prose*. Trans. Richard Howard. Ithaca: Cornell UP, 1977. 42–52. Rpt. in Lodge and Wood 137–44.

Togeby, Knud, and Pierre Halleux, eds. Karlamagnús Saga. Branches 1, 3, 7 et 9. Copenhagen: CA Reitzel, 1980.

Tolan, John V. Saracens: Islam in the Medieval European Imagination. New York: Columbia UP, 2002.

Treitler, Leo. "Saint Martial of Limoges." Medieval Lyric, anthology 1, 1–3.

Trinh T. Minh-Ha. Woman, Native, Other: Writing Postcoloniality and Feminism. Bloomington: Indiana UP, 1989.

Tusiani, Joseph, trans. Luigi Pulci: Il Morgante: The Epic Adventures of Orlando and His Giant Friend Morgante. Bloomington: Indiana UP, 1998.

Uitti, Karl D. Story, Myth, and Celebration in Old French Narrative Poetry, 1050–1200. Princeton: Princeton UP, 1973.

van Dijk, Hans, ed. Het Roelantslied. 2 vols. Utrecht: HES, 1981.

van Emden, Wolfgang. " 'La bataille est aduree endementres': Traditionalism and Individualism in Chanson-de-geste Studies." Nottingham Mediæval Studies 13 (1969): 3–26.

———. La chanson de Roland. Critical Guides to French Texts 113. London: Grant, 1995.

———. Girart de Vienne, par Bertrand de Bar-sur-Aube. Paris: Société des Anciens Textes Français, 1977.

———. "The Reception of Roland in Some Old French Epics." Roland and Charlemagne in Europe: Essays on the Reception and Transformation of a Legend. Ed. Karen Pratt. London: King's Coll. London, Centre for Late Antique and Medieval Studies, 1996. 1–30.

———. Was Roland? Perf. Gary Bond, Michael Laird. Prod. Judith Bumpus. BBC, Radio Three. 15 Aug. 1978.

Vance, Eugene. Reading the Song of Roland. Englewood Cliffs: Prentice, 1970.

Vielliard, Jeanne. Le guide du pèlerin de Saint-Jacques de Compostelle. 1978. Paris: Vrin, 1990.

Verbruggen, J. F. The Art of Warfare in Western Europe during the Middle Ages: From The Eighth Century to 1340. Trans. Sumner Willard and S. C. M. Southern. Europe in the Middle Ages Selected Studies 1. Amsterdam: North-Holland, 1977.

Viscardi, Antonio. "Canzoni di gesta." Enciclopedia Dantesca. Vol. 1. Rome: Istituto della Enciclopedia Italiana, 1970. 809–12. 6 vols.

Vitet, Ludovic. "La chanson de Roland." Essais historiques et littéraires. Paris: Lévy, 1862. 1–82.

Vitz, Evelyn Birg. Orality and Performance in Early French Romance. Cambridge, Eng.: Brewer, 1999.

-Waldman, Guido, trans. Orlando Furioso. By Ludovico Ariosto. Oxford: Oxford UP, 1983.

Walter, Philippe, trans. Aucassin et Nicolette. Paris: Gallimard, 1999.

Warren, Michelle R. History on the Edge: Excalibur and the Borders of Britain, 1100–1300. Minneapolis: U of Minnesota P, 2000.

———. "The Noise of Roland." Exemplaria 16 (2004): 277–304.

Watson, Rowan. Illuminated Manuscripts and Their Makers. London: V&A, 2003.

Weiss, Judith, trans. *The Birth of Romance: An Anthology: Four 12th-Century Anglo-Norman Romances*. London: Dent, 1992.

Werner, Wilfried, ed. Das Rolandslied *in den Bildern der Heidelberger Handschrift*. Wiesbaden: Reichert, 1977.

Whitehead, Frederick, ed. *La chanson de Roland*. 2nd ed. Oxford: Blackwell, 1946.

William of Malmesbury. "The Battle of Hastings, 1066." *Medieval Sourcebook*. Ed Paul Halsall. 24 Apr. 2006. 22 May 2006 <http://www.fordham.edu/halsall/source/1066malmesbury.html>.

———. *Gesta Regum Anglorum: The History of the English Kings*. By William of Malmesbury. Ed. R. M. Thomson and Michael Winterbottom. 2 vols. Oxford Medieval Texts. Oxford: Clarendon, 1998–99. Vol. 1.

Wilson, David, ed. *The Bayeux Tapestry: The Complete Tapestry in Color*. New York: Knopf, 1985.

Young, Robert J. C. *Postcolonialism: An Historical Introduction*. Oxford: Blackwell, 2001.

Yudkin, Jeremy. *Music in Medieval Europe*. Englewood Cliffs: Prentice, 1989.

Zamora Vicente, Alonso, ed. *Poema de Fernán González*. Madrid: Espasa-Calpe, 1946.

Zink, Michel. *Littérature française du moyen âge*. Collection Premier Cycle. Paris: PUF, 1992.

———. *Medieval French Literature: An Introduction*. Trans. Jeff Rider. Vol. 110. Pegasus Paperbooks 19. Binghamton: Medieval and Renaissance Texts and Studies, 1995.

———. *Le moyen âge et ses chansons, ou un passé en trompe-l'oeil*. Paris: Éditions de Fallois, 1996.

Zumthor, Paul. *Toward a Medieval Poetics*. Trans. Philip E. Bennett. Minneapolis: U of Minnesota P, 1990.

# INDEXES

## Manuscript Index

## Name Index

# Approaches to Teaching World Literature
*Joseph Gibaldi*, series editor

---

*Achebe's* Things Fall Apart. Ed. Bernth Lindfors. 1991.

*Arthurian Tradition*. Ed. Maureen Fries and Jeanie Watson. 1992.

*Atwood's* The Handmaid's Tale *and Other Works*. Ed. Sharon R. Wilson, Thomas B. Friedman, and Shannon Hengen. 1996.

*Austen's* Emma. Ed. Marcia McClintock Folsom. 2004.

*Austen's* Pride and Prejudice. Ed. Marcia McClintock Folsom. 1993.

*Balzac's* Old Goriot. Ed. Michal Peled Ginsburg. 2000.

*Baudelaire's* Flowers of Evil. Ed. Laurence M. Porter. 2000.

*Beckett's* Waiting for Godot. Ed. June Schlueter and Enoch Brater. 1991.

Beowulf. Ed. Jess B. Bessinger, Jr., and Robert F. Yeager. 1984.

*Blake's* Songs of Innocence and of Experience. Ed. Robert F. Gleckner and Mark L. Greenberg. 1989.

*Boccaccio's* Decameron. Ed. James H. McGregor. 2000.

*British Women Poets of the Romantic Period*. Ed. Stephen C. Behrendt and Harriet Kramer Linkin. 1997.

*Brontë's* Jane Eyre. Ed. Diane Long Hoeveler and Beth Lau. 1993.

*Emily Brontë's* Wuthering Heights. Ed. Sue Lonoff and Terri A. Hasseler. 2006.

*Byron's Poetry*. Ed. Frederick W. Shilstone. 1991.

*Camus's* The Plague. Ed. Steven G. Kellman. 1985.

*Cather's* My Ántonia. Ed. Susan J. Rosowski. 1989.

*Cervantes'* Don Quixote. Ed. Richard Bjornson. 1984.

*Chaucer's* Canterbury Tales. Ed. Joseph Gibaldi. 1980.

*Chaucer's* Troilus and Criseyde *and the Shorter Poems*. Ed. Tison Pugh and Angela Jane Weisl. 2006.

*Chopin's* The Awakening. Ed. Bernard Koloski. 1988.

*Coleridge's Poetry and Prose*. Ed. Richard E. Matlak. 1991.

*Collodi's* Pinocchio *and Its Adaptations*. Ed. Michael Sherberg. 2006.

*Conrad's* "Heart of Darkness" *and* "The Secret Sharer." Ed. Hunt Hawkins and Brian W. Shaffer. 2002.

*Dante's* Divine Comedy. Ed. Carole Slade. 1982.

*Defoe's* Robinson Crusoe. Ed. Maximillian E. Novak and Carl Fisher. 2005.

*DeLillo's* White Noise. Ed. Tim Engles and John N. Duvall. 2006.

*Dickens'* David Copperfield. Ed. Richard J. Dunn. 1984.

*Dickinson's Poetry*. Ed. Robin Riley Fast and Christine Mack Gordon. 1989.

Narrative of the Life of Frederick Douglass. Ed. James C. Hall. 1999.

*Early Modern Spanish Drama*. Ed. Laura R. Bass and Margaret R. Greer. 2006

*Eliot's* Middlemarch. Ed. Kathleen Blake. 1990.

*Eliot's Poetry and Plays*. Ed. Jewel Spears Brooker. 1988.

*Shorter Elizabethan Poetry*. Ed. Patrick Cheney and Anne Lake Prescott. 2000.

*Ellison's* Invisible Man. Ed. Susan Resneck Parr and Pancho Savery. 1989.

*English Renaissance Drama*. Ed. Karen Bamford and Alexander Leggatt. 2002.

*Works of Louise Erdrich*. Ed. Gregg Sarris, Connie A. Jacobs, and
    James R. Giles. 2004.

*Dramas of Euripides*. Ed. Robin Mitchell-Boyask. 2002.

*Faulkner's* The Sound and the Fury. Ed. Stephen Hahn and Arthur F. Kinney. 1996.

*Flaubert's* Madame Bovary. Ed. Laurence M. Porter and Eugene F. Gray. 1995.

*García Márquez's* One Hundred Years of Solitude. Ed. María Elena de Valdés and
    Mario J. Valdés. 1990.

*Gilman's "The Yellow Wall-Paper" and* Herland. Ed. Denise D. Knight and
    Cynthia J. Davis. 2003.

*Goethe's* Faust. Ed. Douglas J. McMillan. 1987.

*Gothic Fiction: The British and American Traditions*. Ed. Diane Long Hoeveler
    and Tamar Heller. 2003.

*Hebrew Bible as Literature in Translation*. Ed. Barry N. Olshen and
    Yael S. Feldman. 1989.

*Homer's* Iliad *and* Odyssey. Ed. Kostas Myrsiades. 1987.

*Ibsen's* A Doll House. Ed. Yvonne Shafer. 1985.

*Henry James's* Daisy Miller *and* The Turn of the Screw. Ed. Kimberly C. Reed and
    Peter G. Beidler. 2005.

*Works of Samuel Johnson*. Ed. David R. Anderson and Gwin J. Kolb. 1993.

*Joyce's* Ulysses. Ed. Kathleen McCormick and Erwin R. Steinberg. 1993.

*Kafka's Short Fiction*. Ed. Richard T. Gray. 1995.

*Keats's Poetry*. Ed. Walter H. Evert and Jack W. Rhodes. 1991.

*Kingston's* The Woman Warrior. Ed. Shirley Geok-lin Lim. 1991.

*Lafayette's* The Princess of Clèves. Ed. Faith E. Beasley and
    Katharine Ann Jensen. 1998.

*Works of D. H. Lawrence*. Ed. M. Elizabeth Sargent and Garry Watson. 2001.

*Lessing's* The Golden Notebook. Ed. Carey Kaplan and Ellen Cronan Rose. 1989.

*Mann's* Death in Venice *and Other Short Fiction*. Ed. Jeffrey B. Berlin. 1992.

*Medieval English Drama*. Ed. Richard K. Emmerson. 1990.

*Melville's* Moby-Dick. Ed. Martin Bickman. 1985.

*Metaphysical Poets*. Ed. Sidney Gottlieb. 1990.

*Miller's* Death of a Salesman. Ed. Matthew C. Roudané. 1995.

*Milton's* Paradise Lost. Ed. Galbraith M. Crump. 1986.

*Molière's* Tartuffe *and Other Plays*. Ed. James F. Gaines and
    Michael S. Koppisch. 1995.

*Momaday's* The Way to Rainy Mountain. Ed. Kenneth M. Roemer. 1988.

*Montaigne's Essays*. Ed. Patrick Henry. 1994.

*Novels of Toni Morrison*. Ed. Nellie Y. McKay and Kathryn Earle. 1997.

*Murasaki Shikibu's* The Tale of Genji. Ed. Edward Kamens. 1993.

*Pope's Poetry*. Ed. Wallace Jackson and R. Paul Yoder. 1993.

*Proust's Fiction and Criticism*. Ed. Elyane Dezon-Jones and
    Inge Crosman Wimmers. 2003.
*Novels of Samuel Richardson*. Ed. Lisa Zunshine and Jocelyn Harris. 2006.
*Rousseau's* Confessions *and* Reveries of the Solitary Walker. Ed. John C. O'Neal
    and Ourida Mostefai. 2003.
*Shakespeare's* Hamlet. Ed. Bernice W. Kliman. 2001.
*Shakespeare's* King Lear. Ed. Robert H. Ray. 1986.
*Shakespeare's* Othello. Ed. Peter Erickson and Maurice Hunt. 2005.
*Shakespeare's* Romeo and Juliet. Ed. Maurice Hunt. 2000.
*Shakespeare's* The Tempest *and Other Late Romances*. Ed. Maurice Hunt. 1992.
*Shelley's* Frankenstein. Ed. Stephen C. Behrendt. 1990.
*Shelley's Poetry*. Ed. Spencer Hall. 1990.
Sir Gawain and the Green Knight. Ed. Miriam Youngerman Miller and
    Jane Chance. 1986.
Song of Roland. Ed. William W. Kibler and Leslie Zarker Morgan. 2006.
*Spenser's* Faerie Queene. Ed. David Lee Miller and Alexander Dunlop. 1994.
*Stendhal's* The Red and the Black. Ed. Dean de la Motte and Stirling Haig. 1999.
*Sterne's* Tristram Shandy. Ed. Melvyn New. 1989.
*Stowe's* Uncle Tom's Cabin. Ed. Elizabeth Ammons and Susan Belasco. 2000.
*Swift's* Gulliver's Travels. Ed. Edward J. Rielly. 1988.
*Thoreau's* Walden *and Other Works*. Ed. Richard J. Schneider. 1996.
*Tolstoy's* Anna Karenina. Ed. Liza Knapp and Amy Mandelker. 2003.
*Vergil's* Aeneid. Ed. William S. Anderson and Lorina N. Quartarone. 2002.
*Voltaire's* Candide. Ed. Renée Waldinger. 1987.
*Whitman's* Leaves of Grass. Ed. Donald D. Kummings. 1990.
*Woolf's* To the Lighthouse. Ed. Beth Rigel Daugherty and Mary Beth Pringle. 2001.
*Wordsworth's Poetry*. Ed. Spencer Hall, with Jonathan Ramsey. 1986.
*Wright's* Native Son. Ed. James A. Miller. 1997.